Fodor's EXPLORING

ITALY

D0368273

FODOR'S TRAVEL PUBLICATIONS

NEW YORK • TORONTO • LONDON • SYDNEY • AUCKLAND

WWW.FODORS.COM

Copyright © Automobile Association Developments Ltd.
2002
Maps copyright © Automobile Association Developments
Ltd. 2002

Published in the United States by Fodor's Travel
Publications.
Published in the United Kingdom by AA Publishing.

Fodor's is a registered trademark of Random House, Inc.

ISBN 0-676-90178-6
Fifth edition

Fodor's Exploring Italy

Author: **Tim Jepson**
Revisions: **Tim Jepson, Praxilla Trabattoni**
Series Adviser: **Ingrid Morgan**
Joint Series Editor: **Susi Bailey**
Cartography: **The Automobile Association**
Cover Design: **Fabrizio La Rocca, Tigist Getachew**
Front Cover Silhouette: **Kevin Galvin**

Printed and bound in Italy by Printer Trento srl
10 9 8 7 6 5 4 3 2 1

How to use this book

ORGANIZATION

Italy Is, Italy Was
Discusses aspects of life and culture in contemporary Italy and explores significant periods in its history.

A–Z
Breaks down the country into regional chapters, and covers places to visit, including walks and drives. Within this section fall the Focus On articles, which consider a variety of subjects in greater detail.

Travel Facts
Contains the strictly practical information vital for a successful trip.

Accommodations and Restaurants
Lists recommended establishments throughout Italy, giving a brief summary of their attractions.

KEY TO ADMISSION CHARGES
Standard admission charges are categorized in this book as follows:

Inexpensive	under L5,000 (€2.50)
Moderate	L5,000–L10,000 (€2.50–5)
Expensive	over L10,000 (€5)

ABOUT THE RATINGS
Most places described in this book have been given a separate rating. These are as follows:

▶▶▶ **Do not miss**

▶▶ **Highly recommended**

▶ **Worth seeing**

MAPS
To make the location of a particular place easier to find, every main entry in this book has a map reference to the right of its name. This includes a number, followed by a letter, followed by another number, such as 176B3. The first number (176) refers to the page on which the map can be found. The letter (B) and the second number (3) pinpoint the square in which the place is located. The maps on the inside front cover and inside back cover are referred to as IFC and IBC, respectively.

Contents

Piazza Navona, Rome

Tim Jepson acquired his love for travel when he journeyed through Europe as a street performer. Since then, his wanderlust has taken him from the Umbrian hills to the Yukon's windswept tundra. Hopelessly in love with Italy—like many a romantic Englishman before him—he has lived in Rome, Venice and Tuscany. He is also the author of Fodor's *Exploring* guides to *Florence and Tuscany* and *Canada*.

My Italy

It's not difficult to fall in love with Italy, but it is hard to escape its fatal charm once the love affair has matured. No country, in my opinion, is as rich, no people as passionate, no landscapes as beautiful. And if you don't warm to the Italians, or find countryside elsewhere more beguiling, what about the food and wine—some of the world's best—or the art and architecture? The world would be a poorer place without pasta and pizza, not to mention the artistic legacy of the Renaissance, or the cultural patrimony of the Greeks, Etruscans, Romans, Arabs, and other civilizations that have left their imprint on the Italian peninsula.

I first visited Italy some 20 years ago, and have been going back there every year since. Even now there are corners of the country I have yet to explore, churches to discover, paintings to see, seas to swim, mountains to climb, operas to hear, and food to eat. I'm lucky—I've made a start. For those on their first or second trip, the discovery is just beginning. There are many countries that could warrant a lifetime's study, but in how many would you really want to spend a lifetime? For me, Italy is one, although equally I have no desire to "go native," and few illusions about Italy's faults, for no country is perfect.

Yet Italy comes nearer to perfection than most. As recently as the 1950s it was little more than a peasant-based agricultural country, ravaged by war and years of dictatorship. Today, it's one of the world's leading industrial nations, a byword for style, fashion, and flair. Yet vivid slices of the old Italy survive, its perfection being a blend of the old and new, of black-clad peasants and the glories of Rome, Florence, and Venice combined with family, passion, opera, olive oil, Latin lovers, and all those other things that will be forever Italian. Revel in these and other delights, but be warned: once Italy ensnares you, it has you for life.

Tim Jepson

Italy Is

"We have made Italy," said Cavour, founding father of the Italian state, "now we must make Italians." Some 130 years later, how many Italians, from the German-speaking burghers of the Alto Adige to the blue-eyed Sicilians of Norman descent, still believe in a single nation (except when united behind their soccer team)?

STEREOTYPES Everybody has a picture of the typical Italian: philandering Latin lover; son-smothering *mamma*; pasta-bloated patriarch; louche Mafia Godfather; black-clad widow; deranged driver; sensuous sex siren (*à la* Sophia Loren). Picking national stereotypes is always a dangerous game, but in Italy it is especially fraught with pitfalls. The country was fully unified only in 1870, having been divided for centuries, a historical legacy that has produced countless regional variations of character. For every Italian who conforms to a stereotype, there is another who proves the exception to the rule.

❏ "And don't, let me beg you, go with that awful idea that Italy's only a museum of antiquities and art. Love and understand the Italians, for the people are more marvellous than the land."
E. M. Forster, British novelist. ❏

REGION BY REGION As in any other country, the Italians themselves recognize regional stereotypes, based often more on tradition than reality: there are the arrogant Florentines, the fierce Sicilians; the mild-mannered Venetians, the more abrasive Romans; and the dignified reserve of the Piedmontese contrasting with the mannered efficiency of the Milanese. Italians stand by their regions, considering themselves Tuscans first and foremost, or Sicilians, Umbrians, Calabrians…Others are divided from compatriots by language and cultural tradition (German in the Alto Adige, Slovene in Friuli, French in Piedmont, Greek and Albanian in Sicily and Calabria).

CHARACTERISTICS Nevertheless we instinctively recognize Italians, not only from the way they look (fashion is a common denominator in Italy) but also from their outlook on life, whether a pragmatic aptitude for survival—born of constant political upheavals and foreign invasions—or a natural spontaneity and sensual self-indulgence in anything from food and family to soccer. We admire their apparent free spirit while lamenting their occasional inefficiency—and wonder why, when most nations have something to teach, Italians seem to have more.

For all the Italians' intrinsic differences, there is no doubt the family—though diminishing in size and losing its hierarchical rigidity—is still a major influence in the mainstream of Italian life. Mother and son are its pivotal members, children its sentimental axis, and marriage and death its dynastic climaxes.

HISTORY The family, with its ties of loyalty and obligation, is as much a metaphorical as a literal force, binding Italians to nearest and dearest rather than neighbor and nation. Its roots lie in Italy's agricultural past (when survival demanded cooperation), grounded in Catholicism's teachings and reinforced by times when it became essential to preserve family (or family-like) groups — either in the wake of emigration or in the face of outside interference.

ECONOMIC NECESSITY

Demography and social change are weakening family ties—witness Italy's drug problem and the numbers of old people living alone. Divorce and abortion are now readily available, and attitudes have been modified by the student and feminist movements of the last 25 years (less so in the more traditional south). Yet children often continue to live at home into their thirties—unable to move away to study (there are few scholarships) and unable (or unwilling) to buy their first home alone. At least 65 percent of working Italians, moreover, are dependent on a family economy, a structure that strongly binds extended families.

MOTHER AND CHILD Even as society evolves, and with it the life of the ordinary Italian family, even as birth rates drop and increasing numbers of women join the Italian labor force, you will still find *mammismo*. This attachment of Italian men to their mothers, highlighted in Italian pop music, books, and movies, is as real and pervasive as it is stereotypical. Pop psychologists have been known to call it the key to the Italian family: the Italian man's search for a woman who is as selflessly devoted to him as his mother is explains, they say, both his often-caricatured philandering and his eventual return to hearth and home.

The Catholic Church has been bound up with Italian life for almost 2,000 years. Although in apparent decline and no longer enmeshed in political power, it still plays a part in national affairs and influences—however subtly—many aspects of day-to-day life.

DECLINE In many respects Italy is no longer a Catholic country. Although 97 percent of Italians are baptized, only around 10 percent regularly attend Mass. Divorce, abortion, and birth control are freely available, and the Church's political influence is now almost negligible.

CHRISTIAN FOCUS At the same time, Italy qualifies as one of the holiest spots on earth, not only for its saints, shrines, and churches (and myriad religious festivals) but also because it contains the Vatican. Attitudes toward the latter are ambivalent. On one hand, it was Italy's only real unifying force after the fall of the Roman Empire, yet on the other it opposed political unification, only

Religious mementos on sale

reluctantly relinquishing the Papal States in 1870. It is remembered as a poor ruler, bleeding regions dry and giving little in return—still a source of anticlerical feeling in much of Italy.

STRUCTURE It is important to differentiate between the Vatican and the Catholic Church. The Vatican (with the pope at its head) rules 850 million Catholics worldwide (including those in Italy), while the Italian Church is ruled by a cardinal and the Italian Episcopal Council (composed of 29 bishops). Overseeing all is the pope—*Il Papa* in Italian, from the Greek *pappas*, "father" (Pope John Paul II, elected in 1978, is the 263rd such spiritual successor to St Peter). Pontiffs had political power for centuries until 1870, when they retired to the Vatican, only emerging in 1929 after Mussolini's Lateran Treaty (which formalized Church and State relations and created the independent Vatican territory). Once all ten major posts in the Curia, or church government, were held by Italians: now only one or two are native incumbents, a measure of the degree to which Catholicism's hierarchy has expanded beyond Italy.

PAGAN BACKGROUND Italy's religious heritage goes back to ancient Rome's taste for myth, superstition, and pagan observance. Wandering Rome's Forum you might have sampled dozens of recipes for salvation—Mithraism, Judaism, Christianity, Manichaeism, the worship of Isis, Osiris, and Atargatis, even oddities like the cult of the goddess Cybele, whose priests were expected to castrate themselves.

The burial of apostles Peter and Paul in Rome put Christianity on the Italian map. Unable to shake off all its pagan ways, it sometimes incorporated them. Old festivals were replaced by new ones—December's *Saturnalia* by Christmas, Isis' day of the dead by November's All Souls' Day—and churches were raised all over Italy from the ruins of old temples. Even aspects of the marriage rite were adapted from various Roman ceremonies.

Eating is one of Italy's greatest pleasures. Its cuisine—fed by the natural bounty of land and sea—ranks among the world's greatest, and if the applause for its wines is less resounding, there are still good wines that perfectly match the simplicity of the cooking.

A culinary voyage around Italy is a delight. There are many specialties unique to each region—and even if you stick to the classics, pizza or *spaghetti bolognese* taste better in its places of origin.

RESTAURANTS The appearance of a restaurant has little to do with the quality of food offered. *Ristorante*, *osteria*, and *trattoria* are now fairly interchangeable terms; a *tavola calda* or *pizzeria* is more humble (though the food can still be excellent). You don't have to wade through the entire menu (*la lista*)—Italians themselves often stick to a plate of pasta and salad; nor should you overlook bars and markets as sources of cheap snacks. Avoid fixed-price tourist menus—always a false economy.

MEALS More expensive hotels may offer you the breakfast (*prima colazione*) you eat at home, but Italians tend to start the day with sweet croissants (*una brioche* or *un cornetto*) and coffee (*espresso* or *cappuccino* and *caffè latte*). In Sicily or German-speaking Alto Adige, breakfast might include wine, salami, and grilled cheeses.

Lunch (*pranzo*) is no longer the extended, over-blown occasion of days gone by. Save the big meal until evening and stick to something light—a picnic or bar snack with rolls (*panini*) and sandwiches (*tramezzini*). In bars,

pay first for what you want at the cash register (*cassa*) and take your receipt (*lo scontrino*) to the counter, where a tip slapped on the bar works wonders with the staff.

Full-scale meals start with *antipasto* (an hors d'oeuvre), followed by the *primo piatto* (first course), which may be soup, pasta, or rice, and then by the main meat or fish dish (the *secondo*). Vegetables (*contorni*) or salad (*insalata*) follow separately, and the meal is rounded off with cheese (*formaggio*), fruit (*frutta*), and/or a dessert (*dolce*).

13

WASHING IT DOWN Italy produces more wine than any other country. The D.O.C. classification system is no real indicator of quality; ask instead for local wines (*vini locali*) or house wines (*vini della casa*), and treat yourself to famous varieties in the appropriate regions, such as Piedmont (*Barolo* and *Barbaresco*) and Tuscany (*Chianti*, *Brunello*, or *Vino Nobile*). Happily, standards are rising among small, independent producers (notably in Trentino-Alto, Umbria, Adige, and the Veneto).

Try firewaters like *grappa* at least once, and aperitifs (Cinzano, Campari, and Cynar) and liqueurs like *amaro* (a bitter digestive), *amaretto* (a sweet almond-based drink), and the aniseed-flavored *sambuca*.

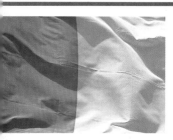

Turnout at Italian elections is higher than elsewhere in Europe, yet for all this apparent enthusiasm most Italians treat politics with the resignation or weary disdain they feel it largely deserves. Only recently have corruption scandals and a crumbling of the old order challenged indifference to the system and made political progress a real possibility.

THE SYSTEM Italy has been a republic since a referendum in 1946, overseen by a largely symbolic president (who occupies Rome's Palazzo del Quirinale) and underpinned by a decision-making lower house, the Chamber of Deputies. Housed in Rome's Palazzo Montecitorio, this has 623 deputies, of whom 24 are ministers. Nearby lies the upper house (Palazzo Madama), composed of 315 senators, made up of six representatives from each Italian region plus various lifelong senators, appointed for their service to the state (such as ex-presidents of the Republic).

LOCAL GOVERNMENT Italy's 20 regions (*regione*) also enjoy a large measure of self-government, some—usually those in politically problematic areas—being semi-autonomous (notably Sicily, Sardinia, Trentino–Alto Adige, and the Valle d'Aosta). Each region is divided into provinces (*provincia*), and each province is then further divided into a series of local councils (*comune*).

Publicity material for the Leghe

DEMOCRACY The Italian postwar political system rose from the ruins of Fascist dictatorship—with all the democratic frailties and insecurities that implies. Despite its many faults, it has been behind (if not always directly responsible for) the transformation of Italy from an agricultural backwater to one of the world's leading industrial nations. Its institutions, if now looking more moribund, were framed to prevent a throwback to Mussolini and seemed initially to match the country's particular needs.

VOTING Voting is written into the Italian constitution as a "civic duty," being seen after the war as an act in support of the very idea of democracy. Failure to vote can in theory be marked on a citizen's criminal record. A complicated system of proportional representation led to the series of coalition governments whose corruption finally brought about their own downfall (see opposite page). In August 1993, parliament voted in an electoral reform bill, whereby 75 percent of both upper and lower houses are elected in a "winner takes all" system, the remaining 25 percent by proportional representation.

Italians also occasionally vote in referendums, held when 500,000 or more signatures are collected on an issue, a democratic device that decided such crucial issues as divorce and abortion in the 1970s and electoral reform in 1993.

A CROOKED WALTZ For all the 50 or so postwar governments in Italy elected under the old voting system, ultimate control remained all but

unchanged, power and position being shared out among the coalitions in a gentle waltz of slowly changing partners.

The largest party, the center-right *Democrazia Cristiana* (Christian Democrats), commandeered the four- or five-party coalitions, sharing the spoils of government with the Socialists (P.S.I.), Republicans (P.R.I.), Liberals (P.L.I.), and Social Democrats (P.S.D.)—and keeping out the popular Communists (later

> ❏ "And what is the prize eventually to be won? The rebirth of democracy. The glorious prospect of being able one day to choose their rulers from a list of powerful men, most of whose corruptions are already known and accepted with weary resignation." Norman Lewis with the Allies in Italy in 1944. ❏

renamed *Partito Democratico della Sinistra*, Democratic Party of the Left). None of these parties has survived untainted by corruption, which has crept in largely under the cover of *clientelismo*—the hidden links, votes for favors, and the like that have characterized Italian political life since Machiavelli, but that now seem to have become too much even for the long-suffering Italians.

In 1993 politicians agonized over the formation of a new electoral system

PRESENT AND FUTURE Italian politics are currently undergoing a sea change. Scandal after scandal has revealed the breadth and depth of corruption, with the highest in the land, in politics and industry, under investigation for bribery, misappropriation of billions of lire—even murder. Such was the disgust with politicians that in April 1993 the president asked the respected governor of the Bank of Italy to form a government. Carlo Azeglio Ciampi was the first nonparliamentarian prime minister of Italy this century. New parties have sprung up, notably the *Leghe* (Leagues), northern coalitions in favor of a federal Italy (see page 16), and *La Rete* (The Network), a southern-based party against political collusion with the Mafia. Further signs of disenchantment with the old parties were seen with the creation of Forza Italia, a center-right party formed by media mogul Silvio Berlusconi, and the center-left coalition under Romano Prodi, both of whom have fallen from power. However, new parties have sprung up before, such as the Radicals and Greens in the 1970s, and there is doubt—given Italian bureaucracy's Byzantine obduracy—whether the present upheavals really mark the end of old-style Italian politics.

Geography and history have always seemed to handicap southern Italy—a region that starts somewhere between Rome and Naples—leaving it poorer than the north and also the victim of an unholy trinity comprising prejudice, corruption, and organized crime.

PROBLEMS Some of the south's problems will never go away. Little can be done to alter Italy's shape, which leaves the region far from markets, thus crippling industrial initiative; nor to alter the south's harsh climate, which leaves agriculture hamstrung; nor to change its geology, which offers few energy sources or raw materials. Nor, it appears, can much be done to tackle the Mafia, whose tentacles continue to strangle legitimate enterprise and discourage long-term investment.

Calabrian women

POTENTIAL FOR CHANGE Other problems that affect the south can perhaps be resolved more easily, principally those that are rooted in the autocratic Spanish regimes (from 1559) that stifled the south for centuries—corruption, poor education, crumbling infrastructure, and latent feudal hierarchies. Money has been thrown at the region for decades, every so often hitting its targets—notably in eradicating malaria and in building new roads—but more often than not falling into the pockets of corrupt Mafia barons.

EMIGRATION The south has known two great periods of emigration: the first to the U.S. at the turn of the century, the second to the industrial heartlands of the north (Milan, Turin, and Venice), where cheap southern labor fueled the economic boom of the 1950–1960s. While boom has hardly turned to bust—they say Italy without the south would be Europe's richest country—southerners are resented by some with a virulence that amounts to racism.

NEW BIGOTRY Northerners have always looked with mock horror on the south. In the wake of recent political disillusionment, however, attitudes have taken a more ugly turn. Graffiti warns *terroni* (peasants) to go home (or worse), and there has been growing support for the *Leghe* (Leagues), increasingly popular political parties who—angered at what they see as the north subsidizing the south—argue for a more federal, even partitioned, Italy. This is unlikely to happen, but the longing—some 140 years after unification—is a symptom of a greater malaise in the Italian soul.

Symbol of the prosperous north

Italy has long hummed with a babel of dialects descended from Greek, Latin, and the languages introduced by foreign invaders over the centuries. Regional differences still define Italian character, but mass media is gradually eroding the country's linguistic diversity.

HISTORY Italian draws the bulk of its vocabulary from Latin and is still the closest of the Romance languages to its Roman roots. It has evolved in its present form from the educated language of Tuscany, primarily because this was the regional dialect used by great medieval writers such as Dante, Petrarch, and Boccaccio. Even today an Italian saying describes how "Tuscans polish the air around them," and the best Italian is said to be *la lingua toscana in bocca romana* (a Tuscan tongue in a Roman mouth).

USAGE For all its occasional verbosity, Italian is one of the world's most beautiful languages, its cadences more seductive to the heart than the mind. Its particular spell was well captured by Charles V, the Holy Roman Emperor, in the famous observation that he spoke Spanish with God, French to his courtiers, German to his horse, and Italian to women. He might have added that Italian is one of the best languages for displays of anger and passion.

DIALECTS Italy's particular shape, its remote mountain enclaves, and its past have all fostered an estimated 1,500 different dialects. In fact, it is estimated only two percent of Italians are unable to speak some form of

dialect. Some even speak a different language, notably in the Valle d'Aosta (French), Friuli (Slovene), and Alto Adige (German). The Venetian dialect has words of Spanish and Portuguese origin (a legacy of its seafaring tradition). Lombardy's has German imports (having been ruled by Austria), while Piedmont's is heavily laced with French. Spanish and French crop up in Neapolitan, while a bastardized Greek and Albanian is spoken in

17

parts of Calabria. Sicily boasts a sprinkling of Arabic, French, and Spanish; so does Sardinia, which has its own language, Sardo (as well as a Catalan enclave in Alghero). And small pockets of *Ladino* (Ladin) are still spoken in certain remote Alpine valleys. In as little as a generation, however, with the leveling influence of television, Italy may find itself speaking a standard Italian, its dialects no more than quaint memories.

Movies are among Italy's major contribution to mainstream modern culture. They not only influenced a generation of postwar film-makers, but also defined a very particular image of Italy with films like La Dolce Vita *and stars such as Sophia Loren, Marcello Mastroianni, and Claudia Cardinale.*

EPICS AND ESCAPISM Italian movie-making launched itself in Turin with blockbusting silent films like Enrico Guazzoni's *Quo Vadis?* (1913) before moving to Rome—to take advantage of its climate and ready-made locations—where lack of funds and its head-on encounter with Fascism saw it crash to near oblivion in the 1930s. Movies made under Fascist auspices were usually ideologically approved propaganda or the so-called *telefoni bianchi*, named after the white telephone that always appeared in the heroine's bedroom—symbol of the exotic Hollywood fairy tale for Italians who didn't own a telephone, much less a white one.

NEOREALISM Rome's great studios, Cinecittà, were opened by Mussolini in 1938 with the words "cinema is our greatest weapon." Cinecittà became Italian cinema's spiritual home, inhabited after the war by a generation of young filmmakers whose newfound freedom produced the revolutionary genre known as Neorealism (which greatly influenced later American *films noirs* and the French New

Wave of the 1960s). Its earliest exponents were Luchino Visconti (*Ossessione*, 1942) and Roberto Rossellini, whose *Roma, Città Aperta* (1945), with its real locations, visceral style, jerky camerawork, and almost documentary footage prepared the ground for classics in the same genre such as Vittorio de Sica's *Ladri di Biciclette* (*Bicycle Thieves*, 1949).

TO THE PRESENT DAY Tastes changed during the boom years of the 1950s and 1960s, when the Neorealists' mantle was taken up by Federico Fellini, Francesco Rosi, and Michelangelo Antonioni (though Pier Paolo Pasolini continued to chronicle the new underbelly of Italian urban life in movies like *Accatone* and *Una Vita Violenta*). Fellini's distinctive view is seen in *La Strada* (1954), *La Dolce Vita* (1960), and *Otto e Mezzo* (*8½*, 1963). Antonioni is perhaps best known for *Blow-Up* (1966), an English-language movie. Later moviemakers such as Bertolucci (*The Last Emperor*, *Last Tango in Paris*) and the Taviani brothers (*Padre Padrone*) also filmed in English. Cinecittà's reputation, meanwhile, grew fat on American epics like *Ben Hur* and *Cleopatra*, before television and rising costs reduced it to peddling so-called "spaghetti westerns," soft porn, and money-making potboilers. Of recent hits, perhaps the most famous are Giuseppe Tornatore's *Cinema Paradiso* and Roberto Benigni's *Life is Beautiful*, though directors like Bernardo Bertolucci are still making films.

Top: Roma, Città Aperta
Left: Ossessione

Italy was

Italy's archeological record goes back over half a million years to early Stone Age hunters. Generations came and went, leaving few traces of their passing, until the advent of the Greeks and Etruscans. Soon a great civilization was born.

PREHISTORY The first modern human remains found in Italy date from paleolithic times around 20,000 BC. More advanced cultures made their appearance between 3000 and 1800 BC, notably the Ligurians (who settled modern-day Liguria), the Siculi (Lazio and southern Italy), and the Sards (who developed a pastoral culture in Sardinia). They were followed by migratory peoples, principally the Picini and Messapians, who crossed the Adriatic from the Balkans, as well as the Veneti, Latins, and Umbrii, who moved down the peninsula from the north.

PHOENICIANS AND CARTHAGINIANS By 800 BC, the Phoenicians had drifted along the African coast and established colonies in Sicily and Sardinia (introducing an alphabet into Italy for the first time). A leading African city, Carthage, eventually became a power in its own right, establishing footholds in southern Italy, Sicily, and Sardinia at about the same time as Greek and Etruscan influence emerged elsewhere.

GREEKS The first Greek colonies on Italian soil were established around 735 BC in Sicily, eventually developing into a network of independent cities all over southern Italy known as Magna Graecia (Greater Greece). Despite internecine wars and conflicts with the Carthaginians (in Sicily) and Etruscans (in Campania), the colonies immeasurably enriched Italy's indigenous cultures in the realms of art and architecture. In agriculture, they introduced two great staples—the vine and the olive.

ETRUSCANS The Etruscans occupied much of present-day Lazio and Tuscany, in an area roughly bounded by the Arno and Tiber rivers (though they occasionally expanded beyond these borders). Where they came from is one of history's great mysteries, but they were probably a mixture of indigenous and foreign peoples, who became linked by a common language. They assimilated neighboring tribes (like the Ligurians and Umbrians) to forge a loose political (and religious) affiliation based on a 12-city confederation. Like the Greeks, they were culturally, technologically, and agriculturally advanced, though militarily they were to prove no match for the Romans, who by about 350 BC had all but defeated their leading cities.

Engraving depicting a Phoenician merchant fleet

After obscure beginnings, Rome conquered its Greek and Etruscan neighbors, its sophisticated republican structure evolving through periods of social disorder into an empire that endured almost 1,000 years and touched almost every corner of the known world.

BEGINNINGS According to legend, Romulus founded Rome in 753 BC. However, the city's earliest archeological remains date from around 1200 BC (though it may be 2,000 years older). By 900 BC, Rome formed the border between the Etruscan and Latin spheres of influence, possibly ruled until around 600 BC by the Tarquins, an Etruscan royal dynasty.

THE REPUBLIC The Etruscan kings were ousted by the Romans in 509 BC and replaced by a republic (*res publica*), where in theory the "people were kings." In practice, the city was riven by disputes between the plebeians (lower classes) and patricians (military and political elite). The plebeians were partly placated by the tribune (494 BC), a magistracy that looked after their interests, and an uneasy consensus allowed Rome to expand, first into Etruscan and Samnite territory, and then into Greek-dominated southern Italy.

*Right: Julius Caesar
Below: The Roman Forum*

THE PUNIC WARS Rome's expansion brought it into conflict with Carthage. The struggle for supremacy took the shape of three protracted campaigns, the Punic Wars—the first of which (264–241 BC) saw Rome seize control of Sicily, Corsica, and Sardinia. In the second (218–202 BC), Carthage dispatched Hannibal and his army—elephants and all—across the Alps to inflict defeats on Rome at Cannae and Trasimeno. Scipio Africanus defeated Hannibal at Zama in 202 BC. The Third Punic War (149–146 BC) left Rome master of the Mediterranean and territories as far flung as Jerusalem and Asia Minor.

JULIUS CAESAR In Rome the city's internal divisions simmered on. Popular revolt exploded in the Social Wars (90–88 BC), bringing about an increasingly authoritarian response from the Senate. The general Sulla was installed to restore order, followed by Pompey, who with two other leading figures—Crassus and Julius Caesar—formed the First Triumvirate (60 BC).

Julius Caesar became dictator of Rome, but it was his grandnephew and adopted son, Octavius, who first assumed the title of emperor as Augustus. He ushered in reforms, public works, and military consolidation that saw Rome emerge as the cultural, religious, and political center of the world.

THE IDES OF MARCH Caesar's military prowess eventually made him preeminent, a dictatorial position he used to heal the scars of a century's civil strife. Institutions were soon reformed, and new temples and civic buildings blossomed. Political jealousy mounted, however, and in 44 BC, on March 15 (the Ides), he was assassinated.

Assassination of Julius Caesar

THE AGE OF AUGUSTUS The Second Triumvirate—Lepidus, Mark Antony, and Octavius—was then formed. Designed to wage war on Caesar's assassins, it soon became a battleground for control of the empire. Antony compromised his chances by dallying with Cleopatra, leaving the field clear for Octavius, who sealed his position with victory at the Battle of Actium in 31 BC. He took the title of *princeps* in 27 BC and changed his name to Augustus Caesar. The Augustan Age marked the high point of Roman civilization.

THE EMPERORS Few subsequent emperors were as successful as Augustus (27 BC–AD 14), but the immense spoils accruing from the empire masked their more grotesque deficiencies. Three of the more decadent incumbents were Tiberius (14–37), Claudius (41–54), and Nero (54–68), followed in turn by the Flavians (Vespasian and his sons Titus and Domitian), under whom the empire enjoyed a period of relative peace and prosperity. This golden age continued under the Antonines, the military emperors Trajan (98–117), Hadrian (117–138), and Marcus Aurelius (161–180).

DECLINE AND FALL After Aurelius' death, revolts broke out against the Roman yoke across the empire; emperors came and went with increasing rapidity; cultural life stagnated; and political, military, and economic institutions teetered on the brink of collapse. Diocletian divided the empire in two (East and West), and the empire briefly stabilized under Constantine, whose Edict of Milan (313) allowed Christians freedom of worship. In time the capital of the Western Empire was moved to Ravenna (with Constantinople the capital in the East).

The Mausoleum of Augustus, Rome

Neither the so-called Dark Ages nor the various waves of barbarians who swarmed into Italy after the fall of the Roman Empire were as black as they are usually painted. Today, however, little evidence remains of the Goths, Franks, and Lombards who dominated the peninsula for more than three centuries.

BARBARIANS Raids by "barbarians" (meaning outsiders) had preoccupied Rome for centuries, but as the empire foundered they became more organized, and the empire did less to withstand them. When Rome itself was sacked in 410 by Alaric the Goth, a tremor was felt around the civilized world. Subsequent incursions came to a head in 476, when Odoacer the Goth displaced the last Western emperor, Romulus Augustulus. In 493 Theodoric, another Goth, managed to seize Ravenna, and with it control of the old empire's valuable western territories.

BYZANTINES Constantinople— modern Istanbul—prospered as the capital of the Eastern Empire (Byzantium), and to a large extent escaped the turmoil that marked the demise of its western counterpart. Between 536 and 552 its emperor, Justinian, retook large areas of Italy (through his famous general Belisarius) in the so-called Gothic Wars. As a result, Byzantine influence dominated parts of the country for centuries, which can be seen in much art and architecture. At a time of political uncertainity, the Church's authority began to have an increasing influence on Italian affairs.

LOMBARDS AND FRANKS Territorial gaps left by the Byzantines were partly filled by the Lombards (568–774), a race from the north, who established three duchies in Italy centered on Pavia, Cividale, and Spoleto. They were later joined by the Franks, a Christian race from Gaul, whose loyalties were divided between two rival factions—the Carolingian and Merovingian dynasties. Pepin the Short, a Carolingian, resolved the division in 754 by appealing to Pope Stephen III, who sanctioned his rule by anointing him with holy oil (a highly symbolic gesture of immeasurable consequence). In return, Pepin and his son, Charlemagne, successfully defeated the Lombards (774), handing over large areas of conquered territory to the papacy. These papal states became the source of the papacy's temporal power. On Christmas Day in 800 Charlemagne was crowned "Emperor of the Romans" by Pope Leo III, an act that forged enduring links between the popes and the northern-based emperors, and guaranteed centuries of conflict.

Charlemagne, Holy Roman Emperor

The centuries following Charlemagne's death saw a struggle for ascendancy between the papacy and the Holy Roman Empire. With the popes claiming the right to crown emperors, and the emperors the right to sanction popes, opposed camps began to emerge across Italy— the Guelphs (who were papal supporters) and Ghibellines (imperial supporters).

RIVAL POWERS The Frankish empire declined, but the office of emperor stayed intact—though emperors increasingly remained in their northern power bases, entering Italy only in attempts to assert imperial authority. While the fortunes of empire and papacy waxed and waned, there were rarely periods when they were not at one another's throats.

TIT FOR TAT The most famous encounter came in 1076, when Emperor Henry IV rejected Pope Gregory VII and his proposals for radical political reforms. Gregory in turn excommunicated Henry, thus— in theory—freeing Catholics from imperial allegiance. This squabble was resolved diplomatically, but others were more violent, notably the rampaging campaigns of Frederick I (Barbarossa) against northern Italian cities from his base in Germany in 1155. Papal fortunes hit rock bottom in the 14th century, with the move of the Church's capital from Rome to Avignon, followed by the Great Schism, when three rival popes vied for recognition.

ARABS AND NORMANS While the north of Italy swayed between pope and emperor, events in southern Italy followed a more orderly path. The Saracens (Arabs) invaded Sicily in 827 and assumed control for two centuries. Elsewhere the Byzantines held sway until supplanted by the Normans (11th century), who arrived in the region as mercenaries. They carved out a kingdom (including Sicily) under Robert Guiscard and his successors Roger I and Roger II.

ANJOU AND ARAGON The marriage of a Norman princess and Emperor Henry VI in 1186 brought the south within the imperial orbit. Unfortunately, the Norman kingdom had been legitimized by the papacy, thus creating the same power struggle that dogged papal and imperial relations in the north. Italian-born emperor Frederick II briefly dominated the south in defiance of the papacy, but his heirs were defeated by Charles of Anjou (1265), brother of the French king, who received Naples and Sicily as a "gift" from the papacy. The Anjous (Angevins) ruled most of the south for two centuries, except for Sicily, which they forfeited to Spain (under Peter III of Aragon) after the uprising known as the "Sicilian Vespers" in 1282. In 1442, Alfonso V of Aragon was named heir to the last of the Angevins, and the south was united under Spanish control for some 300 years until the 18th century.

GREGORIVS·VII·PAPA·SAONENSIS

City states have been a constant feature in Italian history, but they reached their zenith during the 14th century—when 400 of them stretched across the north of the country— riding high on increased trade and the relative decline of papal and imperial authority.

CLIMATE FOR CHANGE Rivalry between pope and emperor left a power vacuum in which cities could evolve independently. This was especially true after 1300, when few emperors could combine control of Italy with their dynastic obligations in northern Europe. As for the papacy, after a dispute with Philip of France, it fell under French domination, and in 1307, compromised and subordinate, moved to Avignon under the protection of the French kings (the Great Schism).

Meanwhile, the maritime republics (Amalfi, Pisa, Genoa, and Venice) and cities that stood on trade routes (Bologna, Milan, Verona, and Florence) grew rich on commerce.

THE *COMUNE* Many cities initially developed a quasi-democratic structure known as the *comune*, a ruling council consisting of merchants,

guildsmen, and minor nobility. As cities prospered, they acquired magnificent *palazzi* and cathedrals. This was the period of Dante (1265–1321), Petrarch (1304–1374), and Boccaccio (1313–1375), all pillars of Italy's literary tradition, and of the first stirrings of artistic change heralding the Renaissance.

25

THE SIGNORE As cities fought one another, or were fractured by internal power struggles, they increasingly abandoned the *comune* and looked to one man (*signore*) to cut through the muddle. Despotic rule followed, usually under a powerful noble, merchant, or *condottiere* (a mercenary employed by the cities to fight on their behalf). Thus rose the Visconti (Milan), Gonzaga (Mantua), Este (Ferrara), Montefeltro (Urbino), Medici (Florence), and many other powerful families.

An agreement in 1455 between Italy's major powers—Milan, Florence, Venice, Naples, and the papal states—cemented a period of calm that lasted until the death of Lorenzo de' Medici in 1492. Thereafter Italy became a pawn in the hands of foreign players—first France and Spain, then Austria.

FRANCE France entered the equation in 1494 when the Duke of Milan, after a quarrel with the Neapolitan king, invited Charles VIII of France to conquer the Kingdom of Naples. Charles, for his part, claimed the throne on the basis that his Anjou ancestor formerly ruled Naples and southern Italy (see page 24). He captured the kingdom easily, but stayed only three months, after which it was regained for Spain by Ferdinand II (Columbus' patron). A later French king, François I, took Milan in 1515, basing his claim on a marriage between a Visconti (former rulers of Milan) and the French royal family.

Napoleon in all his glory

SPAIN Spain joined France in the scramble for territory in Italy in the person of Charles V (1500–1558), Holy Roman Emperor and Habsburg heir to the Austrian and Spanish thrones. His troops ransacked Rome in 1527, and defeated the French at Pavia (1526) and Naples (1529). The Treaty of Cateau-Cambrésis (1559) ratified Spanish rule over Sicily, Sardinia, southern Italy, Milan, and parts of Tuscany for 150 years. France held other pockets, leaving only Venice and the papal states independent of foreign powers. Against this background the religious movements of the Reformation and Counter-Reformation were played out.

AUSTRIA AND NAPOLEON Spain's stranglehold slackened following the War of the Spanish Succession, which saw Lombardy, Mantua, Naples, and Sardinia pass by treaty to the Austrians (1713). Machinations later in the 18th century saw further realignments (Lorraine took Tuscany, Piedmont was ruled by the Savoys, and in 1734 the Spanish Bourbons took southern Italy). Austria controlled the north under Maria Theresa (1740–1780) and her son Joseph II (1780–1792).

All changed with Napoleon's Italian campaigns in 1796 and 1800. He succeeded in conquering the Italian peninsula, establishing a republic. Though it was short-lived, it reduced papal power, reformed feudal hierarchies, and—perhaps most importantly—suggested the potential for a single Italian state. The Congress of Vienna (1815) restored Austrian control, but over the next 50 years did little to halt the momentum of the unification movement.

Three obstacles lay in the path of a unified Italy—Austria (which ruled northern Italy), the papacy (rulers of central Italy), and the Spanish (rulers of Sicily and the south). Although unification was engineered by Italian patriots, it was only made possible by conflict and collusion between foreign powers.

LEADING PLAYERS Unification's Italian protagonists were Giuseppe Mazzini (1805–1872), a political agitator, and Giuseppe Garibaldi (1807–1882), an inspired military leader. Both favored linking royal and republican efforts towards unification, the former spearheaded by Count Camillo Cavour (1810–1861), prime minister of Piedmont, an independent kingdom ruled by the Savoys. Abroad, Napoleon III of France was motivated by concerns for French Catholics and the survival of the papacy. Britain favored the end of Spanish (Bourbon) domination in southern Italy, and Austria was opposed to unification at the expense of its influential position in north Italy.

Garibaldi, military genius of unification

THE 1859 CAMPAIGNS In 1859, Cavour engineered an alliance with Napoleon III against the Austrians, joining the French armies to those of Piedmont (under the Savoy king, Vittore Emanuele II). The Austrians were defeated at Magenta and Solferino, after which Napoleon III—to Cavour's frustration—signed an armistice with them. Meanwhile, revolts elsewhere had gathered a momentum of their own, with uprisings in Tuscany and Emilia, both of which were annexed by Piedmont (along with Lombardy, won at Solferino).

UNIFICATION In 1860 the job of unification was only half complete. To finish it, Garibaldi left Genoa with 1,000 volunteers (the *Mille*) to overthrow the Bourbons in the name of Vittore Emanuele II. Sicily and Naples fell within four months, the papal states surrendered to Cavour, and the Kingdom of Italy was proclaimed in February 1861. The Austrians were removed from Venice and the Veneto in 1866 (defeated following an alliance with Prussia), and Rome and the papacy were taken in 1870 after the withdrawal of the French garrison (precipitated by the fall of Napoleon III, defeated by Prussia that same year in Sedan).

THE 1848 REPUBLICS Unrest swept over all of Europe in 1848. In Italy, it sparked off a war against Austria in Lombardy (under Carlo Alberto, the Savoy king) and the restoration of Venice's Republic of San Marco (also anti-Austria). In Rome, the pope fled from rioting and Mazzini established the Roman Republic (Garibaldi organized the city's defenses). The republics were short-lived. Austria crushed the northern uprisings and French troops relieved Rome, restoring the status quo of a year earlier.

Italy entered both world wars in the hope of territorial gain after piecemeal colonial expansion in Eritrea, Libya, and Abyssinia. Success in 1918 bred only debt and disappointment, and gave rise to Fascism, while failure in 1943—ironically—laid the foundations of progress and the country's present prosperity.

WORLD WAR I At the start of World War I, Italy was neutral, but by 1915 had joined the Allied cause, lured by promises of colonial rewards and the chance of gaining the partly Italian-speaking regions around Trento and Trieste. Its ill-prepared army lost several bitterly fought battles, notably at Caporetto in 1917, before a last-ditch victory at Vittorio Veneto. Although denied certain territories, Italy's gains at the peace conference included (present-day) Trentino-Alto Adige and Friuli-Venezia-Giulia, though at a high cost: national assets fell by 26 percent, and 40 percent of the 5.5 million Italians who fought were killed or wounded.

FASCISM Italy's government was unable to deal with the social and economic chaos unleashed by the war, creating a power vacuum quickly filled by Benito Mussolini, whose high-sounding promises pandered to the panic-stricken middle and upper classes. A threatened general strike in 1922 provided the excuse for his "March on Rome," after which—fearful of civil war—the king handed power to Mussolini (who had an intimidating mob presence on the streets, but still only a tiny showing in parliament itself). By 1925, Italy was ruled by a dictatorship, held together with bluster and brute force, and bolstered by imperial adventures in North Africa.

WORLD WAR II After a hesitant start, Mussolini took Italy to war in June 1940, emboldened by Hitler's success and eager to share in the spoils of victory. After successes in the Adriatic, he suffered defeats in Greece, heavy casualties in Russia, and the loss of Sicily (August 1943), all of which led to his downfall and an armistice with the Allies. The Nazis assumed control, installed Mussolini as the head of a puppet republic, and confronted the Allies—and a force of 450,000 partisans—as they inched up the Italian peninsula to liberate Rome on June 4, 1944. Mussolini's end came in April 1945, when he was shot by partisans and strung up in Milan's Piazzale Loreto.

Fêting the triumphant Mussolini

Italy's progress since World War II has been remarkable. The country has developed in less than a generation from an agricultural backwater to one of the world's leading industrial nations. However, this transformation initially brought social tensions, terrorism, and a rise in organized crime.

THE FIFTIES A referendum in June 1946 voted narrowly (54–46) to replace Italy's monarchy with a republic. With the help of America's Marshall Plan, the hardships of the immediate postwar years gave way to an economic boom bolstered by cheap, compliant labor, and most Italians' thirst for the world of cars, televisions, and material well-being. This was the era of *la dolce vita*, Sophia Loren, baby Fiats, and mass migrations from the south to the industrialized cities of the north. In 1957 the Treaty of Rome was signed, and Italy became a founding member of the European Union.

THE SIXTIES The boom tailed off somewhat in the 1960s, and the orthodoxy of past governments (dominated by the center-right Christian Democrats) gave way to coalitions in which the left demanded a voice. Inflation soared, and social tensions surfaced, the bitter fruit of Italy's sudden wrench from traditional ways of life. Unrest culminated in the *autunno caldo* (hot fall) of 1969, when strikes and student demonstrations crippled the country.

THE SEVENTIES Matters became worse in the next decade, when at times it appeared Italy was on the brink of disintegration. Right- and left-wing terrorism was rife, culminating in 1978 with the kidnap and murder of Aldo Moro, a former prime minister, by the *Brigate Rosse* (Red Brigades). These were the so-called *anni di piombo* (years of lead), named after the amount of bullets used in the period, but also evocative of the gloomy and apocalyptic mood of the times.

THE EIGHTIES AND NINETIES By about 1985 the economy steadied and terrorism was all but defeated. Italy continued to prosper (at least in the north) despite its upheavals and political scandals, progress occurring despite rather than because of its institutions. Today, however, after over 50 years of corrupt government, the country seems to have entered the millennium with a heartfelt desire for institutional reforms. If it succeeds, and the problems of the Mafia and the south are addressed, Italy may finally solve the previous century's problems in this century.

29

Rome, April 1968: student protests were brutally put down by riot police

Italy's artistic heyday may not have been the Renaissance, but the centuries when Greek, Etruscan, and Roman artists and sculptors produced their classical masterpieces. These still lie scattered across the country's many museums and archeological sites.

GREEK INFLUENCES Greek art came to Italy with the colonies of Magna Graecia around 800 BC (see page 231), making its mark on much of south Italy and influencing the Etruscan and Roman cultures that followed for more than a millennium. Particularly influential were the temple architecture of Sicily and southern Italy (Paestum provides supreme examples), and the semicircular Greek theaters, examples of which survive in Taormina and Siracusa. Hellenistic painting, in contrast, has almost vanished, though its influence permeates the tomb paintings and decorated vases of Etruscan culture. Sculpture was very significant, and Greek bronzes and ceramics also served as models for Italian craftsmen.

ETRUSCAN ART While borrowing from Greek models, Etruscan art retained a distinct character, its often earthy naturalism in contrast to the idealized strivings of Greek artists. Tomb paintings survive in Tarquinia and Chiusi, mixtures of visionary, realistic, and superstitious tableaux, testimony to the Etruscans' vivacious and outward-looking culture. Bronze and terra-cotta, rather than marble, were favored for their beautiful and sophisticated sculptures with mysteriously smiling faces, many of which are now on display in the Vatican and Villa Giulia museums. Their goldwork, especially jewelry, was technically brilliant. Little is known of Etruscan architecture, though it probably made use of the arch and vault, forms later adopted by the Romans.

THE ROMANS Roman art's debt to Greece and Etruria was immeasurable, from the use of mosaics and Etruscan sarcophaghus reliefs to the masterpieces of Roman sculpture copied from Greek originals. The derivative nature of Roman sculpture in no way detracts from its often sublime execution, but for originality one must look to Roman architecture (and engineering), with innovations such as the basilica, triumphal arch and commemorative column. There are Greek elements in the Colosseum and Pantheon, and in villas, palaces, and baths, but all are unmistakably Roman. Wall paintings, widespread in their day, but surviving mainly as fragments uncovered at Pompeii and Herculaneum, also showed a Hellenistic bent.

Etruscan vessels of exquisite workmanship

The stylized Madonnas and mosaic tradition of Byzantium were to influence Italian art until the 13th century, and marked an era of great achievement. Together with Roman art and architecture, they formed the basis of Christianity's earliest artistic tradition.

OLD FORMS, NEW THEMES
Christianity presented art with new themes and iconography, and was to be its chief inspiration until the Renaissance. In its earliest incarnations Christian art expressed itself in the prevailing tastes of the day: sculptures graced a few sarcophagi; paintings, except in a handful of catacombs, were rare—though it may be that early Christian artifacts have been lost. Church architecture copied the forms of Roman aisled basilicas, often relying for decoration on mosaics, the most prominent medium of early Christian art. Early mosaics—those of Rome's fourth-century Santa Costanza, for example—followed classical Roman models, but most quickly adopted the more highly colored attributes of the Byzantine models.

BYZANTIUM Byzantine art was a hybrid of classical and oriental influences, introduced by Justinian, emperor of the eastern half of the Roman Empire, when he invaded parts of Italy in the sixth century (see page 23). It was distinguished by abstraction, gold backgrounds, and ornamental motifs, usually seen in the form of mosaics. Notable examples are found in Ravenna (Byzantium's Italian capital), Rome (Santa Maria Maggiore and elsewhere), Milan (Sant'Ambrogio), and Aquileia (the Basilica). Not only did Byzantium's artistic influence spread over a wide area, it also proved remarkably durable, and Byzantine-influenced craftsmen were still producing mosaics in the 12th century (principally in Palermo's Cappella Palatina, the cathedrals of Cefalù and Monreale, and—most famously—in Venice's Basilica di San Marco, the apotheosis of Byzantine art, architecture, and decoration).

31

BYZANTINE PAINTING Byzantium's influence pervades three images that dominated Italian painting until the 14th century: portraits of saints; the

Santa Maria in Trastevere, Rome

iconic Madonna and Child; and *Christus Triumphans*, a large painted crucifix of Christ. All were distinguished by a mystical or reverential tone and stiff, formalized figures. Byzantium is also everpresent in an often overlooked but vital artifact of the Dark Ages—the illustrated monastic manuscripts that carried art's banner for centuries.

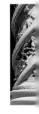

Apart from beautiful mosaics and illustrated manuscripts, Italy's most conspicuous artistic flowering, as the country emerged from the Dark Ages, was primarily in the Romanesque churches and then in the Gothic palaces and cathedrals that accompanied the growth of independent city states.

32

ROMANESQUE Romanesque architecture emerged during the 11th century, fostered by the upsurge of church-building in the emerging city states. Northern European (Lombard) and Italianate influences combined to produce a style distinguished by simplicity, round arches, and thick-walled buildings with cross vaults or exposed beam ceilings. Churches often had a basilical plan, with a raised choir and correspondingly sunken crypt. Decoration was simple, usually confined to the apse or main portal, but often extended to campaniles and baptisteries.

The style emerges all over Italy, particularly in Lombardy (Modena, Parma, and Cremona), around Pisa (Lucca and

Milan cathedral, northern Italian Gothic architecture at its finest

Pistoia), in Sicily (Cefalù, Palermo, and Monreale), and in Apulia, where Arab, Byzantine, and Norman elements combined to create the hybrid known as Apulian-Romanesque (Bari, Ruvo, Trani, Troia, and elsewhere). Masterpieces of Romanesque sculpture include the reliefs of Wiligelmus in Modena, Antelami's work in Parma, the doors of San Zeno (Verona), and the works of the Pisanos across central Italy.

GOTHIC Where Romanesque architecture was robust and earthbound, the Gothic, which originated in 13th-century France, was light and airy. Its emphasis was on verticality, its staples the pointed arch, rose windows, stained glass, rib vaulting, and flying buttresses. In Italy, Milan's Duomo, with its pinnacles and soaring lines, best shows the genre in its characteristic glory.

Elsewhere, a lesser version of the Gothic appeared, its grandeur suited to the desire of cities to make conspicuous displays of their new prosperity. It distinguished the civic palaces (*palazzi pubblici*) of Siena (the Palazzo Pubblico), Florence (Palazzo Vecchio), and Venice, whose Palazzo Ducale captures Italian Gothic style at its most dazzling. The style also emerged in the great cathedrals of central Italy, notably Pisa, Siena, and Florence, and in the Basilica di San Francesco in Assisi (1228), an early Gothic masterpiece.

During the Gothic period, the Renaissance was prefigured by a handful of artists and sculptors who cast off the conventions of Byzantine art to sow the seeds of artistic renewal. Also at this time regional schools began to develop a style that breathed new life into old traditions.

SCULPTORS Nicola Pisano (ca1220–1284) was the first of a trio of 13th-century artists whose marriage of Gothic and classical ideas was a harbinger of things to come. His graceful, sinuous style can be seen in four outstanding works: Fontana Maggiore (Perugia), Arca di San Domenico (Bologna), and pulpits in Pisa (the Baptistery), and Siena (the Duomo). Pisano's pupil and assistant, Arnolfo di Cambio (ca1245–1310), disseminated his influence in works all over central Italy, but the influence of Pisano's son, Giovanni Pisano (ca1248–1314), whose figurative skill was revolutionary, was more significant.

PAINTERS Glimmerings of a new artistic dawn began with men like Pietro Cavallini (active 1273–1308), who began to explore the possibilities of fresco. After working in Rome (Santa Maria in Trastevere), he moved to Assisi, and the Basilica di San Francesco, where he was joined first by Cimabue (ca1240–1302), who

Vasari dubbed the "father of Italian painting," and then by Giotto di Bondone (1266–1337), a seminal figure in the development of Italian art. He introduced emotion, natural settings, three-dimensional figures, and narrative detail into his work (fresco cycles in Assisi and Padua in particular) that broke with the stylized strictures of Byzantine art.

33

Above: Nicola Pisano's Fontana Maggiore in Perugia
Left: detail from Siena cathedral

SIENA While Giotto preached innovation in Assisi's Basilica, the artists of Siena were reinterpreting the Byzantine tradition, forging the most dynamic of the schools of painting that sprang up across central Italy during the 13th and 14th centuries. Glorious swathes of color and gold backgrounds dominated its early masterpieces, exemplified by the works of Duccio di Buoninsegna (ca1255–1318). These features were later wedded to the courtly, detailed style enshrined particularly in the paintings of Simone Martini (ca1284–1344) and Pietro Lorenzetti (active 1306–1345).

A mixture of social, artistic, and intellectual ferment gave rise to the Renaissance, which spread from Florence over the course of 125 years to become one of the greatest periods in the history of Western art.

WHAT AND WHY Several closely related factors helped bring about the Renaissance—the "rebirth" of art and science. Humanist scholarship freed art of its devotional obligations and rediscovered Greek and Roman texts, from which it was a short step to a revival of the classical ideal in art. Where conservative Church patronage had stifled innovation, lay patrons like the Medici provided the financial wherewithal for voyages of artistic discovery. Free-thinking Florence, a prosperous and cosmopolitan city, provided an atmosphere in which creativity could flourish, attracting ever more artists as its reputation snowballed. And as more artists arrived, the exchange of ideas and atmosphere of innovation intensified (particularly in crucial areas such as the study of anatomy and perspective).

FLORENCE Three artists in three key disciplines ushered in the Florentine Renaissance. Filippo Brunelleschi (1377–1446) triumphed as an architect, not only creating a dome for the city's cathedral, but also clarifying ideals of design and advancing the new science of perspective. The sculptor Donatello (1386–1466) produced staggeringly innovative work, returning the nude to the mainstream of artistic expression. And in painting Masaccio (1401–1428)—together with Masolino da Panicale—pioneered techniques of perspective that dazzled contemporaries. An army of hallowed names followed: Paolo Uccello, Fra Angelico, Filippo Lippi, Benozzo Gozzoli, Lorenzo Ghiberti, Luca della Robbia, Verrocchio, Ghirlandaio, and Sandro Botticelli (not to mention architects like Michelozzo, Sangallo, and Leon Battisti Alberti).

OUTSIDE FLORENCE Florence did not have a monopoly on Renaissance talent. Piero della Francesca, from the Tuscan town of Sansepolcro, produced singular works that combined ethereal beauty with compositional precision. In Cortona, his pupil Luca Signorelli painted influential work distinguished by striking nudes. The Marches claimed Venetian-bred Carlo Crivelli, while Umbria had Perugino, responsible for melancholy, soft-edged devotional paintings (sometimes executed in tandem with another Umbrian, Pinturicchio). Siena's masters included sculptor Jacopo della Quercia and painters

Ghirlandaio's Adoration *in Florence's Santa Trinità*

The Raphael Rooms in the Vatican Museum in Rome contain some superb frescoes

Sassetta and Giovanni di Paolo. Other artists of genius included Mantegna (Mantua), Correggio (Parma), Lorenzo Lotto (Lombardy), Tura (Ferrara), Bellini and Carpaccio (Venice), Pisanello (Verona), and Antonello da Messina (Sicily).

HIGH RENAISSANCE As three innovators tower over the Renaissance's formative years, so a trio of artistic geniuses dominate its maturity—the so-called High Renaissance—a period that begins at the turn of the 16th century with the painting of Leonardo da Vinci's *Last Supper* (in Milan). The end of Florence's artistic primacy was marked by Michelangelo (1475–1564), who left his Medici patrons to work in Rome, where papal patronage was the spur for the frescoes of the Sistine Chapel: perhaps the supreme achievement of Western art. Another consummate genius lured to Rome was Raphael, born in Urbino, apprenticed to Perugino, and responsible for such masterpieces as the Vatican's *Stanze di Raffaello* (Raphael Rooms). Paragons of High Renaissance architecture included Bramante, Baldassare Peruzzi, Sangallo the Younger, Sansovino, and the great Andrea Palladio (1508–1580).

MANNERISM Following the sack of Rome by the troops of Emperor Charles V in 1527, Renaissance self-confidence gave way to the self-conscious and disquieting world of Mannerism, a genre—part-inspired by Raphael and Michelangelo—that put art above nature, generally valued style above substance, and flouted the conventions of scale, color, and composition. Its leading lights were Pontormo, Bronzino, Rosso Fiorentino, Benvenuto Cellini, Andrea del Sarto, Domenico Beccafumi (from Siena), Parmigianino (from Parma), and the sculptor Giambologna.

VENICE Venice charted a course of its own during the Renaissance, its artists more concerned with color and atmosphere than the Florentine preoccupations with line and composition. Early on, the Vivarini family of artists (Bartolomeo, Antonio, and Alvise) emphasized the city's debt to Byzantine art and the opulent courtly style known as "International Gothic." Another dynasty, the Bellinis, Giovanni Bellini in particular, marked the city's Renaissance heyday (together with Carpaccio). Venetian painting reached new heights during the High Renaissance with painters like Titian, Tintoretto, Paolo Veronese, and Giorgione—the last as mysterious in his way as Piero della Francesca.

Born in Rome and nurtured by papal largesse, baroque—the artistic expression of Counter-Reformation optimism—may have been named after the irregularly shaped pearls known as perle baroche. *In the words of Luigi Barzini, it "came to be used metaphorically to describe anything pointlessly complicated, otiose, capricious, and eccentric."*

ARCHITECTURE Baroque's first star, Carlo Maderno (1556–1629), responsible for the façade of St. Peter's, was soon outshone by the two giants of the period— Gianlorenzo Bernini (1598–1680) and Francesco Borromini (1599–1667). Bernini transformed the face of Rome, infusing everything—from fountains to St. Peter's monumental piazza—with his exuberant *joie de vivre*. Borromini, his bitter rival, was more tortured and introspective (he eventually committed suicide), but proved the more innovative—even more eccentric—architect. Lacking Bernini's sculptural skill, he was famous instead for his sophisticated geometry and exotic combinations of shapes (best seen in Rome's Sant'Ivo, San Carlo, and Sant'Agnese).

SCULPTURE In sculpture Bernini knew no rivals, his genius apparent from an early age in such works as *Apollo and Daphne* and the *David* in Rome's Galleria Borghese (Italy's first important sculptures since Michelangelo's final works). His masterpiece, *The Ecstasy of St. Teresa* (in Rome's Santa Maria della Vittoria), captures fully the period's emphasis on emotion and stylized

Bernini's St. Teresa, pierced by the arrow of divine love

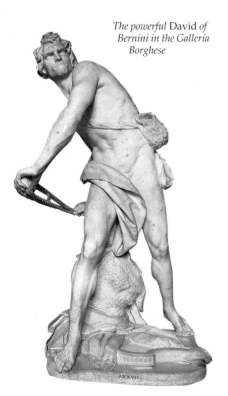

The powerful David *of Bernini in the Galleria Borghese*

PAINTING The baroque period spawned two broad schools of painting, the first dominated by Caravaggio (1573–1610), whose realistic works displayed virtuoso effects of light and shade (*chiaroscuro*), the second championed by the Carracci family (Ludovico, Annibale, and Agostino), whose works signaled a return to the clarity of classical models. Ornate and illusionist ceiling frescoes were also a feature of the age, and Pietro da Cortona (1596–1669) was their chief exponent, best known for work in Rome's Palazzo Barberini (other masters of the art included Bernini's protégé G. B. Gaulli and Andrea Pozzo). Naples proved a hotbed of baroque endeavor, producing artists such as Luca Giordano, Salvator Rosa, and Artemesia Gentileschi, one of Italy's finest woman painters.

37

drama, his passion for illusion and sensuality, and—above all—the spirituality of Teresa's ecstatic vision of God. Alessandro Algardi challenged Bernini briefly, but the period's other principal players operated outside Rome—in Turin (Guarini and Juvarra), Lecce (Zimbalo), and in Catania, Noto, and Ragusa in Sicily.

St. Peter's, Rome. Above: the baldacchino; *below: the piazza*

The last three centuries of Italy's artistic history are often written off as a sad anticlimax, yet Italian artists produced two new styles—neoclassicism and futurism—and excelled in another (rococo). Today, Italian artists still manage to make Italy one of Europe's leading centers of fashion and design.

THE 18TH CENTURY Art and architecture reacted in different ways to the baroque. While architecture turned away from its excesses to find refuge in neoclassicism, a return to the most basic of classical principles (notably in Rome), painting turned to the still more florid and opulent world of rococo, a sensually obsessed style born in France that in Italy found its greatest expression in Venice. Though stripped of its political preeminence, the city was still a wealthy, even decadent retreat, capable of producing and patronizing artists such as Sebastiano Ricci, the great Giovanni Battista Tiepolo (1696–1770), and three leading landscapists, Francesco Guardi, Bernardo Bellotto, and Canaletto (1697–1768). Neoclassicism's more restrained outlook found its way into painting, but was more marked in sculpture, as in the erotic works of Antonio Canova (1757–1822).

THE 19TH CENTURY The march of neoclassicism continued in the 19th century, but in painting it was largely outflanked by the Europe-wide Romantic movement, whose Italian trendsetter was Francesco Hayez (1791–1882)—almost the country's

only notable artist for several decades. The middle of the century saw the emergence of the *Macchiaioli* (from the Italian *macchia*—spot or stain), a group of painters whose use of color marked a reaction against the polish of neoclassicism and shared the modern outlook of the French Impressionists (leading artists included Lega, Fattori, and Signorini). All were overshadowed by Amedeo Modigliani (1884–1920), the best known of Italy's more recent artists (though most of his life was spent in Paris).

THE 20TH CENTURY Art nouveau took a hold in Italy, where it was known as *Lo Stile Liberty*; examples can still be seen in the galleries of Milan and the interiors of early 20th-century cafés in Turin, Trieste, and elsewhere. In painting, the futurist movement—founded by a group of Italians in Paris in 1909—glorified the mechanical age, pioneered by Umberto Boccioni (1882–1916), and developed by Gino Severini and Giacomo Balla. Futurism fused with cubism are found in the works of Italy's last great "name" in art, Giorgio de Chirico (1888–1978).

Modigliani's Seated Man Leaning on a Table

38

▶ ▶ ▶ CITY HIGHLIGHTS

Rome

PRATI

VIA CRESCENZIO

100 200 300 m
0
0 100 200
300 yards

PIAZZA
CAVOUR

Ara
Pacis
Augustae

Mausoleo
di Augusto

PIAZZA
AUGUSTO
IMPERATORE

VIA TOMACELLI

VIA V. COLONNA

VIA TRIBONIANO

PIAZZA ADRIANA

PIAZZA ADRIANA

VIA VITELLESCHI

Parco Adriano

VIA ULPIANO

PONTE
CAVOUR

Palazzo
di
Giustizia

Casa
Madre
d'Mutilati

Palazzo
Borghese

PIAZZA
BORGHESE

VIA DI CLEMENTINO

VIA DI RIPETTA

LUNGOTEVERE MARZIO

LUNG. VATICANO

E

BORGO
SANT'ANGELICO

PIAZZA
PIA

Castel Sant'Angelo

VIA DELLA
CONCILIAZIONE

Musei Vaticani
San Pietro

PONTE
VITTORIO
EMANUELE II

PONTE
SANT'
ANGELO

VIA PACIS

LUNGOTEVERE CASTELLO

PONTE
UMBERTO I

Tevere

PIAZZA
NICOSIA

VIA DELLA SCROFA

CAMPO
MARZIO

LUNGOTEVERE TOR DI NONA

VIA TOMACELLI

Santa Maria
in Campo
Marzio

VIA DI SASSIA

PONTE
PR. AM. SAV.
AOSTA

D

PIAZZA
PAOLI

PONTE
VITTORIO
EMANUELE II

VIA D. ALTOVITI

BANCO S. SPIRITO

PIAZZA
DEL
CORONARI

VIA
SAN SALVATORE
IN LAURO

VIA DEI CORONARI

Sant'
Agostino

Santa Maria
Maddalena

PIAZZA
DELL'ORO

PONTE
PARIONE

PIAZZA
DELL'
OROLOGIO

Santa Maria
della Pace
Santa Maria
dell'Anima

Fontana dei
Quattro
Fiumi

San Luigi
dei Francesi

Palazzo
Madama

PIAZZA
DELLA
ROTONDA

San Giovanni
dei Fiorentini

VIA GIULIA

CORSO VITTORIO EMANUELE

Chiesa
Nuova

PIAZZA DELLA
CHIESA NUOVA

Sant'Agnese
in Agone

Palazzo
Pamphili

PIAZZA
NAVONA

CORSO DEL RINASCIMENTO

Pantheon

PIAZZA SANT'
EUSTACHIO

Sant'Ivo alla
Sapienza

LUNGOTEVERE GIANICOLENSE

C

LARGO
L. PEROSI

Palazzo Braschi
Museo di Roma

Palazzo
della
Cancelleria

Santa Maria
di Monserrato

Sant'Eligio
degli Orefici

REGOLA

CORSO VITTORIO

Fontana
del Moro

PIAZZA
SAN
PANTALEO

Palazzo
Massimo
alle Colonne

EMANUELE II

PI.G

P

LARGO DI
TORRE
ARGENTINA

VIA DEL PELLEGRINO

PONTE
G. MAZZINI

LUNGOTEVERE DEI TEBALDI

Tevere

LUNGOTEVERE DELLA FARNESINA

Villa
Farnesina

Palazzo
Falconieri

PIAZZA
FARNESE

PIAZZA CAMPO DEI
FIORI

Palazzo
Farnese

Sant'Andrea
della Valle

San Carlo
ai Catinari

Templi
Republicani

PIAZZA B.
CAIROLI

V. DELLE

VIA DI TORRE ARGENTINA

B

Palazzo
Corsini

Santa Maria
dell'Orazione
e Morte

Palazzo
Spada

Santi Trinità
dei Pellegrini

VIA ARENULA

GHETTO

LUNGOTEVERE DEI VALLATI

LUNGOTEVERE DEI

PONTE
SISTO

Museo
Torlonia

VIA DELLA LUNGARA

VIA V. BENEDETTA

PIAZZA
TRILUSSA

LUNGOTEVERE SANZIO

PONTE
GARIBALDI

PIAZZA
G. BELLI

Isola
Tiberina

LUNG. ANGUILLARA

PONTE
CESTIO

Gianicolo

Santa
Maria
della
Scala

VIA DELLA SCALA

★

VIA DELLA LUNGARETTA

VIA DELLA LUNGARETTA

A

VIA DI PORTA S. PANCRAZIO

San Pietro
in Montorio

VIA G. GARIBALDI

Fontana
Paola

VIA G. GARIBALDI

Santa Maria
in Trastevere

San Crisogono

VIALE DI

San Benedetto

Santa Cecilia
in Trastevere

PIAZZA
SONNINO

1   T R A S T E V E R E   2   3   E

VIA DI

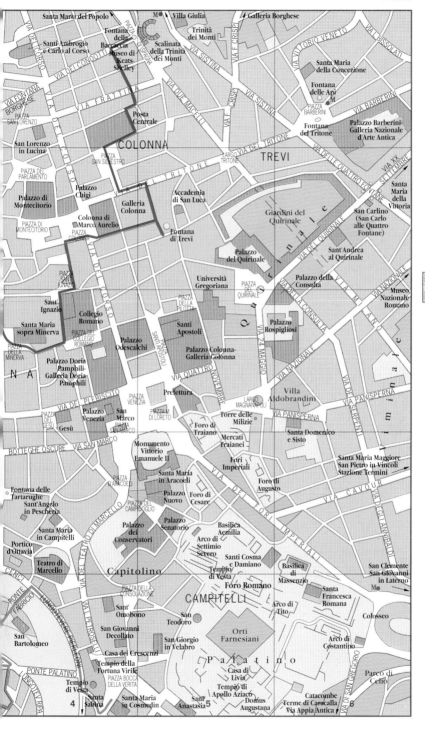

Throw a coin in the famous Trevi Fountain, and legend has it you will return to the city one day

ROME (ROMA) We expect a lot of Rome—seat of empire, mother of civilization, *caput mundi* (head of the world). It is the city of the Caesars, of romance, the city of *la dolce vita* and languorous sunny days, the city of endless art, of churches and museums, of fountain-splashed piazzas and majestic monuments to its golden age of empire. Sadly, it is also the city of uncontrollable traffic, the city of frenetic noise and confusion, the city of wanton crowds, obstinate bureaucracy, and groaning inefficiency. Its modern face is not a pretty one, and to get under its rumpled skin requires an oblique approach to sightseeing.

SEEING THE CITY Head-on confrontation with Rome, however energetically you join the fray, can leave you dispirited and defeated. Plan ahead, therefore, don't attempt too much, don't tackle its streets in the heat of the afternoon. Avoid the temptation to join the trudge around the famous sights. Avoid St. Peter's and the Sistine

Chapel; forget the Colosseum and the Pantheon, at least in the beginning. Reflect instead over a quiet cappuccino in Campo dei Fiori, the city's loveliest square. Forgo the Spanish Steps' aimless mob and climb to the Pincio Gardens for a view over the rooftops to St. Peter's. Thus initiated you can prepare for the assault on the Vatican Museums, or the stroll around the Forum; you can face the traffic and the chaos—and perhaps in time even come to enjoy them as dynamic aspects of a city that is struggling, as it has for centuries, to incorporate the present into its eternal past.

LAYER OF HISTORY Rome belongs to no single historical period. Its sights and quarters are a lavish medley of ancient, medieval, Renaissance, and modern buildings, making it difficult to define areas, or to plan your sightseeing around a single epoch. In the earliest days Rome gathered around seven famous hills—the Aventino, Capitolino, Esquilino, Caelio, Palatino, Quirinale, and Viminale. Later, Augustus created several *rioni*, a series of wards like Paris' *arrondissements*. Neither of these divisions, however, adequately defines the present city.

AREAS OF THE CITY Piazza Venezia is now Rome's hub, a junction of streets that strike off to the four points of the compass. The ***centro storico*** (historical center) is not, confusingly, the Forum and the ancient heart of Rome, but a warren of streets that made up the city's core from the Middle Ages to the last century. Contained between the Tiber and Via del Corso, it divides into a medieval quarter (north of Corso Vittorio Emanuele II), centered around Piazza Navona and the Pantheon, and a Renaissance district (south of Corso Vittorio Emanuele II), centered around Via Giulia and Piazza Farnese. The latter contains the Ghetto, one of the city's most captivating areas (the streets east of Via Arenula). Across the river is **Trastevere** ("across the Tiber"). Once Rome's 19th-century slum— and still seedy in places—it is now generally a charming area, especially good for aimless wandering, restaurants, and evening entertainment. To its north lies **Vatican City**, centered around St. Peter's, an independent state under papal control. Nearby stretch the leafy residential districts of Prati and Parioli.

ROMULUS AND REMUS This is the myth about Rome that everyone knows. It begins in the old Latin capital Alba Longa, where Amulius usurped the throne of his brother Numitor. To avoid rival claims, Amulius forced Numitor's only daughter, Rhea Silvia, to become a vestal virgin. A visit from the god Mars left her pregnant with Romulus and Remus. Amulius cast the twins adrift in a basket, but the gods steered them safely to the Palatine, where a she-wolf cared for the pair until they were found by a shepherd. Told of their destiny by Mars, they founded Rome in 753 BC. The brothers could not agree whether to name the city *Rema* or *Roma*—but Romulus started building his walls regardless. Incensed, Remus jumped over them and was killed by his brother.

WEEKEND'S ITINERARY

SATURDAY
Breakfast in Campo dei Fiori (walk: Ghetto–Isola Tiberina–Piazza Bocca della Verità–Campidoglio).
Morning: Campidoglio, Forum, Colosseum, San Clemente (San Giovanni in Laterano). Lunch (walk: Colle Oppio–Foro Traiano–Fontana di Trevi).
Afternoon: Fontana di Trevi, Santa Maria sopra Minerva, Pantheon, Piazza Navona (walk: Via dei Coronari–Via Governo Vecchio/shopping: Via Condotti, Via del Corso).
Evening: Walk/bus to Trastevere (Santa Maria in Trastevere, Santa Cecilia). Dinner in Trastevere.

SUNDAY
Breakfast in Piazza Navona (walk to Castel Sant' Angelo).
Morning: (Castel Sant' Angelo), St. Peter's, Vatican Museums.
Afternoon: (Walk: to Piazza del Popolo). Pincio, Piazza di Spagna.

43

Etruscan bronze of a she-wolf in the Capitoline Museum. The human twins were added later

VESTAL VIRGINS
Vestal Virgins were the guardians of Rome's sacred flame. They were chosen, before they reached the age of 14, from Rome's leading patrician families. Up to 30 years were spent in service, after which they could retire on a state pension. The only man allowed in their temple was the Pontifex Maximus, or high priest. His title— "Greatest Bridge Builder" —was adopted by the popes, hence the abbreviation *Pont Max* on many of the papal buildings.

44

COLONNA TRAIANO
Trajan's Column was built in AD 113 to celebrate Trajan's victories over the Dacians (tribes from present-day Romania). Its great spiraling frieze contains 2,500 figures and 18 huge drums of Greek marble. The reliefs have provided a wealth of information about Roman arms and modes of warfare.

CLEVER ENGINEERING
The Pantheon's remarkable dome, for centuries one of the world's largest, rests on brick-faced Roman-era concrete walls some 23 feet thick. Its lower drum starts the same width, becoming progressively thinner— and thus lighter—until it is a little over 3 feet thick at its apex. This helped lighten the dome's payload, an effect reinforced by using increasingly lighter materials toward its crown. Heavy travertine mixed with concrete is used at the base; less sturdy volcanic tufa midway, and feather-light pumice at the summit.

Roman monuments

▶▶ Ara Pacis Augustae   40E3
Via di Ripetta
Currently closed for restoration work
The "Altar of Peace" was raised by the Senate in 13–9 BC to commemorate the victories of the emperor Augustus. Its superb reliefs include mythological scenes and episodes from the altar's ceremonial consecration.

▶▶ Arco di Costantino (Arch of Constantine)   41A6
Piazza del Colosseo
The largest and best preserved of Rome's ancient arches was raised to honor the victory of the emperor Constantine over Maxentius in AD 312. Many of its reliefs were taken from earlier monuments, partly for practical reasons, and partly to link the emperor's regime to the glories of the past. The battle scenes, for example, show Trajan at war with the Dacians.

▶▶▶ Castel Sant'Angelo (see page 46)   40E1

▶▶ Catacombe (Catacombs)   *off* 41A6
Rome has over 480 miles of catacombs, the underground tombs of pagans and early Christians. The best of these are the **Catacombe di San Callisto** (Via Appia Antica. *Closed* Wed) with 170,000 graves; others are the nearby **Catacombe di San Sebastiano** (Via Appia Antica. *Closed* Sun), and those of Domitilla (Via Sette Chiese) and Priscilla (Via Salaria).

▶▶▶ Colosseo (Colosseum) (see page 50) 41A6

▶▶ Fori Imperiali   41B5
Via dei Fori Imperiali
Closed for restoration but visible from the road
The five imperial fora were built by successive emperors after the Foro Romano and Palatino became too small. The best are the Foro di Augusto and Foro Traiano. The latter contains the great **Colonna Traiano**▶▶▶ (Trajan's Column) and the **Mercati Traianei**▶ (Trajan's Market).

▶▶▶ Foro Romano (Roman Forum)   41A5
Open: summer, 9–7:30; winter, 9–3:30. Admission free
The old heart of the Roman Empire is crowded with the jumbled ruins of temples, basilicas, and other buildings spanning 1,100 years—a wonderfully evocative place to wander in. Be sure to see the **triumphal arches of Tito and Settimio Severo**▶▶, the mighty **Basilica di Massenzio**▶▶▶, and the **Tempio di Vesta**▶▶▶ (Temple of the Vestal Virgins).

▶▶▶ Palatino   41A5
Via dei Fori Imperiali–Via di San Gregorio Magno
Open: summer, 9–7:30; winter, 9–3:30. Admission: expensive
The Palatine hill was the first of the famous seven hills to be inhabited. In time it became the favored residential district of Rome's élite, including emperors. Most buildings are now badly ruined, or buried under the beautiful 16th-century **Orti Farnesiani**▶▶ (the Farnese Gardens).

▶▶▶ Pantheon   *40C3*

Piazza della Rotonda
Open: Mon–Sat 8:30–7:30, Sun 9–1, 2–6. Admission free
This, perhaps the grandest monument of Roman antiquity, built by Hadrian in AD 128, became a Christian church in 609 (which is one of the major reasons for its remarkable state of preservation). Incredibly, the immense cupola was the largest freestanding dome in the world until as late as 1960.

▶ Terme di Caracalla   *off 41A6*

Via delle Terme di Caracalla
Open: summer, Tue–Sun 9–7, Mon 9–2; winter, Tue–Sun 9–3:30, Mon 9–2. Admission: moderate
The Baths of Caracalla (AD 206) were not as large as the Baths of Diocletian (remains of which you can see around Piazza della Repubblica), but they were more luxurious and are far better preserved. They could accommodate 2,000 bathers, and many thousands more in the complex of sports and leisure facilities nearby.

▶▶ Via Appia Antica   *off 41A6*

Rome's ancient Via Appia Antica, the "Queen of Roads," was built in 312 BC and connected the city with Capua and Brindisi in southern Italy. Today, it still has many of its original cobbles (see below) and is lined by ancient tombs and catacombs. Much of the route is delightful to wander along—a little piece of countryside only a stone's throw from the city.

The classical splendor of the Pantheon

COFFEE AND ICE CREAM
Immediately off the Pantheon's Piazza della Rotonda is La Tazza d'Oro (Via degli Orfani 84), generally considered to sell Rome's best cup of coffee. The best ice cream is to be had at Gelateria San Crispino near the Fontana di Trevi (Via della Panetteria 42; *closed* Tue).

THE GHETTO
The area west of the Teatro di Marcello is the old Jewish Ghetto (created in 1555). The area contains some of the city's quietest and nicest back streets. Wander here during siesta or in the early evening. A recommended stroll is from Campo dei Fiori along Via Giubbonari and Via Portico d'Ottaviano to explore the picturesque streets of the Ghetto. Be sure, too, to see Bernini's delightful Fontana delle Tartarughe (Fountain of the Tortoises) in Piazza Mattei.

The cobbled surface of the 2,300-year-old Via Appia Antica

Elegance and power: the Ponte Sant'Angelo leading to the Castel Sant'Angelo

Museums and galleries

▶▶▶ Castel Sant'Angelo   40E1
Lungotevere Castello
Open: Tue–Sun 9–7:30. Admission: moderate
Built as the tomb of the emperor Hadrian (AD 139), the circular bulwarks of the Castel Sant'Angelo have been used over the centuries as prison, barracks, papal fortress, and now a museum, interesting both for its precious works of art and the labyrinth of imperial tombs, state rooms, and endless nooks and crannies that honeycomb the interior.

TICKETS
For entry to the Galleria Borghese booking in advance is essential; tel: 06/32810.

▶▶▶ Galleria Borghese   off 41E5
Piazzale Scipione Borghese 5
Open: Tue–Sun 9–7:30. Admission: expensive
Only the Vatican offers a grander collection of paintings and sculptures than the Galleria Borghese. Its many highlights include Canova's *Paolina Borghese* and outstanding masterpieces by Bernini: *David*, *Apollo and Daphne*, and *The Rape of Prosperine*. The paintings include Raphael's *Deposition* and works by Caravaggio and Pinturicchio.

▶▶ Galleria Nazionale d'Arte Antica-Palazzo Barberini   41E6
Via delle Quattro Fontane 13
Open: Tue–Sun 9–7. Admission: moderate
This is Rome's foremost picture gallery, most famous for Raphael's *La Fornarina*, but also home to paintings by Fra Angelico, Perugino, Filippo Lippi, Tintoretto, Holbein, and El Greco. The sumptuous rooms are attractions in their own right, notably the **Gran Salone▶▶▶**, dominated by Pietro da Cortona's exuberant ceiling frescoes.

PAOLINA BORGHESE
Numerous myths attach to Canova's erotic statue of Paolina Borghese, doubtless because of the knowing sensuality of its subject—bare-breasted, hips half-draped in veils, and a pose of haughty yet come-hither languor. Paolina was as slyly seductive in life as in art, and caused a lot of gossip with her jewels, her clothes, her long line of lovers, the servants she used as footstools, and the black attendant who carried her from the bath.

▶▶▶ Musei Capitolini (Capitoline Museums)   41B5
Piazza del Campidoglio
Closed: Mon. Admission: expensive
Two museums face one another across Piazza del Campidoglio. **Palazzo Nuovo▶▶▶**, the smaller and

richer of the two museums, contains many masterpieces of classical sculpture, principally the *Dying Gaul*, *Capitoline Venus*, and *Amor and Psyche*. Sculptures in the **Palazzo dei Conservatori**►► across the piazza include the *Spinario*, the *Esquiline Venus*, and the *Capitoline Wolf*. Upstairs, the **Pinacoteca Capitolina**►► has fine paintings by, among others, Caravaggio, Van Dyck, and Titian.

►►► Musei Vaticani (see pages 48–49) *off 40D1*

►► Museo Nazionale Romano *off 41D6*

A magnificent collection of Roman antiquities is housed in two superbly adapted palaces, the **Palazzo Massimo** (Piazza dei Cinquecento 67; open Tue–Sun 9–7:45) and the **Palazzo Altemps** (Piazza di Sant'Apollinare 44; open Tue–Sun 9–7).

►►► Palazzo-Galleria Doria Pamphili *41C4*

Via del Corso-Piazza del Collegio Romano 1a
Open: Fri–Wed 10–5; closed Aug 15. Admission: expensive
With over 1,000 rooms, five courtyards, and four monumental staircases, this is one of Rome's largest palaces. Only part is open to the public, four large galleries crammed with paintings that include works by Titian, Raphael, and Caravaggio. Its most famous canvas is a portrait of *Innocent X* by Velázquez.

►►► Villa Giulia (Museo Nazionale Etrusco) *off 41E5*

Viale delle Belle Arti
Open: Tue–Sun 8:30–7. Admission: moderate
This museum holds the world's most exhaustive collection of Etruscan art and artifacts. The villa in which it is housed is also an attraction. Highlights include the *Sarcofago degli Sposi* (Sarcophagus of the Married Couple); giant terra-cotta statues of *Apollo* and *Hercules*; urns and vases; jewelry, utensils, and other objects.

MUSEO DI PALAZZO VENEZIA
This modern museum (Piazza San Marco 49; *admission: moderate*) houses splendid Italian, German, and Flemish tapestries and a miscellaneous collection of medieval art, sculptures, ceramics, jewelry, and other artifacts.

STROLL
Walk from Piazza Navona to the Pantheon by way of the church of San Luigi dei Francesi, Piazza Sant'Eustachio, and the church of Sant'Ivo alla Sapienza.

47

Inside the Galleria Borghese. Much of its collection was accumulated by Cardinal Scipione Borghese

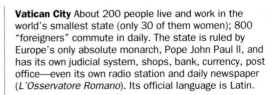

Vatican City is an independent sovereign state in the heart of Rome. Although most of the 106-acre principality is enclosed by high walls and is generally out of bounds, it has superb museums that are open to the public.

THE SWISS GUARD
The Vatican's 90-strong army is designed to protect the papal person. The guards, recruited from Switzerland's four Catholic cantons, must be aged between 19 and 25, be at least 5 feet 9 inches tall, and remain unmarried during their tours of duty. Their striped uniforms, designed by Michelangelo, bear the medieval colors of the Medici popes (red, yellow, and blue).

Vatican City About 200 people live and work in the world's smallest state (only 30 of them women); 800 "foreigners" commute in daily. The state is ruled by Europe's only absolute monarch, Pope John Paul II, and has its own judicial system, shops, bank, currency, post office—even its own radio station and daily newspaper (*L'Osservatore Romano*). Its official language is Latin.

Musei Vaticani (Vatican Museums) The museums, the largest in the world, include the Sistine Chapel, the Raphael Rooms, and at least a dozen self-contained museums. The most important is the **Museo Pio-Clementino**, housing some of the greatest works of classical sculpture. The finest are in the Cortile Ottagono: the *Apollo Belvedere* and the **Laocoön** group. The **Museo Gregoriano-Etrusco** contains some of Italy's best Etruscan artifacts, notably the *Mars of Todi* and *Head of Athene*. The **Pinocoteca** has Rome's best paintings, with works by Giotto, Filippo Lippi, Leonardo, and Raphael.

    The **Cappella di Nicolò V** contains sublime frescoes by Fra Angelico. Five dark rooms with outstanding frescoes by Pinturicchio (1492–1495) form the **Appartamento Borgia**. The **Museo Gregoriano Profano** houses pagan art, mainly classical sculpture. The **Museo Missionario Etnologico** has a fascinating collection of artifacts collected from missionary expeditions all over the world.

Raphael Rooms (Stanze di Raffaello) Raphael's frescoes, commissioned by Julius II in 1503, are one of the masterpieces of the Renaissance. The **Stanza della Segnatura** (Room II) is the most celebrated and was the first to be painted. Its four main frescoes are allegories of Theology, Philosophy, Poetry, and Justice. The **Sala dell'Incendio** (Room I) was the last to be executed, when Leo X was pope, and celebrates Leo's papal namesakes, depicting the *Coronation of Charlemagne* (performed by Leo III); the *Oath of Leo III*; the *Battle of Ostia* (where Leo IV showed mercy to the Saracens); and the *Fire in the Borgo*, where Leo IV (actually a portrait of Leo X) extinguishes a fire by making the Sign of the Cross. Room III's frescoes describe episodes where Divine Providence has intervened to defend the Christian faith, notably Leo I (again Leo X in disguise) *Repulsing Attila the Hun*.

Cappella Sistina (Sistine Chapel) Michelangelo's frescoes in the Sistine Chapel are the pinnacle of European artistic achievement. The 3061-square foot ceiling took four years to complete, the artist lying recumbent most of the time to paint. The restored frescoes divide into nine sections, arranged chronologically. The

A Fra Angelico in the Vatican Museum

first describe five key events from the Book of Genesis: *The Separation of Light and Darkness*; *The Creation of the Heavens*; *The Separation of Land and Sea*; *The Creation of Adam*; and *The Creation of Eve*. After them come: *The Fall and Expulsion from Paradise*; *The Sacrifice of Noah*; *The Flood*; and *The Drunkenness of Noah*. The *Last Judgment* on the rear wall, painted 20 years later, shows Christ in the center with the damned sinking to the right, the saved rising heavenward on the left.

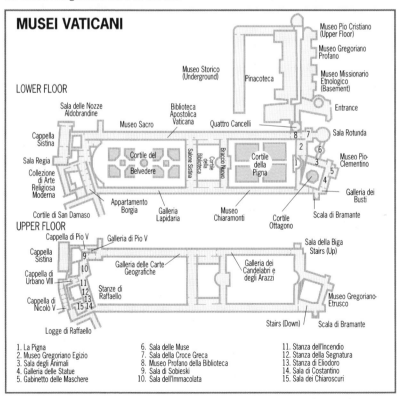

MUSEI VATICANI

Museo Pio Cristiano (Upper Floor)
Museo Gregoriano Profano
Museo Missionario Etnologico (Basement)

LOWER FLOOR

Museo Storico (Underground)
Pinacoteca
Entrance

Sala delle Nozze Aldobrandine
Biblioteca Apostolica Vaticana
Museo Sacro
Quattro Cancelli
8 7 Sala Rotunda
2
Cappella Sistina
Cortile del Belvedere
Salone Sistina
Braccio Nuovo
Cortile della Biblioteca
Cortile della Pigna
1 6
3 Museo Pio-Clementino
5
Sala Regia
Collezione di Arte Religiosa Moderna
4
Galleria dei Busti
Appartamento Borgia
Galleria Lapidaria
Museo Chiaramonti
Cortile Ottagono
Scala di Bramante
Cortile di San Damaso

UPPER FLOOR

Cappella di Pio V
Galleria di Pio V
Sala della Biga
Stairs (Up)
Cappella Sistina
9
Galleria delle Carte Geografiche
Galleria dei Candelabri e degli Arazzi
10
Cappella di Urbano VIII
11
Stanze di Raffaello
12
13
Cappella di Nicolò V
15 14
Museo Gregoriano-Etrusco
Stairs (Down)
Scala di Bramante
Logge di Raffaello

1. La Pigna
2. Museo Gregoriano Egizio
3. Sala degli Animali
4. Galleria delle Statue
5. Gabinetto delle Maschere
6. Sala delle Muse
7. Sala della Croce Greca
8. Museo Profano della Biblioteca
9. Sala di Sobieski
10. Sala dell'Immacolata
11. Stanza dell'Incendio
12. Stanza della Segnatura
13. Stanza di Eliodoro
14. Sala di Costantino
15. Sala dei Chiaroscuri

The most magnificent of Rome's ancient monuments was started by the emperor Vespasian in AD 72 and was completed seven years later by his son, Titus. The Colosseum was inaugurated (in the taste of the times) with a gala in which no fewer than 5,000 animals were slaughtered in one afternoon, followed by over 100 days of games and entertainment.

50

A TRENDSETTER

An architectural and engineering marvel, the Colosseum's arena has provided the model for large stadiums ever since. Over 50,000 spectators could leave their seats within minutes through the 76 numbered exits or *vomitoria*. On the upper levels, a huge movable sailcloth (*velarium*) could be winched into place to shade spectators from the sun.

OPENING TIMES

Open daily, summer, 9–7:30; winter, 9–3:30. Admission: moderate.

Animals and gladiators remained below stage in the Colosseum before fighting in the arena

On stage Contrary to popular myth, the stage was probably not used to kill Christians. It was, however, used for a variety of violent and decadent gladiatorial games (the Romans took the idea of gladiators from the Samnites and Etruscans, who used them originally to train soldiers for battle).

Men, women—even dwarfs—fought each other (and animals) to keep the crowds entertained. The arena could also be flooded to stage mock sea battles. Audiences often exercised the power of life and death. They could reply to a fighter's appeal for mercy (raising a finger on the left hand) with a waving of handkerchiefs (a reprieve), or with the notorious thumbs-down. Survivors, if they were criminals, often had their throats cut anyway.

Days of ruin The games were finally outlawed in AD 438. Fires and earthquakes then began to take their toll on the arena. The clamps holding the massive travertine blocks were removed in AD 662–664, leaving the distinctive holes that punctuate the exterior today. Over the Middle Ages huge amounts of stone were pillaged to build the city's churches and palaces. Preservation only began in 1744 when the area was consecrated and a cross erected in memory of murdered Christians.

Churches

▶ Sant'Andrea al Quirinale   41D6
Via del Quirinale
Open: Wed–Mon 8–12, 4–6
Sant'Andrea is a baroque jewel. It was designed by Bernini and was one of his favorite churches. Many of its ideas were unique at the time (1658–1671), notably the two-columned portico and stretched-oval floor plan. The aristocratically elegant decoration, including gilding and lush red *cottanello* columns (a marble from Sicily), largely relates to the martyrdom of Sant'Andrea (St. Andrew).

▶ San Carlino
(San Carlo alle Quattro Fontane)   41D6
Via del Quirinale
Open: Mon–Fri 10–1, 3–5, Sat 10–1. Sun Mass at 10
Bernini's great rival, Borromini, designed San Carlino (1634–1638), which was his first church in Rome. It is another baroque masterpiece, but expresses the idiom in a different style from that of neighboring Sant'Andrea. The interior is crammed with details and symbols, all bound with precise geometrical patterns. The same use of space is found in the cloisters.

▶▶ Santa Cecilia in Trastevere   41A3
Piazza di Santa Cecilia
Open: daily 9:30–12, 3:45–6:30
Santa Cecilia dates largely from 824, but the interior was disastrously remodeled between 1725 and 1823. However, part of Santa Cecilia's considerable charm is in its gardens and 12th-century portico. The apse contains 9th-century mosaics and an altar canopy by Arnolfo di Cambio (ca1293). There is a fine statue of St. Cecilia by Stefano Maderno (1600), and the church is believed to have been built on the site of her house. The cloister (*admission: inexpensive*) has fresco fragments of Pietro Cavallini's *Last Judgment* (1293).

▶▶▶ San Clemente   *off 41B6*
Via di San Giovanni in Laterano
Open: daily 7:30–12, 3–6
San Clemente comprises three distinct levels. The present church has the city's finest medieval interior (1130), with superb 12th-century mosaics, pulpits, and frescoes by Masolino da Panicale (ca1428). The lower 8th-century church has faded (but important) early frescoes. Below it lie the ruins of a Mithraic temple, open to the public (*Open daily 9–12, 3–6. Admission: inexpensive*).

▶▶▶ San Giovanni in Laterano   *off 41B6*
Piazza di San Giovanni in Laterano.
Open: (Church) daily 7–6; (Baptistery) daily 7–12, 3:30–6:30
San Giovanni (not St. Peter's) is Rome's cathedral church. It was founded by Constantine in 313, and has been much restored. The **cloisters▶▶▶** (*admission: inexpensive*), with their Cosmati marblework, are one of Rome's loveliest spots. The much-copied octagonal **Baptistery▶▶▶**, adapted from 5th-century Roman baths, is the earliest in Christendom. The church was damaged by a terrorist bomb in 1993.

Santa Cecilia in Trastevere, which contains a beautiful apse mosaic as well as works of art by Pietro Cavallini and Arnolfo di Cambio

BOCCA DELLA VERITÀ

The "Mouth of Truth" is a weather-beaten stone face once used by the Romans as a drain cover. According to tradition, anyone suspected of lying would have their hand forced into the gaping mouth (*bocca*). If they were lying the mouth would clamp shut, severing their fingers. A priest supposedly hid behind the stone to chop the hands of those known to be lying. Oaths and business deals were sworn and settled here.

▶▶▶ San Luigi dei Francesi   41D3
Piazza di San Luigi dei Francesi
Open: daily 8–12:30, 3:30–7 (subject to alteration)
The French church of Rome (1589) has a single great treasure: a chapel that contains three paintings by Caravaggio (5th chapel on the left). All three deal with events from the *Life of St. Matthew*, showing the painter's realism and *chiaroscuro* techniques to virtuoso effect.

▶▶ Santa Maria in Aracoeli   41B5
Piazza del Campidoglio
Open: daily 7–6
This church occupies Rome's Holy of Holies—the crown of the Capitoline Hill that once housed the city's first *Arx* (Citadel) and Temple of Juno Moneta. Founded in the 6th century, or possibly earlier, the church has a dazzling interior with ancient columns, chandeliers, and a magnificent wooden ceiling. Its main treasures are Pinturicchio's *Life of San Bernardino* frescoes (first chapel in the right-hand aisle) and, until it was stolen, the *Santo Bambino*, a miracle-working statue carved from an olive tree in Gethsemane.

Nightlife outside Santa Maria in Trastevere

BERNINI'S ELEPHANT

Piazza della Minerva's famous statue of an elephant with a small Egyptian obelisk on its back was designed by Bernini for Pope Alexander VII. The inscription states that it takes the massive strength of the elephant to sustain the weight of true wisdom.

▶▶ Santa Maria in Cosmedin   41A4
Piazza Bocca della Verità
Open: summer, daily 9–6; winter, daily 9–5
Though it lacks great treasures, few Roman churches are as beautiful as Santa Maria in Cosmedin, one of a few medieval buildings in the city to have escaped the baroque style. The portico contains the *Bocca della Verità* (see panel), while the interior boasts lovely pulpits and choir screens, patches of fresco, and an 8th-century mosaic.

▶▶▶ Santa Maria Maggiore   off 41B6
Piazza di Santa Maria Maggiore
Open: daily 7–7
Rome's finest early Christian basilica is the largest and most important of the 80 churches dedicated to the Virgin. The interior is magnificent, graced with 40 ancient columns and restored mosaics from the 5th and 13th centuries. The Paolina and Sistina chapels are also outstanding.

▶▶ Santa Maria sopra Minerva   *41C4*
Piazza della Minerva
Open: daily 7:30–7:30

Rome's only Gothic church lies behind the Pantheon, built over (*sopra*) the ruins of a temple dedicated to Minerva. It contains many fine works of art: Filippino Lippi left frescoes in the Cappella Carafa and there is a statue of *The Redeemer* by Michelangelo to the left of the altar. A number of famous people are buried here.

▶▶▶ Santa Maria del Popolo   *off 40E4*
Piazza del Popolo
Open: Mon–Sat 7–7, Sun 4:30–6

Bramante and Bernini designed much of this church, which contains frescoes by Pinturicchio and two masterpieces by Caravaggio. The **Cappella Chigi**▶▶, which was commissioned by a Sienese banker, was designed by Raphael. The choir boasts tombs by Andrea Sansovino.

▶▶ Santa Maria in Trastevere   *40A2*
Piazza di Santa Maria in Trastevere
Open: daily 7:30 AM–9 PM

Providing the backdrop to Trastevere's liveliest piazza, the church's mosaic-covered facade (12th century) is floodlit at night. Inside are more mosaics, the work of Pietro Cavallini (1290) and earlier Byzantine craftsmen. The ancient columns are from the Terme di Caracalla.

▶▶▶ San Pietro (see page 55)   *off 40D1*

▶▶ San Pietro in Vincoli   *off 41B6*
Piazza San Pietro in Vincoli
Open: summer, daily 7–12:30, 3:30–7 (winter, until 6)

The chains (*vincoli*) are the links that bound St. Peter in Jerusalem, and to which were later added those that shackled him in Rome's Mamertine prison. Both sets of chains, miraculously fused together, can be seen below the high altar. The church is renowned, however, for Michelangelo's monumental statue of *Moses* (1503–1513).

The sumptuous interior of Santa Maria Maggiore

NERO'S TOMB
Santa Maria del Popolo was supposedly built on the site of Nero's tomb in 1099. The Virgin appeared to Pope Paschal II and ordered him to chop down a great walnut tree that had grown from the grave. Paschal obliged, then built a chapel. The emperor's ghost reputedly wandered the area, *en route* to the pyramid tomb that contained the remains of his wife. Today it is the stylish *Rosati* café, a fashionable spot frequented by the city's artists and literati.

STROLL
From Piazza Santa Maria in Trastevere, wend through the streets to the south and climb the Gianicolo hill for views over the city.

54

Piazzas and fountains

►►► Fontana di Trevi 40D5
Piazza Fontana di Trevi
Rome's most famous fountain lives up to expectations as it foams dramatically from a whole wall of the Palazzo Poli. Its central figure, Neptune, is flanked by figures representing a calm and stormy sea. The tradition is to throw a coin into the fountain if you wish to return to Rome. It is one of the city's main meeting places.

►►► Piazza Campo dei Fiori 40C2
This lovely square is as picturesque as any in Italy, with its colorful street market (Mon–Sat 7–2), crammed with stalls selling flowers, fish, and mounds of fruit and vegetables. Take some time to sit out at one of the cafés and enjoy the bustling street life.

►►► Piazza Navona 40C3
Rome's social center is Piazza Navona, an exhilarating spot thronged with life and edged with elegant ocher *palazzi* and outdoor cafés. Its contours match exactly the outlines of the emperor Domitian's *circo* (stadium), built to hold games and horse races in AD 86. It was transformed in 1644 by Pope Innocent X. Bernini designed two of its fountains, the **Fontana dei Quattro Fiumi** (Fountain of the Four Rivers) and the **Fontana del Moro**.

►►► Piazza di Spagna 41E4
At the heart of Rome's best shopping area, and backed by the famous **Spanish Steps►►►**, this colorful square rivals Piazza Navona and the Fontana di Trevi as the city's most popular meeting place. It is named after the palace of the Spanish ambassador to the Vatican. The **Museo di Keats-Shelley** is also to be found here, together with the eccentric **Fontana della Barcaccia►**.

Piazza Navona: the heart of Rome

One of the most famous churches in Christendom and Catholicism's most important point of pilgrimage, St. Peter's sees visitors from all over the world, drawn to the spot where St. Peter was buried after his crucifixion in AD 64 or 67. Few remain unimpressed by the basilica's size and spiritual significance, though many perhaps come away disappointed by its chill interior and—for a church of such fame—its lack of great art.

The first St. Peter's was built in 326 by Pope Sylvester I with the backing of the emperor Constantine. It was to survive until 1452, when Pope Nicholas V and then Julius II began to consider plans for a new basilica.

The new church Designs were drawn up by Bramante, then Antonio da Sangallo. Michelangelo, aged 72, was asked to correct mistakes, which he did by removing much of Sangallo's work and redesigning the dome. Carlo Maderno (1605) made more additions and in 1637 Bernini was called in to act as the interior's architect.

Piazza San Pietro, Bernini's great square framing St. Peter's

Highlights Inside, the overall impression is of size, with little of real artistic merit among the gloomy tombs, heavy marble, and baroque decoration. The exceptions are Michelangelo's *Pietà* (1499), behind glass at the beginning of the right aisle, and Bernini's bronze *baldacchino* (altar canopy) in the crossing. See also the two finest tombs, della Porta's for Paul III and Bernini's influential tomb of Urban VIII. They lie at the rear of the apse, flanking Bernini's *Cathedra Pietri*, designed to encase a chair reputedly used by St. Peter to preach to the Romans.

Climb the dome for breathtaking views, and visit the piazza's tourist office to organize a trip to the crypt, where early Christian tombs possibly include St. Peter's.

OPENING TIMES
Church: summer, daily
7–7; winter, daily 7–6
Dome: summer, daily 8–6;
winter, daily 8–5
Treasury: summer, daily
7–6; winter, daily 9–5
Last tickets 1.25 hours
before closing.
Church: *Admission free*
Dome/Treasury:
Admission: moderate

Walk

Three walks through Rome's streets and piazzas

For routes see map on pages 40–41

Trastevere Start from Piazza Santa Maria in Trastevere and take Vicolo delle Cinque to explore the pretty back streets. Return to the piazza and follow Via della Lungaretta to Piazza Piscinula. Cross to the Isola Tiberina to wander the promenades and see the church of San Bartolomeo. Head south for the Roman temples and church of **Santa Maria in Cosmedin** (page 52) in Piazza Bocca della Verità. Cross back to Trastevere and wind through the streets to **Santa Cecilia in Trastevere** (page 51). Return to Santa Maria in Trastevere.

Piazza Navona–Castel Sant'Angelo
See the church of Sant'Agnese in Agone and Piazza Navona's fountains and walk to **Piazza Campo dei Fiori** (page 54). Stroll through Piazza Farnese (with detours to Palazzo Spada and Santa Maria dell'Orazione e Morte) and then follow Via Giulia before cutting up to the Chiesa Nuova (worth a look for frescoes by Pietro da Cortona). Next door see Borromini's idiosyncratic facade for the Oratorio dei Filippini and his clock tower in Piazza dell'Orologio. Walk to Via dei Coronari and across the Ponte Sant'Angelo to **Castel Sant'Angelo** (page 46).

Piazza Navona–Piazza di Spagna
Walk to the **Pantheon** (page 45) via **San Luigi dei Francesi** (Caravaggio frescoes, see page 52). Then see **Santa Maria sopra Minerva** (page 53) and Sant'Ignazio (for Andrea Pozzo's ceiling frescoes) *en route* for Piazza Colonna and the elegant Colonna di Marco Aurelio.

Head for the **Fontana di Trevi** (page 54) and stroll through the grid of shopping streets around Via dei Condotti toward **Piazza di Spagna** (for the Spanish Steps, see page 54).

Accommodations

Where to look Rome has the range of accommodations you can expect of any great city, from squalid *pensioni* to palatial luxury hotels. The best part to stay in is around Piazza Navona, although it is an area with relatively few hotels. More establishments cluster around Piazza del Popolo and Piazza di Spagna, both pretty and central but a notch below the top hotels on Via Veneto and the area south of the Villa Borghese. The hotels near the Stazione Termini (on Via Magenta, Via Amendola, Via Principe Amadeo) are a cheap last resort. More pleasant *pensioni* are dotted around Prati and Borgo (near the Vatican).

Prices and booking Rome lacks charming hotels in the mid-range. The best in this bracket are booked up months in advance, so reserve well ahead during the city's peak season (Easter to mid-October). Even off season (when reservations are still recommended), prices in Rome are high, and you often get less for your money than elsewhere. Anywhere with a garage is worth its weight in gold. It usually pays to eat in restaurants, rather than choosing full or half-board. Watch out for breakfast and air-conditioning supplements, and remember that prices vary even within a hotel—ask to see a variety of rooms.

TOURIST OFFICES
Avoid the con artists and the long lines at the station's tourist office if you need help finding accommodations. Try instead to use the booths at Fiumicino airport; at the Roma-Nord service station on the A1; the Roma-Sud Frascati service area on the A2; or the EPT office at Via Parigi 5, near Piazza della Repubblica (tel: 06/488991 or 06/4889 9253).

GUIDED TOURS
The best guided tours of the city are offered by American Express from Piazza di Spagna 38, tel: 06/67641. Itineraries usually last around four hours and start at 9:30 AM and 2:30 PM.

57

Noise and appearance Rome is one of Europe's noisiest cities, and you will never entirely escape the cacophony of the streets. Many hotels have double-glazed windows, but unless they are also air-conditioned you will need the windows open in summer. Avoid Termini and the main thoroughfares in favor of back streets or hotels near the parks. Also ask for a room away from the front of the hotel or facing a courtyard. When choosing a hotel do not judge by the exterior, as many a crumbling facade conceals a sumptuous interior. Finally, if you arrive in Rome at Termini you may be approached by touts working for hotels. Only accompany them as a *last resort*. Check prices first and confirm *exactly* where the hotel is situated.

Le Grand Hotel is one of Rome's classiest hotels, and a favorite home away from home for visiting VIPs and royalty

WINE

Rome's local wine is the amber-colored bianco of the Castelli Romani. Frascati is the most famous version, though most varieties are fairly similar. Good wine bars to try include *Cul-de-Sac*, Piazza del Pasquino 73; the intimate *Enoteca Piccola*, Via del Governo Vecchio 75; and the relaxed *Enoteca Cavour*, Via Cavour 313. Also visit the *Antica Enoteca*, Via della Croce 76, a lovely shop where you can buy or drink wine.

CAFÉS AND COFFEE

Rome's best cups of coffee are to be had at *La Tazza d'Oro*, Via degli Orfani 84, and *Sant'Eustachio*, Piazza Sant'Eustachio 82. Other famous bars include the 18th-century *Caffè Greco*, Via dei Condotti 86, a Roman institution; *Columbia*, Piazza Navona 88; the trendy *Bar della Pace*, Via della Pace 5 (off Piazza Navona); and two bars on Piazza del Popolo—*Canova* and *Rosati*.

Sidewalk dining in Rome

Food and drink

What to eat Few things—perhaps only cars, soccer, and families—come between Romans and a good meal. Eating out is all the nightlife many of them need, and a summer evening's meal *al fresco* can be one of Rome's most memorable experiences. The city's specialties may not always be appetizing—things like tripe, brains, salt cod, veal, and offal—but more common Italian staples can be found in most restaurants. Favorite pasta dishes include *bucatini all'amatriciana, spaghetti alla carbonara, fettucine, gnocchi,* and *penne all'arrabiata. Stracciatella* is the classic soup, a clear broth with egg, pasta, and cheese. The best-known main course is *saltimbocca alla romana* (veal with ham and sage cooked in wine and butter). Grilled meats—lamb and beef—are also common. Purple Roman artichokes are renowned, as are asparagus and leaf vegetables like spinach and rocket (*rucola* or *rughetta*), deep-fried Jerusalem artichokes, and zucchini. The best desserts are simple like ice cream or fruit salad (*macedonia*).

Where to eat Trastevere and the streets around Piazza Navona contain many restaurants, though few areas are without their quiet neighborhood *trattorie* and pizzerias. It is often in these places, away from tourist areas, that you will enjoy your best (and most reasonably priced) meals. Rome has more than its share of deceptively chic restaurants where the food and the prices are equally appalling. At the other extreme, do not overlook bars as a source of cheap snacks, and bear in mind that Rome now has many fast-food outlets (there are large branches of McDonald's in Piazza di Spagna and Piazza della Repubblica). Tourist menus are as cheap as elsewhere, but the standard of food is as low as anywhere in Italy.

The tradition of making lunch (*pranzo*) the main meal of the day is slowly dying out—though you can still indulge heavily between 1 PM and 3 PM. In the evenings, Romans eat dinner (*cena*) from around 8 PM, a little earlier in pizzerias, a little later (and longer) in summer.

Shopping

Shopping districts Though not a city to compare with London, Paris, or New York, Rome still has much to satisfy the wealthy or discerning shopper. It's best known for luxury goods—its silks, leather, jewelry, shoes, and accessories are of the highest quality. The most exclusive stores cluster in the grid of streets around Via dei Condotti and Piazza di Spagna. Less expensive streets include Via del Corso, Via Nazionale and Via del Tritone, Via Cola di Rienzo, and the areas around Campo dei Fiori and the Fontana di Trevi.

Markets Rome's most attractive food and vegetable market is in Piazza Campo dei Fiori. Piazza Vittorio Emanuele, however, is the city's main market, selling food and general goods. Via Andrea Doria is another large market (north of the Vatican Museums). Porta Portese is the city's most famous flea market (Sunday only), but there are few bargains and the crowds are overwhelming (be on special guard against pickpockets). Via Sannio next to San Giovanni in Laterano has a smaller junk and second-hand clothes market on Saturday.

Leather goods Shoe stores almost outnumber food shops in Rome. For quality look on and around Via dei Condotti; for low prices try Via Nazionale. Leather shops are similarly numerous. **Sergio Rossi** (Piazza di Spagna) has a high-quality selection. For gloves visit **Sergio di Cori** (Piazza di Spagna 53).

Department stores La Rinascente is Rome's grandest department store and is the largest of the department store chains with branches at Piazza Colonna and Piazza Fiume. It sells clothes, cosmetics, household items, furniture, and much more besides. **Coin**, considered to be the more fashionable store at Piazzale Appio, is best for clothes and kitchenware (five minutes from San Giovanni in Laterano).

Fruit stall in Rome's Campo dei Fiori

59

ANTIQUES
Antique shops with breathtaking pieces and prices to match concentrate on Via del Babuino and Via Monserrato. Via Giulia's stores specialize in furniture, those on Via dei Coronari offer items a touch below Via Babuino in cost and quality.

CHINA, FABRICS, AND LINEN
For china try *Ginori*, Piazza Trinità dei Monti 18b and Via del Tritone 177, or the 19th-century *Cavatorta*, Via Veneto 157. For silks and fabrics visit *Bises* (Via dei Due Marcelli 80), *Meconi* (Via Cola di Rienzo 305), or *Galtrucco* (Via del Tritone 23). *Frette* (Piazza di Spagna 11) is famed for its household linens.

INFORMATION

Newspapers like *La Repubblica* and *Il Messagero* contain daily nightlife listings. *La Repubblica's* Thursday edition also contains a free weekly listings magazine called *Trovaroma*.

TICKET AGENCIES

Rome's leading agency is Box Office, Viale Giulio Cesare 88 (tel: 372 0216); also at Via del Corso 506 (tel: 06/320 2790). Orbis also has tickets for most events (Piazza Esquilino 37, tel: 06/474 4776).

Nightlife

Rome's *dolce vita* days are all but over, and nightlife for many Romans means a meal at a sidewalk café (though there are more active nightspots if you want them). Cultural entertainment through movies and theater hold few rewards for non-Italian speakers.

Concerts and recitals The **Accademia di Santa Cecilia** stages concerts by its own and visiting orchestras at Via della Conciliazione 4 (box office Via della Conciliazione 4, tel: 06/6880 1044, www.santacecilia.it). The **Accademia Filarmonica** (tel: 06/320 1752) holds a major recital series at the Teatro Olimpico, Piazza Gentile da Fabriano 17 (tel: 06/326 5991). The **Oratorio del Gonfalone** stages baroque and chamber recitals at Via del Gonfalone 32A (tel: 06/6880 5637). A wealth of classical music can also be heard free of charge in churches throughout the year.

Music clubs Jazz and Latin music clubs are especially popular in Rome. For Latin music try **Caffè Caruso** (Via Monte Testaccio 36). **Yes! Brazil** is also a lot of fun (Via San Francesco a Ripa 103). The best overall spot must be **Big Mama** (Vicolo San Francesco a Ripa 18), with both jazz and blues; **Caffè Latino** (Via Monte Testaccio 63) and **Alexanderplatz** (Via Ostia 9) are both extremely popular. Most of these late-night clubs offer light meals, drinks, and music.

Beer and bars Sitting at cafés until the small hours is a feature of Rome's summer nightlife. **Caffè della Pace** (Via della Pace 5) is the most popular. Pubs and beer halls (*birrerie*) are also well patronized. Try the **Fiddler's Elbow** (Via dell'Ormata 43, near Santa Maria Maggiore); **Tempera** (Via San Marcello 19, behind Piazza Venezia); **Taverna del Campo** (Campo dei Fiori 16); or Trastevere's **La Scala**, Piazza della Scala.

Discos and nightclubs Discos and clubs are subject to sudden changes of fashion (and ownership), so consult *Trovaroma* magazine for the places of the moment. Admission is often expensive and dressing up *de rigueur*. Longer-established places include **Piper** (Via Tagliamento 9), the **Drunken Ship** (Campo dei Fiori 20–21), and **Alien** (Via Veletri 13), all of which attract a young crowd. **Gilda** (Via Mario de'Fiori 97) and **L'Alibi 2000** (Via Monte Testaccio 44–57) are celebrity spots.

Transportation

Buses Rome's orange buses are run by A.T.A.C. Most services start from Piazza dei Cinquecento, in front of the Stazione Termini. You must buy tickets before boarding, at shops with an A.T.A.C. sticker, or at automatic ticket machines at booths at major stops. Tickets are valid for any number of journeys during 75 minutes. You can get a day pass or a weekly tourist ticket (B.I.G.) (also valid on the *metro*). Board buses at the back and leave at the center. Cancel tickets in the machine near the rear doors. There is a patchy night service (*notturno*) on main routes.

Metro Rome's subway (*la metropolitana*) is fast and easy to use, but it has only two lines. **Line A** connects Battistini Terminal to Ottaviano (for the Vatican), Flaminia (for Piazza del Popolo and the Villa Borghese), Piazza di Spagna (Spanish Steps), Piazza Barberini (for the Galleria Barberini), Termini, Vittorio Emanuele, and beyond. **Line B** is useful for Piramide (Protestant Cemetery), Circo Massimo (the Aventino and Santa Sabina), Colosseo (Colosseum), Cavour (the Roman Forum), and Termini. Overground trains to Fiumicino airport leave from Termini railroad station. Tickets are obtainable from booths at the main stations and from machines (exact change essential).

Taxis It is hard to hail Rome's yellow cabs on the street. Most gather at taxi stands or can be called by phone (tel: 3875, 3570, or 4994). Useful stands are at Piazza Venezia, Termini, Piazza San Silvestro, and Piazza Sonnino (Trastevere). Use only metered yellow cabs (ensure the meter is running). Supplements are charged for phoning for a taxi; after 10 PM; on Sundays; and for each piece of luggage.

Bicycles Bike rental outlets are springing up all over the city, in Via del Corso, Piazza Navona, Viale del Bambino (Pincio), Piazza San Silvestro, and near the Piazza di Spagna and Piazza del Popolo (Flaminia) metro stops. Try Romarent (Vicolo dei Bovari 7A), near Campo dei Fiori.

Yet another way to see Rome

TRAINS AND STATIONS
Most trains arrive and leave from Stazione Termini, Piazza dei Cinquecento (usually called "Termini").
Lines for tickets are long, especially on Friday evening and Saturday morning. Afternoons are the quietest times. Be sure to validate all tickets in the yellow-gold platform machines prior to travel. You will be fined on board if you fail to do so. International tickets, ferries, reservations, and couchettes (sleeping compartments) are all dealt with by separate booths. Only a few trains use Tiburtina, Ostiense, or Trastevere stations.

USEFUL BUS ROUTES
No. 64 Termini–Via Nazionale–Piazza Venezia–Piazza Navona–St. Peter's;
No. 81 Colosseum–St. Peter's/Vatican Museums (Piazza del Risorgimento).
No. 116/117 Small electric buses that cover the city center.

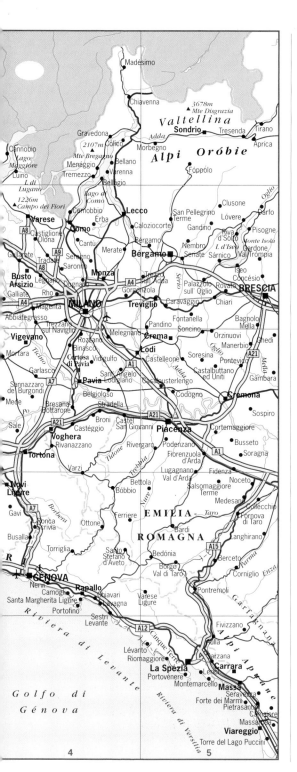

64

SCENIC DRIVES
(*Piedmont*) SS 21
Cuneo–Vinadio–Argentera;
Cuneo–Valdieri–Parco
Naturale dell'Argentera;
Turin–Lanzo Torinese–Val
Grande–Val di Ala; SS 460
Turin–Locana–Ceresole
Reale; (*Valle d'Aosta*)
SS 26 Pont-St.-Martin–
Aosta; SS 505 Pont-St.-
Martin–Val di Gressoney;
SS 506 St. Vincent–Val
d'Ayas; (*Liguria*) SS 530
La Spezia–Portovenere;
La Spezia–Lerici–
Montemarcello.

TOURIST INFORMATION
Aosta: Piazza E. Chanoux
8 (tel: 0165/236 627).
Asti: Piazza Alfieri 34
(tel: 0141/530 357,
538 200 or 582 007).
Levanto (Cinque Terre):
Piazza Cavour (tel:
0187/808 125).
Genoa: Palazzina Santa
Maria, Via al Porto Antico
(tel: 010/248 711).
Turin: Piazza Castello 161
(tel: 011/535 901);
Porta Nuova Station
(tel: 011/531 327).

THE NORTHWEST The regions of Piemonte (Piedmont), Valle d'Aosta, and Liguria have riches to offer every kind of visitor, with a combination of mountain scenery, beaches, fine food, and historic towns.

PIEMONTE Cradled by the Alps on three sides, Piedmont—*piede dei monti*, or "foot of the mountain"—is a region of mountains, vineyard-covered hills, crumbling castles, and half-forgotten villages. Scenery is the main attraction for most visitors, principally the upland enclaves of Monviso, Gran Paradiso, and the Alpi Marittime. In the west, France's proximity colors culture, cuisine, and language. At the same time, Piedmont produces such Italian staples as Fiat cars, vermouth, and that mainstay of Italian restaurants, breadsticks (*grissini*).
Torino (Turin), Piedmont's capital, is a refined, baroque city made prosperous by industry. North are the mountains of the Valle d'Aosta and south the rippling hills and vineyards around Asti and Alba, home of great wines like Barolo and Barbaresco.

VALLE D'AOSTA One of Italy's smallest regions, the Valle d'Aosta contains some of the country's most spectacular scenery. Its links with France were reinforced by the opening of the Mont Blanc tunnel in 1965, and increased trade has brought prosperity, along with busy roads and some light industry.
A journey through the Valle d'Aosta, the valley that scythes through the region and gives it its name, provides a fine introduction to the area's mountains and fairy-tale castles. Its focus, Aosta, boasts Roman remains and a splendid cathedral. Almost any of the smaller nearby valleys offers wonderful views, stone-housed hamlets, Alpine meadows, and ice-clear streams. The Val d'Ayas and Val di Gressoney are outstanding, but probably the most rewarding is the Val di Cogne, if only because it leads to Italy's premier national park, the Parco Nazionale del Gran Paradiso.

MARITIME LIGURIA With Genoa (Italy's largest port) as its capital and Christopher Columbus as its most famous son, Liguria is naturally a region dominated by all things maritime. Its beautiful coastline—the so-called Italian Riviera—divides into the Riviera di Ponente (west of Genoa) and the Riviera di Levante (east). Both are sheltered by the Ligurian and Maritime Alps, mountain walls that guarantee mild winters and a long growing season—resulting in the region's nickname of *Riviera dei Fiori* (Riviera of Flowers).
If you have time for only one sojourn on the coast, head for the Cinque Terre, five tiny fishing villages wedged into the cliffs and mountains on the Riviera di Levante. If your itinerary is more leisurely, amble down the entire coast from Ventimiglia, stopping at Alassio for its broad beach, or San Remo for its mixture of old-world charm and tacky modernism. Drive inland to explore the hills, dotted with attractive, little-known villages, and visit the coast's most famous hill towns, pricey Portofino and Portovenere. Spend time in Genoa, a salty and industrialized port, of interest principally for its old quarter and collection of modest galleries.

▶ Alba   62B3

Austere and medieval Alba is renowned above all for its food and wine: wine in the form of Barolo and Barbaresco (both red), and food in the form of white truffles (*tartufi*), culled from the oak woods of the surrounding hills (see page 174). After sampling the town's food shops head for **San Lorenzo▶**, the old cathedral, containing a finely carved and inlaid choir. Another church, **San Giovanni▶**, contains the town's most prized painting, the *Madonna delle Grazie* by Barnaba da Modena (1377).

▶ Aosta   62D2

Capital of the Valle d'Aosta, relaxed and largely French-speaking Aosta is a sedate and historic town whose lightly industrial fringe is redeemed by a tremendous mountainous backdrop. Its **Cattedrale▶** is worth a look for its choir stalls and small museum housing a magnificent early 5th-century ivory diptych. The finest church, however, is **Sant'Orso▶▶**, renowned for its 11th-century crypt and the wonderfully carved columns of its cloister (1133). Also outstanding are the town's Roman remains.

▶▶ Asti   62C3

One-time rival to Milan, Asti is well worth a visit, and deserves to be known for more than Asti Spumante, its famous (if unsophisticated) sparkling wine. Most of its best monuments—towers, palaces, and churches—are on or near the main street, Corso Vittorio Alfieri. The Gothic Duomo (1309–1354) has a checkered facade of red and white stone, but is less interesting than the church of **San Pietro in Consavia▶**, whose little circular baptistery dates from around the 12th century. Look, too, at **San Secondo▶**, a looming Gothic church with numerous frescoes, the most noted a polyptych by Gandolfino d'Asti.

   You could make an excursion to Albugnano to see the **Abbazia di Vezzolano▶▶**, the finest Romanesque building in Piedmont (13 miles from Asti). Reputedly founded by Charlemagne, it has a remarkable 12th-century facade, magnificent carved rood screen, and lovely cloister.

Sant'Orso church below the snowcapped mountains of the Valle d'Aosta

THE WINES OF PIEDMONT
Piedmont produces some of Italy's most famous wines, from its noble, tannic reds, Barolo and Barbaresco, to semisweet and sparkling whites like Asti Spumante and Moscato d'Asti. Other outstanding reds include Gattinara, Ghemme, Lessona, Barbera, and Dolcetto d'Alba. Whites are less renowned, though Gavi is fashionable (if sometimes bland) and Arneis has a good reputation.

BAGNA CAUDA
Meaning literally a "hot bath," *bagna cauda* is a type of Piedmontese fondue, a spicy dip made by simmering together a mixture of butter, olive oil, garlic, white truffle, anchovies and cream. It is a common wintertime dish all over the region.

WINES OF THE CINQUE TERRE

Cinque Terre Bianco is the basic white; Pigato and Vermentino are generally superior. Rossese and Dolceacqua are good reds. The best wine of all is the rare amber-colored Sciacchetrà, made from semi-dried grapes. Dry versions are drunk as an aperitif, sweeter variations as a fine dessert wine.

EATING OUT

Take advantage of the Cinque Terre's often romantically located restaurants to sample Liguria's culinary special-ties. *Cacciucco* is a rich fish soup, *cappon magro* a fish and vegetable dish eaten in Lent; *burrida*, fish in a spicy sauce; and *ciuppin*, a minced fish sauce. *Pansôti* are ravioli stuffed with ricotta cheese and chard, then topped with a walnut cream sauce. *Cima* is meat—usually veal—stuffed with vegetables, herbs, nuts, eggs, and cheese.

Vernazza's pretty fishing harbor

▶▶ Cinque Terre 63A5

The Cinque Terre (Five Lands) are five tiny seafront villages strung along one of the most dramatic stretches of the Ligurian coast. Each is a picturesque jumble of pastel-colored houses gathered around a small fishing harbor (though tourists these days heavily outnumber fishermen). Above the huddle of houses, mountains covered in woods and lush vegetation provide a beautiful backdrop. Savage cliffs tumble to the sea on all sides, cut by terraces of vines and olives that date back thousands of years. Well-marked and panoramic paths follow the coast and crisscross the hinterland.

Access to the region for centuries was possible only by sea, and even today some of the villages have no road links to the outside world. Boats connect them all, and this is a fine way of seeing the coast. The train, however, is the most practical way of moving from village to village. Any one of the villages makes a fine place to stop, though most people base themselves in **Levanto**, a town just to the north with plenty of hotels and services—as well as a fair amount of charm in its own right.

The villages Each of the villages has its own attractions, and if you get tired of one, it is only a few minutes by rail to the next. From north to south you will find: **Monterosso**, the largest and perhaps least charming of the five, but with the biggest beach and most hotels; **Vernazza**, a tangle of tiny streets, alleys, and arcades; **Corniglia**—the smallest—sitting high above the sea, but with a long, if pebbly beach; **Manarola**, the jewel in the crown, clustered behind a sickle of sand and hemmed in by precipitous mountains, with charming, steep cobbled streets and a harbor that is a rustic picture of bobbing fishing boats and seamen mending nets in the sun; and **Riomaggiore**, which also sits behind a sliver of sand, and has a more generous range of rooms on offer than most of the villages.

PESTO
Liguria's best-known culinary specialty, pesto, was created around Genoa, but is now eaten the world over. It is made from basil, olive oil, garlic, parmesan, and pine nuts, all ground in a mortar and pestle (hence its name). The Ligurians claim that only the region's special, smooth basil and highly prized olive oil are good enough for the real thing.

The striped facade of Genoa's cathedral

▶ Genova (Genoa)   63B4

Italy's premier maritime city, Genoa receives relatively little attention from visitors, most of whom are put off by its lack of famous sights and by the grim suburbs that spread in a confused sprawl over the surrounding hills. Away from the vibrant—and sometimes sordid—waterfront, however, the *centro storico* (historic center) is a medley of teeming streets, some best avoided after dark, but all a joy to explore. Public elevators and railways transport you around the city's multitude of levels.

The proud city One of Italy's four medieval maritime republics, Genoa in the 14th century claimed territories stretching from North Africa to Syria and the Black Sea. It became Europe's most densely populated city, nicknamed *La Superba*, "The Proud," by the poet Petrarch.

Much of the city's wealth went to build the imposing patrician palaces lining **Via Garibaldi▶▶**, one of Italy's most impressive streets. Two house important art galleries: the **Palazzo Bianco▶▶** (*Closed* Mon all day and Tue, Thu, Fri PM. *Admission: moderate*) contains works mainly by Genoese masters, with additional pieces by Veronese, Pontormo, and Filippino Lippi, plus an outstanding medley of Dutch and Flemish paintings. The **Palazzo Rosso▶▶** (*Closed* Mon all day and Tue, Thu, Fri PM. *Admission: moderate*) offers canvases by Caravaggio, Dürer, and Van Dyck, and the masterpiece of Genoa's own Bernardo Strozzi, *La Cuoca*. There is a joint ticket available for Palazzo Rosso and Palazzo Spinola. Other museums are the **Museo Chiossone▶** (*Closed* Mon, Wed, and PM. *Admission: moderate*), home to Italy's foremost collection of Far Eastern art, and the **Galleria Nazionale di Palazzo Spinola▶** (*Closed* Sun AM and Mon. *Admission: moderate*), crammed with sculpture and Renaissance paintings.

San Lorenzo▶▶ is the city's cathedral. Inside, the Museo del Tesoro contains gold and silverware for which medieval Genoa was renowned. **Piazza San Matteo▶▶** is an ensemble of medieval buildings.

CHRISTOPHER COLUMBUS
Columbus spent his childhood in Genoa, in the ivy-clad *palazzo* in Piazza Dante (close to Porta Soprana). For centuries, however, scholars have sought to prove he was born elsewhere. Several towns in Liguria claim him, as does Piacenza in Emilia-Romagna. Some historians say he was a Jewish convert of Spanish origin, forced by religious persecution to flee to Liguria. A 17th-century English manuscript claims he was English, while the Corsican town of Calvi is sure he was born there. Other theories have him as Swiss (Geneva), French, or the Levantine corsair, Giorgio Bissipat. In the *Mayorazgo* (a will made in Seville in 1498), however, Columbus himself wrote that he was "born in Genoa."

CABLE CARS

If you want views of the mountains without having to work up a sweat, several ski lifts and cable cars operate during the summer. One of the most convenient is the tele-cabina from Cogne, which climbs to Montseuc (6,930 feet), just a half mile south of the town. A couple of little paths from its upper station offer easy strolls in the woods, or to the upper summit of Montseuc (7,699 feet).

▶▶ Parco Nazionale del Gran Paradiso   62D2

Italy's first ever national park is also its most spectacular. Ranged around the Gran Paradiso massif (13,401 feet)—the only mountain over 13,200 feet solely in Italy—the park started life as a hunting reserve for the Savoys in the 19th century. In 1919 the family donated the area to the state, thus helping to preserve not only the area's stupendous scenery, but also the ibex, a type of wild goat, for which the park is now best known. Snowcapped mountains, vast glaciers, verdant valleys, and deep-green forests lie within easy reach of drivers and walkers alike.

Three valleys push into the park from the Valle d'Aosta—the Val di Rhêmes, Val Savarenche, and Val di Cogne. Roads run up each one, offering superlative views and many opportunities for walks into the mountains. The best approach overall, though, is via the Val di Cogne and its main center, **Cogne**▶▶, just half an hour from Aosta. A pleasing little winter and summer resort, it has plenty of places to stay and makes a perfect base for exploring the whole of the park. It is a particularly good launchpad for walks. For details of the best hike see "Hiking in Northwest Italy," pages 70–71.

The Gran Paradiso National Park has a wide variety of landscapes, from barren mountain uplands to verdant, flower-filled meadows

Just south of the village is the hamlet of **Valnontey**, a little too swamped by visitors for its own good, but home to the Giardino Alpino, a botanical garden that contains examples of much of the park's outstanding alpine flora. Come in June to see the flowers at their best, and try a few walks up to mountain meadows to see them in their natural habitat. The same walks will also reward you with sightings of ibex as well as the more numerous chamois (a goatlike antelope) and a range of smaller fauna and alpine birds. Around 3,500 ibex and some 6,000 chamois now thrive within the park's confines. Their numbers are slightly worrying, as they have no natural predators; plans have been put forward to reintroduce wolves or lynx to reestablish a natural equilibrium.

▶ Riviera di Levante   63A4

The Riviera di Levante is the less developed and more spectacular half of the Italian Riviera. Like the Riviera di Ponente, however, it is a region where you have to choose carefully if you want to avoid overpriced or overpopular resorts. Almost any town will suffice, though, if all that

you are looking for from a resort is noisy nightlife and lively beachlife.

A general tour by car or train gives you marvelous glimpses of turquoise sea, tiny fishing villages, and a romantic medley of cliffs and mountains. Pine forests plunge to pebbly beaches, interspersed with luxuriant and herb-scented swathes of *maquis*. The best section is the Cinque Terre (see page 66).

Moving east from Genoa, however, the first stop is **Camogli▶**, little changed since Charles Dickens described it as the "saltiest, roughest, most piratical little place." Clustered around a pleasant harbor, it is quieter than many spots on the coast, full of steep streets, brightly painted houses and *al fresco* restaurants. Beyond lies **Rapallo▶**, once a fashionable Edwardian resort, now rather spoiled by modern building and the crush of summer tourists. People come to enjoy its mild climate, beaches with long promenades and its cultural events.

From Rapallo or nearby Santa Margherita Ligure you can reach **Portofino▶▶▶**, one of Italy's most beautiful but also most exclusive seafront villages. The country's rich and famous treat this as their personal playground, with the result that prices are high and the atmosphere select. Nevertheless, the village's sheer prettiness makes it well worth a day trip. Escape the crowds by walking to the Castello di San Giorgio and the little church of San Giorgio just beyond. Most of the Portofino promontory is protected as a *parco naturale*, designed to preserve one of the few unspoiled stretches of the Italian Riviera.

A little farther around the coast, **Sestri Levante▶** has one of the area's better beaches, the Baia di Silenzio, edged around one of the town's two large bays. **Portovenere▶▶** is almost as pretty as Portofino, but not as expensive. It has plenty of restaurants and bars, a ruined fortress and a beautiful sanctuary believed to stand on the site of a temple to Venus. Italians in the know go to **Lerici▶**, an attractive and unpretentious resort with sheltered beaches and a 13th-century Pisan castle.

Portofino's colorful waterfront

PARCO NATURALE DI MONTE DI PORTOFINO
Portofino's hills are cloaked in *macchia* (like the French *maquis*), a thick vegetation of aleppo and maritime pines, and a fragrant undergrowth of herbs, juniper, heathers, and cistus. Tranquil paths crisscross the park's hilly interior. Boat trips from Portofino and Camogli offer views of the often dramatic coastline.

THE GOLFO DEI POETI
The area around Lerici has been praised for its beauty for centuries, never more enthusiastically than by Byron and Shelley, the two poets after whom the area—the Golfo dei Poeti—was named. In one noted incident, Byron swam from Portovenere across the Gulf to visit Shelley in San Terenzo, a quaint fishing village across the bay from Lerici. It was here in 1822 that Shelley started the fateful voyage to Livorno that ended in shipwreck and his death by drowning.

Northwest Italy offers some of the country's best walking, from the spectacular high Alps of the Gran Paradiso National Park to the cliffs of the Cinque Terre and the Portofino peninsula.

LA MORRA AND LE LANGHE

The lovely hilly countryside around Alba is known as Le Langhe, a region swathed in vineyards and dotted with castles and hilltop villages. La Morra is one of the finest, enjoying all-embracing views (hence its nickname, the *Belvedere delle Langhe*). It also boasts a wine museum and a series of walks following designated wine routes. Each path is color-coded according to its destination and takes you past vineyards, wine cellars and rustic inns where you can sample the local vintages.

Explore the Italian countryside on foot

Hiking is not always easy in Italy. The Alps, however, have well-marked trails and are covered by up-to-date and readily available maps. This also applies to less well-known areas, foremost of which are the scarcely explored mountains of the Parco Naturale dell'Argentera in southwest Piedmont. Walking possibilities are endless throughout the Alpine areas of Piedmont and Valle d'Aosta. Below are a few of the finest to get you started.

Parco Nazionale del Gran Paradiso To explore this park buy the Kompass 1:50,000 map *Gran Paradiso-Valle d'Aosta* (No. 86) or IGC *Parco Nazionale del Gran Paradiso* (No. 3). The most popular walk in the area starts from Valnontey, south of Cogne. From the village (5,497 feet) take trail 106/36 to the *Rifugio Vittorio Sella* (8,527 feet). The path climbs through pine forests, with grand views of the surrounding mountains and glaciers, as well as excellent opportunities of seeing ibex and chamois. At the *rifugio*, take trail 39 south toward Lago di Lauson (8,764 feet) and follow it to the *Rifugio Sella Herbetet* and the head of the valley. Then walk down the valley on trail 33 back to Valnontey. Allow a full day for the walk, and try to avoid August and summer weekends, when the route is extremely popular.

Parco Naturale dell'Argentera This walk starts from Terme di Valdieri, a hamlet at the heart of the park (20 miles southwest of Cuneo in southern Piedmont). Use the IGC 1:50,000 map *Alpi Marittime e Liguri* (No. 8). Pick up the N8 trail that strikes west up the Valle di Valasco from immediately south of Terme di Valdieri (4,514 feet). Follow the well-made mule track to the upper part of the valley, which flattens out into one of the most beautiful upland meadows in the Alps (5,817 feet). At the small Savoy hunting lodge, the ruined *Casa di Caccia*, take the trail over the river and follow the main path into the mountains to the Lago di Valscura (7,504 feet). Descend via trails N22, N20, and N18 to the *Casa di Caccia* and thus back to Terme di Valdieri. Allow a full day for the walk.

Parco Naturale del Monte di Portofino All sorts of marked walks, long and short, are possible on the Portofino promontory. The most popular depart from Portofino itself, whose tourist office has several maps and guides covering many local hikes. The neatest circuit, a marked trail, leaves the village and climbs to San Sebastiano (630 feet), continuing to Monte delle Bocche (1,702 feet) before dropping down to the little fishing village of San Fruttuoso. Here you can either take one of the regular boats back to Portofino, or walk back along a quite magnificent coastal path via Punta Carega and the

Val Ruffinale. You should allow four hours to follow the complete circuit from Portofino.

Cinque Terre Numerous paths have been marked and mapped around the Cinque Terre villages and their mountainous hinterland. Maps and details are available from all local tourist offices, and the Italian Alpine Club (CAI) produce their own 1:40,000 *Carta dei Sentieri delle Cinque Terre*, available in local bookstores. Trains linking all the villages mean you can easily return to base without having to retrace your steps. The most obvious walks link the coastal villages, traversing breathtaking scenery, often by means of precipitous terraces or thousands of tiny steps cut into rocks. Any stretch between two villages has its rewards, though it is also worth exploring the mountains to the rear, where paths run along the entire summit ridge (linked by transverse trails to the coast).

The Castello di Verres lies in the Valle d'Aosta, northeast of the Parco Nazionale del Gran Paradiso

SAN REMO'S FLOWER MARKET

Every morning except Sunday, at around 6:30, traders gather in San Remo's Corso Garibaldi for one of Europe's largest flower markets. Over 20,000 tonnes of roses, carnations, mimosa, and other flowers change hands here every year.

A SCENIC TRAIN JOURNEY

The railway from Ventimiglia to Limone Piemonte is one of Italy's most scenic, passing through French territory as it climbs from the coast into the heart of the Alpi Marittime. An engineering marvel, the line was badly damaged in World War II and only reopened as late as 1979. Around ten trains daily ply the route. The journey takes 70 minutes.

THE PALMS OF BORDIGHERA

Bordighera has the unique privilege of supplying the Vatican with palms for Palm Sunday, the week before Easter, a tradition said to go back to 1586, and the raising of the Egyptian obelisk in front of St. Peter's, Rome. The supporting ropes threatened to break, but a sailor from Bordighera shouted "Water on the ropes," despite an order that the watchers should stay silent on pain of death. The pope, Sixtus V, awarded the village the palm concession in gratitude. Sadly, the story is probably a myth.

▶ Riviera di Ponente   62A3

The Italian Riviera's western portion stretches from Ventimiglia on the French border to Genoa. For the most part it is an unbroken chain of popular beach resorts, all far cheaper and more down-to-earth than their neighbors across the border.

Ventimiglia has a passable old quarter, but remains essentially a border town, crammed with dreary hotels, garages, and duty-free shops. **Bordighera**▶ ▶, beyond, is more refined, one of the first resorts to attract well-heeled British and Continental visitors in the 19th century. The beach is good and the historic center still boasts several medieval monuments.

San Remo▶ was once the Nice of the Italian Riviera, its mild climate, gardens, and genteel charm the magnet for the cream of European aristocracy. These days its appeal combines ritz with kitsch, though the old town (La Pigna), flower market and palm-lined promenades are all worth an hour's exploration. The cable car up Monte Bignone also makes a good excursion, offering views on clear days as far as Cannes. The town hosts a famous song festival every February.

Diano Marina and Laiguelia are both functional, family-oriented resorts, overshadowed by **Alassio**▶, a large, affluent, and lively town with the best beach in Liguria (more than 2 miles of fine sand).

Albenga▶ only has a pebbly foreshore, but its old town is the most historically rewarding on the Riviera. Its chief draws are the 5th-century baptistery—Liguria's most important early Christian building—the cathedral, the Museo Igauno, the intimate Piazza dei Leoni, and the Palazzo Peloso-Cipolla, whose Museo Navale Romano contains finds from a Roman galley sunk nearby in the 1st century BC. The Museo Diocesano, behind the Baptistery, is also worth a quick visit.

Finale Ligure▶ is among the Riviera's most pleasant spots, less crowded than Alassio. There is an interesting old-town area (Finalborgo) 1 mile inland. Little **Noli**▶ is a picturesque resort-cum-fishing village, with a good beach and interesting Romanesque church, San Paragorio. The last town before Genoa is the industrial port of Savona.

Elegant San Remo's palm-fringed harbor

The Hanbury Gardens (Giardino Hanbury) lie near the village of Mortola Inferiore, 4 miles from Ventimiglia. Founded in 1867 by Sir Thomas Hanbury, a wealthy English tea merchant, they were acquired by the Italian state in 1960. They are now ranked as some of the most important gardens in Italy.

The Ligurian coastline has one of the mildest winter climates in the country. Flowers of all varieties flourish here even in February, a natural bounty that has been turned to commercial advantage by the region's market gardeners. All down the coast you see chequered fields of brightly colored blooms, or row upon row of cavernous greenhouses.

At Mortola, Sir Thomas Hanbury took advantage of the region's benign climate to produce Italy's largest botanical gardens, planting out over 5,000 species of plants and flowers from all corners of the globe. Many were exotic specimens from Africa and Asia, carefully acclimatized to grow alongside the staples of Mediterranean and Alpine flora. The palms together with succulents and cacti are particularly outstanding. These days the garden is past its prime, over three-quarters of the species having been lost over the years (restoration work is now in hand). Nonetheless it still remains worth visiting, particularly if you come armed with a picnic.

The Hanbury Gardens are among Italy's finest, their mild climate making them worth a visit throughout the whole year

At the gardens' center is an extravagant Islamic-style mausoleum, Sir Thomas Hanbury's final resting place. From here the gardens fan out on steep terraces, a clever piece of design that constantly unfolds new vistas as you walk from level to level. The gardens' partial ruin in places only adds to their atmospheric appeal, creating overgrown nooks and hidden corners among the more formal settings. The terraces fall away to the sea in a mixture of unkempt arbors and riotous pergolas, occasionally revealing an artificial grotto or crumbling fountain.

The gardens are open Thu–Tue, Apr to mid-Jun, 10–5; summer, 9–6; winter, 10–4. Closed on Wednesdays; admission is expensive.

DRINKING IN STYLE

Turin is famous for its elegant *fin-de-siècle* cafés and coffeehouses. The best known include *Caffè Torino*, Piazza San Carlo 204; *Caffè San Carlo*, under the arcades of Piazza San Carlo (across the street from *Stratta*, the city's top chocolate shop); *Mulussano* in Piazza San Carlo; and *Baratti e Milano*, just off Piazza Castello in the gallery leading to Via Po.

BASILICA DI SUPERGA

In 1706, King Vittorio Amedeo II, surveying the positions of the French and Spanish armies besieging Turin, promised to build a basilica in honor of the Virgin if she came to the city's rescue. Turin was duly spared and the pledge fulfiled in the shape of the Basilica di Superga.

The old center of Turin, capital of Piedmont

►► Torino (Turin)   62C2

Piedmont's capital is a mixture of industrial hinterland—the domain of Fiat and Lancia—and a gracious city center of gardens, arcades, and boulevards. A quiet university town during the Middle Ages, it acquired a French flavor it has never entirely lost when the Savoys moved from Chambéry to establish their capital here in 1574. The city is undervisited—dreary suburbs tend to put people off—but the old core is worth a morning's exploration.

The two main sights gather under one roof in Piazza San Carlo's Palazzo dell'Accademia delle Scienze: the **Museo Egizio**►► (*Closed* Mon. *Admission: expensive*), considered the most important museum of Egyptian antiquities outside Egypt, and the **Galleria Sabauda**►► (*Closed* Mon. *Admission: moderate*), an outstanding art gallery built around the Savoys' family collection. Nearby, visit the **Museo Nazionale del Risorgimento**► (*Closed* Mon. *Admission: moderate*), for more background on Turin's pivotal role in Italian unification.

A little to the north lies Piazza Castello, home to a trio of sights. Most prominent is the **Palazzo Reale**► (*Closed* Mon. *Admission: moderate*), a Savoy royal palace crammed with gaudy state apartments, of less interest than the gardens to the rear, the Giardino Reale. Across the piazza stands the **Palazzo Madama**►► (partially closed for restoration), fronted by a fine baroque facade. Inside is the Museo Civico dell'Arte Antica, an eclectic collection of glassware, ceramics, jewelry, and paintings. On the square's north side the **Armeria Reale**► (*Closed* Mon) offers one of the world's greatest collections of arms and armor. The **Duomo**►►►, off Piazza Castello, is best known for the Turin Shroud (see opposite page). For an overall view, climb **Mole Antonelliana**►►, a 19th-century folly, also home to the excellent **Museo del Cinema**►.

Turin's cathedral contains one of the most famous—and controversial—relics in Christendom: the Holy Shroud, the cloth reputedly used to wrap Christ for His burial.

The Turin Shroud is a 4-yard length of linen, unremarkable except for the fact that it contains an imprint of what the faithful claim is an image of the crucified Christ. It first appeared in Europe around the middle of the 15th century, when it was presented to Ludovico of Savoy in Chambéry. In 1578 it was brought to Turin by another member of the Savoy family, Duke Emanuele Filiberto.

It is only in recent decades that rigorous scientific study of the shroud has been possible. The results have been double-edged. On the one hand, three separate university teams—in Italy, Britain and the United States—have concluded, as a result of carbon-14 dating, that the shourd is a forgery dating from between 1260 and 1390. On the other, they are unable to explain how the shroud's image, which is like a photographic negative, could have been created.

Housing the Shroud The Holy Shroud (or *Sindone*) is only brought out for display on special occasions. The original is kept in the Cappella della Sacra Sindone, locked securely away in a silver casket, which in turn is protected inside an iron box, a marble coffer, and a heavy urn on the chapel's main altar. Although Filiberto intended to build a new church to house the relic, his successors commissioned first Amedeo di Castellamonte and then Guarino Guarini (1624–1683) to design a chapel within the cathedral (badly damaged by fire in April 1997).

One of the baroque school's leading lights, Guarini has monuments built to his designs in places as far afield as Lisbon, Paris, and Prague. The chapel in Turin, however, is his masterpiece; a consummate piece of late-baroque frippery, notable especially for the exuberant excess of its unusual cupola.

THE SHROUD'S IMAGE
A photographic replica of the shroud on display in the cathedral shows the face of a bearded man, wounds from a possible crown of thorns, plus front and rear images of a body displaying spear wounds, the marks left by a whip and bruises compatible with carrying a cross.

75

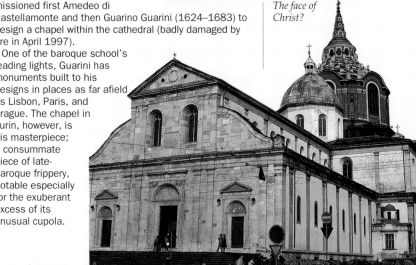

The face of Christ?

Drive

The Valle d'Aosta

See map on pages 62–63.

A spectacular drive through one of Italy's major Alpine valleys, full of magnificent castles, old stone villages and Europe's highest mountains, Mont Blanc, the Matterhorn, and Monte Rosa.

Note: although this drive follows the valley floor, be sure to explore the minor roads that strike off into scenic side valleys along the way—Val di Gressoney, Val d'Ayas, Valtournenche, and Val di Cogne.

Pont-St.-Martin, gateway to the valley, is a fine old village, surrounded by vineyards and known for its 1st-century BC Roman bridge. Bard offers the first of the valley's castles, most of which were built by the Challant family who ruled the region for seven

centuries. The stark fortress at Verres comes into view soon after, but is perhaps less interesting than the castle at **Issogne▶**, which is a plain affair from the outside, but inside full of fascinating apartments and sumptuous period furnishings.

St.-Vincent is a fashionable spa with one of Italy's largest casinos. Farther west, **Fenis▶▶** is the one castle to visit if you visit no other, a fairy-tale fortress of towers and turrets, its court, chapel, and loggias covered in 14th-century frescoes.

Fairy-tale Fenis Castle

Aosta is the region's focus (see page 65), an interesting town in its own right and a good base for trips to the **Parco Nazionale del Gran Paradiso** (see page 68) and **Valle del Gran San Bernardo** (see page 77). Beyond it, the castles come thick and fast, with particularly fine examples at Sarre, St.-Pierre, and Avise—all of them pretty villages as well.

Round off a drive by taking the cable car ride over Mont Blanc, the **Funivia del Monte Bianco▶▶▶** (*Open* daily). It leaves from La Palud, a hamlet 2 miles to the north of Courmayeur. You can ride to 10,960 feet at Punta Helbronner, press on over the Géant Glacier, or cross the mountain (Apr–Sep only) to Chamonix over the French border.

Farming in the Valle d'Aosta

▶▶ Val d'Ayas — 62D2

The Val d'Ayas is one of the prettiest of the valleys that branch off the Valle d'Aosta: broad, heavily wooded, and crowned by the colossal peaks of Monte Rosa and the Matterhorn (Cervino in Italian). Champoluc is the chief resort, departure point for mountain hikes and the cable car to Testa Grigia (11,000 feet), one of the most spectacular vantage points in the Alps. Brusson, to the south, is a base for easier walks, the best being the trail to the coronet of mountain lakes below Punta Valfredda (3hr 30min).

▶ Valle del Gran San Bernardo — 62D2

Easily seen from Aosta (see page 65), this valley is best known for its pass and famous St. Bernard dogs (see panel). Along its entire length, however, it is a scenic delight, well worth traveling for the ride alone. For still grander scenery, take the tortuous mountain road east of the valley into the wild reaches of the Valpelline.

▶ Val di Gressoney — 62D3

So perfect an alpine valley it is almost a cliché, the Val di Gressoney is a vision of emerald-green meadows, snow-capped peaks, shimmering glaciers, and geranium-hung wooden houses. Its inhabitants, the Walser, speak an obscure German dialect, having migrated here from the Swiss Valais in the 12th century. The main centers, Gressoney-St.-Jean and trendier Gressoney-La-Trinité, offer plenty of hiking and skiing opportunities.

▶ Valle di Susa — 62C1

The Valle di Susa lacks the drama of smaller alpine valleys, and is spoiled in places by light industry and its busy road and rail links. It has, however, one or two highlights, notably the dramatic abbey of **Sacra di San Michele**▶▶▶ (*Closed* Mon), just west of the pretty lakeside village of Avigliana. **Susa**▶ features a scattering of Roman remains and several ancient churches. Close by, roads lead into glorious scenery, particularly around the nature reserves of Salbertrand and Orsiera-Rocciavré.

Bridge leading to the
St. Bernard Tunnel

THE ST. BERNARD PASS
The 8,148-foot pass has long been one of the Alps' most important routes, used by Roman legions, Celts, Charlemagne, and Napoleon. Today, its chief attraction is the Hospice of St. Bernard, founded in 1050. It is just over the border in Switzerland, so take your passport. Part of the monks' vocation involved ministering to weary and snowbound travelers, helped by a uniquely robust type of dog. The souvenir shacks are stuffed with china, plastic, and fluffy versions of the famous brandy-carrying St. Bernard dog.

Lombardy and Emilia-Romagna

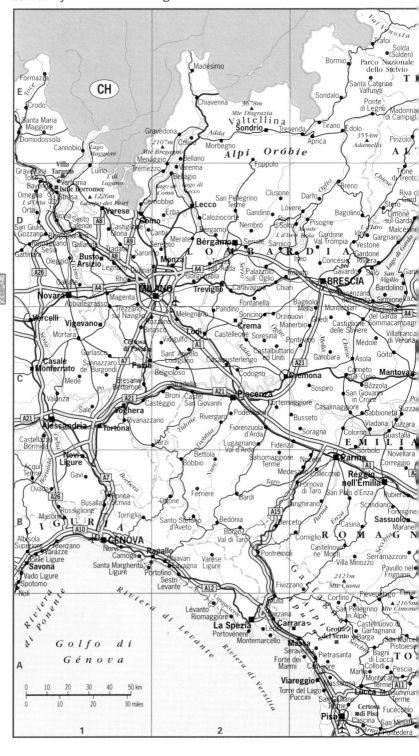

Merano (Meran)
Sarentino (Sarnthein)
Naturno (Naturns)
Chiusa (Klausen)
Val di Funes
Val Badia
Santo Stéfano di Cadore
Bolzano (Bozen)
Ortisei (Sankt Ulrich)
Val Gardena
Cortina d'Ampezzo
Auronzo di Cadore
Appiano (Eppan)
Canazei
Dolomiti
Pieve di Cadore
ENTINO
Láives
3343m
Marmolada
Alleghe
Málé
Cles
Moena
3220m
Mte Civetta
Forno di Zoldo
Dimaro
Egna
Predazzo
Ágordo
Longarone
Cavalese
San Martino di Castrozza
3150m
C. Brenta
Ardoino
Mezzombardo
Ariso
2847m
Cima d'Asta
Belluno
Ponte nelle Alpi
Molveno
Lavis
Cembra
Sédico
O ADIGE
Trento
Pergine
Valsugana
Val Sugana
Borgo Valsugara
Fonzaso
Grigno
Arsiè
Mel
Trichiana
A22
Arco
Rovereto
Asiago
575m
M Grappa
Feltre
Vittório Véneto
Mori
Valdobbiádéne
Conegliano
Negrar
Arziero
Val Sugana
Brenta
Piave
Maser
Cornuda
Spresiano
Odezzo
A27
Grezzana
Arzignano
Maróstica
Ásolo
Montebelluna
Ponte di Piave
Ala
Schio
Thiene
Bassano del Grappa
Castelfranco Véneto
Treviso
San Doná di Piave
Valdagno
Malo
Dueville
Cittadella
Roncade
A4
Bosco Chiesanuova
Chiampo
Montécchio Maggiore
V E N E T O
Scorzè
Frèganziol
Negrar
Arzignano
A4
Longare
Cadóneghe
Torcello
VERONA
San Bonifácio
Rubano
Mira
VENÉZIA
Lonigo
PADOVA
Dolo
A22
San Giovanni Lupatoto
Noventa Vicentina
Abano Terme
Albignasego
Laguna Véneta
Isola della Scala
Cologna Véneta
Montagnana
Monsélice
Piove di Sacco
Bovolone
Cerea
Este
Conselve
Chioggia
Nogara
Legnago
Cavázere
San Benedetto Po
Badia Polesine
Lendinara
Rovigo
Adige
Rosolina
Póggio Rusco
Castelmassa
Adria
Po
Táglio di Po
Sérmide
Occhiobello
Polesella
Pontarina
Móglia
Novi di Modena
Bondeno
Copparo
Iolanda di Savóia
Mésola
Porto Tolle
Mirandola
Camposanto
Finale Emilia
Mirabello
Ferrara
Tresigallo
Migliarino
Codigoro
Carpi
Solera
Cento
Malalbergo
Portomaggiore
Comacchio
Crevalcore
San Giovanni in Persiceto
Reno
Argenta
Valli di Comácchio
Módena
Castelfranco Emilia
Castel Maggiore
Molinella
A1
Spilamberto
Búdrio
Medicina
Consélice
Alfonsine
Vignola
Casalecchio di Reno
BOLOGNA
Bagnácavállo
Ravenna
Pántaro
Sasso Marconi
Castel San Pietro Terme
Lugo
Russi
Sant'Apollinare in Classe
Pianoro
Imola
A14dir
Montone
Vergato
Monzuno
Faenza
A14
Cérvia
A1
Brisighella
Castrocaro Terme
Forlì
Cesenático
Castiglione dei Pépoli
Modigliana
Forlimpopoli
Bellária
Porrétta Terme
Firenzuola
Predáppio
Méldola
Cesena
Savignano sul Rubicone
Vérnio
Marradi
Rocca San Casciano
Bidente
Santarcángelo di Romagna
Verúcchio
CANA
Pistoia
San Piero a Sieve
Borgo San Lorenzo
Santa Sofía
Mercato Saraceno
SAN MARINO
Prato
Sesto Fiorentino
Dicomano
165m
Mte Falterona
Sársina
Bagno di Romagna
Novalféltria
San Marino
San Leo
Lastra Signa
Fiésole
Stia
Camaldoli
Monte Feltro
Vinci Sieno
Óntassieve
Chiusi della Verna
Badia Prataglia
Pennabilli
Sassocórvaro
Scándicci
FIRENZE
Reggello
Poppi
1591m
Bibbiena
Pieve Santo Stéfano
Sant'Angelo in Vado
Urbánia
Émpoli
San Casciano in Val di Pesa

80

TOURIST INFORMATION
Bellagio (Lake Como): Piazza della Chiesa 14 (tel: 031 950 204).
Bergamo: Via Aquila Nera 2 (tel: 035 242 226).
Bologna: Piazza Maggiore 1 (tel: 051 239 660).
Como: Piazza Cavour 17 (tel: 031 269 712).
Malcesine (Lake Garda): Via Capitanato del Porto 6-8 (tel: 045 740 0044).
Mantova: Piazza A. Mantegna 6 (tel: 0376 328 253).
Milano: Via Marconi 1 (tel: 02 7252 4301); Stazione Centrale (tel: 02 669 0532 or 02 7252 4360).
Parma: Via Melloni 1B (tel: 0521 218 889).
Pavia: Via Fabio Filzi 2 (tel: 0382 22 156).
Ravenna: Via Salara 8–12 (tel: 0544 35 404).
Stresa (Lake Maggiore): Via Canonica 8 (tel: 0323 30 150).

LOMBARDY AND EMILIA-ROMAGNA Italy's richest regions are a perfect balance of city and countryside. Lombardy is divided between the plains of the Po and the mountains of the high Alps (Emilia-Romagna is mainly plain). Two cities lie at their heart: Milan, Italy's fashion and finance capital; and Bologna, ancient seat of learning and gastronomic star. Elsewhere, scattered small cities combine medieval centers with industrial hinterlands. Immense agricultural riches spring from the plains, creating, sadly, unlovely landscapes. If it's fine scenery you want, head for the Italian Lakes, a dozen or more lakes that fill the great Alpine valleys north of Milan.

MILAN Italy's capital by rights is Rome, but these days it could as easily be Milan (Milano), a major industrial center and a flourishing hotbed of fashion, design, and high technology. Visitors often find its modern face less appealing than more obviously historic cities like Venice and Florence, yet the city's sights include a grand cathedral, the world-class Brera art gallery—and Leonardo da Vinci's *Last Supper*. The city also makes a good touring base: the lakes and mountains are surprisingly close, and fascinating towns like Bergamo and Pavia—with its magnificent abbey—are less than an hour away.

THE ITALIAN LAKES Celebrated for centuries for their great natural beauty, the lakes these days are slightly sullied by people and pollution, but for the most part they remain a romantic medley of mountains, forests, lakeside villas, and mild-weathered resorts. The big three—Como, Garda, and Maggiore—are well known; slightly less frequented are Iseo and Orta. The latter, in particular, is still largely unspoiled by crowds and commercialism. Como takes most of the scenic plaudits, and Maggiore is a must, if only to visit the Isole Borromee (Borromean Islands).

You really need a car to do the lakes justice (though trains offer firsthand views of them all, save Garda). If possible try to avoid July and August, and weekends in particular, when many of Lombardy's cities empty

northward toward the region. Ideally, make base camp near a lake, then take boat trips to its other towns—by far the best way to see the scenery. Stresa is the best overall center on Lake Maggiore; Como the best on Lake Como; and Malcesine the first choice on Garda. All these places are popular, of course, and smaller villages are always worth checking out. If in doubt, head north, away from the spots easily reached from Milan.

CITIES Northern Italy's plains offer next to nothing in the way of scenery. Their tedium is relieved only by some of Italy's finest medium-sized cities, places that most people pass by as they rush to Florence or Venice. Lombardy's are perhaps the least known, and as a result can make surprisingly peaceful spots to while away a couple of days. Mantova is the best, a perfect medieval city in a strange, lagoon-circled setting. Cremona is a little too provincial, but attracts attention as the birthplace of the great violin-maker Stradivari. Bologna and Parma are the big draws in Emilia-Romagna, prosperous cities renowned for their cuisine and wide range of interesting medieval monuments.

RICE AND RISOTTO It comes as a surprise to many people to see the vast paddy fields that spread over large areas of Piedmont and Lombardy. Rice—and not pasta—is the mainstay of the Milanese diet (the area is Europe's largest rice producer). No one knows when or why cultivation started, though the theory is that the grain spread from Asia to Egypt and was then brought by Arabs to Sicily. The classic recipe for risotto uses rice fried with butter and onions, then cooked with stock, marrow, and saffron (butter and parmesan are added before serving). Other versions include *certosa*, with crayfish (invented by Carthusian monks); *monza*, with sausage; *comasco*, using perch; *lomellina*, with frogs; and *alla pilota*, from Mantova, with salami. Do not worry if none of these dishes takes your fancy; pasta is as popular here as it is elsewhere in Italy.

Bellagio, the jewel of Lake Como

SCENIC RAILWAYS
Europe's highest and most spectacular railway, the "Red Train," runs from Tirano (near Sondrio) to St. Moritz. Special tourist trains operate in summer, carrying observation cars for better views of the peaks and glaciers of the Bernina Alps. Almost equally spectacular is the two-hour run through the mountains from Domodossola to Locarno.

SCENIC DRIVES
SS 229 Lago d'Orta; SS 337 Domodossola–Santa Maria Maggiore–Locarno; SS 659 Domodossola–Crodo–Formazza; (*Lake Como*) SS 340/SS 583 Como–Gravedona–Bellano–Lecco–Bellagio–Como; SS 38/SS 39 Sondrio–Aprica–Edolo; (*Stelvio National Park*) SS 300 Bormio–Santa Caterina–Ponte di Legno: (*Adamello Regional Park*) SS 345 Breno–Collio–Iseo.

The Colleoni Chapel, Bergamo

DONIZETTI

Gaetano Donizetti, master of *bel canto*, the style of virtuoso aria that characterized his operas, was born in Bergamo in 1797. Around 60 operas and 51 years later he also died there, riddled with syphilis and certifiably insane.

EATING AND EPITHETS

Bologna has many nick-names: *La Dotta* (The Learned), after the university; *La Turrita* (The Turreted), after its towers; and *La Grassa* (The Fat), after a cuisine widely considered Italy's finest. Besides *bolognese* sauce (or *ragù*), specialties include bologna sausage; *mortadella* (a kind of Italian cold cut); *tortellini*; and *tagliatelle*, reputedly invented for the wedding feast of Lucrezia Borgia and the Duke of Ferrara. The long, straw-colored strands of pasta were said to have been inspired by the bride's flowing locks.

▶▶ **Bergamo**   78D2

Bergamo is in two parts: an old hill town, Bergamo Alta, and the more modern Bergamo Bassa. Most of the sights cluster in Bergamo Alta's Piazza Vecchia and the adjoining Piazza del Duomo. The French writer Stendhal thought the Piazza Vecchia "the most beautiful place on earth…the prettiest I have ever seen." Gracious medieval buildings fill both squares, notably the Romanesque church of **Santa Maria Maggiore**▶▶, its riotously overdecorated interior distinguished by a magnificent wooden choir. Flanking the church is the even more impressive **Cappella Colleoni**▶▶▶ (*Open* Mar–Oct, daily 9–12:30, 2–6; Nov–Feb, Tue–Sun 9:30–12:30, 2–5. *Admission free*), designed in 1476 for the Venetian *condottiere* Bartolomeo Colleoni by G. A. Amadeo (also responsible for Pavia's Certosa, see page 91). Its ceiling frescoes, by G. B. Tiepolo, depict the life of John the Baptist. Nearby, see also the **Baptistery**▶, and climb to the **Cittadella**▶ for beautiful views over the town.

Walk towards Bergamo Bassa on Via Pignolo to take in the **Accademia Carrara**▶▶▶ (*Closed* Mon. *Admission: moderate*), one of northern Italy's most important—and least-known—art galleries. Many of the Italian masters are represented (Botticelli, Titian, Raphael), as well as other European "greats."

▶▶▶ **Bologna**   79B4

Capital of Emilia-Romagna, wealthy Bologna is known for its cuisine, its left-leaning politics, Italy's oldest university and its mellow-bricked palaces and arcades. It centers around Piazza Maggiore and Piazza del Nettuno, home to Giambologna's 1556 Fontana del Nettuno, the medieval Palazzo Comunale, and **San Petronio**▶▶▶, one of Italy's greatest Gothic churches (note its portal in particular, by the Sienese sculptor Jacopo della Quercia). The nearby **Museo Archeologico**▶ (*Closed* Mon. *Admission: moderate*), has a wide-ranging collection, best seen in conjunction with the **Archiginnasio**▶▶ (*Closed* Sun and Sat PM. *Admission free*), part of the city's original medieval university.

No trip to the city is complete without climbing the leaning Torre degli Asinelli, but leave time also for the **Pinacoteca Nazionale**▶▶ (*Closed* Sun PM, Mon. *Admission: moderate*), with its important collection including Raphael's famous *Ecstasy of St. Cecilia*; **San Giacomo Maggiore**▶▶ for its Bentivoglio chapel; the Gothic church of San Francesco; Santo Stefano, a group of ancient churches; and the art-crammed **San Domenico**▶▶▶, with the Arca di San Domenico, the saint's sarcophagus, bearing sculpted decoration by Nicola Pisano and Michelangelo.

▶ **Brescia**   78D3

Lombardy's second city is disappointing, its historic center tarnished by hideous Fascist architecture, its sights scattered around chill modern streets. **Piazza della Loggia**▶ has a delicately festooned loggia, a palace designed in part by Palladio and Sansovino (1492–1570). The nearby Piazza del Duomo has two cathedrals, one drab, the other—the **Rotonda**▶—a more interesting 12th-century affair. Via dei Musei contains several Roman remains and the **Museo della Città**▶ (*Closed* Mon). The **Pinacoteca Tosio-Martinengo**▶▶ (*Closed* Mon. *Admission:*

moderate) offers the works of local artists (plus Raphael, Tiepolo, and Tintoretto). The city's masterpiece—Titian's *Annunciation*—can be seen in the church **San Nazario**▶▶.

▶ Como   78D1

Como, on the shores of Lake Como, is part elegant resort, part industrial town. Parks and bustling cafés line its lake-front promenades, all a stone's throw from the splendid 15th-century Renaissance-Gothic **Duomo**▶▶. Other frag-ments of old Como include San Fedele (once the town's cathedral), at the heart of the medieval quarter, and the Porta Vittoria, the late 12th-century city gate. Brave the industrial quarter to see **Sant'Abbondio**▶▶, a beautiful 11th-century church, and ride the funicular to hilltop Brunate for views of the lake. When you tire of Como, you can drive 12 miles west to **Castiglione Olana**▶▶▶, to see the Gothic Collegiata, with its glorious frescoes by Giotto's pupil, Masolino da Panicale.

▶▶▶ Como, Lago di (Lake Como)   78D2

Edged by mountains, Lake Como is the most dramatic of the Italian lakes. True, its waters are often polluted and its resorts thronged by tourists, but despite this, its lush setting, villas, gardens, and views make a visit essential. Take a boat tour (special passes available at Como allow you to stop wherever you please). **Bellagio**▶▶▶ is the most picturesque village (see panel), but Cernobbio, Tremezzo, and Menaggio all have their charms.

BELLAGIO

Lake Como's jewel has been called the prettiest village in Europe. From its promontory, it looks out over both arms of Lake Como, commanding peer-less views, and is best approached by boat from either Como or Menaggio. Wander the cobbled streets, almost too quaint for their own good, and visit the gardens of the Villa Melzi (*Open* mid-Mar–Oct, daily 9–6:30. *Admission: moderate*) and Villa Serbelloni (*Open* Apr–Oct, Tue–Sun; guided tours twice daily 11 AM, 4 PM. *Admission: moderate*). The apse and capitals of San Giacomo, a 12th-century church, both have some good carvings. From the village you can also visit Varenna, with the Villa Monastero and its lovely garden.

83

THE DEATH OF MUSSOLINI

Lake Como's beautiful surroundings were the incongruous setting for the capture and killing of Benito Mussolini by partisans in 1945, when the Fascist leader was attempting to flee to Switzerland. He was caught at a roadblock near Mezzegra (just south of Tremezzo). The partisan leader, Waltger Audasio, tried to shoot Mussolini, but the Duce's mistress Claretta threw herself on the gun, which jammed. Audasio then took his driver's gun and shot Claretta before complying with Mussolini's last request to shoot him in the chest.

The Neptune Fountain, or Fontana di Nettuno (1556), is the work of local sculptor Giambologna

▶ Cremona 78C2

A quiet provincial town, Cremona is synonymous with violins, and in particular with Antonio Stradivari (1644–1737), the greatest violin-maker of all time. The town honors its most famous son with a museum, the **Museo Stradivariano▶** (*Closed* Mon. *Admission: moderate*), complemented by the adjoining Museo Civico, both crammed with violins and miscellaneous memorabilia (as well as displays devoted to Roman Cremona).

Violins apart, Cremona can seem a little stultifying: too quiet to hold your interest for long. The Romanesque **Duomo▶ ▶** and medieval **Piazza del Comune▶ ▶**, however, are superb, and in the **Torrazzo▶ ▶** (*Open* daily. *Admission: moderate*), the town boasts the tallest medieval tower in Italy (369 feet).

▶ Faenza 79B5

You visit Faenza, an otherwise melancholy town, for one thing only: the vast **Museo delle Ceramiche▶ ▶** (*Open* Tue–Sun AM and Sat PM; *Admission: moderate*), one of the most comprehensive ceramic collections in Italy. The town's pottery (majolica), with its characteristic blue and ocher coloring, has been famed throughout Europe for over 500 years. Today it is still produced and sold in numerous workshops. The museum displays not only native ware, but also pottery from many periods and countries—from Roman majolica and Renaissance sculpture to the modern ceramic art of Pablo Picasso, Henri Matisse, and Marc Chagall.

Faenza's distinctive ceramics have been celebrated for their beauty for centuries

84

▶ ▶ Ferrara 79B4

In its day, Ferrara—a lovely and relatively unvisited town—could claim one of Europe's most dynamic Renaissance courts. Its driving force was the Este family, a dynasty who ruled and rebuilt the city over several hundred years. Their dynastic seat, the **Castello Estense▶** (*Closed* Mon. *Admission: moderate*), still lords it over the town, worth seeing for its decorated apartments and atmospheric dungeons. Another Este retreat, the **Palazzo Schifanoia▶ ▶** (*Closed* Mon. *Admission: moderate*), is noteworthy for its Sala dei Mesi, a roomful of fine frescoes illustrating the twelve months of the year.

Other worthy paintings, including works by Bellini and Mantegna, reside in the gallery of the early Renaissance **Palazzo dei Diamanti▶ ▶** (*Closed* Mon and PM daily; *Admission: moderate*). The attractive **Duomo▶ ▶** also contains a jewel of a museum, the Museo del Duomo (*Open* daily. *Admission: donation*), full of precious works of art.

The town's major sights apart, it's pleasant simply to stroll along Ferrara's pretty streets—Via delle Volte and the distinct medieval and planned Renaissance quarters in particular.

THE VIOLINS OF CREMONA
Cremona's Andrea Amati produced the first modern violin in 1566, handing down his techniques to his son Nicolò, who passed them in turn to his pupils, Antonio Stradivari and Giuseppe Guarneri. Stradivari's career spanned 68 years, during which time he made an estimated 1,200 violins, violas, cellos, harps, guitars, and mandolins. He reputedly kept instruments in his bedroom for a month before completion. In this way, he claimed, his dreams imparted "soul" to his creations. Between 800 and 1,000 violins annually are still produced in Cremona's 60 workshops (*botteghe liutarie*). Europe's foremost violin-making school, La Bottega, is also here.

▶▶▶ Garda, Lago di (Lake Garda)   78D3

Garda is the largest of the Italian Lakes, its landscapes divided between gentle plains in the south and hills and mountains in the north. Its most popular spot is **Sirmione**▶▶, enchanting off-season, tourist-choked in summer. The castle **Rocca Scaligera**▶ (*Closed* Mon. *Admission: moderate*), is the most memorable sight. Out of town you should also see the **Grotte di Catullo**▶, the ruins of a Roman spa on a hillside of ancient olive trees.

Midway up the lake's eastern shore, stop off at **Punta di San Vigilio**▶▶, the lake's prettiest spot. After enjoying its views and cypress-filled gardens, go to **Malcesine**▶, one of Garda's more sedate and appealing villages. Like Sirmione, it, too, has an evocative castle, though more people go for the cable car ride to the 6,600 feet summit of Monte Baldo for its views and hiking opportunities. It is known as the "Garden of Italy" for its botanical variety.

Riva del Garda▶ is the lake's best-known resort, a young and lively spot, though its crowds and commercialism weigh against its prettiness. Nearby, visit the 313-foot waterfall, Cascata del Varone. Moving around to the lake's less ravaged western shore, drive into the hills above Limone sul Garda for a network of scenic roads (via Vesio Pieve and Tignale). Views from the church of Madonna di Monte Castello (near Tignale) are especially good. **Gardone Riviera**▶▶ was once the lake's most fashionable resort and still retains much of its erstwhile elegance. Nearby stands the not-to-be-missed **Il Vittoriale degli Italiani** (see panel).

▶ Iseo, Lago di   78D2

One of the quieter Italian Lakes, Iseo has few sights but shares its neighbors' beauty and mountainous surroundings. **Monte Isola**▶▶, an island in the center of the lake, is known for its panoramic views.

POETIC ECCENTRICITY
The extraordinary villa called Il Vittoriale (*Closed* Mon. *Admission: expensive*) was presented by Mussolini to Gabriele d'Annunzio, larger-than-life poet, soldier, socialite, and aristocratic womanizer. The gift was ostensibly in recognition of d'Annunzio's patriotism, but was also designed to keep him quiet (his claim to have eaten dead babies can hardly have helped the Fascist cause). The poet transformed the villa into a kitsch palace, filling it with souvenirs of his military, literary, and amatory accomplishments. Furnishings include an embalmed tortoise, a bath surrounded by 200 pieces of bric-à-brac and a World War I biplane.

Sirmione is one of the prettiest and most popular towns on Lake Garda

The plains of Emilia-Romagna have little to offer the walker, but there are hikes to suit all abilities in Lombardy's Lakes region, the Alpine foothills, and mountain wilderness of the Stelvio National Park.

86

Lago di Como On Como's western shore, try the hike that starts from the hamlet of Breglia above the lakeshore town of Menaggio. The trail reaches the *Rifugio Menaggio* after about an hour and a quarter, and from here several trails lead into higher terrain. The best option (weather allowing) is the path to Monte Bregagno (6,950 feet), a breathtaking viewpoint.

Lago di Garda Monte Baldo on Lake Garda's eastern shore has several easily accessible high-level hikes (take the cable car from Malcesine or minor roads into the mountains from the lakeshore). The best of these follows the mountain's main ridge, heading for the *Rifugio Telegrafo* (7,095 feet). To plan this and other local walks use the Kompass map *Lago di Garda-Monte Baldo* (No. 102).

Malcesine's cable car offers an easy way to see the fine views of Lake Garda

Parco Nazionale dello Stelvio Italy's largest national park has over 600 miles of marked trails. The classic hike for first-time visitors is along the Valle dello Zebrù, a spectacular valley due east of Bormio, a town on the park's western flanks. Immediately to the south, the parallel Valle dei Forni has a great walk to the *Rifugio Branca* from Forni, with magnificent views of the Cevedale glaciers (use Kompass map *Ortles–Cevedale*, No. 72).

Practicalities Hiking is best in the Alps from June to September, but the season is longer in the Lakes, where snow on low ground melts sooner. Most of the area is well-mapped, the most comprehensive coverage being provided by the 1:50,000 Kompass series. Tabacco maps are even better, but they cover fewer areas. Both brands are widely available on the spot. Tourist offices often have guides to easier hikes, particularly in the Lakes.

▶▶▶ Lago Maggiore (Lake Maggiore)   78D1

You need choose what you see on Lake Maggiore. Much of the shore is flat and disrupted by factories, the mountains are far away, and the towns crowded. But the villas, lush gardens, and vestigial 19th-century elegance of the lake's resorts continue to draw visitors.

Refined **Stresa▶▶**, though busy, is the best center. An important international music festival takes place here annually in late August. A cable car runs from the town to Monte Mottarone for stunning views. Pick up boats at Stresa for the **Isole Borromee▶▶▶**, an exquisite archipelago of islands. Isola Bella's villa and gardens make it the most visited of the group (see panel), but **Isola Pescatori▶▶** and the quieter **Isola Madre▶▶▶** should not be missed. The pleasant town of Cannobio is a good place to stay on the western shore; it has little to see, but is connected by buses and ferries to other points on the lake.

More intimate **Baveno▶** was once patronized by Queen Victoria. Near Verbania is **Villa Taranto▶▶** (*Open* Apr–Oct, daily. *Admission: expensive*), the most famous of all the Lakes' botanical gardens. Resorts farther north and on the lake's eastern (Lombardy) shore have little to recommend them other than tranquility. The best are **Cannero Riviera▶**, Ghiffa, Cervo, and **Angera▶**.

▶▶▶ Mantova (Mantua)   78C3

Once past Mantova's grim outskirts you can see why Aldous Huxley described it as the most romantic city in the world. Surrounded by lakes (it is sometimes known as *piccola Venezia*—little Venice), the city has a skyline of ancient towers and a center of medieval perfection.

The top sight is the astounding **Palazzo Ducale▶▶▶** (*Open* Tue–Sun 8:45–7:15. *Admission: expensive*), home of the Gonzagas, one of the Renaissance's foremost dynasties. In its day it was the largest palace in Europe. When it was sacked in 1630, 80 carriages were required to remove the 2,000 works of art contained in its 500 rooms. Be sure to see the Camera degli Sposi and its Mantegna fresco cycle, the palace's real treasure, and the family's summer residence, the **Palazzo Te▶▶▶** (*Open* Tue–Sun 9–6, Mon 1–6. *Admission: expensive*), designed by Giulio Romano and with wonderful frescoes by him.

Highlights continue with **Piazza delle Erbe▶▶**, a lovely square; **Sant'Andrea▶▶**, a Renaissance church by Alberti; the 11th-century Rotonda; and the Torre della Gabbia, a medieval prison.

Top: Isola Bella
Above: neighboring Borromean island, Isola Pescatori

ISOLA BELLA
Isola Bella (*Open* daily. *Admission: expensive*), was no more than a barren rock until the 17th century, when Count Carlo III Borromeo decided to convert it into a garden paradise for his wife, Isabella. The island is spoiled only by the artificial grottoes, kitsch statues, and badly decorated villa—described by Robert Southey as "one of the most costly efforts of bad taste in all Italy."

Milan's magnificent Gothic cathedral

MILANESE FOOD
Milan's gastronomic specialties include *polenta*, a type of cornmeal-based mush, a staple of northern Italy—trendy today, but quite bland. More mouth-watering are breaded cutlets, *cotolette alla milanese*—*wiener schnitzel* by another name (a legacy of Milan's period under Austro-Hungarian rule). *Risotto alla milanese* is also common, traditionally made with saffron and broth. *Panettone*, a Milanese cake with fruit and raisins, is a Christmas treat now eaten all over Italy.

LOCAL WINES
The closest wine zones to the city produce Oltrepò Pavese and San Colombano. From farther afield look for Pino and Rosso di Franciacorte; the fine white, Lugana; the reds Groppello, Buttafuoco and Barbacarlo; and the wines from the Valtellina, a high Alpine valley—Grumello, Valgella, and Sassella.

▶ ▶ ▶ **Milano (Milan)**   78D2

There is little *dolce vita* in Milan: busy and work-oriented, Italy's capital of fashion and high finance is a slick and businesslike city—and firmly European in outlook (a "southern suburb of Paris," according to some, while Rome is a "northern suburb of Cairo"). Modern in appearance as well as outlook, Milan is perhaps less fun to wander in than some cities—though its main sights are as compelling as any in the country.

The finest of these is the **Duomo**▶ ▶ ▶, Italy's largest Gothic building, and Europe's third largest church (after St. Peter's and Seville cathedral). The exterior's forest of spires and intricate decoration—a "poem in marble," said Mark Twain—compensates for a disappointing interior. The highlight is a trip to the roof, a magical world of spires and turrets, with views—smog allowing—that extend as far as the Matterhorn.

West of the Duomo, stroll through the **Galleria Vittorio Emanuele**, a Belle Epoque shopping arcade, to reach La Scala, Milan's famous opera house, and then Via Manzoni, one of the city's most fashionable and frenetic streets. Partway up it stands the **Museo Poldi Pezzoli**▶ ▶ (*Closed* Mon. *Admission: moderate*), a collection of antiques and paintings, the best of which are in the Salone Dorato (Golden Room). Antonio Pollaiuolo's *Portrait of a Young Woman* is here, one of Italy's most renowned portraits, together with works by Raphael, Mantegna, Botticelli, Giovanni Bellini, and Piero della Francesca.

For the city's single most famous work of art, however, you need to trek across the city to the church of **Santa Maria delle Grazie**▶ ▶ ▶ (*Closed* Mon; you must book at least two days in advance). Partly designed by Bramante, the church is a Renaissance tour-de-force, though few people give it more than a passing glance. Most are intent on seeing Leonardo da Vinci's *The Last Supper*, on a wall of Santa Maria's old refectory (*Open* Tue–Sun 8:15–7. *Admission: expensive*) (see page 90).

The colossal size of the **Castello Sforzesco** (*Closed* Mon) makes it the city's principal landmark after the **Duomo**.

Built by the Viscontis, Milan's medieval overlords, and enlarged by their successors, the Sforzas, it became the seat of one of Europe's leading courts of the Renaissance period. Now its rambling inner courtyards house two average art galleries: the **Pinacoteca**►► (*Closed* Mon) and **Museo d'Arte Antica**►► (*Closed* Mon). The latter's collection is a mishmash of sculpture, dominated by Michelangelo's unfinished last work, the *Pietà Rondanini*. The former includes a fresco cycle from Boccaccio's *Decameron*, a plethora of medieval *objets d'art* and works by Mantegna, Crivelli, Bellini, and Filippo Lippi.

Ten minutes away is the **Pinacoteca di Brera**►►► (*Closed* Mon. *Admission: moderate*), one of Italy's top galleries, and one that is so rich that it probably requires several visits. Among the feast of paintings on display are Mantegna's famous *Cristo Morto* and Veronese's equally well-known *Supper in the House of Simon*. Other treasures include Raphael's *Marriage of the Virgin*, Piero della Francesca's *Pala di Urbino*, Giovanni Bellini's superlative *Pietà*, and works by Caravaggio, Carpaccio, Tintoretto, El Greco, Rembrandt, and many more.

For still more art, visit the **Palazzo dell'Ambrosiana**►► (*Closed* Mon. *Admission: expensive*), home to a fabulous 17th-century library and a distinguished art collection, including Botticelli's *Tondo* and *Madonna del Baldacchino*; Caravaggio's *Fruit Basket* (Italy's first and the artist's only still life); Giorgione's *Page*; Leonardo's *Portrait of a Musician*; and the cartoon for Raphael's *School of Athens*.

If looking at paintings begins to wear a little thin, you could make for the most eminent of Milan's many churches, **Sant'Ambrogio**►►►, founded in 379 by St. Ambrose, Milan's first bishop and the city's patron saint. Most of the present structure dates from the 11th century. Inside the church, its chief treasures are a handsome pulpit, one of Italy's finest Romanesque works, the apse's 11th-century mosaic, and the sanctuary's 9th-century gold and jewel-studded ciborium.

SHOPPING
Milan is tops for high fashion, accessories, and luxury goods. The big-name shops cluster in the so-called *Quadrilatero d'Oro* (Golden Quadrangle)—the area defined by Via Monte Napoleone, Via della Spiga, Via Borgo Spesso, and Via Sant'Andrea. For more affordable prices you could do worse than visit *La Rinascente* in Piazza del Duomo, Milan's largest and oldest department store—and a city institution. Many of the glass-domed *gallerie* off Galleria Vittorio Emanuele have interesting, high-quality shops.

89

TOURIST OFFICE
This can be found at Via Marconi 1 (Piazzale Duomo); tel: 02 7252 4300.

High-class shopping in the Galleria Vittorio Emanuele

Asked to name the world's most famous paintings, many people would cite first the **Mona Lisa** *and then another Leonardo da Vinci masterpiece—*The Last Supper, *painted in the refectory of Milan's Santa Maria delle Grazie.*

THE SEARCH FOR JUDAS

The 16th-century painter and art historian Giorgio Vasari tells us that the figure of Judas gave Leonardo great problems in the two years he worked on the painting. He scoured Milan's streets and prisons for models, casting around for someone with a face of sufficient venality. The result, said Vasari, was "the very embodiment of treachery and inhumanity."

The Last Supper, *during the restoration process*

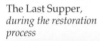

Leonardo's vision of the beginning of Christ's agony is one of European art's best-known images, yet until recently *L'Ultima Cena (The Last Supper)* had been allowed to fade and deteriorate badly, to the extent that Aldous Huxley called it "the saddest painting in the world." Even then, for all the decay, it remained a startling work, capturing the moment Christ announces that He will be betrayed by one of His disciples.

Leonardo chose to apply oil and tempera to a dry surface, rather than the accepted fresco method of painting pigment onto wet plaster. This allowed him greater flexibility of tone and color, but moisture soon began to corrode the painting. Over the centuries the fresco suffered further from clumsy attempts at restoration. At one point, the monks gave up on the project altogether—and whitewashed part of the painting. On another occasion, Napoleonic troops used the fresco for target practice. In 1943 a bomb hit the building, destroying everything but *The Last Supper*.

Modern restoration techniques have attempted to turn back the years. The fresco's details are now vivid, gestures and expressions captured in almost photographic detail, although some critics feel the colors have been made too bright. Look for the figure of Doubting Thomas and his raised finger; the hangdog profile of Philip, fearful that he may be the betrayer; and Peter, partly blocked by Judas hurrying forward with his 30 pieces of silver.

▶ Modena 79B4

A long-time rival to Bologna, Modena is a northern city in the classic mold: provincial and quietly prosperous, its outskirts industrial, its tight center a medieval delight. Pride of place goes to the **Duomo▶▶**, a 12th-century Romanesque masterpiece, known for its *tribuna* (rood screen) and a lurching campanile, the **Torre Ghirlandina▶**. In the maze of appealing old streets nearby, make a point of visiting the Palazzo dei Musei, home to three museums: the Biblioteca Estense (*Closed* PM *and Sun. Admission free*), its prize exhibit the *Bibbio Borso*, a sumptuously decorated medieval Bible; the Museo d'Arte Mediovale e Moderna e Etnologia (*Closed* Mon. *Admission: moderate*); and the Galleria Estense (*Closed* Mon. *Admission: moderate*), with paintings, many by local Renaissance masters.

▶▶ Orta, Lago di 78D1

Lake Orta's tranquil beauty is the perfect antidote to the commercialism and tainted charms of the larger Italian lakes. Its main center, **Orta San Giulio▶▶**, is a peaceful small town, a base for boat trips out to the **Isola San Giulio▶▶**. This is a dream of an island, its hamlet capital dominated by a brilliant white Romanesque church, the Basilica di San Giulio. For views, walk up the Sacro Monte above Orta San Giulio, or drive to Madonna del Sasso and Quarna, perched above the lake's western shore.

▶▶▶ Parma 78B3

Italy's most prosperous town, Parma is a monument to good living, with fine food (it is the home of Parma ham and Parmesan cheese), an excellent opera house, and a wealth of elegant cafés and shops. The **Duomo▶▶▶** is one of the country's finest Lombard-Romanesque churches, distinguished by the 16th-century painter Correggio's dome frescoes of the *Assumption of the Virgin*. Nearby, the 12th-century octagonal **Baptistery▶▶▶** contains some of the most expressive Romanesque sculptures in Italy, a series of reliefs on the exterior, and 12 carvings inside depicting the months of the year. Behind the Duomo, **San Giovanni Evangelista▶▶▶** (the Abbey of St. John) boasts a baroque front and more superlative frescoes by Correggio. The Galleria Nazionale, the antiquities museum, and the extraordinary Teatro Farnese are all housed in the vast **Palazzo della Pilotta▶▶** (*Open daily* AM *only. Admission: expensive*).

▶ Pavia 78C1

A day trip from Milan, Pavia—where kings and emperors were crowned in the Middle Ages—has a sleepy collection of medieval streets, with something of interest at every turn. Most of the sights, however, are overshadowed by the nearby **Certosa di Pavia▶▶▶** (*Open Tue–Sun*, Oct–Mar, 9–11:30, 2–4:30; Apr, 9–11:30, 2:30–5:30; May–Sep, 9–11:30, 2:30–6. *Admission: donation*), one of the most dazzling monasteries in Europe, set in a former hunting ground of the Visconti family and rich in Renaissance and baroque art. Nevertheless, do not miss two outstanding churches; **San Michele▶▶▶** and **San Pietro in Ciel d'Oro▶▶**, both Romanesque masterpieces. The austere 14th-century **Castello Visconteo▶** also houses a trio of art and archeology museums.

Your table is ready in Parma's Piazza Garibaldi

Ravenna: Basilica di San Vitale

▶ Piacenza   78C2

Unassuming Piacenza stands in the shadow of better-known cities like Parma and Cremona. Few people visit its sleepy medieval center, still laid out on the gridiron pattern of the old Roman colony (the city marked the end of the old Roman road, the Via Aemilia). Piazza dei Cavalli, the central square, is dominated by the crenellated **Palazzo del Comune▶▶**, the council chamber of the medieval city. At its center are two equestrian statues, some of Italy's finest baroque sculptures.

▶▶▶ Ravenna   79B5

Most people come to Ravenna expecting only mosaics (see opposite page) and are surprised to find as appealing a small town as any in Italy. True, the mosaics are virtually the only things to see, but the center's tangle of streets are a pleasure to wander. You might also spend a happy hour in **Piazza del Popolo▶**, a square filled with outdoor cafés and noble medieval *palazzi*. Close by, be sure to visit the **Tomba di Dante▶** (*Open* daily. *Admission free*), burial place of the famous medieval poet. He died in Ravenna in 1381 after being exiled from Florence, his home town.

▶ Rimini   149D5

Rimini is nirvana for beach enthusiasts who like their resorts big and brash (none come bigger—this is Europe's largest coastal town). Crammed with Italian families, and German and Scandinavian students, it is known for sun, sea, and sex for dusk-to-dawn nightlife, and for huge, heavily commercialized beaches. Given all this, it remains surprisingly unsleazy—though it is not the place for quiet sunbathing. Smaller resorts in a similar mould run all the way down Italy's Adriatic coast.

Ravenna boasts the finest Byzantine mosaics in the world outside Istanbul, a legacy of its role as capital of the Western Roman Empire in the 5th century. Its history made it a meeting place of artistic trends.

Honorius moved the seat of empire to Ravenna around AD 403, prompted by Rome's stagnation and by Ravenna's convenient location near *Classis*, the Romans' main port on the Adriatic coast. The city boomed and continued to thrive after the empire's fall, first under the barbarian leaders Odoacer and Theodoric, and later as a Byzantine vassal ruled by the emperor Justinian.

Mosaics The most breathtaking mosaics—"monuments to unageing intellect," in the words of W. B. Yeats—are to be found in the **Basilica di San Vitale** (*Open* daily. *Admission: moderate*—includes Mausoleo di Galla Placidia), a magnificent Byzantine-style church (built in 547) in the city center. Two strands can be identified in the mosaic panels, the first the Byzantine scenes depicting Justinian, Theodora, and their court, the second the more classically inspired episodes taken from the Old Testament. Both sets date from as early as the 6th century.

Across the grassy piazza outside the church stands the **Mausoleo di Galla Placidia** (see panel. *Admission: moderate*), a tiny chapel studded with mosaics of ethereal blues and glittering golds—one of the most intimate and impressive buildings in Italy. The nearby **Museo Nazionale** (*Closed* Mon. *Admission: moderate*), also boasts many Roman, Byzantine and early Christian mosaics. The church of **Sant'Apollinare Nuovo** (*Open* daily. *Admission: inexpensive*), contains two further mosaic cycles. Both show processions, one of virgins and the other of martyrs, gliding toward the altar against a beautiful background of gold and green-leafed palms. On a smaller scale, the 6th-century **Cappella di Sant'Andrea** (*Open* daily. *Admission: inexpensive*) contains mosaics from two eras; one from the building's period as a Roman bathhouse, the other executed when the building became a Christian baptistery.

Three miles from Ravenna, the church of **Sant' Apollinare in Classe** (*Open* daily. *Admission: inexpensive*) is all that survives of ancient Classis. Consecrated in 549, its mosaics are as impressive as any in the city, particularly those in the apse of *The Transfiguration of Christ*.

Peacock mosaic in San Vitale

GALLA PLACIDIA

Galla Placidia was one of the most remarkable women in ancient Rome's history. Daughter of Theodosius, the father of Emperor Honorius, she was kidnapped when the Goths sacked Rome. Almost immediately she married Ataulfo, one of her kidnappers—who was promptly assassinated. She then sought refuge with her half-brother Honorius. Forced to marry Constantius, a Roman general, she contrived to have her husband made joint emperor with Honorius. Widowed again, she had her son, Valentinian III (aged six), made emperor (with herself as regent). She died and was buried in Rome in AD 450, leaving open the question of who instigated her mausoleum in Ravenna.

TICKETS

You can buy a combined entry ticket (from the tourist office) for San Vitale, Galla Placidia, Sant'Apollinare Nuovo, Sant'Apollinare in Classe, and Sant'Andrea.

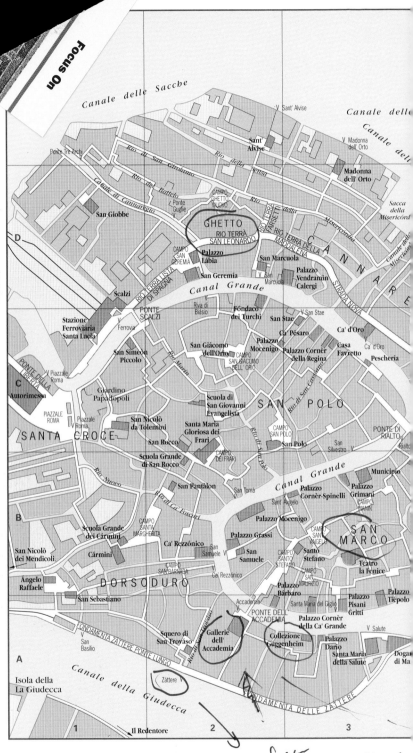

Canale delle Sacche

V Sant' Alvise

Canale delle

Canale delli

Ponte Tre Archi

Rio di San Girolamo

Rio della Sensa

Sant' Alvise

V Madonna dell' Orto

Madonna dell' Orto

Rio del Battello

Ponte Guglie V

CAMPO GHETTO NUOVO

Rio Terra Farsetti detta

Rio Terra della MADDALENA

Miserícordia

Sacca della Misericórd

San Giobbe

GHETTO

RIO TERRÀ SAN LEONARDO

CAMPO SAN GEREMIA

Palazzo Làbia

San Marcuola

V San Marcuola

Palazzo Vendramín Calergi

C A N N A R E

Scalzi

RIO TERRA LISTA DI SPAGNA

San Geremia

Canal Grande

Riva di Biásio

Fóndaco dei Turchi

San Stae

V San Stae

STRADA NOVA

Stazione Ferroviaria Santa Lucía

PONTE SCALZI

Ferrovia

Ca' Péesaro

Ca' d'Oro

Ca' d'Oro

San Simèon Piccolo

Rio Marín

San Giácomo dell'Ório

Palazzo Mocenigo

Palazzo Cornèr della Regina

Casa Favretto

Pescheria

V Piazzale Roma

CAMPO SAN GIACOMO DELL' ORIO

PONTE DELLA LIBERTA

Giardino Papadópoli

Scuola di San Giovanni Evangelista

SAN POLO

Rio di Sant Cassiano

Autorimessa

PIAZZALE ROMA

Piazzale Roma

San Nicolò da Tolentíni

Santa Maria Gloriosa dei Frari

CAMPO SAN POLO

PONTE DI RIALTO

SANTA CROCE

San Rocco

CAMPO DEI FRARI

San Polo

San Silvestro

Rialto

Scuola Grande di San Rocco

Rio Nuovo

Canal Grande

Municipio

San Toma

Palazzo Cornèr-Spinelli

Palazzo Grimani

CAMPO MANIN

Scuola Grande dei Cármini

Ca' Foscari

San Pantálon

Sant Angelo

Palazzo Mocenigo

CAMPO SANTA MARGHERITA

Palazzo Grassi

CAMPO SAN ANGELO

SAN MARCO

San Nicolò dei Mendícoli

Cármini

Ca' Rezzónico

San Samuele

CAMPO SANTO STEFANO

Santo Stefano

Teatro la Fenice

Ángelo Raffaele

CAMPO SAN BARNABA

Ca' Rezzónico

CAMPO SAN MAURIZIO

DORSODURO

San Sebastiano

Palazzo Bárbaro

Santa Maria del Giglio

Palazzo Pisani

Palazzo Tiépolo

Accademia

PONTE DELL' ACCADEMIA

Gritti

A

FONDAMENTA ZATTERE PONTE LUNGO

San Basilio

Squero di San Trováso

Gallerie dell' Accademia

Collezione Guggenheim

Palazzo Cornèr della Ca' Grande

Palazzo Dario

V Salute

Palazzo Pisani

Santa Maria della Salute

Doga di Ma

Isola della La Giudecca

Canale della Giudecca

Zàttere V

FONDAMENTA DELLE ZATTERE

1

Il Redentore

2

3

Ice Cream
Zattere -
Gelateria -
Nico
Giand

Venice

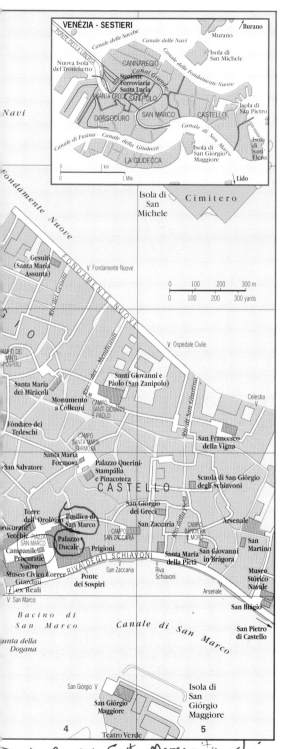

VENÉZIA - SESTIERI

PONTE DELLA LIBERTÀ

Canale delle Sacche
Canale delle Navi
Canal Grande
Canale delle Fondamente Nuove

Murano
Burano
Isola di San Michele

Nuova Isola del Tronchetto
CANNAREGIO
Stazione Ferroviaria Santa Lucía
SANTA CROCE
SAN POLO
DORSODURO
SAN MARCO
CASTELLO
Isola di San Pietro

Navi
Canale di Fusina
Canale della Giudecca
Canale di San Marco
Isola di San Elena

Isola di San Giórgio Maggiore
Isola di Santi

LA GIUDECCA
Lido

0   1 km
0   1 Mile

Isola di San Michele
Cimitero

Fondamente Nuove

Gesuiti (Santa María Assunta)
V Fondamente Nuove

0   100   200   300 m
0   100   200   300 yards

V Ospedale Civile

Rio dei Gesuiti
FONDAMENTE NUOVE
Rio dei Mendicanti

CAMPO DEI SANTI APÓSTOLI

Santa María dei Mirácoli
Santi Giovanni e Páolo (San Zanipolo)

Monumento a Colleoni
CAMPO SANTI GIOVANNI E PAOLO

Celestia V

Fóndaco dei Tedeschi

CAMPO SANTA MARIA FORMOSA

San Francesco della Vigna

Santa María Formosa
Palazzo Querini-Stampália e Pinacoteca

San Salvatore

Scuola di San Giórgio degli Schiavoni

C A S T E L L O

San Giórgio dei Greci

Torre dell'Orológio
Basílica di San Marco
ocuratie Vecchie PIAZZA SAN MARCO
Palazzo Ducale
Campanile
Procuratie Nuovo
Museo Civico Correr
ex Reali
Ponte dei Sospiri
San Zaccaria
RIVA DEGLI SCHIAVONI
CAMPO SAN ZACCARIA
San Zaccaria
Prigioni

San Martino
CAMPO BANDIERA E MORO
Arsenale
San Giovanni in Brágora
Santa Maria della Pietà
Riva Schiavoni
Arsenale
Museo Stórico Naválé
San Biágio

Bacino di San Marco
Canale di San Marco
unta della Dogana
San Pietro di Castello

San Giórgio V
San Giórgio Maggiore
Isola di San Giórgio Maggiore
Teatro Verde

4   5

#1 or 82
Vaporetti
Boat trip
Bridge of sighs

→ Campo Santa Margarita -slice pizza

Chiesa della Salute

ARRIVING

Venice's main Marco Polo airport is at Tessera (8 miles away) linked by ATVO buses (25 minutes) to Piazzale Roma. Treviso airport, 18 miles north of Venice, is the main airport for charter flights. Cars must be parked in Piazzale Roma or the Tronchetto. From here you must walk or take a *vaporetto* to the center of the city.

▶▶▶ CITY HIGHLIGHTS

VENICE (VENEZIA) Not everyone falls in love with Italy's most idiosyncratic city. Its decay can seem sinister, its crowds unendurable, its canals dark, and its alleys claustrophobic. Yet there are few people who remain unmoved by it. No matter how you picture the city, be prepared for the reality to be stranger—and probably lovelier—than you imagined. It is no use pretending that you can do justice to its treasury of sights on a short visit. Most of the time it is best simply to wander at random, for Venice is as much a city of atmosphere as it is of museums and monuments.

A WORD OF WARNING Visit Venice in the frenetic months of July and August and you risk coming away disappointed. Venice has no real off-season, but during these months the city becomes a travesty (crowds, high prices, packed hotels). Although it sounds like heresy, therefore, give careful thought to taking a room outside Venice in high summer—perhaps in Padua, Treviso, or Verona—and making several day trips by train. Leave cars behind—parking is a nightmare and long lines of traffic develop on the causeway from the mainland. The train services are excellent and link directly to the heart of the city.

THE CITY'S ORIGINS The Venetian lagoon was probably first settled around the time of Christ. More sustained settlement took place during the barbarian invasions (when this little group of islands in the lagoon became a safe haven). By the 6th century a loose confederation of communities had formed, initially under the firm hand of Byzantium (with its rule based in Ravenna), but by 726 under the autonomous control of an elected leader—the Doge. Trading links with the East soon brought great wealth, particularly during the Crusades, and by the 13th century the city owned territories stretching to the Black Sea (a domain "one quarter and one half-quarter of the Roman Empire"). These included a sizeable mainland empire (present-day Veneto and beyond).

CONFLICT Venice's prestige inevitably led to conflict with the papacy and other leading European powers. The League of Cambrai, formed in 1508, united the major European powers against the city, an alliance the city withstood, but only at the cost of sacked territories and an exhausted treasury. In the East, the Ottoman empire had been an increasing threat since early in the 15th century. Even at sea, Venice faced competition, the opening up of the Americas having tilted world trade away from Venice's traditional eastern markets.

DECADENCE AND DECLINE The Sack of Rome in 1527 left most of Italy except Venice under the control of Charles V. Stranded on the country's periphery, the city declined, its fall hastened by the Turks, who continued to nibble away at its overseas empire. Napoleon demolished the moribund state in 1797, leaving the city to pursue its own decadent devices (casinos, brothels, and endless festivities). It passed to the Austrians who, in moving their trade through Trieste, further quashed any hope of Venice's re-emergence. Through the 20th century, tourism developed apace (to around 20 million visitors a year). The expanding industrial towns of Mestre and Marghera on the mainland have helped reduce the city's population from 180,000 in 1945 to its present level of around 60,000.

ORIENTATION Venice has six districts (*sestieri*), hundreds of canals, thousands of streets and *campi*, and just one "piazza" (Piazza San Marco). Addresses include the name of the relevant *sestieri* (see map, pages 94–95). The main canal, the Canal Grande, has only three bridges (at the train station, the Rialto, and the Accademia). Often the best way of finding your way back to Piazza San Marco, the heart of Venice, is by a public canal boat, called a *vaporetto*—so carry a map of the stops and routes.

TOURIST INFORMATION
The main tourist office is at the Venice Pavilion, Palazzina dei Santi (tel: 041 522 5150) by the Giardinetti Reali (2 minutes' walk from St. Mark's). There are smaller offices at Piazza San Marco 71c (tel: 041 529 8730); Santa Lucia station (tel: 041 529 8711); Marco Polo airport (tel: 041 541 5887); and the Tronchetto parking lot. American Express is at Salizzada San Moise 1471 (tel: 041 520 0844), useful for currency exchange and a variety of organized guided tours.

STROLL–RIVA DEGLI SCHIAVONI
Running along the waterfront from the Palazzo Ducale, this is one of the most popular strolls in the city. Despite the crowds and occasional commercialism, it still makes an outstanding walk—particularly at sunset.

The Canal Grande

Although Venetian painting followed the currents of Italian art, it always plotted its own distinct course, influenced by ideas from East and West. It was distinguished by an emphasis on color, landscape, texture, and the use of light to evoke atmosphere (in contrast to Florence's preoccupations with structure and perspective). The result was an artistic patrimony unequaled by any other city.

98

SCULPTURE

Venice differed from central Italy in its lack of indigenous sculptors or sculptural masterpieces (the Colleoni statue—see page 109—is a notable exception and was sculpted by a Florentine, Verrocchio). Instead, the medium tended to be an integral part of larger architectural projects. Its principal exponents were Jacopo Sansovino, the Republic's foremost architect (who came from Rome in 1527), and Alessandro Vittoria, a member of Sansovino's workshop, who dominated Venetian sculpture in the latter part of the 16th century.

WHERE TO SEE—
GIOVANNI BELLINI

The Accademia contains several Madonnas, a series of allegorical panels, and a pair of altarpieces by Bellini. Elsewhere in the city the best of his work is to be found in San Zaccaria, San Pietro (Murano), Santa Maria Gloriosa dei Frari, Madonna dell'Orto, and San Zanipolo.

Byzantine and Gothic Venice's earliest artistic influences came from the East, fostered by the city's close political and commercial links with Byzantium. The greatest evidence of this is the major church, Basilica di San Marco. Byzantine elements continue in the Gothic splendor of the Ca' d'Oro palace, and in the 14th-century paintings of Paolo Veneziano. Over time the Orient's influence was married to the Gothic by the paintings of Lorenzo Veneziano and Michele Giambono.

Early Renaissance painters The Renaissance was slow to take hold in Venice, but the city's artists—with a distinctive use of color—molded Renaissance tenets into a style of painting that was distinctly Venetian. Some of Venice's most celebrated artists belonged to families that produced generation after generation of painters. The first was the Vivarini family: Antonio (ca1419–1480), his brother Bartolomeo (ca1430–1391), and son Alvise (ca1445–1505). The most prominent were the Bellinis;

Generations have tried—and failed—to find a precise meaning in Giorgione's mysterious painting The Tempest

The Miracle of the Cross on San Lorenzo Bridge *by Gentile Bellini, in the Galleria dell'Accademia*

THE ISTORIA
Narrative fresco cycles, or *istorie*, were a distinctive part of the Venetian Renaissance. Although often concerned with lives of the saints, they also wove depictions of contemporary Venetian life into their narrative thread. Only three of the ten cycles commissioned between 1475 and 1525 survive: the Accademia has two; Carpaccio's *St. Ursula* and the *Miracles of the Relic of the True Cross* (executed by five artists, including Carpaccio and Gentile Bellini). The third, Carpaccio's *St. George and St. Jerome*, is in the Scuola di San Giorgio degli Schiavoni.

father Jacopo (ca1400–1470), a pupil of Gentile da Fabriano, and sons Gentile (ca1429–1507) and Giovanni (ca1430–1516), the latter among the greatest of all the Venetian painters. Gentile is best known for his *istoria* or narrative cycle (see panel). Another artist involved in the same genre was Vittore Carpaccio (ca1465–1526), famous for the color and vivid detail he brought to paintings depicting the Venice of his day.

High Renaissance Two pupils of Giovanni Bellini marked Venice's artistic zenith. Giorgione (1475–1510) is one of art's most mysterious figures. His poetic paintings are as enigmatic as his short life, their strange, unsettling qualities exemplified by *The Tempest* (in the Accademia). Tiziano Vecelli, known as Titian (ca1485–1576), is among the finest painters of any age, and is renowned for a robust style, brilliant color and technical skill. Initially in thrall to Titian, Tintoretto (1518–1594) became his chief competitor. His dynamic paintings were more vivid and concerned with show than Titian's, where the sensuousness is expressive of an event's inner drama. Paolo Veronese (1528–1588), by contrast, is less turbulent, his works harmonious blends of warmth, light, and color. Both artists worked on huge canvases, often playing visual games—juggling viewpoints and perspective—as they strove for drama and effect.

Baroque and rococo Artistically, the 17th century was a fallow period, dominated by the baroque, a largely Roman preoccupation. In the 18th century, though, Venetian artists adopted rococo, a softer and riper style whose approach emphasized sensuality for its own sake. It was taken up by Sebastiano Ricci, Giambattista Tiepolo, and his son Giandomenico Tiepolo. They produced brilliant, almost decadent works, and their trademark, like that of so many other artists in Venice, was their dazzling use of color. Venice's artistic last gasp came with Antonio Canal, better known as Canaletto (1697–1768), and Pietro Longhi (1702–1785), both of whom painted often frivolous or idealized portraits of Venice itself.

Self-portrait by Titian

WHERE TO SEE—TITIAN
Despite his long life and prodigious output, Titian is badly represented in his home city (many of his works were stolen by Napoleon and now form the cornerstone of the Louvre's fine collection). In Venice his greatest works are in Santa Maria Gloriosa dei Frari, the Accademia, and Santa Maria della Salute.

A quite literally glittering repository of art and an extravagant mixture of differing architectural styles, the Basilica di San Marco is one of Europe's most exotic cathedrals as well as being Venice's single most famous building.

FOUR HORSES
San Marco's most famous statues, the four gilded bronze horses that stood above the portal, are kept inside the basilica to protect them from atmospheric pollution (the ones outside today are copies). No one is certain whether the originals are 4th-century BC Hellenistic bronzes or statues from a Roman triumphal arch cast seven centuries later. They were stolen from Constantinople by the Venetians during the Crusades.

100

THE PALA D'ORO
Made in Constantinople in 976, this gold altar panel is encrusted with 300 sapphires, 300 emeralds, 400 garnets, 15 rubies, 1,300 pearls, and countless lesser stones, figures, roundels, and enamel plaques.

OPENING TIMES
Summer, Mon–Sat 9:45–5, Sun 2–4:30; winter, Mon–Sat 9:45–4, Sun 2–4. *Admission free* to Basilica; *inexpensive* to each of Treasury, Pala d'Oro, and Loggia dei Cavall

Origins The basilica was conceived to house the body of St. Mark, the city's patron saint, stolen from Alexandria by Venetian merchants in 828. Completed in its basic form in 1094, the church was then embellished over nine centuries, creating a unique blend of Islamic, Byzantine, and European art and architecture. The decoration is completely overwhelming—so it is best to pick your way through it selectively.

The exterior The most noteworthy details of the exuberantly decorated exterior are the Romanesque carvings of the main portal. In particular, look closely at the central arch's *Months and the Seasons* (1225) and the outer arch's *Trades of Venice*. The mosaics above the doorways (1260) describe the story of St. Mark's abduction and the arrival of his body in the city.

The interior Beyond the vestibule, or narthex, the main body of the basilica is dominated by 13,200 square feet of mosaics—a kaleidoscope of color and Biblical anecdote dating mostly from the 12th and 14th centuries. Be sure also to see the Treasury and its collection of gold and silverware: the rood screen (1394); the 10th-century pulpits; the icon known as the *Madonna di Nicopeia*; and, most importantly, the famous Pala d'Oro (see panel).

Part of the flamboyant facade of San Marco

Churches

All these churches are outstanding, but the top three are the Basilica di San Marco, Santi Giovanni e Paolo (San Zanipolo), and Santa Maria Gloriosa (I Frari).

▶▶▶ Basilica di San Marco   95B4
Piazza San Marco
Open: see panel opposite
Venice's cathedral and finest church (see opposite page).

▶▶▶ Campanile di San Marco   95B4
Piazza San Marco
Open: Jul–Aug, daily 9:30–7:30; Sep–Jun, daily 9:30–3:30 or 7 depending on month. Admission: moderate
Venice's tallest building rises 326 feet above Piazza San Marco, offering views over the city, the lagoon, and—on clear days—the distant Dolomite mountains. The original tower collapsed in 1902, but was rebuilt over the next ten years. At its base stands the beautifully decorated **loggetta▶▶**, built 1537–1549 by Jacopo Sansovino.

▶▶ Madonna dell'Orto   94D3
Fondamenta della Madonna dell'Orto.
Open: Mon–Sat 10–5. Admission: inexpensive
Tintoretto was a parishioner of this little church in the north of the city (and is buried here). Several paintings by him decorate the walls, including *The Presentation of the Virgin* (right aisle), *The Last Judgment*, and *The Adoration of the Golden Calf* (both in the chancel). Also here is Cima da Conegliano's *St. John the Baptist* (to be found in the first chapel on the right).

▶▶▶ San Giorgio Maggiore   95A4
Isola di San Giorgio Maggiore
Open: daily 9:30–12:30, 2:30–6 (4 in winter). Admission to campanile: inexpensive
This church is one of Palladio's two Venetian master-pieces (the other is Il Redentore). It occupies its own small island, and the views from its campanile are some of the most celebrated in the city. The interior is the setting for two Tintoretto masterpieces, the *Last Supper* and *Shower of Manna*. His *Deposition* is in the Cappella dei Morti.

▶▶ San Giovanni in Bragora   95B5
Campo Bandiera e Moro, Castello
Open: Mon–Sat 3:30–5:30. Admission free
Vivaldi was once the organist in this Gothic church, rebuilt in 1475, whose paintings include the *Baptism of Christ* by Cima da Conegliano, the *Risen Christ* by Alvise Vivarini, and Bartolomeo Vivarini's lovely *Madonna*.

▶▶▶ Santi Giovanni e Paolo (San Zanipolo)   95C4
Campo Santi Giovanni e Paolo, Castello
Open: Mon–Sat 9–12, 2:30–6, Sun 3–6. Admission free
Venice's largest church is renowned for the tombs of the 25 doges buried here, including Pietro Mocenigo and Michele Morosini. Other works of art include a polyptych by Giovanni Bellini, *St. Vincent Ferrer*, and an altarpiece, *St. Antony and Supplicants* by Lorenzo Lotto.

THE BELLS OF THE CAMPANILE
Each of the campanile's five bells had a special function: the Marangona marked the beginning and end of the working day; the Trottiera summoned the members of the Maggior Consiglio to council meetings; the Nona rang midday; the Mezza Terza proclaimed a session of the Senate; and the Renghiera (or Maleficio) tolled after executions.

The imposing bulk of Santi Giovanni e Paolo (San Zanipolo in the Venetian dialect)

101

A GRISLY EPISODE
Marcantonio Bragadin was a Venetian general captured, tortured, and executed by the Turks in Cyprus in 1571. He was chained to a stake and flayed alive in front of the Pasha. His peeled skin was then stuffed with straw, mounted on a cow, and paraded around the streets. It was then hung from the bowsprit of the admiral's ship for the return voyage to Constantinople. Later the skin was returned to Venice, and is now in San Zanipolo, in the urn next to the first altar of the right aisle. The general's death was avenged at the Battle of Lepanto in 1571 by Doge Venier, whose bronze statue is also in the church.

SANTA MARIA FORMOSA
The church stands close to the Miracoli. *Formosa* means "most beautiful" and refers to an apparition of the Virgin on this site in the 7th century. The present church dates from 1492 (the facades are neo-classical, the campanile baroque). Paintings include a triptych by Bartolomeo Vivarini (1473, first chapel right) and Palma Vecchio's fine *St. Barbara and Four Saints* (right transept). Outside is a lively square, with a few cafés and a small vegetable market.

▶▶ Santa Maria Assunta (Gesuiti) 95D4

Near the Fondamente Nuove, Cannaregio
Open: daily 10–noon, 5–7. Admission free
Fronted by a soaring facade, and obviously built to impress, this Jesuit church (1714–1729) has a quite awe-inspiring interior, its pillars, pulpits, and floor draped in what appears to be swathes of green and white damask. All the hangings, however, even down to the tassels and fringes, are made from the most delicately carved marble.

▶▶▶ Santa Maria Gloriosa dei Frari (I Frari) 94C2

Campo dei Frari, San Polo
Open: Mon–Sat 9–6, Sun 1–6. Admission: inexpensive
Known as *I Frari* (The Friars) after its Franciscan founders, this cavernous church is a treasury of exceptional paintings and sculpture. Its main glories are three of the greatest paintings in Italian art: Titian's *Assumption of the Virgin* (behind the high altar); his *Madonna di Ca'Pesaro* (second altar of the left aisle); and Giovanni Bellini's sublime *Madonna and Child* (in the sacristy). Elsewhere the church is loaded with paintings and sculptures that could occupy you for an hour or more. They include works by Donatello, Antonio Canova, Sansovino, Bartolomeo Vivarini, and many more.

▶▶ Santa Maria dei Miracoli 95C4

Campo dei Miracoli, Cannaregio
Open: Mon–Sat 10–5. Admission: inexpensive
One of the most exquisite small churches in Venice, the Miracoli is a tiny masterpiece of classical architecture. It is the work of Pietro Lombardo, aided by his sons, and was built between 1481–1489. Elegant and refined in exterior form, its interior contains some of the city's most intricate decorative sculpture.

▶▶▶ Santa Maria della Salute 94A3

Campo della Salute, Dorsoduro
Open: daily 9–12, 3–5:30. Admission free
Salute means health, and this church was built as thanks for the city's deliverance from the plague of 1630, when 45,000 Venetians died. (A similar pledge 54 years earlier had resulted in the building of Palladio's Redentore.) Built on 100,000 wooden piles, the church occupies a prime position on the Grand Canal, making it one of the city's great landmarks. The sacristy contains several paintings by Titian and Tintoretto's *Marriage at Cana*.

▶▶ San Pantalon 94B2

Campo San Pantalon, Dorsoduro
Open: daily 8–11:30, 3:30–7 (except Sat 4:30–7). Admission free
A shortage of money left San Pantalon with an unfinished facade, a deficiency for which the interior more than compensates. Its melodramatic ceiling contains some 60 panels depicting a mass ascent into Heaven: *The Martyrdom and Apotheosis of San Pantalon*, painted by Antonio Fumiani between 1680 and 1704. Smaller paintings include Veronese's last work, *San Pantalon Healing a Boy*, and Antonio Vivarini's *Coronation of the Virgin*, painted in 1444.

IL REDENTORE
Leading Italian architect Andrea Palladio designed two churches in their entirety in Venice. One was San Giorgio Maggiore (see page 101), the other Il Redentore, commissioned in 1576 by the Senate to mark the end of a plague. Its prominent position on the Giudecca and eye-catching facade make it one of the city's landmarks, best seen across the water from Dorsoduro.

SAN STAE
San Stae is close to a *vaporetto* stop on the Grand Canal, and at the heart of a neighborhood of tiny squares and narrow canals that sees relatively few tourists. Its statue-filled baroque facade is one of the Grand Canal's most striking sights.

▶▶ San Sebastiano
94A1

Campo San Sebastiano, Dorsoduro
Open: Mon–Sat 10–5. Admission: inexpensive

San Sebastiano belongs almost entirely to Paolo Veronese, who is buried in the church and left in it the greatest single collection of his work. The best are: three ceiling panels depicting the *Life of St. Esther*; two paintings in the sanctuary, *San Sebastian* and *St. Mark and St. Marcellian*; the walls of the *barco* (nuns' gallery); the painted organ doors; and the ceiling panels of the sacristy.

▶▶ Santo Stefano
94B3

Campo Francesco Morosini, San Marco
Open: Mon–Sat 10–5. Admission: inexpensive

As well as being a handsome, highly decorated church, Santo Stefano is notable for its Gothic portal, its "ship's keel roof" (like an upended wooden hull), and a calm, airy interior whose sacristy contains late works by Tintoretto.

▶▶▶ San Zaccaria
95B4

Campo San Zaccaria, Castello
Open: daily 10–12, 4–6. Admission: free; Cappellas inexpensive

San Zaccaria is full of paintings, the most celebrated being Giovanni Bellini's *Madonna and Four Saints*. It is worth paying the small fee to see Tintoretto's *Birth of John the Baptist* (Cappella di Sant'Atanasio). The Cappella di San Tarasio has altarpieces by Antonio Vivarini and Giovanni d'Alemagna (1443).

CAMPO SAN ZACCARIA
The square outside San Zaccaria has a checkered past. San Zaccaria itself was built as a shrine for Zaccharias, father of John the Baptist, who is buried under the second altar on the right. The convent alongside was once notorious for its licentiousness. Most of the nuns were reluctant internees, incarcerated because of parental pressure or because their fathers were too poor to provide them with dowries.

Scattered across the 520 square miles of Venice's lagoon (Laguna Veneta) are some 40 islands, many of them deserted, others meriting as much attention as the city itself.

GETTING THERE
To reach the islands of the lagoon, take *vaporetti* from Piazzale Roma or the Fondamente Nuove: many lines run to the Lido; line 42 goes to San Michele and Murano; line 12 from the Fondamente Nuove takes in Murano, Burano, and Torcello. A 12-hour pass is available for boat travel to the islands.

Burano►► While Burano's menfolk attended to the fishing, the island's women spent hours making the famous Burano and Venetian-point lace. Traditionally each woman specialized in a single stitch (there are seven in all), passing the lace between one another during its creation. Today the island's many craft shops sell local and factory-made foreign lace. Before leaving, visit the **Scuola del Merletto**, an interesting lace museum and school, and allow time to wander the village's streets of neat and brightly painted houses.

Lido► Ranged over the lagoon's largest sandbank, the Lido is a full-fledged seaside resort, once Europe's most fashionable (Thomas Mann's *Death in Venice* is set here) but now a more downbeat—and in places dingy—conglomeration of big hotels, crowded beaches, and murky water. It is, however, worth taking the *vaporetto* here from San Marco for the sublime spectacle of the Venetian skyline—one of the world's great views.

Murano►► Murano is a workaday and slightly down-at-the-heel place dedicated almost entirely to glass-blowing. The glass furnaces moved here from the city in 1291 as a precaution against fire. For centuries thereafter the island's craftsmen were European leaders in their field. Nowadays the streets are crammed with shops hawking glassware—some of it exquisite, some of it cheap and hideous by turns. Be sure to visit the furnaces themselves to see glass being blown—admission to most is free (many lie along the Fondamenta dei Vetrai). To see examples of Murano glass past and present, and to learn about glass techniques, visit the glass museum, the **Museo Vetrario**. The church of **San Pietro Martire** has two good paintings: Veronese's *St. Jerome* and Giovanni Bellini's *Madonna and Child.*

Murano glass; not to everyone's taste, but certainly distinctive

Torcello►►► The best day trip from Venice, this rustic and peaceful little island is easily explored. Most people are here to see **Santa Maria Assunta**, Venice's first cathedral, home to magnificent 11th- and 12th-century mosaics, but the 11th-century church of Santa Fosca and the small Museo dell'Estuario are both also worth a visit.

Venice is in more peril than most historic cities, threatened by air and water pollution, sinking foundations, flooding, and the constant assault of mass tourism.

Subsidence Around 30 years ago, Venice was threatened with catastrophe. The main culprits were the water-hungry industries on the mainland, whose exploits lowered the water table and threatened to undermine the city's foundations. Two large aqueducts to pipe water from mainland rivers saved the day in 1973.

Local subsidence, though, continues to be a threat. Most of the city's buildings rest on pilings driven into the mudflats of the lagoon—or in the case of poorer houses, shored up on a loose cement of rubbish and rubble. With the lagoon now subject to increasingly frequent low tides, air can reach the pilings and accelerate their rate of decay.

Flooding Floods in Venice are nothing new, but severe inundations in 1966, 1979, and 1986 have made them the focus of the city's planners. Winter flooding is caused by strong southeast winds and seasonally high tides. Recently they have grown more frequent—not, research shows, because of global warming, but through human interference in the lagoon over the last century in the form of land reclamation and the deepening of channels.

Solutions The proposed solution is a tidal barrier built across the lagoon's three main entrances. Opinion of the boom's likely efficacy is divided and many conservationists argue it does not address the city's basic problems: the more general but ultimately more critical ones of a declining population, slowly stagnating lagoon, and the choice between preserving Venice for the Venetians—more housing and industry—and turning the city into a historical fossil preserved for profit and posterity.

THE FLOOD OF 1966
On November 4, 1966, Venice's sea walls (*murazzi*) were breached by the combined effects of gale-force winds, an earth tremor, and two successive high tides, and the city found itself under 3 feet of water. There were no injuries and no paintings lost (unlike Florence, flooded on the same day).

AIR POLLUTION
Smog is another problem. Sulphur dioxide from mainland factories combined with the lagoon's humid and salty air produce an intensely corrosive combination. The conversion of domestic heating systems from oil to gas has lessened the problem, but local industry still pumps 50,000 tons of toxins into the atmosphere annually.

WATER POLLUTION
Venice's sewage is treated, but most of the city's sinks and baths empty straight into the lagoon. For years the cleansing effects of daily tides and the work of natural biological agents (marine life) preserved the ecological equilibrium. The increased use of phosphate-rich detergents and fertilizers, however, has upset this, and the possible building of the barrier, which will further disturb tides, does not augur well for the lagoon's health.

You may need waterproof shoes on even the sunniest days in Venice

STROLL—DORSODURO
Walk on the waterfront along Fondamenta delle Zattare for lovely views across the lagoon to the Giudecca. Finish at Santa Maria della Salute.

Museums and galleries

▶▶▶ Accademia ✂ 94A2

Campo della Carità, Dorsoduro
Open: Mon 8:15–2, Tue–Sun 8:15–7:15. Admission: expensive
The Accademia is Venice's greatest art gallery, a superlative collection of Venetian paintings, many gathered from churches and palaces around the city. Masterpieces by all Venice's painters adorn its walls, the highlights of which include Giovanni Bellini's *Madonna Enthroned* and Carpaccio's *The Presentation* (Room II); Mantegna's *St. George*, Giorgione's *Tempest*, and some of Bellini's *Madonnas* in Rooms IV–V; Titian's *St. John the Baptist* (Room VI); three Veronese masterpieces in Room XI; six *Scenes from Venetian Life* by Longhi (Room XVII); fresco cycles—*The Miracles of the Relics of the Cross* (Room XX) by Gentile Bellini and others; and Carpaccio's *The Legend of St. Ursula* (Room XXI). There is a Canaletto in Room XVII.

▶▶ Ca' d'Oro e Galleria Franchetti 94C3

Calle di Ca' d'Oro, off Strada Nova
Open: Mon 8:15–2, Tue–Sun 8:15–7:15. Admission: moderate
Named after the now-vanished gilding (*oro*—gold) that covered its elaborate facade, this is Venice's most famous *palazzo*, currently home to a well-presented and varied art collection. Its showpieces are Mantegna's *St. Sebastian* and A. Vivarini's polyptych of *The Passion*. There are also lesser pieces by Titian, Giorgione, and Tintoretto, and many rewarding works by less prominent Venetian artists and sculptors.

Inside the Doge's Palace

►► Ca' Rezzonico e Museo de Settecento Veneziano 94B2

Fondamenta Rezzonico, Dorsoduro
Closed for restoration until Spring 2002
This palace's "Museum of 18th-century Venice" evokes the splendor of the city's last great flowering through its magnificent rooms crammed with original tapestries, furniture, costumes, silks, brocades, lacquerwork—even a contemporary puppet theater and chemist's shop.

You may find some of the trappings gaudy, but the frescoes of the Tiepolo family and the touching Venetian scenes by Longhi and Guardi alone make the entrance price worth paying.

►►► Collezione Guggenheim 94A3

Calle Cristoforo, Dorsoduro
Open: Apr–Oct, Wed–Fri, Sun–Mon 10–6, Sat 10–10;
Nov–Mar, Wed 10–6. Admission: expensive
Millionairess Peggy Guggenheim's gallery—housed in an 18th-century *palazzo* on the Grand Canal—has one of the world's most important collections of modern art. Rooms are arranged by style (Dadaism, cubism, surrealism) and contain all 20th-century art's top names.

►► Museo Civico Correr 95B4

Procurative Nuove, Piazza San Marco
Open: Apr–Oct, daily 9–7; Nov–Mar, daily 9–5. Last ticket sold 3:30. Admission: expensive (see panel)
This is Venice's main historical museum, a vast and generally fascinating showcase for documents, weapons, coins, ducal regalia, and a wealth of miscellania. Some knowledge of Venetian history is needed to get the most from the exhibits. The fine art gallery upstairs is second only to the Accademia.

►► Museo Storico Navale 95B5

Campo San Biagio, Castello
Open: Mon–Fri 8:30–1:30, Sat 8:30–1. Admission: inexpensive
Housed near the Arsenale (the Republic's old naval base), this museum is Italy's best collection of all things maritime. With plenty of background on the famous gondolas, the displays range from models of galleys used against the Turks to manned torpedoes from World War II.

►►► Palazzo Ducale ✗ (The Doge's Palace) 95B4

Piazzetta San Marco
Open: Apr–Oct, daily 9–7 (last ticket sold 5:30); Nov–Mar, daily 9–5 (last ticket sold 3:30). Admission: expensive
The Doge's Palace was the seat of power in Venice for almost 1,000 years, but most of the present building dates from the 15th century. You need at least a morning to do it justice (arrive early to avoid the crowds). Tarry over the main entrance (Porta della Carta) and courtyard; the staircase (Scala dei Giganti); the Anticollegio, with paintings by Titian and Veronese; and the Sala del Maggior Consiglio, the council chamber, famous for Tintoretto's huge oil painting, *Paradiso*. The interiors of the Bridge of Sighs and the prisons are also superb.

THE BRIDGE OF SIGHS ✗
The famous Ponte dei Sospiri links the Palazzo Ducale with its prisons (the name supposedly comes from the sighs of condemned prisoners). For the most part the prisons harbored only petty criminals (Casanova was imprisoned here in 1755 for 15 months). Hardcore convicts were kept in the less salubrious Piombi (the Leads), under the palace's roof, or in the Pozzi (Wells): 18 dark and dank cells deep in the palace's bowels.

107

The Bridge of Sighs, reputedly named after the sighs of condemned prisoners

TICKETS
Admission to the Museo Civico Correr also includes entry to the Palazzo Ducale and other city museums.

CAMPO SANTA MARGHERITA

This square, ringed by 14th-century houses, is the social heart of the Dorsoduro district. It has an attractive food and vegetable market, and lots of relaxed bars, haunts of students from the university. Nearby is the Scuola Grande dei Carmini, rich in Tiepolo frescoes.

THE SCUOLE

The *scuole* of Venice were religious confraternities administered by wealthy Venetians as charities for the needy. The main ones took their names from their patron saints or from the nationality of their founders. Many acquired tremendous prestige, reflected in their works of art, among the most remarkable in Venice.

SAN ROCCO

The *scuola* of San Rocco was always chiefly concerned with the relief of the sick—as was its patron, San Rocco (or St. Roch). The saint was held especially useful in cases of bubonic plague, an illness from which he was saved by divine intervention. Paintings all over Italy (and especially in Venice) often show him pointing to a plague sore on his thigh.

The Torre dell'Orologio, Piazza San Marco

▶▶ **Palazzo Mocenigo** 94C2

Salizzada San Stae, Santa Croce
Open: Tue–Sun 10–5. Admission: moderate
Once owned by one of Venice's grandest families, this palace's nine rooms still look much as they did in their 18th-century heyday. Each is gilded, painted, and decorated with period furniture and Murano glass chandeliers.

▶▶ **Palazzo Querini-Stampalia** 95B4

Campiello Querini, Castello
Open: Tue–Sun 10–1, 3–6. Admission: moderate
The splendor of this 16th-century *palazzo* suggests the scale of Venice's former wealth and power. Its 20 rooms contain the art collection and furnishings of one of the city's leading 18th-century families. The paintings are not the city's best, but there are one or two notable works, such as the chronicles of Venetian life by Pietro Longhi, Giovanni Bellini's *Presentation in the Temple*, and popularist portrayals of *Venetian Festivals* by Gabriele Bella.

▶▶▶ **Scuola di San Giorgio**
 degli Schiavoni 95B5

Calle Furlani, Castello
Open: Apr–Oct, Tue–Sat 9:30–12:30, 3:30–6.30,
Sun 9.30–12.30; Nov–Mar, Tue–Sat 10–12:30, 3–6, Sun 3–6.
Admission: moderate
Schiavonia (the name refers to Slavic peoples) was what Venetians called Dalmatia, a coastal strip along the eastern Adriatic, and once a dominion of the Republic. The *scuola* set up by the city's resident Slavs contains Vittore Carpaccio's poetic frieze of frescoes illustrating the lives of St. George, St. Tryphon, and St. Jerome (all of them patron saints of Dalmatia).

▶▶▶ **Scuola Grande di San Rocco** 94B2

Campo San Rocco, San Polo
Open: Apr–Oct, daily 9–5:30; Nov–Mar, daily 10–4
"One of the three most precious buildings in Italy," said John Ruskin of San Rocco. He was referring to Tintoretto's series of over 50 biblical scenes that took 23 years to complete, executed after the artist won the commission in a competition. In the Sala dell'Albergo, one wall is covered in a magnificent *Crucifixion*. The entrance wall depicts scenes from *The Passion* (1567). In the upper hall, the wall panels, and ceiling (1581) contain New Testament scenes. There are more Tintorettos on the ground floor (1587).

Landmarks

▶ Arsenale 95B5

Walk to Campo dell'Arsenale to admire the arch and flanking towers that mark the entrance to the Arsenale. This vast naval dockyard in the east of the city was where the great ships of the Venetian empire were built and berthed. Most of the old basins and docks are now deserted or used by the Italian navy, but glimpses from the outside still evoke their past scale and splendor.

▶▶▶ Monumento a Colleoni (Colleoni Statue) 95C4

Campo Santi Giovanni e Paolo, Castello

Bartolomeo Colleoni, a native of Bergamo, served Venice as one of its leading *condottieri*, or mercenaries, from 1448. At his death he left a portion of his wealth to the state, on condition that a statue of him be raised in front of the Basilica di San Marco. The Republic took the money, but cheated by erecting the statue in front of the Scuola di San Marco. In the statue itself, however, they did Colleoni proud, commissioning the Florentine sculptor Andrea Verrocchio to produce one of the masterpieces of Renaissance sculpture (1481–1488).

THE RIALTO

Venice's earliest settlers were drawn to the stable land and defensive position on the Grand Canal's *rivo alto* (high bank). In time the area (and name) developed into the Rialto, the city's commercial heart. In the "Bazaar of Europe," textiles, precious stones, silks, spices, and exotica from the Orient were traded. Europe's first state bank opened here in the 12th century, and finance flourished—as did prostitution. The Rialto still has a busy market, concentrated on the Ruga degli Orefici (souvenirs), Campo San Giacomo (fruit and meat), and Campo Battisti (fish).

109

▶▶▶ Ponte di Rialto (Rialto Bridge) 94C3

The Rialto Bridge is one of the city's best-known landmarks. Built between 1588 and 1591, it replaced a wooden bridge whose central portion could be raised to allow the passage of ships (many paintings, like Carpaccio's contribution to the *Miracles of the True Cross* cycle in the Accademia, show what this and earlier bridges originally looked like).

The elegant Rialto Bridge, once the only crossing of the Grand Canal

▶▶ Torre dell'Orologio (Clock Tower) 95B4

Piazza San Marco

Crowds invariably gather around this curio, a brightly enameled clock face and digital clock linked to moving statues. The face indicates the hours, phases of the moon, and movement of the sun through the signs of the zodiac. Two bronze figures of Moors strike the hours.

In a city as beautiful and free of cars as Venice, walking makes the perfect option for getting around. One of Venice's greatest pleasures is escaping the crowds to lose yourself in its magnificent labyrinth of alleys and canals, so treat the suggestions below as no more than starting points for your own exploration.

VENETIAN WORDS

An open space (piazza) in Venice is called a *campo*, *campiello* or *campazzo*. Alleys are *calle*, *calletta* or *callesella* (occasionally *ruga*, analogous to the French *rue*). A *ramo* is the branch of a *calle*. *Salizzada* refers to the first alleys paved with stone; *fondamenta* (or *riva*) means the path alongside a canal. A canal is a *rio*; a *rio terrà* is a canal which has been filled in.

Visitors outside St. Mark's

Canal Grande Venice's single best excursion is not a walk at all, but a boat trip on one of the *vaporetti* that ply up and down the Grand Canal (Nos. 1 or 82). Buy one of the many guides or maps devoted solely to the canal to identify its key buildings (there are 200 separate palaces alone). Boats make frequent stops if you want to get off and see anything on the way.

Piazza San Marco In and around Piazza San Marco you can wander between some of the city's most famous sights—the Basilica di San Marco, Campanile di San Marco, Palazzo Ducale, Museo Correr, Libreria Sansoviniana, and the Ponte dei Sospiri ("Bridge of Sighs").

The west Start at the Accademia and head west toward the Fondamenta Gheradini, which is home to a lovely fruit and vegetable market, and then make for the Scuola Grande dei Carmini, San Pantalon, the Scuola Grande di San Rocco, and Campo San Polo. Afterward, head north toward the Grand Canal (where you will be able to catch a boat to the center) via Campo San Giacomo dell'Orio and the churches of San Giacomo and San Stae.

The east Eastern Venice is one of the city's quieter areas. Start at Campo Santa Maria Formosa and its eponymous church, located just northeast of Piazza San Marco. Then take in Santi Giovanni e Paolo and its lovely square and Colleoni monument. Proceed to San Francesco della Vigna, the Arsenale, the Museo Storico Navale, and the Scuola di San Giorgio degli Schiavoni.

The Ghetto Venice's was the world's first ghetto (the term comes from the Italian word *getar*, to found, or *geto*, foundry, after the metal-working industry that dominated the area until 1390). Jews were segregated here from 1516 on. The district's low, crowded houses are distinctly different from the rest of the city. The heart of the Ghetto is in Cannaregio, north of the Rio Terrà San Leonardo.

Transportation and shopping

Getting around The *vaporetto*, or water bus, is the principal means of traveling Venice's canals (*motoscafi*, or motor launches, are similar but quicker). The system is initially confusing, but you soon get the hang of the numbered routes. The city map (pages 94–95) shows the main stops, each of which usually has a ticket office, route maps, and timetable. Tickets can also be bought in shops with an A.C.T.V. sign (the public transportation company). Tickets cost a flat fare, though if you are making several journeys buy 24- or 72-hour tourist tickets or a discounted 10-ticket block (a *blochetto*). A 12-hour island pass allows you to visit Murano, Burano, and Torcello. Remember to date-stamp your ticket at each pier before boarding. Tickets must also be bought for large pieces of luggage. Services run about every 10 minutes. Seats in the prow are the most coveted spots—they offer the best views.

Walking—the city's only other means of getting around—is helped by yellow signs pointing directions to the main destinations. Given Venice's complexity, no map is totally accurate: Hallweg, Falk, FMB, or Kummerly and Frey are the best.

Shopping Venice has always been a city where goods are bought and sold. These days, the vast number of visitors means prices are inflated and much of its merchandise just tourist junk. But quality crafts for which the city has traditionally been renowned—fabrics, glass, leather, metalwork, paper, and woodwork—can still be found. The island of Burano is especially known for its lace, Murano for its glassware. Metalwork and woodwork shops are found around Campo San Barnaba. For Venetian carnival masks and hats visit **Tragicomica** (Calle Nomboli, San Polo 2800) and **Mondonovo** (Rio Terrà Canal, Dorsoduro 3063, off Campo Santa Margherita).

Fashionable shopping areas are the Mercerie—the streets between Piazza San Marco and around the Rialto bridge. The busiest area is the Strada Nova, from the train station to the heart of the city.

RENTING A GONDOLA
Gondola fares are priced at a set rate—though few gondoliers adhere to this, so confirm the price *and* duration of a trip before setting off. Rates are doubled between 8 at night and 8 in the morning. Useful tips are to take rides in the late afternoon, when the Grand Canal is less crowded, and to start from a station on the Canal (rides on the lagoon are more choppy).

111

The gondolier still provides the most romantic—if most expensive—way of seeing Venice

TRAGHETTI
Since the Grand Canal has only three bridges, it can often save time to use the *traghetti* (two-man gondola ferries) that cross the canal between special piers (at several points). Fares are very inexpensive (you pay the boatman). Visitors usually sit, but Venetians like to stand for the short crossing.

Carnival masks make stylish and unusual souvenirs

Venice

ALTERNATIVES TO VENICE

Price and availability of hotels can be a problem in Venice, and though it may not be an ideal arrangement, you might consider seeing the city as day trips from a base in nearby towns. Padua (see page 124) and Treviso (see page 125) are good options, both less than half an hour by train from Venice.

Accommodations

Reservations and peak season Venice has around 200 hotels. While most are well run, a few have become slovenly, taking for granted the constant flow of visitors who fill the city virtually year round. It is almost essential to reserve a room in advance during July and August, and wise to do so for the rest of the peak season—which runs from mid-March to late October. Christmas and Easter must also be considered peak periods—together with the two weeks of Carnevale in February.

Prices Hotel rates are higher than in Rome or Florence, which in the upper brackets puts them among the highest in western Europe. Off-season rates can be far more reasonable—but this is when many hotels close. It is often impossible to avoid paying for breakfast, whether you take it or not, and charges for air-conditioning—a plus in summer—can be hefty. Few hotels have restaurants, but where they do, they often involve unappetizing dinners.

Many visitors willingly pay extra for a room with a canal view

Rooms Because of the constraints imposed by planning regulations, Venice's old hotels often have a wide variety of rooms, good and bad, so ask to see several before parting with any money. Rooms with canal views command a premium, worth paying only if it avoids a dark and miserable back room. Singles are notoriously bad, so lone travelers might consider taking a double room in a cheaper hotel. Lounges are frequently minimal in all but the grandest hotels.

FINDING A ROOM

If you arrive without a room, head straight for one of the tourist offices run by the A.V.A. (the Venetian Hoteliers' Association). They have booths at the Santa Lucia train station, Marco Polo airport, or the Autorimessa Comunale in Piazzale Roma. The lines may be long, but each will find you a room, taking a deposit according to the category of hotel (deductible from your first night's bill).

Noise and location The best hotels lie close to the Grand Canal near San Marco; the cheapest in the streets around the train station off Rio Terrà Lista di Spagna. Wherever your hotel, be certain when making reservations to find its exact location (and remember you may need to carry your luggage). Even without cars, Venice has its share of nocturnal traffic. Church bells and pedestrian chatter can also reverberate noisily in narrow streets. Dorsoduro is one of the quieter areas.

Food and drink

Restaurants Mass tourism has not been good for Venetian cuisine. Restaurant prices are high, cooking unimaginative, and service indifferent. Good restaurants can be found—usually in the upper price bracket—and even an average meal can be made memorable by a water-front setting. Places away from San Marco and in the quieter eastern and northern parts of the city are good areas to search out cheaper and more authentic *trattorie*.

If you are watching your budget, most restaurants offer a *menù turistico*, a fixed-price menu. Quality and quantity, however, are usually inferior to eating *à la carte*. Most places close once a week, often on Sunday or Monday.

Cafés and bars Given Venetian prices, cafés and bars are more than ever the great standby if you want inexpensive snacks and sandwiches. Between-meals nibbles in the city are known as *cichetti*, typically including *polpette* (meat-balls) and *carciofi* (artichoke hearts), eggs and anchovies. All are traditionally washed down with *un ombra*, a glass of wine—literally a "shadow," from the idea of coming out of the sun for light refreshment. For a treat, indulge yourself in one of the city's more famous and venerable bars (see panel).

Venetian cuisine Fish and seafood form the basis of Venice's cuisine: as prawns, squid, and octopus in *antipasti*, in *zuppa di pesce* (fish soups), or as *granseola* (Murano crabs), *sarde in saor* (marinated sardines), *baccalà* (salt cod), and *seppioline nere* (cuttlefish cooked in its own ink). *Risotto* is the first course *par excellence*, whether with seafood, vegetables, or ingredients like snails, tripe, and quails. *Bigoli* is a local pasta, often served with a tuna (*tonno*) sauce. Thick soups are also popular, especially *pasta e fagioli* (pasta and beans). Cornmeal *polenta* is another staple, often an accompaniment to the famous *fegato alla veneziana* (calves' liver and onions).

WINE
Good local wines include Friulian whites like Tocai and Pinot Bianco and reds like Merlot, Refosco, and Raboso. The best drink is *prosecco*, a delicious, light sparkling wine. It is inexpensive and available in any bar—simply ask for *un prosecco*.

BARS—THE TOP THREE
Venice's most famous café is *Florian* in Piazza San Marco, opened in 1720 and patronized ever since by the famous and notorious—Proust, Wagner, and Casanova included. Both Florian and its competitor, the less pretty but equally notorious *Quadri* across the square, charge stratospheric prices—but they are worth it for a once-in-a-lifetime treat. Much the same goes for the legendary *Harry's Bar*, at Calle Vallaresso, San Marco.

113

One of the world's great settings for an al fresco meal

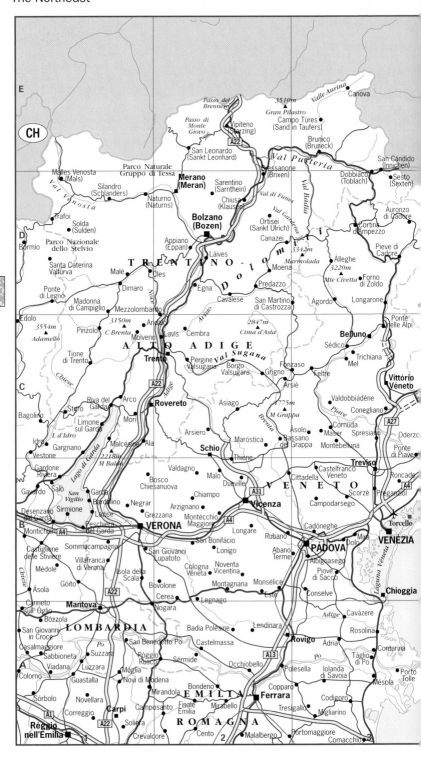

A

2780m
▲ Mte Coglians

Santo Stéfano
di Cadore

Paluzza

Pontebba

Tarvisio

Ampezzo

Tolmezzo

Chiusaforte

FRIULI -

VENÉZIA

A23

Venzone

Gemona
del Friuli

GIULIA

Tarcento

Maniago

San Daniele
del Friuli

Tricésimo

Cividale
del. Friuli

SLO

Spilimbergo

Aviano

Udine

Pordenone

Codróipo

Gorizia

San Vito
al Tagliamento

Castions
di Strada

Palmanova

Gradisca
d'Isonzo

Azzano
Décimo

A28

A4

Cervignano
del Friuli

Monfalcone

Latisana

Aquileia

A4

Duino

**Borgo
Grotta Gigante**

Portogruaro

Laguna di
Marano

Santo Stino
di Livenza

Lignano
Sabbiadoro

Grado

**Castello
di Miramare**

TRIESTE

San Donà
di Piave

*Golfo di
Trieste*

Múggia

Eraclea

Cáorle

Iésolo

Lido di Iésolo

HR

*G o l f o
d i   V e n é z i a*

0	10	20	30	40	50 km
0	10		20		30 miles

TOURIST INFORMATION

Bolzano: Piazza Walther 8 (tel: 0471/307 000). Cividale del Friuli: Corso d'Aquileia 10 (tel: 0432/731 461). Padua: (Padova) Train Station (tel: 049/875 2077). Trento: Via Alfieri 4 (tel: 0461/983 880). Trieste: Via San Nicolò 20 (tel: 040/679 611) and Riva 3 Novembre 9 (tel: 040/347 8312). Verona: Palazzo del Municipio, Piazza Bra, Via Alpini 11 (tel: 045/806 8680). Vicenza: Piazza Matteotti 12 (tel: 0444/320 854).

SCENIC DRIVES

(*Veneto*) SS 48/SS 51 around Cortina d'Ampezzo; SS 203 Belluno–Agordo–Cortina d'Ampezzo; SS 141 Bassano del Grappa–Monte Grappa; (*Trentino*) SS 612 Trento–Cembra–Cavalese–San Martino di Castrozza; SS 421/ SS 237/SS 239 Mezzolombardo–Andalo–Molveno–Tione di Trento–Madonna di Campiglio; (*Alto Adige*) SS 241/ SS 48 Bolzano–Canazei–Cortina d'Ampezzo; SS 508 Bolzano–Val Sarentina–Vipiteno; SS 44 Vipiteno–Passo di Monte Giovo–Merano; SS 621 Brunico–Valle Aurina–Canova.

▶▶▶ REGION HIGHLIGHTS

THE NORTHEAST Venice exerts such a pull that few visitors escape its clutches to explore the rest of northeast Italy—the regions of the Veneto, Trentino-Alto Adige, and Friuli-Venezia Giulia. Yet in many ways this is a region whose attractions are among the best of their kind. Among its landscapes are the Dolomites, the most spectacular mountains in Europe. Architecturally, the region contains the villas of Andrea Palladio, one of the most influential of all architects. Padua has one of Italy's great fresco cycles, and Verona is undoubtedly among the country's finest Roman and medieval cities. Ethnically, too, the region is fascinating, a melting pot of Italian, Slav, and German-speaking peoples. Even some of Italy's most famous wines originate in the northeast—notably the ubiquitous Soave and Valpolicella.

THE VENETO Modern-day Veneto is the heartland of Venetia, the mainland territories ruled by the Venetian Republic between the 14th and 18th centuries (though Venetia's domain also included much of present-day Friuli-Venezia Giulia). Like most northern regions it divides neatly into plain, low hills, and mountains. The plain is prosperous and densely populated, which means sightseeing involves braving sprawls of industry and modern housing. Any unpleasantness, however, is worth enduring to see Verona, Shakespeare's setting for *Romeo and Juliet*, and as beautiful today as it must have been when the play was written. Vicenza, too, deserves a day's visit, mainly for its Palladian architecture, and wonderfully prosperous and tight-knit little city center. Padua, by contrast, is disappointing, though its modern horrors should be overlooked for as long as it takes to see Giotto's frescoes and the Basilica di Sant'Antonio. Few places stand out among the lesser towns, though Asolo provides a restful retreat from the bustle of the cities.

TRENTINO–ALTO ADIGE This strange, multicultural hybrid is a region where unresolved historical problems have come home to roost. Southern Trentino (capital Trento) is Italian-speaking, while Alto Adige, or Sudtirol (capital Bolzano), is mainly German-speaking. Alto Adige was ceded to Italy at the end of World War I, having previously been part of the Austro-Hungarian Empire. As a result, everything here has more than a tinge of the Teutonic. Ethnic differences have led to inevitable tensions (including acts of terrorism), though a large measure of autonomy has, for the most part, kept the lid on nationalist ambitions.

While the disputes are generally out of sight, the region's bilingualism and brisk efficiency are immediately noticeable. Most of the area's pleasures, however, are those that transcend cultural differences. Trento and Bolzano both have their charms (along with Merano), but the mountains of the Dolomites provide the region's main attraction. Their magnificent scenery can be enjoyed by car or train, but hiking (and skiing) facilities are so outstanding in this area that it would be foolish not to attempt a little walking.

Alto Adige's cuisine has a decidedly Teutonic and Middle European flavor. Be prepared for *knödel* (dumplings), often in a clear broth (*suppe*); *wiener schnitzel* (breaded veal cutlets); *sauerkraut; blau forelle* (mountain trout); *speck* (a special ham); *gröstl* (a meat, onion, and potato pie); goulash; and—of course—the ubiquitous apple strudel. Delicatessens are full of excellent cheeses, pickles, hams, and sausages. Bakeries have many types of black and rye bread, as well as Viennese-type pastries (be sure to try *krapfen*, a cake with jam and whipped cream). Most Italian culinary staples are usually also available.

FRIULI-VENEZIA GIULIA This region is more ethnically jumbled than Trentino-Alto Adige, comprising a cocktail of Italian, Slavic, and central European cultures that fills Italy's extreme northeastern corner. A fascinating area, its peripheral position puts it beyond the ambitions of most visitors. Its coastal plains are not much to look at (though the lagoons have a beauty of sorts), but two of their little towns—Aquileia and Cividale del Friuli—can hold their own with any in Italy. The old Austro-Hungarian port of Trieste has an old world atmosphere and makes a perfect base for local excursions.

Piazza delle Erbe, the social heart of Verona

117

CATERINA CORNARO
Caterina Cornaro was a scion of one of Venice's most powerful families. Through marriage she became queen of Cyprus, but was eventually duped by Venice into abdicating. In return she received Asolo, where she lived and held court for 30 years. In 1509 she was forced out by Emperor Maximilian, and fled to Venice, where she died a year later.

GRADO
Isolated in the heart of the Venetian lagoons (6 miles from Aquileia) is Grado, a wonderfully atmospheric place. The town's centerpiece is Sant'Eufemia, a church that has changed little since it was built in 579, its highlight a 6th-century mosaic floor. Grado is also a beach resort, with enormous beaches, warm water, and safe swimming (the town's name comes from its gently graded shoreline). Boats run here from Trieste (four per week), a lovely way to visit the town.

VILLA BARBARO
The Villa Barbaro at Maser, northeast of Asolo, is not only one of Palladio's finest villas, but also contains a virtuoso group of frescoes by Veronese, considered one of Italy's finest examples of trompe l'oeil.

▶▶ **Aquileia**   115C5

Today Aquileia is a sleepy agricultural town. Little at first glance suggests it is the region's most significant archeological site. In its day, however, its trading links and defensive position made it the fourth most important Italian city in the Roman Empire (after Rome, Milan, and Capua). By the 4th century, it was also a patriarchate, a region ruled by a bishop-prince, or patriarch.

The first patriarch, Teodoro, built a sumptuous **Basilica**▶▶▶ (*Open* Mon–Sat 8:30–7, Sun 8:30–7:30. *Admission free*) in 313, remodeled in the 10th century and now—despite damage from earthquakes—the region's most impressive medieval building. Its most breathtaking feature is a vast mosaic floor, considered among the world's finest early Christian mosaics. Almost as noteworthy are the Cripta degli Scavi, a crypt containing parts of the 4th-century church; the tombs of several patriarchs; and the crypt's 12th-century frescoes.

Elsewhere there are numerous **Roman remains**▶▶, together with two intriguing museums—the **Museo Paleocristiano**▶ (*admission free*) and **Museo Archeologico**▶ (*admission: moderate*; both *closed* Mon PM).

▶▶ **Asolo**   114C3

Asolo is a romantic medieval hill town, full of churches and tiny squares, and set in the Dolomites' bucolic foothills. Of all the Veneto's small towns, it is perhaps the most beautiful, and its wooded and villa-studded countryside the most charming. Fittingly, it lends its name to an Italian verb, *asolare*, meaning to pass one's time in pleasant aimlessness.

The actress Eleonora Duse was born in Asolo in 1859. Notorious as much for her tempestuous love affairs as for her performances, she frequently retreated to the town to escape scandal, and after her death in Pittsburgh during an American tour was returned to her birthplace to be buried. The **Museo Civico**▶ (*undergoing renovation; partially open 10–7; due to open fully May 2002*) houses many mementos and memorabilia connected with the English poet Robert Browning, one of the town's other notable inhabitants.

▶ **Bassano del Grappa**   114C2

Formerly renowned for its school of painting, this town in the foothills of the Alps is now known for its pottery and—as its name suggests—a noted *grappa* (a type of *eau de vie*). Local-born painter Jacopo Bassano (1516–1592) dominates the **Museo Civico**▶ (*Closed* Mon. *Admission: moderate*), which includes his *St. Valentine Baptizing St. Lucilla*. More famous is the town's wooden bridge, the much rebuilt 13th-century **Ponte Coperto** or **Ponte degli Alpini**▶.

▶ **Belluno**   114C3

Belluno's old town occupies a lofty position high above the confluence of the Ardo and Piave rivers. To the west it is framed by the Dolomiti Bellunesi, the most southerly and least explored of the Dolomite ranges. For the rest, the town is full of old arcaded streets and Renaissance *palazzi*. **Piazza del Duomo**▶ is the most beautiful square, the Venetian-style Palazzo dei Rettori the best-known palace. The Gothic church of **Santo Stefano**▶ and the Museo Civico (*Closed* winter Sat, Sun, and Mon PM; summer Sun and Mon PM) are also worth a visit.

► Bolzano (Bozen)   *114D2*

Capital of the mostly German-speaking Alto Adige, Bolzano is a congenial base for exploring the Dolomites (see pages 120–121). Over the centuries it has been controlled by the Counts of Tyrol, the Habsburgs, the Austrians, and the Bishops of Trento. Its Gothic **Duomo►** (repaired after World War II) neatly combines modern altars with fragments of medieval fresco. Its carved spire and green-tiled roof are eye-catching, but less interesting than the fine sandstone Gothic pulpit and famous *Porta del Vino* (Wine Door). This is embellished with reliefs of vines and peasants tending their vineyards, commemorating a special licence granted to the church to sell wine in 1387.

Elsewhere, the **Chiesa dei Domenicani►** contains the town's best paintings, several 14th-century Giottoesque frescoes. Also visit the **Chiesa dei Francescani►**, known for its carved altarpiece and gracious frescoes. The **Museo Civico►►** (*Closed* Mon. *Admission: moderate*) offers archeological fragments and a folklore section, with costumes, woodcarvings, household objects, and reconstructed interiors. Take the *funivia* (cable car) to Soprabolzano (literally "over Bolzano"), from where a tiny tramway takes you 4 miles to the hamlet of Collalbo and the "Earth Pyramids," a bizarre rock "forest" of eroded spires and pinnacles.

MONTE GRAPPA
From Bassano del Grappa take the winding mountain road 19 miles north to Monte Grappa, 5,857 feet high, where you can take in some of the grandest panoramas in the area.

CASTELLO RONCOLO
You can visit one of several castles in the Val Sarentina valley north of Bolzano. Castello Roncolo (13th- to 19th-century) is the nearest and most impressive, with guided tours of its rooms, many decorated with 15th-century frescoes. (*Open* Mar–Nov. *Closed* Mon. *Admission: moderate*)

Above: market day in Bassano del Grappa Left: elegant traditional houses in Bolzano

DRIVE
One of the best of the many scenic drives near Bolzano is the SS 508, which follows the Val Sarentina to Vipiteno (62km).

WHAT'S IN A NAME
The Dolomites are so-
called because of the
dolomite rock, or magne-
sium limestone, which
is their main constituent.
The rock itself was
named after the 18th-
century French geologist
Diendonne Sylvain
Guy Tancrède de Gratet
de Dolomieu.

*The Tre Cime di
Lavaredo with the*
Rifugio Locatelli
(refuge) beneath

▶▶ Cividale del Friuli   115C5

Important as one of the few places in Italy where there is
some tangible record of the Lombards (see panel),
Cividale is a lovely place, filled with a tangle of medieval
streets, ancient bridges, and interesting churches.

The 15th-century **Duomo▶▶** boasts several remarkable
works, including an embossed early 13th-century *pala*, or
silver altarpiece. Off the right aisle, the Museo Cristiano
contains the octagonal *Baptistery of Callisto*, commissioned
in the 8th century by Cividale's first bishop-patriarch and
made from 5th-century Lombard marble and stonework.
The *Altar of Ratchis*, carved in 749, is one of the few surviving masterpieces from the Lombard era.

To the Duomo's left, the **Museo Archeologico▶▶**
(*Closed* Mon PM. *Admission: inexpensive*) houses Lombard
weapons, tools, and jewelry, but the town's finest monument to the era is the **Tempietto Longobardo▶▶** (*Open
daily. Admission: inexpensive*), an old temple whose carved
stucco arch is a peerless example of Lombard sculpture.

**THE COMING OF THE
LOMBARDS**
The Lombards swept into
Italy after the fall of the
Roman Empire. A Teutonic
warrior race, they had
descended from
Scandinavia to occupy the
Danube. They came south
in AD 568, under their
king, Alboino. The
entourage included
40,000 men, women, and
children, supported by a
huge retinue of slaves,
wagons, and livestock.
They established three
Italian dukedoms, the first
of which had Cividale as
its capital (the other two
were Pavia, in Lombardy,
and Spoleto, in Umbria).

▶▶▶ Dolomiti (The Dolomites)   114D2

No other European mountains approach the scenic
spectacle of the Dolomites, a group of 30 or so self-
contained massifs in a wide arc from Lake Garda to the
Austrian border. Set apart from the rest of the Alps by
their geology, they are ancient coral reefs that have been
compressed, uplifted, and weathered. This largely
explains the incredible crags and rock pinnacles that are
their hallmark, and the peculiar, pinkish-orange limestone
that forms most of the massifs.

Many mountain roads offer views unparalleled in Italy
(see page 121), but it would be a shame to come here and
not attempt a little walking (see pages 122–123). On a first
visit, the best way to come to grips with the area is to concentrate on one or two massifs. The most famous is the
Dolomiti di Brenta▶▶▶ in the west, with Madonna di
Campiglio as the best base. Several massifs are also easily
accessible from Bolzano (Sciliar, Puez-Odle) and from
Cortina d'Ampezzo (Sesto, Cristallo, Marmarole, and
Fanes-Sennes-Braies).

THE GREAT DOLOMITES ROAD

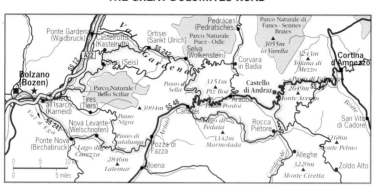

Drive

La Grande Strada delle Dolomiti

La Grande Strada delle Dolomiti—the Great Dolomites road—was opened in 1909 to link Bolzano with Cortina d'Ampezzo and runs for 66 miles through some of the most spectacular mountain scenery in Europe. You can add many scenic options to this itinerary, especially if you make the return loop to Bolzano.

From Bolzano the road enters the Val d'Ega, a corridor of gorges and beautiful waterfalls that offers thrilling views of the Catinaccio and Latemar massifs. Mountain-cradled Lago di Carezza is one of the road's more famous viewing spots.

The road then continues over high passes, skirting thick forests and wild countryside, and constantly unfolding yet more breathtaking vistas as it twists and turns around hairpin bends toward Canazei. Here the SS 641 offers a tortuous alternative to the Strada, touching the Marmolada massif, glaciers, and Lago di Fedaia before extending to the last leg to Cortina d'Ampezzo.

The Passo Sella with Sassolungo in the background

Anyone who loves mountains and the activities associated with them will be entranced by the Dolomites. They offer an unbeatable combination—stupendous scenery, hikes to suit every ability, and some of the best skiing in Europe.

MONTE CIVETTA WALK
Start from the village of Alleghe, 23 miles south-west of Cortina (use the SS 638 and SS 203). Take the path from the village to the *Rif. A. Tissi* via Lago Coldai and *Rif. Sonino* (tremendous views of Civetta's huge rock walls). For a longer walk continue from *Tissi* south to *Rif. Vazzoler* and thus to Listolade on the SS 203 (9 miles south of Alleghe). Use Kompass map *Alpi Bellunesi* (No 77).

The Passo di Giau, La Gusela

Walking On no account should you come here without tackling at least one walk. It need not be difficult: there is ample choice between easy low-level strolls and more demanding high-level walks. Towns and starting points are often high up, so even what look like "mountain climbs" are usually easier than they first appear. Access to all the main centers is straightforward; maps are excellent and widely available; paths are well-marked and well-trodden; and hotels are inexpensive and plentiful. Refreshment stops (*rifugi*) are rarely more than an hour apart, and there are numerous cable cars to take the sting out of the longer, more arduous ascents.

The only problem is knowing where to start. Numerous guidebooks are published, and tourist offices have lists of walks. The best approach is to settle on one massif and a single base, and start with a recognized "classic." At the same time, you should not take the mountains lightly. Go equipped with boots or stout shoes, carry food and water,

and take adequate warm clothes and rain gear: the weather can change quickly at high altitudes.

Dolomiti di Brenta Use Madonna di Campiglio (4,950 feet) as your base. It offers plenty of hotels and numerous circular walks you can complete in a day. The easiest is to take the Grostè ski lift to *Rif. G. Graffer* (7,748 feet) and follow trail 316 to the *Rif. Tuckett* (7,498 feet). From here you can follow paths 317 or 328/318 back to Madonna. Alternatively, walk from Madonna to *Rif. Vallesinella* (an easy hour's stroll on trail 375), then climb to the *Rif. Brentei* (317/318), one of the Dolomites' most popular refuges. For a longer walk, continue on path 318 up the spectacular Val Brenta Alta toward *Rif. Pedrotti*. Double back the same way to the *Brentei* or drop to the Val Brenta and back to Madonna on trail 323 or 391 (all walks are clearly marked on the Kompass map *Dolomiti di Brenta* No. 73).

Dolomiti di Sesto This is the easternmost Dolomite massif. Cortina is a good overall base, but Sesto and Dobbiaco are the closest villages to the best-known walk, which follows path 5/102 up the Val Fiscalina from San Giuseppe (south of Sesto) to the *Rif. Locatelli* with extraordinary views of the much photographed Tre Cime di Lavaredo (see page 120). Paths 101/104 give closer views of these peaks and longer walks. There is another, easier approach to the Tre Cime from *Rif. Auronzo* to the south (reached by road from Cortina). The Tabacco map *Cortina-Dolomiti di Sesto* (No. 1) covers the whole area.

Skiing In the Dolomites, the choice of both ski slopes and resorts is almost endless. Even the tiniest of villages has some slopes on offer, together with general stores, hotels, and skiing outfitters.

The main centers for skiing are perhaps **Cortina d'Ampezzo**, east of Bolzano in the heart of the mountains, and **Madonna di Campiglio**, west of Trento, on the fringe of the Dolomiti di Brenta. Both towns are crowded and decidedly upscale, but for your money you get all the trappings of top-class international resorts.

For similar facilities—but in less chic surroundings—try the resorts in the Val Gardena (such as **Ortisei Canazei**) or in the **Val Badia** south of **Brunico** (itself one of several modest resorts in the Val Pusteria). There are also good cross-country skiing (*sci di fondo*); two of the best centers are Ortisei and Dobbiaco in the Val Pusteria.

ACCOMMODATIONS
Almost every hamlet in the Dolomites has a superb range of accommodations. Most are aimed at skiers, which means that summer rates are very competitive. Hotels are comfortable and of higher overall quality than in much of Italy. Do not be afraid to spend a night in a mountain refuge—they are not the preserve of hardened mountaineers. Rooms are in dormitory form, but they are snug and friendly places. Most open daily from June to September. Details from tourist offices.

Skiing in the Dolomites at Vigo di Fassa

123

SETTIMANE BIANCHE
Ski resorts' bargain periods are known as *settimane bianche* (white weeks). They usually fall in January and February when slopes are at their emptiest and snow conditions are often unreliable. Prices on passes and hotels are reduced.

EXCURSION FROM MERANO

The tiny church of San Procolo lies in the hamlet of Naturno in the lovely Val Venosta (9 miles west of Merano). It contains exceptional wall paintings from the 8th century—the oldest in the entire German-speaking world. The trip is best combined with a drive into the Tessa mountains, an Alpine massif northwest of Merano. From Naturno, pick up the road west of the hamlet, which strikes north up the Val di Senales. This provides a breathtaking 15-mile route into the mountains.

▶▶ **Merano (Meran)** 114D2

Sedate, mountain-ringed Merano is a fossil from a bygone age, full of *belle époque* memories, leftovers from the turn of the century, when its mild climate, thermal springs, and "grape cure" made it a favored spa with monied Europeans (the cure, reputedly used since Roman times, involves a two-week diet of fresh grapes). Among the many parks and promenades, the most famous is the **Passeggiata d'Inverno e d'Estate▶**, a path by the banks of the Passirio River. Above the town is the Passeggiata Tappeiner, a path that winds through gardens and vineyards offering views of Merano and its valley.

The town center is at its best around Via dei Portici, where rustic houses sit alongside more recent neoclassical and art nouveau buildings. Nearby are the Gothic **Duomo▶** and ivy-clad **Castello Principesco▶** (*Closed* Mon)—the main things to see—together with a handful of churches and the modest Museo Civico. But Merano is mainly a place to relax in, preferably, if you can afford the cures, at the **Terme**, the largest of the town's spa facilities.

The condottiere *Gattamelata rides proudly outside St. Antony's Basilica, Padua*

▶▶▶ **Padova (Padua)** 114B3

Padua is worth enduring for two not-to-be-missed sights. The **Cappella degli Scrovegni▶▶▶** (*Open* Feb–Oct, Tue–Sun 9–7; Nov–Jan 9:30–5:30. *Advance booking essential, tel: 820 4550. Admission: moderate*) is home to one of Italy's greatest fresco cycles: Giotto's 32-panel series of paintings on the lives of Christ and the Virgin Mary (1303–1309). Like the artist's cycle in Assisi (see page 168), it marked a turning point in Western art, introducing a fluency and naturalism into painting that departed from the formality of Byzantine art.

St. Antony of Padua, one of Italy's most revered saints, is buried in the **Basilica di Sant'Antonio▶▶** (*Open* daily). Donatello's statue of Gattamelata, a Venetian *condottiere*, stands outside. Inside are his bronze reliefs of St. Antony's life; high altar figures of the *Madonna and Saints* (also by Donatello); St. Antony's votive-filled chapel; and 14th-century frescoes in the Beato Luca and San Felice chapels.

▶ Trento (Trent) 114C2

Italian-speaking capital of Trentino, Trento is best known for the Council of Trent, a meeting at which the Catholic hierarchy between 1545 and 1563 debated ways to turn Europe's rising tide of Lutheranism. Its opening and closing sessions took place in the **Duomo▶▶**, heart of the present town, whose austere nave contains an unusual arcaded stairway, traces of old fresco, and a modest copy of Bernini's *baldacchino* in St. Peter's, Rome. Outside, on the east wall, look for the church's famous "knotted columns," a memorial to the skill of the town's medieval masons. Alongside the Duomo, the Palazzo Pretorio contains the **Museo Diocesano▶** (*Closed* Sun. *Admission: moderate*), a small museum displaying 16th-century Flemish tapestries, carved altarpieces, and painted chronicles of the Council of Trent.

Elsewhere, Trento is nicely uncommercialized, and a pleasure to wander through for an hour or so. Via Belenzani, with its rows of Renaissance *palazzi*, is the most singular street. As you explore, try to take in the church of Santa Maria Maggiore and the **Castello del Buonconsiglio▶▶** (*Closed* Mon. *Admission: moderate*), for centuries the home of Trento's prince-bishops. Inside, it houses the Museo Provinciale d'Arte and the *Ciclo dei Mesi*, a lovely 15th-century fresco cycle by unknown artists depicting the months of the year.

▶ Treviso 114B3

Drawn away by Venice's siren call, few people have much time for Treviso. Yet its old center is an alluring mixture of canals, frescoed facades, shady porticoes, and medieval fragments. The churches of **San Nicolò▶▶** and **Santa Caterina▶▶** are the main monuments, both filled with frescoes and decorated tombs. The **Duomo▶**, which has paintings by Tintoretto and others, is also diverting, while **Via Carlo Alberto▶**, heart of an appealing market district, is the best single street to wander for its own sake. Also explore the central Calmaggiore area, with many old *palazzi*, the Peschiera (Fish Market), and two excellent museums: the **Museo Civico▶** (*Closed* Sun PM and Mon. *Admission: inexpensive*) with works by, among many others, Titian and Bassano.

For wine lovers, the wine roads known as the Strada del Vino Rosso and Strada del Vino Bianco (the "Red" and "White" wine roads, respectively) start out from Conegliano, just 14 miles north of Treviso, with plenty of opportunities to sample the local wines.

125

An evocative glimpse of Treviso

*Trieste's harbor was
once one of the most
important ports in the
old Austro-Hungarian
empire*

MIRAMARE
The most popular excursion from Trieste is to Miramare, a beautifully located castle built for Archduke Ferdinand Maximilian between 1856 and 1870 (located 4 miles north of the city). It is a marvelously kitschy and eclectic building (open to the public), though Triestini prefer to come here for the beaches (*Open* daily. *Admission: moderate*).

GROTTA GIGANTE
Borgo Grotta Gigante (*Closed* Mon), 9 miles from Trieste, is near the largest publicly accessible cave in the world. The Grotta Gigante can reputedly accommodate St. Peter's, Rome, with room to spare (it is 353 feet deep by 686 feet wide).

▶▶ Trieste   115B5

Trieste has little to see, if truth be told, but it rates as one of northern Italy's most atmospheric and distinctive cities (it also has lovely surroundings and a rugged coastline). At the crossroads of three cultures, it has been shaped by Italian, Slavic, and middle-European influences. Once the chief port of the Austro-Hungarian Empire, its most tangible memorials relate to this golden age—notably several neoclassical districts and a handful of wonderful turn-of-the-century coffee houses (**San Marco** in Via G. Battisti and **Tommaseo** in Piazza Tommaseo are the most famous). To glimpse the city's earlier past, visit **San Giusto▶▶**, the Romanesque-Gothic cathedral (with its origins in the 6th century), filled with frescoes and some outstanding 12th-century mosaics. Close by, the **Museo di Storia e d'Arte▶** (*Closed* Mon and PM daily. *Admission: inexpensive*) chronicles the city's history from Roman times (the city was the Roman port of Tergeste). It is easily seen in conjunction with the **Museo Sartorio▶** (*Closed* Mon and PM daily; *Admission: moderate*), a series of gloomily decorated rooms redeemed by a ceramics collection and some 270 Tiepolo drawings. Climb to the Castello (1470–1630) for its views and small museum of weapons and armour.

▶ Udine   115C4

Once a bastion of the Roman Empire's northern frontier, Udine is today one of Italy's more urbane and airy little towns. At its heart lies the monumental **Piazza della Libertà▶▶**, dominated by the Palazzo del Comune, one of many buildings around the town to bear a Venetian stamp (the town was ruled by Venice from 1420 to 1797). To the south, the main attractions of the **Duomo▶** are several paintings by Giovanni Battista Tiepolo, a painter who also left frescoes in the **Oratorio della Purità▶** opposite (entry with sacristan) and **Palazzo Arcivescovile▶** (*Open* Wed–Sun. *Admission: moderate*), which contains the Museo Diocesano and Gallerie del Triepolo.

Be sure to climb to the 16th-century **Castello▶** (*Closed* Mon)—from the Piazza della Libertà (you pass the lovely Loggia del Lionello *en route*). Paintings in the castle's museum include works by G. B. Tiepolo, Caravaggio, Carpaccio, and Bronzino. Also leave time for San Francesco, a neat little Renaissance church.

Opera's emotional drama and sensuality are perfectly suited to the Italian temperament—"more heart than mind," said Giacomo Puccini—and there is nowhere better to enjoy a performance than in Italy itself, whether under the stars in Verona's amphitheater or in one of the country's many great opera houses.

Opera's roots lie in the traditional Italian mystery plays, the *maggi*, and the madrigal comedies of the 16th century. The composer Jacopo Peri produced the first *opera in musica*, literally a "work in music," in 1600, a performance of *Euridice* to mark the marriage of Maria de' Medici to Henry IV of France. This and other early pieces were little more than spoken recitals with a light musical backing. The first composer to use a full orchestra was Claudio Monteverdi (1567–1643), whose *La Favola d'Orfeo* (1607) is held to be the first operatic masterpiece.

The first public opera house, the Teatro di San Cassiano, opened in Venice in 1637, followed by others all over the country. By 1700 there were 17 in Venice alone. About 2,000 new operas were staged during the 18th century.

The golden age Opera's 19th-century golden age was heralded by the almost simultaneous arrival of Rossini, Donizetti, and Bellini. All enjoyed success at an early age, were often in fierce competition, and burned out quickly, the first two dying relatively young (Rossini's last triumph came at the age of 40). Italian opera's greatest genius was perhaps Verdi. The son of a semi-literate peasant, Giuseppe Verdi (1813–1901) wrote such masterpieces as *Rigoletto* (1851), *La Traviata* (1853), *Aida* (1871), and *Otello* (1887).

HARSH CRITICS
In the 19th century, Italian audiences were notorious for their rowdiness and uncompromising criticism. Charles Dickens noted their "uncommonly hard and cruel character" and thought them "always to be lying in wait for an opportunity to hiss."

GIACOMO PUCCINI
The curtain fell on the golden age with the death of Verdi's successor, Giacomo Puccini, responsible for many highlights of the operatic canon, such as *La Bohème* (1896), *Tosca* (1900), and *Madame Butterfly* (1904).

The Roman Arena in Verona, scene of a summer opera season

Even if you are no fan of opera, seeing a performance in Verona's Arena is an unforgettable experience. The season runs throughout July and August, when the city is crowded and hotels difficult to find. You can get tickets from the box office (Arch 6 of the Arena); from the *Ente Lirico*, Piazza Brà 28 (tel: 045 800 5151)—or from scalpers outside the Arena (who sell at little over face value). Most seats are unnumbered, so arrive early—the build-up is fun anyway—and be sure to rent a cushion and bring a sweater.

The imposing exterior of Verona's Duomo

ROMEO AND JULIET

Shakespeare's Capulets and Montagues were based on true families (the Cappelli and Montecchi). Their feuds were also real enough, though the characters of Romeo and Juliet are fictional inventions. Nonetheless, it is hard to resist the so-called *Casa di Giulietta* (Juliet's House) (*Closed* Mon. *Admission: moderate*) on Via Cappello. The house and courtyard are pretty and there's even a balcony, though, as Arnold Bennet pointed out, it is "too high for love, unless Juliet was a trapeze artist, accustomed to hanging downwards by her toes."

"There is no world without Verona walls, /But purgatory, torture, hell itself./ Hence—banished is banish'd from the world—And world's exile is death..."
William Shakespeare (*Romeo and Juliet*).

►►► Verona   *114B1*

Verona is one of northern Italy's loveliest and most artistically alluring cities. You should try to spend several days here—a couple seeing the city sights and soaking up the atmosphere, and a few exploring nearby towns like Vicenza, Padua, and Mantua. Verona's picturesque center, set on the fast-flowing Adige river, is scattered with Roman and medieval remains, churches, monuments, and a labyrinth of old streets—as romantic as when it was chosen by Shakespeare as the setting for *Romeo and Juliet.*

In the center Start a tour in Piazza Brà, the city's mammoth main square. It holds the 1st-century AD **Arena**►►► (*Open* Tue–Sun 9–6:30; Jul–Aug, 8–3:30. *Admission: moderate*), one of the largest surviving amphitheaters of the Roman world. Built to hold 20,000 spectators, it still provides the stage for the city's famous summer opera season (see panel). You need not pay for a performance, however, to see its interior or enjoy the city from its upper tiers.
Via Mazzini►, the center's elegant main street, leads to a far more intimate square: **Piazza delle Erbe**►►, the city's heart and social meeting place. Renaissance palaces and medieval town houses surround it on all sides, echoing to the bustle of a colorful fruit and vegetable market.
 Alongside it lies one of Italy's most magical piazzas, the **Piazza dei Signori**►►►, once the city's chief public piazza, hence its trio of 12th-century civic buildings: the Loggia del Consiglio, a council meeting chamber; the Palazzo del Governo, seat of Verona's medieval rulers; and the Palazzo della Ragione, a Gothic ensemble whose **Torre dei Lamberti**►► offers dizzying views of the city.

In its lower corner are the **Arche Scaligere►►►**, among the most accomplished Gothic funerary monuments in Italy. They are the tombs of the Scaligeri, principally Cangrande I ("The Big Dog"), a protector of Dante and patron of the arts. His grinning figure looks down from the equestrian statue atop his tomb, distinct from other clan members, whose canopied graves lie behind a palisade (decorated with ladders, the family's emblem, and a pun on their name—*scala* is Italian for "ladder").

Going north Not far away is **Sant'Anastasia►**, Verona's largest church, the focus of the city's most captivating medieval quarter. Here, too, is the **Duomo►**, distinguished by its exterior carvings and Titian's *Assumption* (first altar on the left). Behind the church, cross the river for the **Teatro Romano►**—a ruined Roman theater—and the modest Museo Archeologico (*Closed* Mon and PM in winter. *Admission: moderate;* includes ticket for the Teatro Romano). Above the museum, climb the steps to the Castel San Pietro to enjoy one of the city's best views. **San Giorgio in Braida►**, just to the west, is worth a look if only for the *Martyrdom of St. George* by Veronese.

Going west The **Castelvecchio►►►** (*Open* Tue–Sun 9–6:30. *Admission: moderate*), a fortress and former Scaligeri seat, is now home to the Museo Civico d'Arte. Before you reach its paintings, the castle's maze of courtyards, chambers, and passages is a fascinating diversion in its own right. Foremost among the artworks are Madonnas by Pisanello, Carlo Crivelli, and Giovanni Bellini; Tiepolo's *Heliodorus*; and Tintoretto's *Nativity* and *Concert in the Open*. Behind the castle the fortified Ponte Scaligero (1355) crosses the river to Piazza Arsenale, part of a city park where you can take a break from sightseeing.

Wander north and recross the river and you come to **San Zeno Maggiore►►►** (*Open* Mon–Sat 8:30–6, Sun 1–6. *Admission: inexpensive; discount ticket for five churches available*), widely regarded as northern Italy's most magnificent Romanesque church. Exterior details to admire include the ivory-colored facade; the huge rose window and its *Wheel of Fortune*; the reliefs of the main portal; and the extraordinary 12th-century bronze panels of the door. Inside are frescoes and, even more impressive, Mantegna's compelling *Madonna and Saints* above the high altar.

A GLASS OF WINE
Verona is known for its historic *osterie*, old-fashioned wine shops, popular stops for a glass of sparkling *prosecco*, Soave, or one of the cheap Bardolino or Valpolicella reds. Try *Bottega dei Vini*, Vicolo Scudo di Francia (off Via Mazzini); *Cacciatore*, Piazza Isolo; and *Osteria delle Vecete*, Via Pellicciai; or *Osteria del Duomo*, Via Duomo.

WINE FAIR
Italy's biggest wine fair, *Vinitaly*, takes place in Verona every April, with ample opportunities for the public to sample wines from all over Italy.

RULERS AND PATRONS
Though ruthless in pursuit of power, the Scaligeri were great patrons of the arts. Both Giotto and Dante were guests of the family: Dante dedicated his *Paradiso* to Cangrande I.

The splendid tomb of Cangrande I

VILLA VALMARANA AI NANI

Hundreds of villas are scattered around Vicenza's countryside. Some of the best—like the Villa Valmarana (*Open* Mar 15–Nov 15, Wed–Sun 10–12, 2:30–5:30, Tue 2:30–5:30. *Admission: moderate*)—are only a stone's throw from the city. Valmarana is known for its fresco cycles by Giambattista and Giandomenico Tiepolo, poetic and cheerful depictions of classical stories and idealized country life.

BASILICA DI MONTE BERICO

This gaudy 17th-century basilica commemorates two apparitions of the Virgin, held to signal Vicenza's deliverance from the plague in 1426. Pilgrims throng its interior, but for other visitors its lures are its views of the city and two exceptional paintings: Montagna's *Pietà* and Veronese's handsome *Supper of St. Gregory the Great* (*Open* Mon–Sat 6:15–12:30, 2:30–7:30, Sun 6:15–8 PM. *Admission free*).

Setting up shop: a craft fair in Vicenza's Piazza dei Signori

▶▶▶ Vicenza   114B2

Vicenza is a showcase for the architectural genius of Andrea Palladio (see opposite), who designed or restructured most of the city's finest buildings. Otherwise, it is a wealthy city, grown fat on a booming electronic sector, Italy's largest textile industry, and the printing business. **Piazza dei Signori▶**, site of the old Roman forum and still the city center, contains the **Basilica▶▶▶** (*Closed* Mon and Sun PM in winter. *Admission: moderate*), Palladio's first project and the building with which he made his reputation. Its tremendous colonnades buttress the earlier Palazzo della Ragione, a medieval law court whose crumbling exterior had defied all previous attempts at repair. The **Loggia del Capitano▶** across the piazza is also by Palladio, though never completed. Before leaving the square, enjoy the Piazza delle Erbe's fruit and flower market, and have a drink in the old world Gran Caffè Garibaldi coffeehouse.

Corso Andrea Palladio▶▶, the center's main street, is lined with palaces, some by Palladio, some by Vincenzo Scamozzi, his chief disciple: the best are Bonin-Thiene (No. 13); Capra (No. 45); Pagello (No. 47); Thiene (No. 67); Braschi (No. 67); the **Palazzo del Comune▶** (No. 98); and the **Palazzo da Schio▶**. To complete a Palladian tour, visit the **Teatro Olimpico▶▶▶** (*Closed* Mon. *Admission: expensive, includes entry to Museo Civico*), Europe's oldest indoor theater and perhaps Palladio's finest work. The tourist office alongside has information on the architect's villas around Vicenza. The most famous of Palladio's villas, **La Rotonda**, was a pavilion whose design was widely copied, particularly in the United States at Thomas Jefferson's home, Monticello.

No visit is complete without seeing the church of **Santa Corona▶▶** (*Closed* Mon AM), site of Veronese's *The Adoration of the Magi* and Giovanni Bellini's *The Baptism of Christ*. The **Museo Civico▶** (*Closed* Mon. *Admission: expensive, includes entry to Teatro Olimpico*) houses works by Veronese, Bassano, Montagna, and Tintoretto.

Andrea Palladio counts as one of the most significant Italian architects of the 16th century. Through his reinterpretation of classical idioms he became an influential figure in the development of Western architecture.

Born in Padua in 1508, Palladio was apprenticed to a sculptor at an early age. At 16 he moved to Vicenza and enrolled in the guild of bricklayers and stonemasons. He soon found employment as a mason in a workshop specializing in monuments and decorative sculpture. He later became the protégé of Count Giangiorgio Trissano, a humanist poet and scholar, who guided his studies, directing him to the works of ancient Roman architects like Vitruvius (active 46–30 BC). During this period Palladio probably met Alvise Cornaro, the architect responsible for importing the Roman Renaissance style into northern Italy. He also came into contact with Vicenzan high society, whose leading pillars were to employ him to design their palaces and country villas. He embarked on the first of these— the Villa Godi—in 1540.

The legacy of Rome In 1541 and again in 1547 Palladio visited Rome, studying not only the works of Rome's High Renaissance masters— men like Bramante and Peruzzi—but also the city's Roman antiquities, whose classical forms were to inspire much of his work. The fruit of his studies appeared in the variety and proportional

subtlety of the palaces he built over the next 30 years. Of the many classical ideas that informed his buildings, the most distinctive was the use of the ancient Greco-Roman temple front as a portico (as in La Rotonda).

Another visit to Rome in 1554 produced his book *L'Antichità di Roma*, which for 200 years remained the standard guidebook to Rome. Even more influential still were *I Quattro Libri dell'Architectura* (1570), four books that together form perhaps the most important architectural treatise ever published.

The last years After 1570, Palladio was preoccupied with church design in Venice, producing Il Redentore, San Giorgio Maggiore, and the facade of San Francesco della Vigna. Remarkably, he never received a civic or private commission from the city. His last work was Vicenza's Teatro Olimpico in 1580, the year of his death.

Top: La Rotonda, near Vicenza
Above: Palladio's Venetian masterpiece, San Giorgio Maggiore

Handwritten notes (top left):
1. Novella
2. Academia - Mus. Duomo - 3.
4. Santa Croce
5. Ponte Vecchio

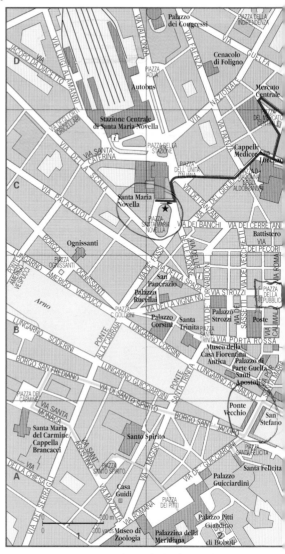

Above: Florentine monk,
a link with the past
Below: Florence's
unmistakable roofscape

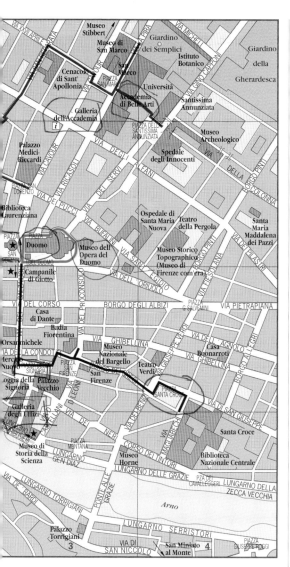

FLORENCE (FIRENZE) Tuscany's main attraction is as a city-sized shrine to the Renaissance. Florence's churches, palaces, and museums are crammed with enough fine art to last a lifetime. Its streets, on the other hand, are surprisingly dour, hunched up with dark *palazzi* and filled with traffic and tourists. One or two notable exceptions aside, therefore, it is a city where your time is best spent indoors, poring over paintings or sculpture. Not that the city is without its visual appeal. Few sights are as impressive as a first view of Piazza del Duomo, the Ponte Vecchio, or the Piazza della Signoria. But these are aberrations—more points of departure than places to linger. Florence has cafés for relaxation and outstanding gardens such as the Giardino di Boboli, but head for Siena if you want atmospheric streets and medieval charm.

▶▶▶ CITY HIGHLIGHTS

Florence

FESTIVALS

Florence's foremost event is the **Maggio Musicale Fiorentino**, one of Europe's leading festivals of opera and classical music (April–early July). The **Estate Fiesolana**, a festival of chamber and symphonic music, is held at Fiesole (June–late August). The Box Office at Via Alamanni 39 (055 210 804) and in Chiasso dei Soldanieri 8r, off Via Porta Rossa (055 219 402) has information and provides tickets for most events.

TOURIST INFORMATION

The main tourist offices are at Via Cavour 1r (tel: 055 276 0381), north of the Duomo, and at Borgo Santa Croce 29r (tel: 055 234 0444 or 055 226 4524). There is another office just outside the Santa Maria Novella train station (tel: 055 238 1226).

HIGHLIGHTS Piazza della Signoria offers the Palazzo Vecchio and the Loggia della Signoria (or Loggia dei Lanzi), Piazza del Duomo, the Duomo and Baptistery, while Piazza della Repubblica, located between the two, is a 19th-century square on the site of the Roman forum. From these central piazzas it only takes a matter of minutes to reach the city's three great galleries: the Uffizi (paintings), the Bargello, and Museo dell'Opera del Duomo (sculpture). Other buildings offer similar star attractions—Michelangelo's *David*, housed in the Accademia, for example, or the sculpture-filled facade of Orsanmichele. The city is so rich in art that its second-ranked picture gallery—the six-museum complex of the Palazzo Pitti, surrounded by the Boboli Gardens—is better than most cities' best.

CHURCHES Where Florence's galleries chronicle the Renaissance in its entirety, its churches tend more to be monuments to particular artists. Most contain individual works of genius by the great masters: San Marco (Fra Angelico); San Lorenzo (Michelangelo); Santa Croce (Giotto); Santa Maria del Carmine (Masaccio and Masolino); and Santa Maria Novella (Masaccio, Ghirlandaio, and Filippino Lippi).

ORIGINS Ancient *Florentia* was reputedly founded in 59 BC by Julius Caesar (though there was an earlier Etruscan settlement in the hills at nearby Fiesole). Florence emerged from the Dark Ages as an independent city state, prospering through banking and trade in wool and textiles. Ruled first by mercantile elements (the Primo Popolo), it later passed to the guilds (the Secondo Popolo) and, in 1293, to the quasi-republican Signoria (a council drawn from the major guilds).

GUELPH AND GHIBELLINE Florence's rise to power, however, was blighted by the Guelph and Ghibelline conflicts that affected many Italian city states (fights between supporters of the pope and emperor respectively). Often these were a cover for local rivalries, the most famous being the divisions in the Guelph camp between "Black" and "White" factions (Dante belonged to the latter, and along with many others was expelled from the city in 1302).

THE MEDICI A single family emerged triumphant from Florence's conflicts—the Medici, a banking dynasty founded by Giovanni de' Medici. Its members were to control Florence—and later Tuscany—for over three centuries. Their power reached its zenith under Giovanni's son Cosimo, and Cosimo's grandson Lorenzo il Magnifico (1449–1492), under whose enlightened patronage Florence became the greatest city of the Renaissance. Influence slipped when Lorenzo's son, Piero, surrendered to the French in 1494, leaving the way open for Savonarola, a charismatic monk who held the city in thrall until executed by the papacy in 1498.

LAST OF THE MEDICI The family returned in 1512 with reduced power, only to be removed again in 1527 when Charles V overran Rome (ousting Clement VII, a Medici pope). They were back again just three years later, and under another (distantly related) Cosimo declared themselves Grand Dukes of Tuscany in 1569. The last of the Medici died in 1737, and the city passed by treaty to the future Francis I of Austria. Except for 15 years of Napoleonic rule, Florence remained under Austrian control (with nominal independence) until Italian unification in the mid-19th century. The city was capital of Italy from 1865 to 1871.

The view from Florence cathedral's dome

Italy's many ghosts include the poets, painters, and men of letters lured by what Keats called a "beakerful of the warm south." The years between about 1720 and 1790 marked the halcyon days of the Grand Tour, a route through several European cities culminating in Rome and Naples. Without this journey no gentleman's (rarely lady's) education was complete.

Top: Thomas Cook's first tour group in the ruins of Pompeii

MODERN VISITORS
The Grand Tour's turning point came in 1864 when a Mr. Thomas Cook ran the first package tour from London to Naples. He provided food, travel, entertainment, and hotels for some 50 people, thus ushering in the era of mass tourism. With at least 50 million visitors a year, tourism is now among Italy's top money-earners, a boon and a bane for residents—and, perhaps, for foreigners too, who are now left with only scraps of the old Italy captured in the poems, paintings, letters, and journals of travelers past.

San Giorgio from the Dogana, Sunrise, *by J. M. W. Turner*

136

Early visitors After those who came for the purposes of plunder and pillage, Italy's earliest visitors were pilgrims, drawn by Rome's shrines and churches. Their greatest incursion occurred during the Holy Year proclaimed by Boniface VIII in 1300. Although doubtless designed to line papal coffers rather than provide spiritual solace, Boniface's offer of plenary indulgences attracted some two million visitors.

Pilgrims continued to outnumber tourists until about the 16th century, when gentlemen of substance turned to Italy to add the final polish to their courtly and cultural education. Castiglione's famous book *Il Cortegiano* (*The Courtier*) was translated and became a bible of behavior for English courtiers. However, this was also the period in which Italy acquired its reputation for intrigue, corruption, and diabolic debauchery.

Paradise of exiles By the 18th century, Italy had come to be seen either as a museum of the past, or a country where foreigners could cast off their inhibitions and indulge in its more sensuous diversions. Some came for art and inspiration; some sought escape, others health; and many were lured by the idea of a warm climate stimulating the passions.

However, the journey to the promised land often turned out to be fraught with incident and difficulty. Joseph Addison arrived at Calais and fell into the harbor; Casanova was apparently sexually molested by a policeman; and Tobias Smollett, perhaps the most miserable man ever to travel, found dirt and disappointment at every turn. Goethe wisely observed that "every foreigner judges by the standards he brings with him."

Italy worked its spell on countless others, among them Milton, Montaigne, Rubens, Turner, Velázquez, Poussin, Liszt, Nietzsche, Robert Browning, Alfred Lord Tennyson, Keats, Ruskin, Whistler, Shelley, Herman Melville, Mark Twain, and Henry James.

Churches

▶▶▶ Battistero (Baptistery)   133C3

Piazza San Giovanni
Open: Mon–Sat 12–6:30, Sun 8:30–1:30. Admission: inexpensive
The 11th-century Baptistery is most famous for its bronze doors, whose creation is considered to have marked the start of the Florentine Renaissance. The south (entrance) doors by Andrea Pisano were already in place when the 20-year-old Lorenzo Ghiberti won a competition to design the others in 1401. His north doors have panels illustrating the Life of Christ; the east doors show Old Testament scenes. Inside are a 13th-century mosaic ceiling, and Donatello and Michelozzo's tomb of the antipope John XXIII (a landmark of early Renaissance sculpture).

▶▶ Campanile   133C3

Piazza del Duomo
Open: daily. Ticket office closes 6:50. Admission: expensive
"The model and mirror of perfect architecture," said Ruskin of the Duomo's bell tower, begun in 1334 to a design by Giotto. It was finished by Andrea Pisano and Francesco Talenti, and decorated with reliefs by Pisano, Donatello, and Luca della Robbia (most of the originals are now in the Museo dell'Opera del Duomo). Climb the 414 steps to the top for the vertiginous views.

▶▶▶ Duomo (Santa Maria del Fiore)   133C3

Piazza San Giovanni-Piazza del Duomo
Open: Mon–Wed, Fri–Sat 10–5, Thu 10–3:30, Sun 1:30–5.
Admission free
The cathedral was started in 1296 following a design by Arnolfo di Cambio, but consecrated in 1436, after contributions by several more architects—notably the magnificent dome by Brunelleschi. The interior's only major works are restored frescoes in the dome by Vasari and two equestrian frescoes: *Sir John Hawkwood, a famous English mercenary* by Uccello and *Niccolò da Tolentino* by Andrea Castagno.

137

The Duomo, Florence

THE ANNUNCIATION
Until the end of the 18th century, the Florentine New Year began on March 25, the Feast of the Annunciation—hence the popularity of paintings of the Annunciation and of the church of Santissima Annunziata, a fashionable spot for society weddings. The feast day is still marked by a large annual fair in Piazza Santissima Annunziata.

MICHELANGELO'S TOMB
Michelangelo's body was brought back from Rome in 1574 and buried in Santa Croce following a magnificent memorial service in San Lorenzo. His tomb is immediately on the right of the church as you enter. Michelangelo is said to have chosen this spot personally. The reason? On the Day of Judgment, when the graves of the dead fly open, the first thing he would see would be Brunelleschi's dome on the Duomo.

Santa Croce's 19th-century facade

MERCATO CENTRALE
Be sure to visit this market near San Lorenzo, the largest covered food hall in Europe (built in 1874). It is a fantastic medley of fruit, vegetable, meat, and fish stalls, plus all kinds of bars and specialty food shops (tripe, pasta, olive oil, etc). It is open Mon–Sat 7–2 (mid-Sep–mid-Jun, Sat 4–8 PM). The streets around it are crammed with stalls selling cheap bags, belts, shoes, and clothes.

▶▶ **Orsanmichele**   *133B3*

Via dei Calzaiuoli
Open: Mon–Fri 9–12, 4–6, Sat–Sun 9–1, 4–6. Admission free
Once a granary, Orsanmichele became a trade hall for the city's guilds and later a place of worship. Each guild commissioned a sculpture for the church's exterior, from artists such as Ghiberti, Verrocchio, and Donatello. Inside is an ornate tabernacle by Andrea Orcagna (1355–1359).

▶▶▶ **Santa Croce**   *133A4*

Piazza Santa Croce
Open: summer, Mon–Sat 9:30–5:30; winter, 8–12:30, 3–5:30; Sun year round 3–5:30. Admission free
Florence's most famous church is renowned for its frescoes and the tombs of some of the city's most illustrious

personalities. The key frescoes are two cycles by Giotto, painted in the Peruzzi and Bardi chapels right of the altar. One has scenes from the life of St. Francis, the other from the lives of St. John and John the Baptist. Painted in the early 14th century, their lifelike portrayal is a radical departure from the Byzantine style of the day. The frescoes of the Virgin nearby, also 14th-century, are by Taddeo Gaddi and son. Among the church's 270 tombs are shrines to Machiavelli, Michelangelo, Galileo, and Rossini.

Donatello has two exceptional works in the church, a relief of the Annunciation and a wooden Crucifixion. If you revel in Renaissance architecture, Brunelleschi's Cappella dei Pazzi chapel is a masterpiece of the genre.

▶▶▶ **San Lorenzo**   *132C2*

Piazza San Lorenzo
Open: daily 7–12, 3:30–6:30. Admission free
Founded in the 4th century as the city's first cathedral, San Lorenzo later became the parish church of the Medici.

Most people come here for the **Cappelle Medicée**, the family's mausoleum (entered via a separate entrance behind the church). It contains four tombs, two of them sculpted by Michelangelo: one for Lorenzo (grandson of Lorenzo the Magnificent), carved with reliefs representing *Dawn and Dusk*, the other for Lorenzo the Magnificent's youngest son Giuliano, decorated with figures representing *Night and Day*. Michelangelo also designed the Biblioteca Laurenziana, an extraordinary Medici library (in the cloister off the main church).

▶▶▶ Santa Maria del Carmine   *132A1*
Piazza del Carmine
Open: Mon, Wed–Sat 10–5, Sun 1–5. Admission: moderate
This church contains Masaccio's famous Brancacci fresco cycle, one of the great Renaissance masterpieces. Masolino da Panicale started the cycle in 1425, and was joined by Masaccio (then aged 22), first as an assistant, later—when his genius became apparent—as an equal. The paintings were a turning point in Renaissance art, demonstrating innovative use of perspective, drama, naturalism, light, and space. They were completed by Filippino Lippi 60 years after Masaccio's untimely death (at the age of 25).

▶▶▶ Santa Maria Novella   *132C1*
Piazza Santa Maria Novella
Open: Mon–Fri 7–12, 3:30–6, Sat 7–12, 3:30–5, Sun 3:30–5. Admission free
Santa Maria Novella's gloomy interior hides several of Florence's foremost frescoes, most notably Masaccio's 1428 *Trinity*, one of the first Renaissance paintings to master the principles of perspective. Crowds gathered at its inauguration, unable to believe a painting could create a "recession" in a solid wall. The Cappella Strozzi is lavishly frescoed by Filippino Lippi, and the apse contains frescoes by Domenico Ghirlandaio. Be sure to see the richly decorated **cloisters▶▶**, the Chiostro Verde, with frescoes by Paolo Uccello and the Cappella degli Spagnuoli.

▶▶▶ San Miniato al Monte   *133A4*
Open: summer, daily 8–12, 2–7; winter, daily 8–12, 2:30–6. Admission free
This fine Romanesque church perches above **Piazzale Michelangelo▶▶**—a stunning vantage point that offers some of the city's most memorable panoramas. If you do not relish the walk up the hill, take the regular No. 13 bus from the station or Piazza del Duomo. The beautiful multicolored facade dates from the 11th century, its pediment crowned by an eagle, a symbol of the guild entrusted with the church's well-being. The interior is distinguished by the unusual raised choir and large crypt, by an old pulpit and fragments of inlaid pavement (1207), and by the walls' 15th-century frescoes.

SAN MINIATO
San Miniato (St. Minias) belonged to a Christian community that settled in Florence in the 3rd century. After his martyrdom (he was beheaded), his corpse is said to have carried his severed head across the Arno to the site of the present church.

139

Stained glass in Santa Maria Novella

Florence

Italy's most famous gallery, the Uffizi. Most of its contents were left to the city by the Medici family

PALAZZO DEL BARGELLO
The building housing the Bargello's collection was once home to the *Podestà*, the city's chief magistrate, its courtyard the site of numerous executions. It was the Florentine custom to paint the condemned prisoners, artists as eminent as Botticelli undertook the commissions, whose portraits were hung on the palace's exterior walls. The building took its present name in the 16th century, when the chief of police, the *Bargello*, took up residence.

Art galleries

▶▶▶ **Bargello, Museo Nazionale del**   *133B3*
Via del Proconsolo 4
Open: Tue–Sun 8:15–1:50, plus 1st, 3rd, and 5th Mon of month. Admission: moderate
Italy's preeminent collection of Renaissance sculpture opens with four Michelangelo masterpieces, including *Apollo*, before moving on to Cellini and Giambologna. Second-floor highlights include works by Donatello, and reliefs by Brunelleschi and Ghiberti.

DAVID'S DEFORMITIES
Michelangelo's *David* was originally destined to reside in front of the Duomo. It was intended as a piece of public sculpture, not a gallery exhibit, which explains its deliberate deformities—the huge head, overlong arms, and overlarge hands—all of which serve to increase its monumental effect. Started when the artist was 26, it took three years to complete, and when finished was the largest statue sculpted since Roman times.

▶▶▶ **Galleria dell'Accademia**   *133D3*
Via Ricasoli 60
Open: Tue–Sun 8:15–6:50. Admission: expensive
Most visitors come here for one thing—Michelangelo's *David*, the most famous nude in art history. The gallery has six other Michelangelo figures—a *Pietà*, an unfinished *St. Matthew*, and *Four Slaves* "imprisoned" in stone.

▶▶▶ **Galleria degli Uffizi**   *133A3*
Piazzale degli Uffizi
Open: Tue–Sun 8:15–6:50. Admission: expensive
Some of the best-known Renaissance paintings are here. Altarpieces by Cimabue, Duccio, and Giotto open proceedings, followed by six rooms of Sienese and Gothic art. Then come the familiar names: Room VII (Fra Angelico, Paolo Uccello, and Piero della Francesca); VIII-IX (Pollaiuolo and Filippo Lippi); and X-XIV (Botticelli). Later rooms include Caravaggio, Raphael, Michelangelo, and da Vinci.

Museums and palaces

▶▶ Casa Buonarroti (Michelangelo Museum)   *133B4*

Via Ghibellina 70
Open: Mon, Wed–Sun 9:30–2. Admission: expensive
Michelangelo never lived in this house, which belonged to his nephew, and its jumble of memorabilia includes only two accredited original works: the *Madonna della Scala*, his earliest known sculpture (executed when he was 16), and the *Battle of the Centaurs*, carved soon after. He is also credited with a *Crucifix*, discovered in Santo Spirito in 1963.

▶▶ Museo dell'Antica Casa Fiorentina   *133B2*

Via Porta Rossa 13. Closed for long-term restoration
The museum occupies the Palazzo Davanzati, part of which has been furnished and decorated to suggest the appearance of a 14th-century Florentine house. Its rooms range from a typical kitchen to a frescoed bedchamber, all filled with period detail, including art, furniture, tapestries, and domestic objects from the 14th to 18th centuries.

▶ Museo Archeologico   *133C4*

Via della Colonna 36
Open: Mon 2–7, Tue, Thu 8:30–7, Wed, Fri–Sun 8:30–2.
Admission: moderate
The Archeological Museum's collection embraces Greek, Roman, and Egyptian objects, but is of most interest for its Etruscan exhibits. It suffered terribly in the 1966 flood, and restoration work means many treasures are not on show.

MARKETS
Two of Florence's markets lie close to the Casa Buonarroti: Piazza dei Ciompi's Mercato delle Pulci, the city's flea market, and the Mercato di Sant'Ambrogio, a rumbustious food market missed by most tourists.

STROLL—GIARDINO DEI SEMPLICI
Close to San Marco and the Archeological Museum is the Giardino dei Semplici, created by Cosimo I as a medicinal and botanical garden in 1545. A peaceful spot for a stroll, it retains its original layout, with medicinal herbs, Tuscan plants, flowers, and shady avenues. The entrance is at Via La Pira 4.
Open Mon–Sat 9–1.
Admission free.

▶▶▶ Museo dell'Opera del Duomo   *133C3*

Piazza del Duomo 9
Open: Mon–Sat 9:30–6:30, Sun 8:30–2. Admission: expensive
Literally meaning "the work of the Duomo," the Opera del Duomo's sculpture collection is drawn from works removed from the Duomo, Campanile, and Baptistery. On the ground floor are reliefs from the cathedral's first facade (the present facade is 19th-century). Upstairs (after passing a *Pietà* by Michelangelo) are two sculptures by Donatello, the *Prophet Habakkuk* and *Mary Magdalene*, and two *cantorie* (choir lofts), by Donatello and Luca della Robbia. In the last room stand several of Ghiberti's original bronze panels from the Baptistery doors.

Sculpture in the Museo dell'Opera del Duomo

MUSEO STIBBERT

One of the city's more off-beat museums lies a half mile north of San Marco at Via Stibbert 26. Its 64 rambling rooms contain a 50,000-piece private collection, ranging from snuffboxes to paintings, but best known for one of the world's greatest assemblages of armor and militaria. *Closed* Thu. *Admission: moderate*.

HENRY JAMES ON FRA ANGELICO:

"He apparently never received an...impression of evil; and his conception of human life was a perpetual sense of sacredly loving and being loved..."

FILIPPO LIPPI

Filippo Lippi (1406–1469) was a notorious womanizer—despite being a monk. Vasari said he was "so lustful that he would give anything to enjoy a woman he wanted...and if he couldn't buy what he wanted then he would cool his passion by painting her portrait." On one occasion, Cosimo de' Medici—despairing of a commission ever being completed—locked him in the studio of the Palazzo Medici, only for Lippi to escape down a rope of knotted sheets.

LOGGIA DELLA SIGNORIA

Many of the statues outside the Palazzo Vecchio are copies—not those in the nearby Loggia della Signoria, however, an open loggia that contains two great originals: Benvenuto Cellini's bronze *Perseus* and Giambologna's *Rape of the Sabine Women*.

Part of the grounds behind the Pitti Palace, home to members of the Medici family

▶▶▶ **Museo di San Marco (Fra Angelico Museum)**   *133D3*

Piazza San Marco
Open: Tue–Fri 8:15–1:50, plus 1st, 3rd, 5th Mon and 2nd and 4th Sun of the month, Sat 8:15–6:50. Admission: expensive
Cosimo de' Medici rebuilt the monastery of San Marco for the Dominicans in 1437. During the work, Fra Angelico—himself a Dominican monk here from 1436 to 1447—frescoed much of the building, creating the paintings as a hymn to God. The peaceful ex-monastery is now a veritable memorial to this most sublime of Renaissance painters. The Ospizio dei Pellegrini (Pilgrims' Hospice) near the entrance contains around 20 works, mostly collected from churches around Florence. The Sala Capitolare (Chapterhouse) across the cloister contains a powerful *Crucifixion*, but Fra Angelico's single greatest work, the *Annunciation*, is on the stairs leading to the monks' dormitory cells, all 44 of which contain Biblical vignettes frescoed by the artist and his assistants.

▶ **Museo di Storia della Scienza (History of Science Museum)**   *133A3*

Piazza dei Giudici 1
Closed: all day Sun, Thu; Tue, Sat PM. Admission: expensive
This fascinating little museum explores the technological side of the Renaissance and its links between art and science. It includes antique clocks, a reconstructed alchemical laboratory, surgical and anatomical models, and material connected with Galileo.

▶▶ **Palazzo Medici-Riccardi (Medici Palace)**   *133C3*

Via Cavour 1
Open: Mon, Tue, Thu–Sun 9–7. Admission: moderate
This vast Renaissance palace was designed for Cosimo il Vecchio in 1444 and enlarged two centuries later by the Riccardi family. Two windows in the ground floor arches are attributed to Michelangelo, and copied in numerous *palazzi* around the city. The only part of the Medici wing to survive is the chapel, which contains frescoes of *The Journey of the Magi* by Benozzo Gozzoli, a pupil of Fra Angelico (its figures are portraits of members of the

Medici family). The second floor has a painting by Filippo Lippi, for whom Cosimo established a workshop here.

▶▶ Palazzo Pitti 132A2

Piazza de' Pitti
Closed: Mon. Combined and individual tickets available
The Pitti family commissioned this colossal palace around 1460 to outdo the Medici—only for the Medici to buy them out in 1541. It now houses six separate museums. Of these the Galleria Palatina is the most important. Its highlights include 11 Titians and 14 Raphaels, a selection of works by Andrea del Sarto, Perugino, Caravaggio, Velásquez, Rubens, and Van Dyck, plus ceilings by Pietro da Cortone.

▶▶ Palazzo Vecchio 133B3

Piazza della Signoria
Open: daily. Admission: expensive
What this palace lacks in grace it makes up for in grandeur. Its imposing bulk and campanile loom over Florence's main piazza. Started in 1299, it was built to house the *signoria*, the ruling council, whose members

MUSEO DI ZOOLOGIA
This museum (also known as *La Specola*) is a stone's throw from the Palazzo Pitti (at Via Romana 17). Most visitors come for the *Cere Anatomiche* or Anatomical Waxworks (*Open* Tue and Sat 9–noon. *Admission: moderate*). It contains over 600 models made between 1775 and 1814, ranging from entire corpses to arms, legs, and organs, each minutely dyed and detailed to reveal nerves, muscles, and blood vessels. The most famous room shows four wonderfully graphic tableaux of Florence during the plague.

143

were selected from Florence's seven major guilds. Its public apartments are worth a look, particularly the *Salone dei Cinquecento*, full of statues and frescoes by Vasari. Off the *Salone* lies the *Studiolo*, a tiny masterpiece of Mannerist decoration. The *Sala dei Gigli* features a statue of *Judith and Holofernes* by Donatello and frescoes by Ghirlandaio.

▶ Ponte Vecchio 132A2

This bridge and its picturesque huddle of overhanging shops is one of the city's most familiar landmarks. It was built in 1345, and its shops once included butchers, grocers, and blacksmiths, all of whom were removed in 1593 on the orders of the Medici Ferdinand I. The bridge had a private corridor containing artists' self-portraits between the Medici offices in the Uffizi (*ufficio*—office) and the Palazzo Pitti. Ferdinand objected to slabs of meat as not fitting for the ducal passage. Since then the bridge has been the preserve of jewelers and goldsmiths.

Top: Ponte Vecchio
Above: buildings on the 14th-century bridge

Florence's occasionally gloomy streets are not as appealing to wander through as those of some other cities, but almost any itinerary takes you to churches, palaces, art galleries, and museums of immense individual interest.

STROLL—GIARDINO DI BOBOLI

The Boboli gardens behind the Palazzo Pitti have innumerable peaceful corners for quiet strolls or leisurely picnics. Above the gardens looms the Forte di Belvedere, from where there are unforgettable panoramas of the city. Access to the Belvedere is possible from the Costa San Giorgio, a lane behind Santa Felicità.

144

A dramatic corner of Santa Maria Novella

Piazza del Duomo A wander around Piazza del Duomo and the adjacent Piazza San Giovanni introduces you to three of the city's landmarks—the Duomo, Battistero, and Campanile. Stroll along the cathedral's southern exterior and you come to the Museo dell'Opera del Duomo.

Piazza della Signoria to Santa Croce From Piazza del Duomo follow Via dei Calzaiuoli, Florence's main street. Stop off at Orsanmichele, and in Piazza della Signoria, the city's main square. The piazza contains the Palazzo Vecchio and Loggia della Signoria (and the Uffizi is nearby). Heading east you can then take in the Bargello and some of the most attractive streets that lead to the church of Santa Croce.

Santa Maria Novella to the Museo di San Marco Start at the church of Santa Maria Novella. Cross Piazza dell'Unità Italiana to its east and take Via del Melarancio to San Lorenzo and the Cappelle Medicée. See the Palazzo Medici-Riccardi before cutting up to look around the Mercato Centrale, Florence's busy covered market. Then head north to see Sant'Apollonia and Andrea del Castagno's important but surprisingly little known fresco of *The Last Supper*. The Galleria dell'Accademia and Museo di San Marco lie a short distance east.

If you have time, this walk can also encompass a trio of more minor sights around Piazza della Santissima Annunziata: the Museo Archeologico, Santissima Annunziata, and the Spedale degli Innocenti.

Oltrarno This walk takes in some of the city's quieter reaches south of the River Arno. Start either at the Museo di Storia della Scienza or the Ponte Vecchio. Pop into the church of Santa Felicità to see one of Florence's greatest Mannerist masterpieces, Pontormo's *Deposition*, and then walk west to see Santo Spirito and Santa Maria del Carmine. Finish at the Palazzo Pitti and Giardino di Boboli (see panel).

Transportation and shopping

Getting around Walking is the most practical way to see Florence—most of the sights are close together. Orange A.T.A.F. **buses** can be used to cover larger distances or to visit outlying spots like San Miniato al Monte. Most services stop in Piazza del Duomo (see panel). There are four basic ticket types: one valid for any number of trips in one hour; one valid for three hours; a 24-hour pass; and a *multiplo* of four one-hour tickets. They must be bought before boarding from *tabacchi* or automatic machines around the city.

If you are **driving**, the **zona a traffico limitato** (Z.T.L.)—the city traffic restrictions—prevent you taking your car into the center between specific periods throughout the day. You can enter to unload luggage at hotels but must then leave and park elsewhere. The main parking lots are Fortezza da Basso (which is behind the train station), Piazza Beccaria, Piazza Porta Romano, Piazza Liberta, and Lungarno della Zecca Vecchia. All of these become busy and all are pay parking lots.

Shopping Florence is an excellent shopping center, and is particularly known for its **leather goods**. The most exclusive shops, including the big-name designer boutiques, are concentrated on Via de' Tornabuoni and its two smaller tributaries, Via Strozzi and Via della Vigna Nuova (**Gucci** among them, which was founded in Florence). Borgo Ognissanti is also crammed with top-quality shops. Visit **Cellerini**, Via del Sole 37r, for a huge selection of purses. For slightly cheaper clothes and leatherware visit the market stalls around San Lorenzo or **Beltrami** for shoes, clothes, and accessories (branches around the city).

Jewelry is also of a high standard, with many of the best shops on and around the Ponte Vecchio (though prices are high—and beware the inevitable fakes sold by some of the street traders). For **antiques** visit Via Maggio, Borgo Ognissanti, or the riverside streets such as Lungarno Corsini. Specialty **food** shops can be found around the Mercato Centrale. For one of the best delicatessens in the city pay a visit to **Pane & Co.**, Piazza di San Firenze 5r, a gastronomic heaven.

USEFUL BUS ROUTES
No. 7 Station–Duomo–Fiesole;
No. 10 Station–Duomo–Museo di San Marco;
No. 13 Station–Duomo–Piazzale Michelangelo–San Miniato;
No. 15 San Marco–Via del Proconsolo–Ponte alle Grazie–Palazzo Pitti–Piazza Santo Spirito–Piazza del Carmine–Fortezza da Basso.
Maps and timetables are available from the A.T.A.F. office at Piazza del Duomo 57r.

BICYCLE RENTAL
Bicycles can be rented from several points in the city. Try *Alinari*, Via Guelfa 85r (tel: 055 280 500) or *Florence by Bike* Via San Zanobi (tel: 055 488 992).

145

FARMACIA S. M. NOVELLA
Be sure to visit this shop (Via della Scala 16), an original monastic chemist almost unchanged since the 16th century. It is as famous for its furniture and décor as for its products, which include soaps, face creams, medieval cures, and herbal remedies.

Quality does not come cheap in Florence

MARBLED PAPER
Florence is one of the few places where you can find marbled paper, a craft brought to Venice from the Orient in the 12th century. The oldest outlet (1856) and the place to buy is **Giannini**, Piazza Pitti 37r.

DEPARTMENT STORES
Upscale **Coin** is at Via dei Calzaiuoli; and mid-range **Rinascente**, Piazza della Repubblica 1.

HOTEL AGENCIES

In addition to the ITA agency you might try **Florence Promhotels**, Viale A. Volta 72 (tel: 055 570 481); **Family Hotels**, Via Faenza 77 (tel: 055 292 864); and **COOPAL**, Via il Prato (tel: 055 292 192).

PICNICS

Picnics cut costs and make pleasant outings in their own right. Buy food from *alimentari* or markets like the Mercato Centrale, Sant'Ambrogio (in Piazza Ghiberti near Santa Croce), or Piazza Santo Spirito. Then retire to the Semplici or Boboli gardens, or squares like Santissima Annunziata, Santa Croce or Santa Maria Novella.

The terra-cotta pantiles of a Florentine roofscape

Accommodations

Florence is undeniably one of Europe's most popular tourist destinations, and although it has well over 400 listed hotels, it is a city where peak-season accommodations are at a premium. If you arrive late in the day during July and August, you may find it difficult to secure a room in almost any category of accommodations.

Ideally, of course, you should reserve well in advance, but all is not necessarily lost even if you turn up in the city without a reservation. Florence has several agencies that find rooms at a set price for a small commission (which can usually be deducted from your first night's bill). Vacant rooms may only be available on the outskirts of the city, so make sure that you know where your hotel is and how to get to it. If possible, arrive early in the morning, for most spare room will have gone by mid-afternoon

Informazioni Turistiche Alberghiere (ITA) is the best-known of these agencies (for similar agencies, see the panel on this page). They have two year-round offices: the most useful of these is inside the main train station, *open* daily 9 AM–9 PM (tel: 055 282 893), while the other is in the AGIP service station at Peretola on the A11 highway west of the city (tel: 055 421 1800).

Choosing a hotel Most budget hotels are located near the station, predominantly on Via della Scala, Via Nazionale, and Via Faenza. Some—but not all—are fairly grim, and certain areas are best avoided at night. The district around Ognissanti has the plusher hotels. The quietest spots to stay are in Oltrarno (where there is also more chance of finding a room). The area around the Teatro Comunale is another good base (Corso Italia).

Do not judge a hotel by its exterior, for plain facades on gloomy palazzi often conceal wonderful Renaissance interiors. Atmospheric and charming villa and palace hotels are widespread in the city center. Rooms can vary greatly within a building, so ask to see a selection before parting with any money. Noise is as much a factor as it is in any Italian city.

Food and drink

Florence likes to claim it introduced cooking to the French—when Catherine de' Medici took a group of Florentine chefs to Paris on the occasion of her marriage to the future Henry II of France. The city's cooking is now wholesome and down-to-earth, centered around basic ingredients like olive oil, top-quality meat, and fresh vegetables. Restaurant prices are a little high, as you would expect in a tourist town, but the overall quality is usually reliable and occasionally exceptional. Florentines eat a bit earlier than some other Italians—around 12:30 for lunch, 7:30 for dinner. As a general rule, inexpensive places cluster around the station, the top spots on the main streets, and the quieter *trattorie* in Oltrarno.

Anyone at all interested in Tuscan food should be sure to visit the Mercato Centrale, a superb covered food market on Via dell'Ariento near San Lorenzo.

Specialties Florence's most famous dish is the ubiquitous *bistecca alla Fiorentina*, a thick, heavily seasoned Val di Chiana steak grilled over an open fire. Appetizers are likely to include *crostini* (toasts covered in truffle, olive, or liver paste) or strong hams and salamis (boar sausage is common—*salsiccia di cinghiale*). First-course favorites are thick soups such as *ribollita* (literally "reboiled"), *pappa al pomodoro,* and *panzanella*, all variations on a theme of vegetables, beans, oil, and bread. The city's most traditional dishes are today rather scarce—things like tripe, pumpkin soup, cocks' combs, and kidneys—though they can still be found.

Drinking The best place to sample wine is in a traditional *vinaio*, or wine shop, which—like most bars—often also sells snacks (see panel). Chianti is the obvious local drink, but most Tuscan wines are usually available—Brunello, Vino Nobile, and many others. Outdoor cafés are not as big a feature as in some cities, but they do exist, together with several famous but touristy bars that thrive on their past reputations.

BARS AND CAFÉS
Piazza della Signoria's Rivoire is the city's most elegant café, closely followed by Piazza della Repubblica's grand but more sterile Gilli, Giubbe Rosse, and Paszkowski. Giacosa, Via de' Tornabuoni 83r, is good (and claims to have invented the Negroni cocktail). Manaresi, Via de' Lamberti 16r, claims to serve Florence's best cup of coffee. Caffè Amerini, Via della Vigna Nuova 63r, is a welcoming place for a break.

147

ICE-CREAM
Florence's—some say Italy's—best ice cream is found at Vivoli, Via Isola delle Stinche 7r (between the Bargello and Santa Croce). Follow the crowds.

ENOTECA PINCHIORRI
This is among Europe's finest restaurants, with excellent food and wine. Prices are stratospheric, but for a one-time treat this cannot be beaten (Via Ghibellina 87; tel: 055 242 777).

Taking a break in Piazza della Signoria

Ottone
Ferriere
Taro
Fornova di Taro
Reggio nell'Emilia
Crevalcore
San Giovanni in Persiceto
Móndena
Castelfranco Emilia
Castel Maggiore
San Polo d'Enza
Bardi
Langhirano
EMILIA-
Rubiera
Scandiano
Formigine
Santo Stefano d'Aveto
Bedónia
Parma
Berceto
Casina
Sassuolo
Maranello
Spilambergo
A1
Borgo Val di Taro
Pontremoli
Corniglio
R O M A G N A
Castelnovo ne' Monti
Serramazzoni
Vignola
Casalecchio di Reno
BOLOGNA

E

Chiavari
Lavagna
Varese Ligure
Villa Minozzo
Pavullo nel Frignano
Sasso Marconi
Pianoro
Sestri Levante
A12
Fivizzano
Enza
2121m
Mte Cusna
Pievepélago
2165m
Panaro
Fanano
Vergato
Reno
Monzuno
A1

Riviera di Levante
Cinqueterre
Corfino
San Pellegrino in Alpe
Mte Cimone
Porretta Terme
Castiglione dei Pepoli
Lévanto
Riomaggiore
Garzana
Castelnuovo di Garfagnana
Mte Cimone

La Spézia
Carrara
Leici
Grotta del Vento
Barga
San Marcello Pistoiese
Vérnio
Firenzuolo
Portovénere
Montémarcello
Massa
Serávezza
Bagni di Lucca
Borgo Sa Lorenzo
San Piero a Sieve

D

Forte dei Marmi
Pietrasanta
Collodi
Pescia
Pistoia
Sesto Fiorentino
Fiesole
Camaiore
Viareggio
Massarosa
Maria
Montecatini Terme
Prato
Torre del Lago Puccini
Lucca
A11
Monsummano Terme
Lastra a Signa
FIRENZE
San Giuliano Terme
Vinci
Scandicci
Pisa
A12
Certosa di Pisa
Fucecchio
Empoli
Cascina
Arno
Pontedera
San Miniato
San Casciano in Val di Pesa
Livorno
Collesalvetti
Ponsacco
Castelfiorentino
Certaldo
Greve in Chianti
Péccioli
C
I di Gorgona
Rosignano Marittimo
San Gimignano
Poggibonsi
Castellina in Chianti
Volterra
Colle di Val d'Elsa
Montengioni
Cécina
Cécina
Siena
Pomarance
Colline Metallifere
T O S C A N A
Marina di Bibbona
Castagneto Carducci
San Galgano
Monticiano
San Vincenzo
Campiglia Marittima
Massa Marittima
Roccastrada
I di Capraia
Populónia
Piombino
Follónica
Cinigiano
Ombrone
B
Isloa d'Elba
Portoferráio
Cavo
Canale di Piombino
Punta Ala
Mte Capanne
1089m
Lacona
Porto Azzurro
Castiglione della Pescáia
Grosseto
Fetováia
Marina di Campo
Capoliveri
Scansano
Marina di Alberese
Magliano in Toscana
I Pianosa
Parco Naturale della Maremma
F
Corse
Orbetello
Porto Santo Stefano
Ansedonia
Monte Argentário
Porto Ercole
A
I di Montecristo
I del Giglio
I di Giannutri

0 10 20 30 40 50 km
0 10 20 30 miles

1   2   3

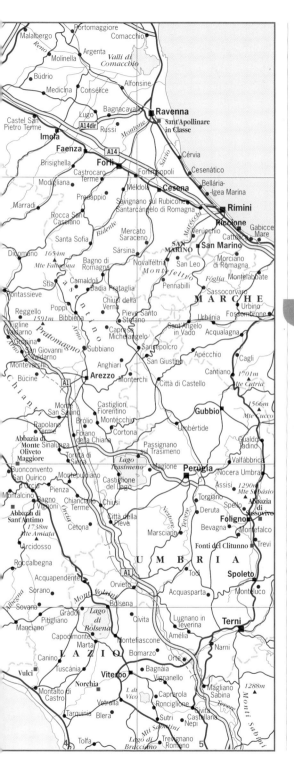

Dawn over a typical Tuscan landscape

TOURIST INFORMATION
Arezzo: Piazza della
Repubblica 28 (tel:
0575 377 678).
Cortona: Via Nazionale 42
(tel: 0575 630 352).
Lucca: Piazza Verdi (tel:
0583 419 689).
Montepulciano: Via
Gracciano Corso 26 (tel:
0578 717 242).
Pienza: Palazzo Civico,
Corso Rossellino 59 (tel:
0578 749 071).
Pisa: Via Carlo Cammo 2
(tel: 050 560 464).
Siena: Piazza del Campo
56 (tel: 0577 280 551).
Volterra: Via Turazza 2
(tel: 0588 86 150).

TUSCANY (TOSCANA) In exploring Florence—with all its treasures—you barely scratch the surface of Tuscany's artistic heritage. Almost every town in Tuscany boasts attractions that could occupy a day's sightseeing. Siena deserves at least that, its calm medieval ambience the perfect foil for tourist-filled Florence's frenetic pace. Little known Lucca is as graceful a town as any in Italy, often overlooked in favor of Pisa, curiously lackluster once you have seen the Leaning Tower and its surrounding ensemble. Lofty Volterra, too, has its medieval moments, but is better known for its fine Etruscan museum. Arezzo might be ignored altogether, except for its great frescoes, while nearby Cortona seduces with its fine and atmospheric streets. Pienza and Montepulciano, too, are both as attractive for their own sakes as for any outstanding art and architecture they offer.

THE VILLAGES The siren call of Tuscany's towns leaves little time for its villages. No trip to the region, though, would be complete without a visit to San Gimignano and its famous towers, still an evocative sight despite thousands of summer visitors. Fewer people find their way to Sovana, well off the beaten track, but well worth a trip for its charm, churches, and Etruscan tombs. Nearby, Sorano and Pitigliano complete a fine trio of villages. South of Siena are more villages (see Drive, page 155), most notably Montalcino—famous heart of the Brunello wine region. In this same area, lost in lovely countryside, stand three beautiful abbeys—Sant'Antimo, San Galgano, and Monte Oliveto Maggiore.

THE LANDSCAPES Chianti encapsulates for many people Tuscany's archetypal landscape. There is more to the region, however, than just vineyards and soft, rolling hills. In the far north, for example, rise the mountains of the Orecchiella and Alpi Apuane, famed for their marble and their scenic splendor. Caught between them is the green valley of the Garfagnana. Along much of the coast stretches the Maremma, an often melancholy but still evocative plain edged with low hills. One corner contains the Monti dell'Uccellina, a glorious pocket of coastal landscapes protected by the Parco Naturale della Maremma. South of Siena lie the *crete*, the region's strangest landscape, bare clay hills checkered with prairies of rippling wheat. In the east are the Casentino, Mugello, and Pratomagno, all Chianti's scenic equals, but all still largely unexplored by foreign visitors.

EATING Italians who should know better dismiss Tuscans as *mangiafagioli*—bean eaters. The region's cuisine may be simple, but it is hearty and varied, based on excellent olive oils and the finest ingredients. Meals often start with *crostini* (small pieces of toast with liver, olive, or tomato pastes), followed by soups like *ribollita* (a thick bread, bean, and vegetable broth). Meat dishes include *lepre* (hare); *arista* (pork loin with garlic and rosemary); *pollo alla diavola* (grilled, marinated chicken); and the famous *bistecca alla Fiorentina* (a steak grilled over charcoal). Meats often appear *alla cacciatore* ("in the way of the hunter"), simple roasts in a rich sauce of tomatoes, garlic, and olives. Wild boar and game birds are also common. For dessert you might find *zuccotto* (sponge cake with cream and chocolate) or *panforte* (a spicy cake of nuts and candied fruit from Siena). Many menus also offer *cantucci*, small almond cookies traditionally served at the end of a meal with Vin Santo (see below).

WINE Chianti needs little introduction, a wine of infinite variety and quality, sometimes sublime, often insipid. Of greater repute is Brunello di Montalcino and its younger cousin, Rosso di Montalcino. Almost as famous is Vino Nobile di Montepulciano, at its best one of Italy's more majestic reds. Less well-known are the excellent Pomino, Carmignano, Cercatoia (from Lucca), and Morellino di Scansano. Whites include the impeccable Villa Antinori Bianco, the rare Torricella, and variable Vernaccia di San Gimignano. The semisweet Vin Santo ("Holy Wine") is a famed dessert wine, though its quality is not always very consistent.

SCENIC DRIVES
SS 146/SS 451 Montepulciano–Pienza–San Quirico–(Montalcino)–Buonconvento–Monte Oliveto Maggiore; SS 222 (*Chiantigiana*) Siena–Castellina in Chianti–Greve–Florence; SS 68 Volterra–(San Gimignano)–Colle di Val d'Elsa; SS 70/SS 208 (Florence)–Pontassieve–Poppi–Camaldoli–Bibbiena–Chiusi della Verna; SS 324 Castelnuovo di Garfagnana–San Pellegrino in Alpe–Pievepelago–San Marcello Pistoiese–Pistoia.

SCENIC RAILWAYS
For a look at the Garfagnana and its mountains, ride the little branch line from Lucca to Aulla (two hours). For a plodding journey around the *crete*, some of the region's most distinctive scenery, take the trains from Siena to Grosseto.

151

Miniature garden in Castellina in Chianti

Part of The Legend of the Holy Cross *by Piero della Francesca in Arezzo's San Francesco church*

152

THE PIERO DELLA FRANCESCA TRAIL
To see more famous Piero della Francesca paintings drive 10 miles east of Arezzo to Monterchi. The old village school hall at Via della Reglia (tel: 0515 900 404. *Closed* Mon. *Admission: inexpensive*) contains his *Madonna del Parto*, the only image of the pregnant Madonna in Italian art. Another 8 miles on, the Museo Civico in Sansepolcro houses the *Resurrection* and the *Madonna della Misericordia*, plus several minor works.

▶▶ **Arezzo**   *149C4*

An otherwise unexceptional provincial town, Arezzo is distinguished by one of Tuscany's most famous fresco cycles—Piero della Francesca's *Legend of the Holy Cross* in the **church of San Francesco**▶▶▶ (*Open* daily 8:30–12, 2:30–6:30. *Admission: moderate*). The frescoes, created between 1452 and 1466, tell the story of the cross used to crucify Christ, and represent one of the largest collections of this artist's work (see panel). Elsewhere the town offers the **Pieve di Santa Maria**▶▶, an attractive Romanesque church with a striking facade and a high altar polyptych by Pietro Lorenzetti, a *Madonna and Child with Saints* (1320). Behind the church rises the **Piazza Grande**▶, a dramatically sloping medieval square, best known for the apse of Santa Maria (see above), which backs onto the square, and the superb carved **doorway**▶▶ (1434) by Bernardo Rossellino on the Palazzetto della Fraternità dei Laici, in the piazza's northwest corner. Above the square sits the **Duomo**▶, which contains another Piero della Francesca fresco, *Mary Magdalen*. Alongside stand some lovely stained glass and the tomb of Guido Tarlati, perhaps designed by Giotto. The **Fortezza Medicea**▶ provides a belvedere for views over the hills of the Casentino.

▶ **Casentino**   *149D4*

The Casentino is one of Tuscany's hidden corners. A large, mountain-ringed basin, it embraces the Arno's upper reaches—an undulating agricultural region—and the huge tracts of one of Italy's wildest primeval forests, the **Foresti Casentinesi**▶▶ (a proposed national park). Most of the little villages have something of interest, and away from the slightly spoiled valley floor the upland roads are a scenic delight. **Poppi**▶ is a picturesque village, centered on a 13th-century castle and fine 12th-century abbey, the Badia di San Fedele. Beautifully situated **La Verna**▶ near Chiusi della Verna has a monastery founded by St. Francis—it was here he received the stigmata. A breezy walk behind it leads to La Penna (4,234 feet) for some fine views. The village of Caprese Michelangelo, birthplace of the great artist whose name it bears, lies 7 miles south.

▶▶ Chianti 148C3

The vineyards and wooded hills of Chianti form the quintessential Tuscan landscape. They also form a veritable "Paradise of Exiles" for hordes of foreign expatriates, an influx that has undoubtedly spoiled certain hill towns (in summer at least). Some are tarnished by light industry. The region's real pleasures, therefore, are to be found in driving the back roads, exploring the small villages and sampling wine at any one of several hundred vineyards open to the public. **Greve in Chianti▶** lies at the heart of Gallo Nero ("Black Cockerel") country; the consortium is responsible for some of the region's better wine. The village holds a large wine fair every September, and is full of wine shops (the best is Piazzetta Santa Croce's Enoteca di Gallo Nero). Elsewhere, one of the most interesting *cantinas* to visit is the Castello di Brolio at **Brolio▶**.

▶▶ Cortona 149C4

Legend claims hilltop Cortona to be older than Troy, though today the town's appearance is medieval, with old churches and ancient corners dotted around its precipitous cobbled streets. The Renaissance church of **Santa Maria del Calcinaio▶▶**, one of the finest in this part of Italy, stands out as you approach. Piazza della Repubblica forms the town center, which is close to the **Museo dell'Accademia Etrusca▶▶** (*Open* Apr–Oct, Tue–Sun 10–7; Nov–Mar, 10–5. *Admission: moderate*), a fine little Etruscan museum, and to the **Museo Diocesano▶▶▶** (*Open* Apr–Sep, Tue–Sun 9:30–1, 3:30–7; Oct–Mar, 9–1, 3–5. *Admission: moderate*), a small but superlative gallery that contains Fra Angelico's *Annunciation* and *Madonna and Child*.

STRADA CHIANTIGIANA
For a representative slice of Chianti scenery follow the *Strada Chiantigiana*, the name given to the SS 222 road from Siena to Florence. Designed as a *Strada del Vino* (Wine Road), it also cuts through some of the region's less spoiled countryside by way of Castellina and Greve in Chianti.

153

WINE
Chianti was the world's first officially designated wine-producing area. In 1716 Cosimo III defined the boundaries within which vineyards could claim the *Chianti* name. Now there are seven separate wine-producing zones and over 7,000 registered vineyards. As a result, Chianti is not one wine, but many, with great variety in taste, type, and quality. Standards have improved recently, with the best wines most often found in the *Chianti Classico* (*Gallo Nero*) and *Chianti Rufina* zones. Better Chiantis mature at between four and seven years. Recent vintage years have been 1985, 1986, and 1990.

The Piazza della Repubblica in the hilltop town of Cortona

Tuscany

154

CAPRAIA
Capraia, largely a nature reserve, is by far the most appealing of the several small islands off Tuscany's coast (it is linked by ferry to Livorno and Portoferraio). There is only one small town, Capraia Isola, busy in summer, sleepy off-season. Footpaths crisscross the mountainous interior and boat trips operate around the rocky coastline.

Portoferraio on Elba

▶▶ Elba, Isola di   148B2

The island of Elba is a world unto itself within Tuscany, hardly a part of the region at all. Its excellent white-sand beaches, limpid waters, and lush interior landscapes attract a flood of visitors (over a million in August alone). **Portoferraio▶▶** is the capital, reached by ferry from Livorno and Piombino on the Tuscan mainland. **Marina di Campo▶** on the south coast has the largest beach, but is also the island's biggest and brashest resort. The beautiful part of the island centers around its highest point, Monte Capanne (3,362 feet), close to two lovely hill towns—Poggio and **Marciana▶▶**—and on the spectacular cliff scenery of the west coast. In the southeast corner, **Capoliveri▶▶** provides access to a string of small popular resorts.

▶ Forte dei Marmi   148D2

Forte dei Marmi was once the main port for exports of marble from the Alpi Apuane. Today it is the most upscale town on the Riviera della Versilia, the string of resorts that line the Tuscan coast north of Pisa. Palm-lined boulevards and a first-rate beach are hardly enough to explain why the town has such an exalted reputation. It is, however, a favored retreat for writers and artists, and a good base for visiting the eastern Alpi Apuane.

▶ Garfagnana   148D2

North of Lucca, the Garfagnana embraces the Serchio valley and the staggering mountain ranges of the Alpi Apuane and the Orecchiella. Its towns are undistinguished, though **Bagni di Lucca▶** preserves something of the romantic beauty that attracted Byron, Browning, and Shelley in the 19th century. **Barga▶▶** has a Romanesque gem in its honey-stoned cathedral. The Grotta del Vento, about 6 miles west of Barga, is Tuscany's most spectacular cave. In the **Orecchiella▶▶** drive the magnificent mountain roads to San Pellegrino in Alpe with its **Museo della Campagna▶▶** (*Closed* Mon, except Jul–Aug. *Admission: moderate*), an outstanding ethnographic museum.

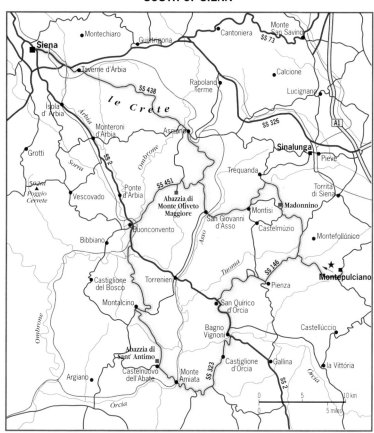

SOUTH OF SIENA

155

Through Tuscany's heart

A glorious drive that takes you through the heart of the Tuscan countryside, visiting vineyards, abbeys, Roman baths, and historic hill towns.

Start in **Montepulciano** (page 158), and after a look around take SS 146 west to **Pienza** (page 158), an essential stop, then drive down to **San Quirico d'Orcia**▶ for its Romanesque church, the Collegiata. Just south, detour to **Bagno Vignoni**▶▶ to see

the sulfurous hot springs in the village square. Continue past the hilltop village of Castiglione d'Orcia to the romantic ruined abbey of **Sant'Antimo**▶▶. After **Montalcino** (page 157), wind down to Buonconvento, home to an excellent art gallery, the **Museo d'Arte Sacra**▶▶. Climb through beautiful countryside to the wonderfully situated and remote **Abbazia di Monte Oliveto Maggiore** (page 157). Continue to Siena (SS 438) or return by country roads to Montepulciano.

Note: you can start from Siena, taking the SS 326 toward Sinalunga, then the SS 438 to Asciano, a gorgeous road through the *crete* (bare, deeply fissured hills that are a feature of the landscape south of Siena).

▶▶▶ **Lucca** 148D2

Lucca is Tuscany's most likable town after Florence and Siena. Its Roman grid of streets is enclosed by tree-lined **walls**▶ ▶—that you should walk for the views—and dotted with palaces, museums, and Romanesque churches.

San Michele in Foro▶▶▶ is the most beautiful of the churches, its muted interior overshadowed by perhaps Italy's most intricate and inspired facade. The **Duomo di San Martino**▶▶▶ is home to more precious works of art

Facade of Lucca's San Michele church

CERTOSA DI PISA
You can visit this fascinating 14th-century Carthusian monastery from either Pisa or Lucca (13 miles). Guided tours show you the frescoed main church, 11 tiny chapels, and the cloister, with its three-room suites of cells and gardens. Monks lived here in solitude and silence except on Sundays, when they were permitted to speak and eat together. Note the message above the gate as you leave, *Egredere sed non omnis*: "Leave, but not entirely," addressed to monks sent on missions to the outside world.

(*Open* daily. *Admission: inexpensive* to Carretto tomb). The main portal has carvings by Nicola Pisano, while the nave is dominated by the Tempietto, a gaudy octagon built to house the *Volto Santo*. This highly venerated icon is supposed to be a true effigy of Christ carved at the Crucifixion (it is probably a 12th-century fake). Off the right aisle lies the 15th-century *tomb of Ilaria del Carretto* by Jacopo della Quercia, which is one of Italy's most exquisite Renaissance masterpieces. To the left of the Duomo in the square stands the Museo della Cattedrale, a fine little collection of art and artifacts.

San Frediano▶ ▶ stands in the town's northern reaches, distinguished outside by a 13th-century mosaic, inside by a beautiful 12th-century font and some of the town's best frescoes, a cycle by Amico Aspertini (16th century). Near by is the **Piazza del Anfiteatro**▶ ▶, a medieval square built in and around the old Roman amphitheater.

The **Pinacoteca Nazionale**▶ (*Closed* Mon, Sun PM. *Admission: moderate*) is as interesting for its extravagantly decorated rococo rooms as for its medieval paintings, but best for art lovers is the **Museo Nazionale Guinigi**▶ (*Closed* Oct–Mar, Mon and Sun PM. *Admission: moderate*) with good paintings, sculptures, furniture, and applied arts. The birthplace of composer Giacomo Puccini, Via di Poggio 30, houses a small museum of memorabilia.

▶▶ Maremma   148A3

The Maremma stretches from Pisa to the border with Lazio, an area of empty, often melancholy countryside that for centuries has been covered in marsh and wild tracts of *maquis*. Drainage of the region was started by the Etruscans (and finished by Mussolini). Vestiges of its ancient landscapes, however, are preserved in the beautiful **Parco Naturale della Maremma▶▶**. The park headquarters are at Alberese, from where a bus takes you into the park (private traffic is banned from the area).

Tuscany's finest beach lies north of the park, the almost completely uncommercialized **Marina di Alberese▶▶**. More developed resorts include **Porto Ercole▶** and **Porto Santo Stefano▶**, upscale spots on Monte Argentario, a mountainous promontory close to the Laguna di Orbetello (some of Italy's best bird-watching territory). To the north of here are **Punta Ala▶**, a chic, purpose-built resort, and **Castiglione della Pescaia▶**, a resort and fishing village.

Inland, **Massa Marittima▶▶** offers a perfect medieval piazza, with one of Tuscany's best small cathedrals. Other far-flung villages worth exploring if you have the time are Sovana (see page 163), Pitigliano, Roccalbegna, and Castagneto Carducci.

▶▶ Montalcino   149B4

A lovely, if unassuming hill town, Montalcino produces one of Italy's most prestigious red wines—Brunello di Montalcino. The often busy *enoteca* in the Rocca (castle) is

VINEYARDS
Two outstanding vineyards can be visited around Montalcino: the Fattoria dei Barbi (4 miles to the southeast), which also has a renowned restaurant attached, and the Villa Banfi (11 miles southwest), the area's largest and most modern producer.

157

one spot to sample it (the ramparts offer the bonus of good views). No visit to the town is complete without a drink in the **Fiaschetteria Italiana**, a wonderful 19th-century café in Piazza del Popolo. Around the town there are several little churches and an excellent **Museo Civico▶▶** (*Closed* Mon. *Admission: moderate*).

▶▶▶ Monte Oliveto Maggiore, Abbazia di 149B4

Open: daily. Admission free
No monastery in Italy can have a more beautiful setting than this, founded in the 14th century by the Olivetans, "White Benedictines," a breakaway group who strove to return to the simple ideals of the Benedictine order. Its main treasure is a 36-panel fresco cycle on the life of St. Benedict, by Il Sodoma and Luca Signorelli.

Abbey of Sant'Antimo, south of Montalcino

SANT'ANTIMO
The 12th-century Benedictine abbey of Sant'Antimo (6 miles south of Montalcino) ranks high in Tuscany's pantheon of Romanesque buildings. Its setting, frescoes, and carvings are delightful; on Sunday mornings a small group of French Cistercians often celebrate Mass with a Gregorian chant.

THE LEANING TOWER
Italy's most famous tower started to lean almost from the day it was built (in 1173). The tilt is now around 16.5 feet from the vertical, and increasing by as much as half an inch a month. Cracks are appearing in its 14,000 tons of marble, one reason why entry to the tower was restricted for many years. The area's sandy subsoil is the main culprit, having proved unsuitable bedding for the tower's foundations. Engineers succeeded in reversing the lean in a project completed in 2001.

*The Leaning
Tower of
Pisa*

▶▶ Montepulciano 149B4

Hilltop Montepulciano is a perfect blend of medieval, Renaissance, and baroque ingredients. A further attraction is Vino Nobile di Montepulciano—the "king of wines." An important Renaissance church, Sangallo's **San Biagio▶▶**, stands just outside the walls. Within them, Piazza Grande's ancient *palazzi* compete for attention with the **Duomo▶▶**, best known for its Michelozzo sculpture and a sublime altarpiece by Taddeo di Bartolo. There is also a small civic museum (closed for restoration; contact tourist office for latest details). Be sure to climb the tower of the Palazzo Comunale for its views, and to explore the delightful back streets.

▶▶ Pienza 149B4

Pienza is a planned Renaissance town, created by Pope Pius II (and named after him) out of Corsignano, the village of his birth. The transformation began under Bernardo Rossellino in 1459, the architect responsible for most of the town's buildings. It was cut short by Pius' death, but not before the consecration of the **cathedral▶▶▶**, a handsome pile with a redoubtable wooden choir and five altarpieces by the leading Sienese artists of the day. More paintings (and papal vestments) are displayed in the **Museo Diocesano▶** (*Closed* Tue. *Admission: moderate*), nearby. The **Palazzo Piccolomini▶▶** (*Closed* Mon. *Admission: moderate*) contains richly appointed papal apartments and offers sweeping views from its courtyard. Churches worth a glance include San Francesco and the **Pieve di Corsignano▶▶**.

▶▶▶ Pisa 148D2

Pisa's **Leaning Tower▶▶▶** needs no introduction. A surprising number of people, however, overlook the other magnificent buildings in Piazza del Duomo, otherwise known as the *Campo dei Miracoli* (Field of Miracles). The tower was intended as a campanile for the **Duomo▶▶▶**, a stunning creation famous for its pulpit (by Giovanni Pisano) and paintings by Cimabue and Ghirlandaio. Giovanni's father, Nicola, sculpted a similarly fine pulpit in the **Baptistery▶▶▶** nearby. In the cemetery, or **Camposanto▶▶**, the Cappella Ammannati frescoes illustrate *The Triumph of Death* (many other paintings were lost as a result of bombing during World War II). The **Museo dell' Opera del Duomo▶▶** contains a mixture of sculpture and paintings. The **Museo delle Sinopie▶** contains sketches for the Camposanto's vanished frescoes. You can buy a single ticket to see Piazza del Duomo's main sights.

▶▶ Pistoia 148D3

Pistoia's quiet provincial demeanor conceals a superb medieval interior. Its heart is the **Piazza del Duomo**▶▶, site of several stern *palazzi*, the Gothic Baptistery, and the 12th-century Duomo. The cathedral boasts possibly the greatest piece of silverwork in Italy, the Dossale di San Jacopo. Started in 1287 and not completed until the late 15th century, this amazing altarpiece weighs over a ton and features 628 carefully sculpted figures. Of the town's many churches, two deserve special attention: **San Giovanni Fuorcivitas**▶▶ and **Sant' Andrea**▶▶, the latter home to a pulpit by Giovanni Pisano, a masterpiece of Italian Gothic sculpture.

▶▶ San Galgano, Abbazia di 148B3

San Galgano may not be Tuscany's best-preserved building—the roof has collapsed—but it is by far its most romantic and atmospheric. Founded in 1218 by the Cistercians, it was for a period Tuscany's leading monastic center. Be sure to walk to the nearby **Chiesetta di San Galgano**▶▶. The effort is rewarded by superb views and fragments of 14th-century fresco.

▶▶▶ San Gimignano 148C3

Few places look as thoroughly medieval as San Gimignano. Its famous crop of towers—a "Renaissance Manhattan"—together with its art-filled churches make it one of the most popular excursions from Florence or Siena. Endure the crowds to climb the Torre Grossa (*Open* Mar–Oct, daily 9:30–7; Nov–Feb, times vary. *Admission: moderate*) in Piazza del Popolo, one of the town's 14 surviving towers (out of an original 72). Also fight your way into the **Collegiata**▶▶▶ (*Closed* Sun AM), beautifully and comprehensively frescoed by three artists, including Taddeo di Bartolo, whose *Last Judgment* must be one of Tuscany's most wonderfully gruesome paintings. Climb to the Rocca (castle) for its views, and to the church of **Sant'Agostino**▶▶ (*Open* daily. *Admission free*) for Benozzo Gozzoli's fresco cycle on the life of St. Augustine.

PISTOLS

Pistoia was one of Italy's most violent medieval towns—Michelangelo called its inhabitants "enemies of heaven"— which makes it only fitting that it should be responsible for the word "pistol." A *pistole* was originally a dagger, but the name came to be used for the small firearms made in the town during the 16th century.

VERNACCIA DI SAN GIMIGNANO

Once one of Tuscany's greatest white wines, Vernaccia vintages are these days pale imitations of their former selves. Pale and flowery wines have largely replaced the aged, golden wine of times past. Good wines are still produced, however, notably by Falchini and Teruzzi & Puthod.

159

San Gimignano, a medieval jewel, is celebrated for its towers and beautiful skyline

The Campo, Siena's magnificent heart

▶▶▶ Siena

148C3

Florence's long-term historic rival is still its main rival for the attentions of visitors. Siena is the medieval city *par excellence*, more intimate and, for many who get to know it, ultimately more appealing than the Tuscan capital, notwithstanding all the latter's artistic bounty.

The Campo Siena's heart is the sloping semicircular **Campo**, Italy's greatest square and scene of the famous Palio (see page 162). The **Palazzo Pubblico**▶▶▶ (*Open* mid-Mar–Oct, daily 10–7; Nov–mid-Mar, daily 10–6:30, until 11 PM Jul–Aug. *Admission: expensive*) is Siena's town hall and home to the Museo Civico. Numerous paintings line its walls, including two frescoes attributed to Simone Martini in the Sala del Mappamondo: a *Maestà* (1315) and the *Portrait of Guidoriccio da Fogliano*, a courtly image of a *condottiere* on horseback. Almost as notable are the frescoes in the next room, the Sala dei Nove: Ambrogio Lorenzetti's *Allegories of Good and Bad Government*, panels that entertainingly illustrate their subject matter.

If you can face the 503 steps, climb the adjacent **Torre del Mangia**▶▶ (*Open* Mar–Oct, daily 10–7, until 11 PM Jul–Aug; Nov–Feb, daily 10–4. *Admission: moderate*) next door for views of the town. Before leaving the square, pay through the nose at least once for a drink at one of its many cafés to enjoy the piazza's activity.

MONTERIGGIONI
This must-see village, 7 miles north of Siena on the SS 2, rivals San Gimignano as the most evocative and complete medieval ensemble in Tuscany. Its fame rests on its perfectly preserved 13th-century walls, a formidable set of fortifications that look out from their unspoiled hilltop site over the surrounding countryside.

Siena's cathedral
Below: dome and campanile; bottom: interior

The Cathedral A short walk away the decorated facade of the **Duomo**▶▶▶ makes an exuberant introduction to a still more impressive interior. Of particular note are the inlaid marble pavement, Nicola Pisano's great pulpit, Donatello's bronze pavement (north transept), and the Piccolomini altar, partly sculpted by Michelangelo. Above all, see the Libreria Piccolomini (off the left aisle), with Pinturicchio's frescoes on the life of Pope Pius II.

The baptistery, below the east end of the cathedral, contains one of Siena's leading Renaissance treasures, a baptismal font by Donatello, Ghiberti, Jacopo della Quercia, and other artists. The **Ospedale di Santa Maria della Scala**▶▶▶ (*Open* mid-Mar–Oct, daily 10–6; Nov–mid-Mar, 10:30–4:30. *Admission: moderate*) has superb church fresco cycles.

Located behind the Duomo, the **Museo dell'Opera del Duomo**▶▶ (*Open* daily. *Admission: moderate*) contains the greatest of all Sienese paintings, a *Maestà* by Duccio (1311). Visit the **Pinacoteca Nazionale**▶▶▶ (*Open* Tue–Sat 8:15–7:15, Sun 8:15–1:15, Mon 8:30–1:30. *Admission: moderate*) for a résumé of the city's art. It is crammed with paintings by Duccio, Martini, Pietro and Ambrogio Lorenzetti, Sassetta, and Bartolo di Fredi.

Siena's Palio is no mere tourist attraction. This horse race, run twice yearly in the Campo, is not only Italy's most spectacular festival, but a symbol of the rivalries that still rage between the town's medieval contrade (districts).

SPECIAL EVENTS
Of the 600 or so Palios run since the 17th century—a second annual race was created in 1639 to be run each 16 August—around 60 have been held to celebrate special events. In 1809, races took place to mark Napoleon's victorious return to Paris; in 1849 to celebrate the opening of the Siena–Empoli railway; in 1945 to mark the end of World War II; in 1947 to record the sixth centennial of St. Catherine's birth; and in 1969 to acknowledge the first lunar landing.

162

Origins The Palio has taken place almost every year since medieval times (though the custom may well go back further). It takes its name from the *pallium*, a banner embroidered with an image of the Virgin and presented to the race's winner. Originally run through the town's streets, the pageant moved location to the Campo during the 16th century.

The *contrade* Siena has 17 *contrade* (districts), each with its own flag and heraldic motif (usually an animal), as well as its own church, museum, and social center. (At one time there were reputedly 59 *contrade*.) Allegiance to the *contrada* of your birth is still absolute—after a conventional baptism, children are "baptized" again in their *contrada* fountain. Each *contrada* holds an annual parade, and the *alfieri*, the famous flag-throwers, can often be seen practicing in the streets.

Only ten *contrade* may take part in the race, so lots are drawn to make the selections. Horses are also drawn by lot, though *contrade* select their own jockeys, many of whom are drawn from the *butteri*, the traditional cowboys of Tuscany's Maremma region. Other representatives of the *contrade* well in evidence are the flag-bearers, drummer, captain, grooms, and pages.

The race The races are run on July 2 and August 16, but the days beforehand are filled with numerous processions and pageantry. Trial races are run, parties held and—most importantly—the horses are blessed in church (dung produced in the church is taken as a good omen). Meanwhile, jockeys can be bribed or ambushed before the race, and alliances are forged and broken between different *contrade*. Huge bets ride on the result. In the race itself, which lasts just 90 seconds, anything goes except interfering with a rider's reins.

Anything goes in the world's most colorful horse race

Despite the obvious dangers, no one—supposedly—has ever been killed, thanks, say the Sienese, to the protection of the Virgin Mary (in whose honor the race is run). Even if you are not in Siena on race day—when the town is hugely crowded—you can watch the race live on television.

▶▶▶ Sovana
149B4

Tiny Sovana is as historically interesting a village as you will find in Italy. For centuries it was controlled by the Aldobrandeschi, a noble clan who held sway over much of the region. The election of a family member, Hildebrand, as Pope Gregory VII in 1073, brought it great wealth (reflected in buildings now out of all proportion to the village's size).

There is just one street and one tiny square, Piazza del Popolo. On its left side stands **Santa Maria**▶▶▶, a glorious Romanesque church, remarkable for its frescoes and 9th-century ciborium (altar canopy). Along a country lane lies the **Duomo**▶▶▶, whose 8th- to 12th-century interior contains fascinating early carvings and a wonderfully intimate crypt. The countryside around the village is scattered with hundreds of **Etruscan tombs**▶▶, notably the Tomba della Sileno, Tomba del Sireno, and **Tomba Ildebranda**▶▶, considered Tuscany's finest single tomb.

▶ Viareggio
148D2

Viareggio—Tuscany's "Biarritz"—is almost Florence-on-the-Sea, with Italian families flocking here in summer from the region's landlocked capital. In the 19th and early 20th centuries, Viareggio was a fashionable resort; vestiges of its heyday are still visible in the town's famous Liberty and art deco buildings. It is still a relatively sedate spot, with the Versilia coast's best facilities and beaches.

▶▶ Volterra   *148C3*

Dark and Etruscan Volterra broods over a strange, empty countryside from its magnificent hilltop position. **Piazza dei Priori**▶▶, with its central square of stage-set medieval perfection, is dominated by the Pisan-style Duomo and baptistery, the former noted for its pulpit and *The Magi*, a magnificent 15th-century fresco by Benozzo Gozzoli.

For more paintings, pay a visit to the **Pinacoteca Comunale**▶, the star of which is Rosso Fiorentino's extraordinary *The Descent from the Cross*, a particularly good example of the Mannerist genre. Fans of Etruscan craftsmanship and culture should also take time to visit the **Museo Etrusco Guarnacci**▶▶, one of Italy's most important archeological museums. Also wander the town's outskirts to see its many Roman remains, the *balze*—deeply eroded cliffs and gullies—and the shady gardens of the **Parco Archeologico**▶

163

Some of Volterra's extensive Roman remains

Rocca San Casciano
Savignano sul Rubicone
Santarcángelo di Romagna
Rímini
Riccione
Mercato Saraceno
Verucchio
Cattólica
Gabicce Mare
Santa Sofia
Sársina
SAN MARINO
San Marino
Pesaro
Bagno di Romagna
Novalféltria
San Leo
Morciano di Romagna
Montelabbate
Marotta
Fano
Camaldoli
Pennabilli
Montefeltro
Sassocorvaro
Úrbino
Fossombrone
Mondolfo
Senigallia
Badia Prataglia
Chiusi della Verna
Úrbania
Foglia
Corinaldo
Metauro
Falconara Marittima
Pieve Santo Stefano
Bibbiena
Sant'Angelo in Vado
Ostra
Ancona
Caprese Michelangelo
Acqualagna
Pérgola
Cesano
Portonovo
Sansepolcro
Apécchio
Cagli
Arcévia
Sirolo
San Giustino
1701m Mte Catria
Jesi
Esino
Mte Cónero
Numana
M A R C H E
Anghiari
Subbiano
Cantiano
Sassoferrato
Ósimo
Porto Recanati
Monterchi
Città di Castello
Filottrano
Recanati
Loreto
Arezzo
1566m Mte Cucco
Gubbio
Fabriano
Cingoli
Castiglion Fiorentino
Brólio
Montécchio
Matélica
San Severino Marche
Macerata
Cortona
Umbértide
Gualdo Tadino
Potenza
Porto Sant'Elpídio
Fóiano della Chiana
Passignano sul Trasimeno
Nocera Umbra
Valfábbrica
Corridónia
Porto San Giorgio
Lago Trasimeno
Magione
Perugia
Tolentino
Fermo
Montepulciano
Castiglione del Lago
Assisi
1290m Mte Subásio
Camerino
Chienti
Falerone
Chianciano Terme
Chiusi
Torgiano
Spello
San Ginésio
Sarnano
Ripatransone
Città della Pieve
Deruta
Bevagna
Foligno
Abbazia di Sassovivo
Monti Sibillini
Amándola
Grottammare
Cétona
Marsciano
Montefalco
Trevi
Visso
San Benedetto del Tronto
Fonti del Clitunno
Nestore
Tévere
Ascoli Piceno
Martinsicuro
U M B R I A
Todi
Spoleto
Triponzo
Piano Grande
Norcia
2476m Mte Vettore
Alba Adriática
Acquasanta Terme
Néreto
Montepulciano
Montecchio
Montericone
Monteluco
Cascia
Giuliánova
Acquapendente
Orvieto
Acquasparta
Nera
Amatrice
Teramo
Monti della Laga
Montefiascone
Bolsena
Civita
Lugnano in Teverina
Terni
Monti Volsini
Lago di Bolsena
Capodimonte
Amélia
Montório al Vomano
Vomano
Atri
Gradoli
Marta
Bomarzo
Narni
A B R U Z Z O
Penne
Tuscánia
Orte
2213m Mte Terminillo
Monteréale
Gran Sasso d'Italia
2914m Corno Grande
Norchia
Viterbo
Bagnáia
Vignanello
Tévere
Antródoco
Campo Imperatore
Vetralla
Capránola
1288m
Rieti
L'Áquila
San Vittorino
Blera
Ronciglione
Civita Castellana
Magliano Sabina
Cittaducale
Áterno
Bomínaco
Torre de' Passeri
Sutri
Nepi
L A Z I O
Fiamignano
Salto
San Clemente a Casáuria

0 10 20 30 40 km
0   10   20 miles

A14

A14

A24

A1

164

UMBRIA Umbria has emerged from Tuscany's shadow, no longer its poorer sister, but a beautiful and varied region in its own right. Its narrow borders harbor a dozen or more hill towns, each crammed with treasures. Its pastoral countryside has earned the title *Il Cuore Verde d'Italia* ("The Green Heart of Italy"). It is also Italy's mystical heart, the birthplace of St. Benedict and St. Francis.

THE HILL TOWNS Umbria's hill towns are the highlight of any visit to central Italy. Pink-stoned Assisi, birthplace of St. Francis, is a medieval jewel (though recent earthquakes have severely damaged the town). Perugia, its more stern neighbor, has a warren of dark medieval streets and countless churches and galleries. Orvieto possesses Italy's finest Gothic cathedral. Spoleto and Gubbio (the "Umbrian Siena") are both delightful medieval towns. Lesser and less-visited places also have their charms, notably Todi, the epitome of an Umbrian hill town; Spello, steep and sleepy; and Montefalco, a lofty belvedere with a fine little art gallery.

THE COUNTRYSIDE Part of Umbria's charm is its soft, gentle countryside. Some is spotted with light industry, but off the main roads the region is a picture of pastoral perfection—all olive groves, oakwoods, vineyards, and silver-hazed hills rolling into the distance.

Lago Trasimeno provides a watery contrast close to Perugia, while in the east a wild counterpoint is provided by the Valnerina and Monti Sibillini. The unspoiled scenery around Norcia—the equal of any in Italy—contains the Piano Grande, one of the country's most poetic landscapes.

LE MARCHE (The Marches) Some people predict that the Marches will follow the tourist-filled track of Tuscany and Umbria. Virtually unknown, it has all the ingredients for a popular tourist destination—scenery, beaches, and historic towns. Its landscapes vary from the mountains of the Apennines to the jumbled hills and valleys that lie closer to the coast.

Umbria and Le Marche

Lush vineyards carpet the slopes up to Assisi

Violin workshop in
Ascoli Piceno

166

SCENIC DRIVES
(*Umbria*): SS 209
Terni–San Pietro in
Valle–Triponzo–Visso;
Visso–Castelluccio–Piano
Grande–Norcia;
Spello–Monte Subasio–
Assisi; SS 79 bis
Orvieto–Todi.
(*Marche*): San Leo–
Carpegna–Pennabilli–
SS 258–Sansepolcro;
SS 78 Ascoli Piceno–
Amandola–Sarnano.

Urbino is unmissable, thanks to its great Ducal Palace, while San Leo and Ascoli Piceno are lesser spots of which any region would be proud. On the coast there are good resorts, notably around Monte Conero and Ancona.

GASTRONOMY Umbria's gastronomic credentials are almost unknown to foreigners. It is one of only two areas in the country where truffles are found in abundance (the other is around Alba in Piedmont). These strange delicacies have been prized since Roman times for their aromatic, not to mention aphrodisiac qualities. They grace the dishes of many restaurants, especially around Norcia and Spoleto. In Norcia, too, you can eat wild boar, together with Italy's most celebrated salamis and the miniature lentils of Castelluccio.

The Marches' best-known specialty is Ascoli Piceno's delicious *olive all'ascolana*—hollowed-out green olives stuffed with ground meat and fried in olive oil. Its other great delicacy is *vincisgrassi*, a rich lasagne filled with prosciutto, cream, and black truffles. Up and down the coast, there are also at least seven different versions of *brodetto* (fish stew). Each town claims the perfect recipe. Ancona's is most famous, perhaps because it contains 13 types of fish. South of Monte Conero the broth is thickened with flour, saffron is used, and slices of bread are toasted. To the north, flour is omitted, vinegar is added, and the bread is eaten untoasted and rubbed with garlic.

WINE Tuscany for a long time outranked Umbria in wine as in much else, but Umbria is now at least the equal, and often the superior, of its neighbor. The wines of Torgiano's Lungarotti, the Rubesco Riserva in particular, are among the most distinguished in Italy. Other Umbrian wines are like the region itself—subtle and understated—none more so than the vintages of Montefalco. Try the rare Sagrantino, Rosso di Montefalco, and Grechetto (the classic Umbrian white), preferably from producers like Adanti, Caprai, and Benincasa. Also look for Antinori's Cervaro della Sala (which has the potential to become one of Italy's great whites). More humble but still acceptable drinks include Orvieto (white) or Colli Altotiberini (red).

▶ **Ancona**   *164C3*
Ancona is a busy and unattractive port, worth a call only to see the Romanesque church of **San Ciriaco**▶▶, the **Pinacoteca**▶ (*Closed* Mon PM and Sun AM. *Admission: moderate*), and **Museo Archeologico**▶▶ (*Open* summer daily; winter Tue–Sun AM. *Admission: moderate*), an archeological collection of medieval paintings and paleolithic and Roman remains.

The town takes its name from the Greek *ankon* (elbow), probably after **Monte Conero**▶▶ some 6 miles to the south. This promontory is the only land formation to disturb the straight coastline that runs hundreds of miles from the Venetian lagoons to the Gargano peninsula. You can explore its rugged interior by walking from several centers, or by driving one of two scenic roads to the churches of Santa Maria di Portonovo and Badia di San Pietro. To see its spectacular cliffs and seascapes, take boat trips from Portonovo, Sirolo, or Numana, three popular and picturesque resorts on the so-called **Riviera del Conero▶**.

▶▶ Ascoli Piceno   *164B3*

After Urbino, Ascoli Piceno is the Marches' most enticing historic town. Much of its center still conforms to the layout of the old Roman colony, built after the defeat of the *Picini*, an early Marchese tribe. At its heart lies **Piazza del Popolo▶▶▶**, whose ensemble of medieval buildings creates one of Italy's loveliest squares. Admire it over coffee from the art deco surroundings of the Bar Meletti, then take a closer look at the Palazzo del Popolo and the church of **San Francesco▶▶**. To the south stands the **Duomo▶**, whose prize exhibit is a ten-paneled altarpiece by Carlo Crivelli, the Venetian artist also well represented in the **Pinacoteca Civica▶▶** (*Open daily. Admission: moderate*) nearby.

The most picturesque part of town (with many medieval watchtowers) lies at the top of Via del Trivio above the Tronto River (walk down Via della Luna for the best views). The area harbors the Gothic church of San Pietro Martire and the appealing SS *Vicenzo ed Anastasio*, an 11th-century church built over a 6th-century crypt.

TOURIST INFORMATION
Ascoli Piceno: Piazza del Popolo 1 (tel: 0736 253 045).
Assisi: Piazza del Comune (tel: 075 812 450 or 812 534).
Gubbio: Piazza Oderisi 6 (tel: 075 922 0790 or 922 0693).
Orvieto: Piazza del Duomo 24 (tel: 0763 341 772 or 341 991).
Perugia: Piazza IV Novembre 3 (tel: 075 572 3327 or 573 6458).
Spoleto: Piazza Libertà 7 (0743 220 311).
Urbino: Piazza Duca Federico 35 (tel: 0722 2613 or 0722 2441).

167

Ascoli Piceno's beautiful Piazza del Popolo

SAN DAMIANO
This church lies in a secluded spot amid olive groves, preserving the humility and mystical atmosphere usually associated with St. Francis but absent in much of the town. It was here that the saint received his calling from God, and where he composed his famous *Canticle to the Sun*. St. Clare also lived here, and the smoke-blackened church, cloister, and refectory are little changed from her day. The church is a pleasant 15-minute walk from Assisi.

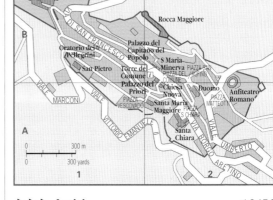

168

ST. FRANCIS'S TOMB
St. Francis was buried in great secrecy to prevent his remains being stolen or desecrated (medieval relics had enormous spiritual and financial value). His tomb was so well hidden that it was only discovered in 1818 after almost two months of excavations.

▶▶▶ **Assisi** _164B2_

A series of earthquakes in late 1997 tragically damaged the lovely medieval town of Assisi. St. Francis's burial place, the beautiful **Basilica di San Francesco**▶▶▶ (*Open* daily. *Admission free*) its premier sight, suffered serious damage to its Upper Church, but, like much else in the town, is now open again after extensive, and loving, restoration.

The walls of the sombre, atmospheric Lower Church are covered in frescoes and decorative motifs including: Simone Martini's impressive frescoes of the life of St. Martin; the ceiling vaults above the high altar (by Giotto and his assistants); and Pietro Lorenzetti's powerful *Deposition* and *Crucifixion*. The walls of the Upper Church are covered by one of Italy's most famous fresco cycles, Giotto's *Life of St. Francis* in 28 huge panels, some of which have also been damaged.

The Basilica di San Francesco contains the tomb of St. Francis and majestic frescoes by Giotto and others

Other sights Elsewhere, see **San Pietro**▶, an expertly restored 11th-century Romanesque church; **Oratorio dei Pellegrini**▶, a lavishly frescoed 15th-century pilgrims' hospice; **Piazza del Comune**▶▶, the town's central square, on the site of an old Roman forum, with the 1st-century Tempio di Minerva; the Basilica di Santa Chiara, St. Clare's burial place; and the **Duomo**▶, dull inside, but fronted by a glorious Romanesque facade. From the Duomo walk up to the Rocca Maggiore (castle) for remarkable views.

Umbria is Italy's mystical heart, the terra dei santi—*land of saints. The region was the birthplace not only of Francis and Benedict, founding fathers of Western monasticism, but also of a multitude of lesser saints including St. Clare, St. Rita, and St. Valentine.*

Light and landscape Few would deny the strange mystical light that illuminates Umbria's gray-hazed hills. Nor would many dispute the soft-edged beauty of the region's countryside—a landscape that epitomizes pastoralism and seems made for peaceful introspection. Could it be that these abstract qualities have helped nurture the region's wealth of saints and mystics?

History Umbria's history and position also have a bearing on its preponderance of saints. One of the Romans' most important consular roads, the *Via Flaminia*, cut through the region, not only linking Rome with the Adriatic, but also providing a conduit for eastern monks and other early Christians fleeing persecution. Umbria's green hills were the first place they came to, many settling in the woods and caves, perfect sanctuaries in which to pursue monastic contemplation.

MONTEFALCO
Nowhere shows Umbria's preponderance of saints better than Montefalco, a little village that produced eight saints. You can see the 3rd-century bones of San Fortunato (abbey of that name) and the mummified bodies of Illuminata and Chiarella (church of Sant'Agostino) and St. Clare (convent of Santa Chiara).

St. Benedict Tiny Romanesque churches all over Umbria mark the graves of the region's holy men and women. Each town had its bishop—who was invariably sanctified—each village its saint (or saints). The caves of three such early hermits can still be seen at Sant'Eutizio, a Benedictine abbey north of Norcia. It was through contact with these men—St. Spes, St. Fiorenzo, and St. Eutizio—that Norcia's St. Benedict (480–547) found his vocation. This apparently minor event was of incalculable importance, for it led ultimately to the creation of the Benedictine Order. (Benedict, incidentally, is the patron saint of Europe.)

St. Francis More than 600 years were to elapse before the birth of Umbria's other great saint, St. Francis (1182–1226). A humble but revolutionary spirit, he took Christianity back to its basic principles—"poverty, chastity, and obedience." Among his many followers was St. Clare, who formed the Poor Clares, the Franciscans' female wing. Like many orders springing from Umbria's soil, it spread throughout Europe and survives to this day. Francis, together with St. Catherine of Siena, is the patron saint of Italy.

St. Francis of Assisi with one of his animal friends

PORTE DELLA MORTE
Gubbio's famous "doors of death" are narrow, bricked-up doors wedged into many of the town's medieval facades. They were supposedly used to carry a coffin out of the house. Having been tainted by death, it is said, they were then sealed. In fact, their purpose was probably defensive, the narrow entrance behind the door being easier to defend than the main doors. The best examples are in Via dei Consoli.

MONTE INGINO
A visit to this hill above Gubbio is a must: walk up the path behind the Duomo or take the cable car from Porta Romana. There are great views and you can see the *ceri*, large wooden "candles" used in the Corsa dei Ceri, a 900-year-old pageant held annually on May 15.

Taking it easy in Gubbio

WINE
Orvieto's fertile volcanic soils partly account for the high reputation of its wine, once so prized that architects working on the Duomo were happy to be paid in it. These days newer and drier Orvietos rank less highly, though the old-style *Orvieto abboccato* is making a comeback through such wines as Decugnano dei Barbi's Pourriture Noble and Bigi's Vigneto Orzalume. Other good producers are Antinori, Dubini, and Barberani.

▶ **Bevagna** *164B2*

Plain-bound Bevagna, ancient *Mevania*, until recently little more than a serene backwater sitting within medieval walls, is today noted principally for its central **Piazza Silvestri▶▶**, one of Italy's most perfect medieval squares. On the *piazza* stand two exquisite Romanesque churches, San Michele and San Silvestro. To one side of the square a monumental staircase leads up to the 13th-century Palazzo dei Consoli.

Near Bevagna are the medieval Foligno, sadly spoiled by World War II bombings, and the 11th-century **Abbazia di Sassovivo▶▶**. This contains Umbria's finest cloister but has been closed since the 1997 earthquake.

▶▶▶ **Gubbio** *164C2*

Umbria has few sights more enchanting than Gubbio's old streets, orange-tiled houses, and mountain-backed setting. Start a tour just below the old town in Piazza di Quaranta Martiri, where the church of **San Francesco▶▶** has an engaging fresco cycle (1510) by Ottaviano Nelli, one of Umbria's earliest important painters. Opposite the church stands the **Loggia dei Tiratori▶**, Italy's best-surviving example of a now rare type of building: here wool was stretched out under its arches to dry evenly.

Up in town, interest centers on the vast **Palazzo dei Consoli▶▶** (*Open* Apr–Sep, daily 10–1, 3–6; Oct–Mar, daily 10–1, 2–5. *Admission: moderate*), a 14th-century palace housing a museum noted for the Eugubine Tablets, seven 2nd- to 1st-century BC bronzes inscribed in Latin and Etruscan. Nearby, the **Duomo▶** and **Palazzo Ducale▶** (*Closed* Mon) are worth a glance. So, too, are the churches of Sant'Agostino and Santa Maria Nuova, decorated with paintings by Nelli.

▶▶ **Montefalco** *164B2*

Known as the *Ringhiera dell'Umbria* (Balcony of Umbria) for its views, Montefalco is a delightful village with a maze of medieval streets. The art gallery in the church of **San Francesco▶▶▶** (*Open* Mar–May, Sep–Oct, daily 10:30–1, 2–6; Jun–Aug, 10:30–1, 3–7; Nov–Feb, 10:30–1, 2:30–5. *Admission: moderate*), is exceptional, built around Benozzo Gozzoli's fresco cycle, *The Life of St. Francis*. Two other churches deserve a look for their paintings—**Sant' Agostino▶** and **Sant'Illuminata▶**.

▶▶ Norcia 164B2

Norcia's stolid mountain- and market-town atmosphere comes as a surprise after the more bucolic charms of Umbria's western hill towns. Although short of sights, it is an agreeable place and, for gourmets, one of the culinary capitals of Italy. Famous for its cheeses and truffles, it also has the reputation for producing the country's best sausages and salami (so widespread is its fame that a butcher's shop elsewhere in Italy is often called *Un Norcino*). Shops around the main square, Piazza San Benedetto, sell all manner of delicacies, from "mules' testicles" to the ubiquitous boars' heads.

The square also contains the town's most notable buildings, namely the Castellina, a papal fortress (1563), and the church of **San Benedetto▶**, reputedly built over the birthplace of St. Benedict. Just off the square is a temple to Umbrian and Norcian cuisine, the wonderful old medieval hotel and restaurant, the **Grotta Azzurra**.

▶▶ Orvieto 164A1

Orvieto's celebrated crag, or *rupa*—the rim of an ancient volcano—attracted the Etruscans (who called it Volsinii), and later the Romans. These days it is perhaps Italy's finest Gothic **Duomo▶▶▶** (*Open* daily. *Admission free*. Frescoes: *closed* Sun AM. *Admission: inexpensive*) that lures the hordes.

The cathedral's awe-inspiring facade alone took over 300 years to complete, employing 33 architects, 152 sculptors, 68 painters, and 90 mosaicists. Started in the 13th century, it was built to celebrate the Miracle of Bolsena (in which the host being used in a Mass at nearby Bolsena dripped blood onto the altarcloth). Inside is Luca Signorelli's *Last Judgment* (1504), one of the great Italian fresco cycles, as well as a wealth of lesser-known paintings by a number of local 14th-century artists.

The rest of the town is less impressive, but it is worth allowing an hour or so to see the sights. These include the frescoed church of **San Giovenale▶▶**; the church of **San Andrea▶** (*Open* daily. *Admission: moderate*); the Museo Faina's Etruscan artifacts; the Etruscan tombs; and the **Pozzo di San Patrizio▶▶** (St. Patrick's Well), an impressively engineered 16th-century well cut into the rock.

Orvieto's great Gothic cathedral glimpsed down a side street

Drive

The heart of Umbria

A short drive that links six hill towns
and climbs over Monte Subasio—wild
uplands with immense views—before
dropping to Assisi.

The direct drive north from **Spoleto**
(page 176) to Trevi on the SS 3 is not
pretty. For a better taste of Umbria's
pastoral countryside, follow the minor
mountain roads to Montefalco via
either Castel Ritaldi or Giano
dell'Umbria (the more scenic route if
you have time).
   Otherwise, start in **Trevi**, (page 177)
which with Todi is perhaps Umbria's
most spectacularly sited hill town.
Then cross the plain to **Montefalco**
(page 170), allowing a good hour for
its churches, views, and art gallery. As
a possible detour, take in **Gualdo
Cattaneo▶**, another perfect little hill
village. Drop down to sleepy Bevagna

(page 170) for its square and
Romanesque churches, and then
circumvent Foligno on your way to
Spello (page 175). Allow an hour or so

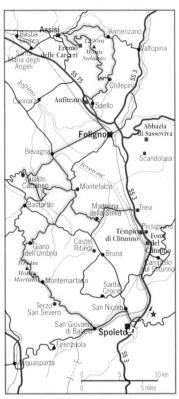

to see Pinturicchio's frescoes and the
town's medieval streets, churches,
and Roman remains.
   North of Spello follow signs to
Collepino▶, an isolated hamlet, and
then cut back to take the well-made
gravel road over Monte Subasio. In
spring the mountain is smothered in
orchids, narcissi, and other wildflowers. Views from the top—the road
reaches 3,960 feet—are exceptional.
As the road drops to **Assisi** (page
168), visit the Eremo delle Carceri,
a beautifully sited Franciscan
monastery. If you do not want to take
the gravel road, use the main SS 3 to
Assisi, or the minor road from
Collepino to Assisi via **Armenzano▶**.

*Trevi, proud on its hilltop above the Vale
of Spoleto*

▶▶ Perugia

Perugia's industrial outskirts are unappealing, but once you are in the old center, Umbria's capital is as attractive as any of the region's hill towns. Much of Perugia is closed to traffic, so leave your car in one of the big parking lots and take the escalators (*scala mobile*) to the center. Alternatively, park at the train station and take a bus to Piazza Italia on Corso Vannucci. Corso Vannucci contains most of the sights, a bustling street, crowned by Piazza IV Novembre, the **Duomo**▶, and **Fontana Maggiore**▶▶▶. The fountain was sculpted by Nicola and Giovanni Pisano. Palazzo dei Priori, a grandiose medieval pile, is home to the **Galleria Nazionale dell'Umbria**▶▶▶ (*Open* daily 8:30–7:30; *closed* 1st Mon of month. *Admission: expensive*), an art gallery documenting the development of Umbrian art. Paintings include canvases by Perugino and Pinturicchio, as well as works by Fra Angelico and Piero della Francesca. More frescoes by Perugino reside in the **Collegio del Cambio**▶▶ (*Open* Mar–Oct, Tue–Sat 9–12:30, 2:30–5:30, Sun 9–12:30; Nov–Feb, Tue–Sat 8–2, Sun 9–12:30. *Admission: moderate*). The **Sala del Collegio della Mercanzia**▶ (*Closed* Mon and Sun PM. *Admission: moderate*), is close by: a 15th-century chamber lined with superb wooden paneling.

Walk down **Via dei Priori**▶ to see the **Oratorio di San Bernardino**▶, adorned with bas-reliefs by Agostino di Duccio. Then visit the Arco di Augusto, an Etrusco-Roman arch, and the outlying churches of Sant'Agostino and **Sant'Angelo**▶. Across the town, **San Domenico**▶ boasts an exceptional Gothic tomb, while its cloisters house the **Museo Archeologico Nazionale dell'Umbria**▶ (*Open* daily. *Admission: inexpensive*). Beyond it lies Perugia's grandest church, the sumptuous **San Pietro**▶▶.

▶ Pesaro

Pesaro's beaches make it a popular tourist destination, but the influx of visitors does little to tarnish the town's style. Behind the white-stucco hotels of the waterfront stands a pleasant old center, its most enticing street the porticoed Corso XI Settembre. Of the sights, the **Museo Civico**▶▶ stands out for Giovanni Bellini's polyptych, *The Coronation of the Virgin*. It also has a ceramics section—Pesaro's majolica once rivaled that of Faenza (see page 84).

Perugia, capital of Umbria, retains its medieval heart

PASTICCERIA SANDRI
Perugia's most atmospheric bar is at Corso Vannucci 32, a turn-of-the-century Viennese-style café with lots of brass, wood paneling, and frescoed ceilings. Try some of the town's renowned Perugina chocolates.

The best place to sample Umbria's wines is the *Enoteca Provinciale*, Via Ulisse Rocchi 16.

ROSSINI
Opera composer Gioacchino Rossini was born in Pesaro in 1792. His home at Via Rossini 34 has a small museum and his works are performed during the town's summer festival.

Weight for weight, truffles are the world's most expensive foodstuff. They have been prized for their earthy and aromatic flavor since Roman times (when they were believed to have been formed by lightning striking the earth). They are subterranean fungi of the class Ascomycetes, *part of the* Tuber *genus.*

SAGRE
You may come across a truffle *sagra* in an Umbrian town or village. This is a festival held to celebrate the truffle harvest (similar festivals take place in honor of many products of the Italian countryside, such as wine, fruit, vegetables—even sausages).

174

What, where, and why Truffles are unable to carry out photosynthesis, and therefore live symbiotically with certain forest plants (using their chlorophyll). Anything from the size of peas to footballs, they thrive best in calcareous soils and amid oak and hazel woods. Numerous other factors influence distribution, however, notably climate and drainage—one of the reasons why commercial production has proved elusively difficult.

Finding truffles Dogs, rather than sows, are now used to hunt truffles (sows are attracted by the truffles' perfume, which closely resembles the musky pheromones of the male pig—unfortunately the sows often become uncontrollably excited when close to the truffle). In order to keep the valuable find secret, a truffle hunter will generally dig only at night. Equipped with torch and trowel, he searches in the spot where his dog sniffed out the truffles earlier in the day.

Types and uses Italy has two key truffle areas—near Alba, in Piedmont, and in Umbria around Norcia and Spoleto. Each has its distinct specialties, for there are at least nine types of edible truffle—though only six are well known. Restaurants usually serve them grated over pasta or omelettes (*frittate*). Shops sell truffle paste or truffles preserved under oil (at a price). The real thing is rare, so beware of substitutes.

Umbrian truffles Umbria's most common truffle is the black winter truffle (*tartufo nero*), gathered from a few inches underground between mid-November and mid-March. The white truffle (the Alba or Acqualagna truffle) is found as much as 20 inches underground (from 1 October to 31 December). The rarer *scorzone*, or summer truffle, occurs near the surface (from May 1 to November 30), rather like the prized *bianchetto* or *marzulo* truffle (November 15 to March 15). Musk and *uncinato* are the other two varieties.

▶▶ Piano Grande   164B2

In the Monti Sibillini, east of Norcia, lies one of the strangest and most magical landscapes in Europe. The Piano Grande is a vast upland plain, 3,960 feet high and covering 16 square miles, surrounded by barren whale-backed mountains. In spring the plain is smothered in poppies, buttercups, and narcissi, as well as rarities like tulips, orchids, and fritillaries. The walking opportunities here are excellent, and the surrounding slopes form an ideal playground for hang gliders.

Hang gliders line up for takeoff on the Piano Grande

175

▶▶ San Leo   164D1

Although less famous than nearby San Marino, San Leo is by far the more attractive destination. Machiavelli thought its **castle**▶▶—hung on a vast cliff—Italy's greatest military fortress, and Dante used it as a model for the landscapes of *Purgatorio*. The little village below has a lovely cobbled square, on which lies a rude 9th-century **Pieve**▶▶, or parish church, and a Romanesque **Duomo**▶.

▶ San Marino   164D1

This independent republic trades ruthlessly on its rather bogus autonomy. According to tradition it was created around AD 300 by a stonemason fleeing religious persecution (with him was Leo, founder of nearby San Leo). This makes it the longest-surviving republic in Europe—its status was acknowledged even by Napoleon. It still has its own mint, postage stamps, and international soccer team. From afar, its tremendous hilltop setting is inviting; close up, the streets are crammed with tourists and souvenir shops. Only the views merit the trip up here.

▶▶ Spello   164B2

Spilling down the lower slopes of Monte Subasio, Spello's pink-stoned medieval houses present an alluring picture from the Vale of Spoleto. Built as a colony on the *Via Flaminia*, the old Roman road between Rome and the Adriatic, it still preserves a modest crop of Roman monuments. The best are two gateways, the Porta Venere and the Porta Consolare, the town's old entrance (across from the Porta Consolare be sure to try the award-winning ice-cream of the *gelateria* across the road). Midway up the street, the church of **Santa Maria Maggiore**▶▶ harbors a fresco cycle by Pinturicchio that ranks with his masterpieces in Rome and Siena's Libreria Piccolomini. Two other little churches are worth a peek: the baroque San Lorenzo and the dark and atmospheric **Sant'Andrea**▶.

EXCURSION FROM SPELLO
Follow signs from Spello's northern gateway to La Baita or Collepino for access to Monte Subasio. The views are magnificent, and there is plenty of opportunity for walking over the mountain's open grassy ridges.

Enchanting Spello

Spoleto's "Festival of the Two Worlds" is Italy's most prestigious international arts festival. It came to the town in 1958 as an Italo-American coventure, a sister festival being held in Charleston, South Carolina. Tickets and information for its performances are available from the tourist office and the festival box office, Piazza del Duomo 9. Be warned, though, that the town is crowded during the festival (late June–July): hotel rooms are at a premium.

Below: frescoes in Todi's cathedral
Bottom: Todi has a dramatic setting

176

▶▶▶ Spoleto 164B2

Spoleto becomes many visitors' favorite Umbrian town. During the 7th century it was the capital of the Duchy of Spoleto, one of the Lombards' three Italian dukedoms. Before that it was a preeminent Roman colony and one of the ancient Umbrians' main citadels (traces of their 6th-century BC walls are still visible).

The largely modern lower town contains a trio of worthwhile churches: **San Gregorio**▶▶; San Ponziano (notable for its crypt and Romanesque facade); and 4th-century **San Salvatore**▶▶▶, one of Italy's oldest churches. In the upper town, picturesque **Piazza del Mercato**▶ is the spot for a cappuccino before taking in its nearby sights—the crypt of **San Ansano**▶ with 6th-century frescoes; the Arco di Druso, a Roman triumphal arch; and **Sant'Eufemia**▶▶, the town's most celebrated Romanesque church, and adjoining **Museo Diocesano**▶▶ (*Closed* Tue. *Admission: moderate*). Unmissable are the **Duomo**▶▶▶, central Italy's loveliest, and the **Ponte delle Torri**▶▶▶, a monumental 14th-century bridge and aqueduct. The Duomo's highlight is Filippo Lippi's apse frescoes. If you cross the *Ponte*, you can walk above Spoleto's breathtaking wooded gorge, or stroll to **San Pietro**▶▶, whose facade's Lombard-Romanesque sculptures are some of Italy's finest.

▶▶ Todi 164B1

Todi is the rising star of Umbrian hill towns, a small market center at heart, but increasingly well known to Italians and foreigners alike. Its position is phenomenal, perched proudly above the Tiber on a great pyramid of a hill. Three sets of concentric walls—Etruscan, Roman, and medieval—center on **Piazza del Popolo**▶▶, a matchless ensemble of medieval palaces crowned by the plain-faced elegance of the Romanesque **Duomo**▶▶. The town's premier church is **San Fortunato**▶▶; its airy interior hidden behind an unprepossessing facade. A stroll through the tranquil public gardens takes you alongside **Santa Maria della Consolazione**▶▶▶, considered by many to be Italy's most perfect Renaissance church.

▶ Trasimeno, Lago (Lake Trasimeno)   *164B1*

Lake Trasimeno

Trasimeno, the largest lake on the Italian peninsula, is only moderately pretty, but is popular with campers, beach addicts, and watersports lovers. **Passignano▶** is the busiest resort. The nicest all-round spot, however, is **Castiglione del Lago▶▶**. Here you can swim off sandy beaches, or take boat trips to **Isola Maggiore▶**, the prettiest of the lake's three islands. North of the lake, roads around the mountains offer quiet drives and marvelous views: **Castel Rigone▶** is the best little village to make for.

▶ Trevi   *164B2*

Trevi's glory is its position, perhaps the most impressive of any Umbrian hill town. The tidy medieval center is a delightful area to wander through, its little alleys known for their intricately patterned cobblestones. The **Duomo▶** retains a Romanesque shell (the interior is baroque). The small **Pinacoteca▶** (*Open* Apr–Jul and Sep, Tue–Sun; Aug daily; Oct–Mar, Fri, Sat, Mon. *Admission: moderate*) has good Umbrian paintings, but for the best art see Perugino's pictures in **San Martino▶** and **Madonna delle Lacrime▶**.

▶▶▶ Urbino   *164C2*

Urbane and majestic, Urbino is one of the least known of Italy's great Renaissance cities. Raphael and Bramante were both born here, and in the 15th century the court of Duke Federico da Montefeltro became one of the most civilized and sophisticated in Europe. Federico's extensive and elegant **Palazzo Ducale▶▶▶** is home to the **Galleria Nazionale delle Marche▶▶▶** (*Open* Mon 8:30-2, Tue–Sun 8:30–7:15. *Admission: moderate*), with two masterpieces by Piero della Francesca: *The Flagellation* and the *Madonna di Senigallia*. Almost as alluring are Raphael's *La Muta*, Uccello's *Miracle of the Host*, and Titian's *Resurrection* and *Last Supper*. Among the rooms, Federico's personal study stands out, renowned for its *intarsia* (inlaid wood).

OLIVE OIL
Although less well known than the oils of Tuscany, Umbria's olive oil is prized by Italians, particularly that of Trevi and the Vale of Spoleto. You need not buy fancy bottles: the widely available *Monini* oils are some of the best.

VALNERINA AND MONTI SIBILLINI

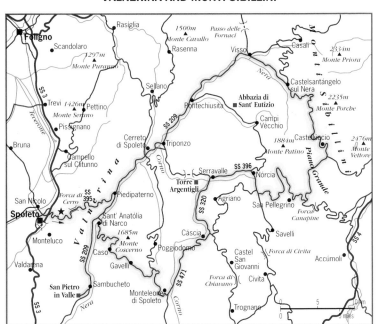

Drive

From Spoleto

A drive through enchanting valleys and along steep mountain roads in Monti Sibillini and across Piano Grande. Start in Spoleto and negotiate the

Historic Spoleto

twisting SS 395 to Piedipaterno (fine views). Follow the Nera river on SS 209 toward its source at the quiet market town of Visso, sometimes through gorges and mountains, elsewhere through farmland and water meadows.

You then climb to the village of **Castelluccio**, one of Italy's highest settlements (4,917 feet), and cross the eerie desolation of the Piano Grande before dropping along a snaking road to **Norcia** (page 171). The gentler terrain from here takes in Cascia, famous as the birthplace of St. Rita. More mountains, pastoral countryside and half-forgotten hill villages follow—Monteleone di Spoleto, Caso, and Gavelli. Few tourists ever see this exceptional countryside and the roads are likely to be deserted.

At **Sant' Anatolia di Narco**, if you have time, detour south before returning to Spoleto. Just after the hamlet of **Sambucheto** watch for the sign to San Pietro in Valle. The 8th-century monastery church is important as one of the few surviving memorials to the Lombards.

Umbria is unusual for central Italy in having several marked trails and detailed maps to make hiking a possibility. There are three main areas: the Monte Cucco park; Gualdo Tadino; and the Monti Sibillini National Park.

Parco Naturale del Monte Cucco This park protects a lovely tract of limestone mountains east of Gubbio. For information visit the Centro Nazionale di Speleologia, Corso Mazzini 9, Costacciaro (on the SS 3, 30 miles north of Foligno). They issue a 1:16,000 map of the 30 marked trails in the area (Kompass sheet No. 664 is also useful). The most popular routes begin in the Val di Ranco: trail 1 climbs to the 5,168-foot summit of Monte Cucco via Pian delle Macinarie: trail 2 is the descent (round trip takes about four hours). Another favorite is the walk along the Valle delle Prigioni from Pascelupo to Pian di Rolla (four-hour round trip).

Gualdo Tadino Gualdo Tadino is on the SS 3, 20 miles north of Foligno. Several marked paths push into the hills east of the town, all marked on the Kompass 1:50,000 map *Assisi-Camerino* (No. 665). The most dramatic climbs the Valle del Fonno gorge, returning via the Passo della Sportella (16 miles: four hours). Another popular route follows the pilgrim trail up Monte Serra Santa (4,696 feet), reached on the extremely well-worn trail No. 122. From the summit you can drop into the Valle del Fonno or follow a path south along the ridges of Monte Nero and Monte Penna. A track drops to Gaifana (16 miles south of Gualdo), or you can continue on the main ridge to Nocera Umbra (via Monte Alago).

Parco Nazionale dei Monti Sibillini
This national park offers some of the best walking in central Italy. You can choose between high mountain routes or easy strolls around the Piano Grande. Numerous trails are marked on the Kompass 1:50,000 map *Monti Sibillini* (No. 666). The most ambitious of these climbs Monte Vettore (8,171 feet) from the road at Forca di Presta. Several paths radiate from Castelluccio: try the pastoral stroll up the Valle di Canatra, or the ridge walk along the western rim of the Piano Grande (via Poggio di Croce and Monte Vetica). On the eastern flanks of the park the classic walks are from the village of Foce to Lago di Pilato, a spectacular hike up a steep valley, and the climb to Monte Sibilla from Montemonaco.

ASSISI
A few paths have been marked from Assisi. The best day's walk follows trail No. 50 from the Porta Cappuccini and Rocca Minore, climbing over Monte Subasio via the Eremo delle Carceri, and dropping down to Spello.

179

The Vale of Spoleto: there are several marked paths (red-and-white marks) around Spoleto

Lazio and Abruzzo

Lazio and Abruzzo

LAZIO AND ABRUZZO Rome cannot help but overshadow Lazio and Abruzzo. There is so much to see in the city you might easily overlook its neighboring regions altogether. But after a few days seeing the capital's sights, it makes sense (if only for a change) to use Rome as a base for day trips into Lazio.

Farther afield, greater relief from Rome's maelstrom awaits in the mountains of the Abruzzo, one of Italy's wildest and least-spoiled regions, and still the largely unexplored haunt of native wolves and the country's last brown bears.

LACKLUSTER LAZIO After the grandeur of Rome, Lazio can seem a trifle anticlimactic. In the north, its melancholy hills are redeemed only by Bolsena and its lake and the nature reserve around Lago di Vico, its generally featureless coastal plains by the Etruscan sites at Cerveteri and Tarquinia. Other historic centers are few and far between in the area, some of the best attractions being provided instead by the villas and gardens, such as Caprarola and the Villa Lante located in the countryside around Viterbo.

▶▶▶ REGION HIGHLIGHTS

Cerveteri *page 186*
Gran Sasso d'Italia
page 188
Ostia Antica *page 190*
Parco Nazionale
d'Abruzzo *page 194*
Tarquinia *page 187*
Tivoli *page 189*

Lake Bolsena, with its islands and Etruscan sites, is one of Lazio's most attractive areas

Take a trip to the Villa d'Este to see its dazzling water gardens

SCENIC DRIVES

(*Lazio*): Viterbo–Lago di Vico–Caprarola–Ronciglione; SS 411 Arsoli–Subiaco–(Filettino)–Campocatino–Fiuggi. (*Abruzzo*): Abruzzo National Park SS 83 Alfedena–Opi–Pescasseroli–Gioia dei Marsi & SS 479 Sulmona–Scanno–Villetta Barrea; SS 5/5bis Sulmona–(Secinaro)–Celno–Rocca di Mezzo–L'Aquila; SS 80/A 24 L'Aquila–Montorio al Vomano–L'Aquila; SS 17bis L'Aquila–Campo Imperatore.

SCENIC RAILWAYS

The main Rome–Pescara line has a picturesque section between Avezzano and Sulmona. The Abruzzo's small branch lines are tempting to ride for their own sake. The short line from Sulmona to L'Aquila, for example (and its continuation to Rieti), runs through good countryside. The best trip of all is from Sulmona to Castel di Sangro, which climbs high into the mountains on the eastern flank of the national park.

St. Benedict's monastery, in the mountains around Subiaco

To the south of the region the countryside is more inspiring, from the tiny Circeo national park with lovely coastal landscapes to the limestone heights of the Ernici and Simbruini mountains (see Subiaco, page 193). Parts of the coast have decent resorts, principally Sperlonga, and if you are feeling more adventurous, the island of Ponza—a great favorite with vacationing Romans—has yet to be fully discovered by most foreign visitors. Few of the region's towns, however, merit a special journey—with the notable exception of those you can see while vacationing in Rome.

EXCURSIONS FROM ROME Most of the excursions you will want to make into the Lazio region are best made as day trips from Rome. Of these the most enticing is Tivoli. Here you can see the famous Villa d'Este, with some of Italy's loveliest gardens, and the ruins of the Villa Adriana (Hadrian's Villa), the largest villa ever built in the Roman Empire. More imperial echoes await in Ostia Antica, Rome's ancient seaport, a collection of ruins as impressive as any in the capital itself. Palestrina, too, has fine old remains, together with a worthwhile museum and tremendous views. Panoramas are also very much a part of Frascati's appeal, the most famous and most easily accessible of the Castelli Romani, a coronet of towns set in the volcanic hills just south of Rome.

All these trips can be made by public transportation, not to be scorned given Rome's traffic problems. The most distant attractions you can see in a day are Cerveteri and Tarquinia's Etruscan tombs (not to mention their museums, and the smaller Etruscan sites at Sutri, Blera, and Norchia). The best of the more remote prospects are the mountains as well as the Benedictine monasteries of Subiaco.

SEASIDE LAZIO Southern Lazio's best beaches are at Sperlonga, Gaeta, Sabaudia, and San Felice Circeo. Rome's coastal resorts (Lido di Ostia, Fregene, and Ladispoli) are not recommended, being largely crowded and polluted. To the north, Santa Severa and Santa Marinella have reasonable beaches and pretty pinewood surroundings. Huge, undeveloped beaches stretch out from the hamlet of Chiarone, where Lazio meets Tuscany. Abruzzo's most pleasant coastal towns are Pineto (13 miles north of Pescara) and Vasto (41 miles south of Pescara).

Sun umbrellas line up on Santa Marinella's popular beach

ABRUZZO Few people venture into the Abruzzo's desolate interior, despite road and rail links that put it within easy reach of Rome. Yet its rewards are immense, particularly if you are in search of wild mountains and villages where life is still harsh and strangers a novelty. Roads lead to the heart of the Abruzzo National Park, which has plenty of well-organized trails and interesting villages, and to the Gran Sasso d'Italia, the highest point on the Italian peninsula. Good paths in both areas allow endless hiking opportunities (see page 194), but there are also plenty of routes into the mountains for drivers. If you are driving, it is rewarding to explore the roads around the Abruzzo's three other great massifs—the Maiella, Monte Velino, and the Monti della Laga (see Scenic Drives panel).

The region is not solely about mountains, however, for as well as any number of remote hill villages, the Abruzzo has a couple of bracing towns that are interesting spots in their own right. Sulmona was the birthplace of Ovid (and where confetti was invented), while L'Aquila contains a neat little museum and several captivating churches.

MOLISE Molise is a tiny region lodged south of the Abruzzo (until 1963 it was part of the old Abruzzi region). Gentler than the Abruzzo, the Matese mountains are still wild and impressive. Towns and villages are less interesting, though Termoli on the coast is a reasonable beach resort, and Isernia has a good archeological museum. Around Isernia there is lovely rolling hill country.

TOURIST INFORMATION
L'Aquila: Piazza Santa Maria Paganicas
(tel: 0862 410 808) and Via XX Settembre 8 (tel: 0862 223 060).
Subiaco: Via Cadorna 59 (tel: 0774 822 013).
Sulmona: Corso Ovidio 208 (tel: 0864 53 276).
Tarquinia: Piazza Cavour 1 (tel: 0766 856 384).
Tivoli: Largo Garibaldi (0774 334 522
Viterbo: Piazza San Carluccio 7 (tel: 0761 304 795).

Early morning in the lively food market in L'Aquila

184

► Alatri   180B3

Alatri's medieval appearance belies its antiquity, for its gateways, Cyclopean walls, and mighty fortified **Acropolis►►** date back to the 6th century BC. The ramparts offer impressive views and the streets are filled with medieval monuments, the most noteworthy being Santa Maria Maggiore, famous for its 14th-century wooden sculpture of the Madonna of Constantinople. While in the area, visit nearby **Anagni►**, another medieval town, renowned for its magnificent Cattedrale.

► L'Aquila   180C3

The Abruzzo's capital was for centuries the second most important town in southern Italy after Naples. Today on first acquaintance it appears dour and depressing. Further exploration reveals a lively mountain town that combines medieval and modern in equal measure. Your first stop should be the castle's **Museo Nazionale d'Abruzzo►►** (*Closed* Mon. *Admission: moderate*), the Abruzzo's foremost museum, a potpourri of exhibits ranging from a stuffed mammoth to displays of sacred art, local pottery, and the cream of the region's paintings.

Close by stands **Santa Maria di Collemaggio►►**, the Abruzzo's premier piece of church architecture, known for its arched portal and pink-and-white marble facade. The church of **San Bernardino►►** contains the tomb of San Bernardino of Siena, who died in the town (the Sienese visit L'Aquila on his feast day, bearing gifts of Tuscan oil).

►► Bolsena, Lago di   180C1

Lake Bolsena is the largest volcanic lake in Italy. One of the best trips locally is the boat ride out to **Bisentina►►**, one of the lake's two islands (the other is Martana—both are probably remnants of the old volcanic crater). Bisentina offers not only views and scenery, but also Etruscan tombs, a Farnese family villa, and five quaint little chapels. Boats run from **Capodimonte►**, an attractive resort that extends into the lake on a castle-tipped promontory. Other towns in the fertile hills around the lake include **Gradoli►**, at the heart of a large wine region, Etruscan **Montefiascone►**, and medieval **Bolsena►**, a relaxed and likeable place that makes the best overall base for excursions around the lake. Civita, 9 miles east of Bolsena, is an eerie and half-deserted ghost town in a lunar landscape.

► Caprarola   180C2

Easily seen in conjunction with Viterbo and Lago di Vico (see page 193), Caprarola is a little village almost entirely given over to the **Palazzo Farnese►►** (*Closed* Mon. *Admission: inexpensive*). One of the high points of 16th-century mannerism, it is a building, said Stendhal, "where architecture married nature." Created as a castle in 1520, it was completed as a Farnese palace in 1559 by Vignola, one of the leading architects of his day. Many rooms are closed to the public and others are missing their period furniture.

Several features, however, still stand out, notably Vignola's famous monumental staircase (the Scala Regia) and the beautifully frescoed Sala del Mappamondo. Outside there is a large park and two gardens—a south-facing summer garden and an east-facing winter terrace.

▶ Castelli Romani   180B2
The 13 villages of the Castelli Romani are descendants of the medieval castles built by the popes and Rome's leading patrician families. They nestle in the Albani hills south of Rome. Although they provide relief from Rome's heat and hassle, many have been spoiled by wanton modern building, but much of the wooded surroundings, and lakes like Albano and Nemi, remain worth seeing; they serve as favorite destinations for Sunday lunch excursions from Rome. **Frascati▶** is the most famous of the villages, thanks to its wine and villas. Castel Gandolfo is well known, mainly as the pope's summer residence. **Rocca di Papa▶**, **Grottaferata▶**, and **Albano Laziale▶**, however, are the most picturesque *castelli*.

▶▶ Circeo, Parco Nazionale del   180A3
The smallest of Italy's national parks, Circeo was created to preserve a portion of the Pontine marshes following Mussolini's 1930s reclamation projects. It is a wonderfully diverse patchwork of lakes, coastal dunes, and forests. Wild boar and fallow deer roam the woods, and the wetland areas are renowned for their resident and migrating species of birds. Walking opportunities are myriad, and you can take boat trips around the lakes and lagoons.

FRASCATI
Frascati's famous and unassuming white wine is the mainstay of simple Italian restaurants the world over. In the Middle Ages, the Albani's foresters built huts of *frascata*, the brushwood that gave Frascati its name and the wine its symbol: the *frasca*, or branch, hung over the doors of taverns when the new vintage was ready.

185

INFORMATION
Parco Nazionale di Circeo's information center is at Via Carlo Alberto 107, Sabaudia (tel: 0773 511 386). It provides a detailed and useful map. Many of the park's gentle marked trails fan out from the center itself. For a more challenging morning's hike climb Circeo's one high spot, Monte Circeo (1,478 feet), a wooded and rocky promontory whose summit affords magnificent views over the park.

Capodimonte on Lake Bolsena. Boat trips on the lake start from here

The Etruscans are one of the most enigmatic and mysterious of ancient civilisations. At their height between 800 and 400 BC they controlled much of central Italy (Etruria) through a 12-strong confederation of cities.

186

DEATH AND LIFE
"Death...to the Etruscans was a pleasant continuance of life, with jewels and wine, and flutes playing for the dance. It was neither an ecstasy of bliss, a heaven, nor a purgatory of torment. It was just a natural continuance of the fullness of life. Everything was in terms of life...the things they did, in their early centuries, are as natural and easy as breathing."
D. H. Lawrence, *Etruscan Places.*

NORCHIA
The ruins of Etruscan *Orcia* lie west of Vetralla, 18 miles east of Tarquinia off the SS 1bis. As well as several monumental tombs, some with great sculpted facades, the village has a medieval castle and 12th-century parish church, San Pietro.

History Where the Etruscans came from is one of history's great conundrums. Most evidence points to a mixture of seafarers and indigenous tribes whose ethnic links were with Asia Minor, and whose trading ties were with Greece. One reason for their shadowy past is depressingly banal—their cities were made almost entirely of wood, so that almost nothing of them remains. The culture's finest memorials are items found in their tombs, and these have left the Etruscans with a reputation for being gloomy and introspective race. In truth, they seem to have been a lively and imaginative people, with highly developed social, cultural, and political systems.

The Etruscan legacy Another reason we know relatively little of the Etruscans is that the Romans deliberately set out to absorb—and then obscure—the culture of their predecessors. Etruscans were probably Rome's earliest settlers (and even provided its earliest kings). Much of their alphabet and language passed into Latin (and thus into other European tongues). The Romans also inherited many of their gods and divinities, rituals and divinations, even their circuses and gladiatorial games. Much of this assimilation had taken place by the 3rd century BC, by which time Rome had defeated most Etruscan cities.

Museums and monuments Grandiose monuments to the Etruscans lie scattered all over ancient *Etruria*, from the stone-cut amphitheater at Sutri to the vivid wallpaintings of Tarquinia. Most of the smaller artifacts have been removed from tombs (*necropoli*), for the Etruscans (like the Egyptians) left the dead with all they would need in the afterlife. Almost every Etruscan site, large or small, has a museum to display them, but their prize exhibits have gone to the Vatican Museums and Rome's Villa Giulia (see page 47). These are the finest Etruscan museums, so try to visit them before exploring the Etruscan sites.

Cerveteri Cerveteri, ancient *Kysry* (Roman *Caere*), was one of the leading Etruscan cities, its pre-eminence based on mineral riches and long-established trading prowess.

No clue to its occupant remains in this empty Etruscan tomb

Over 5,000 tombs lie in the **Necropoli della Banditaccia**, (*Closed* Mon. *Admission: moderate*) laid out as streets and houses to create a literal "city of the dead." Only 50 or so have been excavated (though many have been ransacked over the centuries). Some are curious pillboxes carved from the living rock, others earth-covered tumuli that ripple over the surrounding countryside. Of the 12 show tombs—all near the site's entrance—try to see the *Tomba dei Capitelli* and the *Tomba dei Letti Funebri*. Round off a visit with a trip to the Museo Nazionale Cerite, a modest collection of Etruscan artifacts housed in Cerveteri's 16th-century Castello Orsini.

Tarquinia In its day Tarquinia boasted a population of 100,000 and was probably the Etruscans' cultural and political capital. Now it is a strangely drab and half-derelict town, redeemed only by its museum and tombs, the most famous of any in Italy. The **Museo Nazionale** (*Closed* Mon. *Admission: moderate*) offers a small but excellent collection, its centerpiece, a pair of winged terra-cotta horses, perhaps the most beautiful Etruscan sculpture in existence. Its other exhibits include the inevitable funerary urns, some scintillating jewelry, and several tombs reconstructed to house their wallpaintings under controlled conditions.

The 6,000 original **tombs** (*Closed* Mon. *Admission: moderate*) honeycomb the Monterozzi plateau east of the town. To protect their frescoes only a handful are open to the public at one time (to guided tours). Their Hellenistic-style paintings span around 500 years; the earliest concentrate on mythical and ritualistic scenes, the later on the social (and sexual) context of Etruscan life.

Sutri About 11 miles southeast of Vetralla (on the SS 1bis), Sutri is one of the more rewarding of the lesser Etruscan sites. A picturesque medieval town, it occupies a narrow rocky ridge—the type of site favored by the Etruscans for their cities. Its overgrown amphitheater was carved from the living rock (and seated 6,000 people).

Boxers on an Etruscan vase

In the city of the dead, Cerveteri

Lazio and Abruzzo

Olive terraces backed by the snow-covered Gran Sasso ridge

HIKING
Although it is easy to tour the environs of the Gran Sasso by car, there are numerous straightforward hiking opportunities. For maps and information visit L'Aquila's tourist office at Via XX Settembre 8, or the regional office at Piazza Santa Maria Paganica 5 (tel: 0862 410 808).

ALBERGO CAMPO IMPERATORE
This hotel is famous as the place where Mussolini was imprisoned after the Italian surrender in 1943. He was sprung from the remote eyrie in a daring aerial raid and taken north by the Germans to establish the puppet Salò Republic.

ABBAZIA DI CASAMARI
Take in the Abbey of Casamari as part of a car tour of southern Lazio (it lies just west of Isola del Liri, 25 miles west of Montecassino). Founded by the Benedictines in 1035, rebuilt in 1140, and now fully restored, it is a fine example of French-inspired Cistercian-Gothic architecture. The church (1217) is the three-star highlight, though all the abbey's old components are of interest: these include the cloister, pharmacy, refectory, and chapterhouse. *Open* daily 9–noon, 4–6. *Admission free.*

▶▶ Gran Sasso d'Italia   *180C3*
At 9,610 feet, the Gran Sasso d'Italia (Big Rock of Italy) is the highest point on the Italian peninsula (Etna in Sicily and many Alpine peaks are higher). Thousands of walkers and climbers are attracted to its slopes, drawn by its magnificent snowcapped ridges and the famous **Campo Imperatore▶▶**, a vast, mountain-ringed upland plain.

Access is easiest from L'Aquila. It is only 66 miles on the A24 highway to the turn-off at Assergi and the hamlet of Fonte Cerreto (3,696 feet). Here there are a couple of hotels, a restaurant, and a cable car (*funivia*) that takes you to the **Albergo-Rifugio Campo Imperatore** (7,025 feet), the starting point for most walks. It can also be reached by driving across the Campo Imperatore on the SS 17bis (16 miles from Fonte Cerreto). The easiest of the hikes—no more than a two-hour round trip—is trail No. 10 to Monte della Scindarella (7,336 feet). The classic walk is trail No. 3, which goes close to the summit (Corno Grande).

▶ Montecassino   *181A4*
The huge bulwarks of the abbey of Montecassino (*Open* daily) can be seen from miles around. Its superlative position was perhaps the reason St. Benedict chose it as the headquarters for the Benedictine movement in 529 (though legend said he was guided here by three ravens). For centuries it was one of the most important monasteries in the Christian world, disseminating the Benedictine ideal. It has been rebuilt many times, most notoriously after the entire building—except the crypt—was destroyed by Allied bombing on February 15, 1944. As the Nazis' regional headquarters it was an essential target, yet the abbey's destruction has been a cause for controversy ever since. The old buildings have been faithfully rebuilt, though inevitably the reconstruction is a sterile and soulless affair. The war cemeteries are much visited, and the views—from the middle cloister in particular—are exceptional.

Many visitors to Rome take time out from the sights of the capital to visit Tivoli. The endless cavalcade of tour buses is a small price to pay for the Villa d'Este, Italy's most famous gardens, and the Villa Adriana, the ruins of the Roman Empire's greatest imperial palace.

Villa Adriana (Hadrian's Villa) Tivoli, ancient *Tiber*, was known for its travertine marble—from which much of imperial Rome was built—and as a retirement home for Rome's most prosperous citizens. It had so many villas, wrote Horace, that "the Tibertine soil no longer has ploughland." The greatest, the Villa Adriana (*Open* daily 9 AM–one hour before sunset. *Admission: moderate*), is about 3 miles from the town. Started in AD 125, it was built to Hadrian's own design, his intention being to re-create some of the outstanding buildings he had seen on his travels. Work took ten years, the villa and its gardens extending over a site larger than imperial Rome itself, making it the empire's largest and most costly palace.

To make sense of the ruins, study the model near the entrance, an attempt to reproduce the villa's original appearance. Exploring the lovely site, full of trees and secluded corners, is a pleasure in itself, but make a special point of seeing the Teatro Marittimo, a colonnaded palace built in the middle of an artificial lagoon.

The Villa d'Este The Villa d'Este (*Open* summer, daily 9 AM–one hour before sunset; winter, Tue–Sun 9 AM–one hour before sunset. *Admission: moderate*) started life as a convent, but in 1550 was converted into a country retreat for Cardinal Ippolito d'Este, the son of Lucrezia Borgia and the Duke of Ferrara. The villa now is slightly dilapidated, but its fountains and formal terraces rank as some of the most beautiful in the world.

Their main attractions are the *Viale delle Cento Fontane* (Avenue of a Hundred Fountains), and two outstanding individual fountains: Bernini's *Fontana di Biccierone* and the *Fontana dei Draghi* (Fountain of the Dragons), built for Pope Gregory XIII, whose symbol was a short-tailed dragon. Be sure to find the path leading to the *Rometta*, a model of Rome. Also leave time to visit Tivoli's third and least-known villa, **Villa Gregoriana** (see panel).

VILLA GREGORIANA
The Villa Gregoriana is Tivoli's third and least-known sight, centered on a pair of waterfalls and a deep-cut gorge of lush vegetation. The Grande Cascata, the larger of the falls, was created when the Aniene River was diverted in 1831 by Pope Gregory XVI to protect Tivoli from flooding. The smaller falls, designed by Bernini, are at the narrow head of the gorge. You can walk down a pretty path to the bottom of the 197-foot-deep canyon (currently closed for restoration).

189

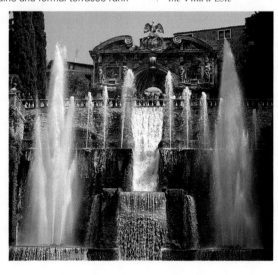

Water is the dominant feature in the gardens of the Villa d'Este

Lazio and Abruzzo

▶▶ Ostia Antica — 180B2

Once ancient Rome's port, Ostia Antica (*Open* daily 9 AM—one hour before sunset. *Admission: moderate*) is now Italy's best-preserved Roman town after Pompeii (its ruins are as good as any in Rome itself). The setting is lovely, with the ruins scattered among vines and wildflowers, the paths shaded by elegant stands of parasol pines.

The colony started life as a fishing village at the mouth (*ostium*) of the Tiber, but grew as the empire expanded, trading a host of commodities with the farthest-flung imperial outposts. In the end, the weight of trade exceeded the port's capacity. Coupled with the accumulation of silt, this led to Ostia's decline and the building of a new port, *Portus Romae* (near present-day Fiumicino).

The sprawling site centers around the Decumanus Maximus, the old main thoroughfare, from which innumerable streets branch off. Each is filled with theaters, temples, workshops, houses, and the famous *horreae*, old warehouses used principally to store grain. Equally interesting are the many *insulae*, old Roman four- and five-story apartment buildings.

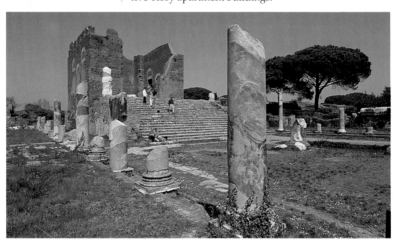

The ruins of Ostia Antica, ancient Rome's most important port

▶ Palestrina — 180B2

Present-day Palestrina is largely medieval in flavor, but it rests over the ruins of *Praeneste*, an important Etruscan site founded in the 7th century BC. The city was famous for the Tempio di Fortuna Primogenia, which was the seat of an ancient cult and important oracle. The temple was enlarged under the Romans in the 4th century BC, the exact scope of the complex only coming to light after bombing during World War II.

The current town is still built on a series of vast terraces, which correspond to the levels of the original temple, fragments of which lie dotted around the streets. Most of the temple treasures have been removed to Rome's Villa Giulia or to Palestrina's own Museo Nazionale Archeologico Prenestino (*Open* daily. *Admission: moderate*). Among the latter's many busts, reliefs, and funerary headstones, the star attraction is the outstanding 1st-century BC *Mosaic of the River Nile*, a detailed narrative describing the story of the river from its source to its delta.

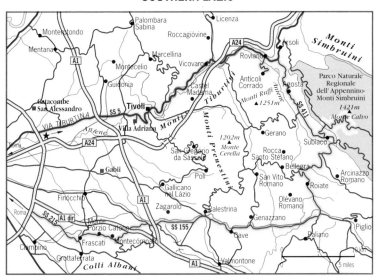

SOUTHERN LAZIO

The Roman countryside

A tour that encompasses pretty pockets of countryside and the most interesting towns within striking distance of Rome.

Make your way from Rome on the Via Tiburtina, not an attractive road—but few in the city's environs are—and see the Villa Adriana and Villa d'Este at **Tivoli** (page 189). Press north and make the short detour to **Anticoli Corrado▶**, an unspoiled hill town, and then follow country roads through the prettiest portion of the journey to **Subiaco** (page 193). Spend time seeing the Benedictine monuments and, if time allows, also explore the wild mountains of the Monti Simbruini to the east.

Monti Simbruini For centuries the Simbruini mountains have supplied Rome with drinking water (their name means "heavy rain"). They are now part of the Apennines Natural Park.

By car you can explore the park's Zompo waterfalls; the Piano di Campoli (one of the region's many impressive karstic plains); and the scenic road from Subiaco to Jenne and Vallepietra, which has fine views over the Aniene gorge, one of the park's several deep ravines.

Continue through the winding hill country to the south to historic **Palestrina** (page 190), birthplace of the great 16th-century composer who took his name from the town, then return to Rome enjoying panoramic views of **Frascati▶** (page 185) and the Colli Albani.

Medieval Anticoli Corrado, with its wonderful hilltop setting

FERRIES TO PONZA
Daily ferries run year-round from Formia and Terracina on the Lazio coast (more frequently in summer). Journey time is 2 hours 30 minutes. Faster hydrofoils run from the same ports in high season, and from Anzio, with connections from Ponza to Ischia and Naples. Connections to Ventotene, the archipelago's other main island—flatter, smaller, and less verdant—run daily from Formia and Ponza (except Sunday).

▶▶ **Ponza, Isola di**   180A1

Romans—but few foreigners—have discovered Ponza, the largest island of the Pontine archipelago off the coast of southern Lazio. Ferries sail to Ponza town, a beautiful fishing village of pastel-colored houses curved around a small harbor. Most people wanting to swim, however, pass over its small beach in favor of Chiaia di Luna, a slender crescent of sand about ten minutes' walk away. To escape the summer crowds, you could take small boats from the port to more secluded coves like Spiaggia Santa Lucia. You can also rent bikes and motor scooters, and a regular bus connects with La Forna, the island's other sizeable village.

▶▶ **San Clemente a Casauria**   181B4

Among the Abruzzo's finest medieval buildings, this Cistercian abbey was founded in the 9th century and restored in the 12th century, creating a beautiful example of transitional Romanesque-Gothic architecture. The splendid portico ushers you into an interior whose simplicity is disturbed only by an elaborate pulpit. Other treasures include a 13th-century Paschal candelabrum and a ciborium taken from an early Christian sarcophagus. The crypt is the most striking feature to survive from the earliest church. San Clemente is located just off the A25 highway near the Torre de' Passeri exit (18 miles north of Sulmona). If the gate is locked, ask the warden in the nearby house to let you in.

▶ **Sperlonga**   180A3

Southern Lazio's most beautiful tract of coastline stretches between Gaeta and Sperlonga. The latter is the area's nicest and most fashionable resort, its whitewashed houses perched high on a rocky promontory. Although it fills up in summer, there is plenty of room on the beach, and if the hotels are full you should find beds at nearby **Terracina▶**, another likeable little resort.

San Benedetto monastery, on a rocky ridge above Subiaco

▶▶ Subiaco   *180B3*

St. Benedict retreated to caves around Subiaco in the 5th century, where he composed his famous *Rule*, one of the cornerstones of Western monasticism. Of 12 monasteries founded in his wake, only two survive. The **Convento di Santa Scholastica**, 25 minutes' walk from the town, has been largely restored, though the beauty of its three cloisters remains unsurpassed; 15 minutes further, the **Convento di San Benedetto** contains the saint's original cave, the *Sacro Speco*, which is adorned with numerous 14th-century Sienese frescoes. Subiaco itself is a winning little hill town.

▶▶ Sulmona   *181B4*

Sulmona is a bracing, mountain-ringed town, ideal as a base for exploring the country around L'Aquila and for excursions into the Abruzzo national park (see pages 194–195). It was the birthplace of both Ovid, the great Roman poet (43 BC–AD 17), and confetti (see panel). Its particular sights are few, but the streets are appealing in themselves. Before you start exploring, take time out in Piazza XX Settembre's **Gran Caffè**, a lovely turn-of-the-century bar. Then see the **Annunziata▶▶** (*Closed* Mon), a mixture of church, palace, and poorhouse; the Gothic Fontana del Vecchio; the Duomo's 12th-century Byzantine relief; and the portal of **San Francesco delle Scarpe▶**.

▶ Vico, Lago di   *180C2*

Lago di Vico is a secret little lake in the crater of an old volcano, surrounded by the forest-covered slopes of the Monte Cimini. The area is a nature reserve, with lots of lovely short walks, and a scenic drive, the **Via Ciminia▶▶**, which traverses the old crater's summit ridges.

▶ Viterbo   *180C2*

Historic towns in northern Lazio are few and far between, which is perhaps why Viterbo has a reputation out of all proportion to its appeal. A favored retreat for numerous medieval popes, today it is a gloomy town, best seen quickly before moving to some of the sights nearby (the Villa Lante, Bomarzo, and Lago di Vico). Most of its old buildings lie on **Piazza del Plebiscito▶** and **Piazza San Lorenzo▶▶**, both fine medieval squares, and in the picturesque quarter around Via San Pellegrino.

CONFETTI
Real *confetti* are sugared almond confections bound with wire and ribbons into elaborate flowers. They have been made in Sulmona since the 15th century. Since then they have played a part in weddings the world over. These days, of course, colored paper is thrown, though traditional white *confetti* are still used at Abruzzese nuptials.

193

Vaulted cloister of Santa Scholastica monastery, near Subiaco

BEAUTY...
Sacheverell Sitwell called the Villa Lante, in Bagnaia, 3 miles east of Viterbo, "the most lovely place of the physical beauty of nature in Italy or in all the world." Its grounds contain some of Europe's most beautiful Renaissance gardens. The formal gardens are seen by guided tour, but you are free to wander in the adjoining parkland (*Closed* Mon. *Admission: inexpensive*).

...AND THE BEASTS
In Bomarzo, 7 miles northeast of Bagnaia, are Lazio's most extraordinary gardens, the Parco dei Mostri (Monster Park), designed in 1552 by the Duke of Orsini. Grotesques, moss-covered sculptures, and huge, fantastical stone creatures give the effect of a surreal 16th-century theme park of fantasy and horror. Though commercialized, the garden is worth the high admission charge.

The Abruzzo national park is central Italy's natural jewel, a superbly administered wilderness area that provides wonderful hiking country and a refuge for wolves and brown bears as well as a host of other flora and fauna.

INFORMATION

For information on the park, visit Pescasseroli's central information office (tel: 0863 91 955) and the large park center and museum close by. Opi, Barrea, Villetta Barrea, and Civitella Alfedena also have smaller, summer-only information centers.

194

Abruzzo national park, one of Europe's last great wildernesses

The lie of the land Most of the park's 98,800 acres comprise a jumbled collection of Apennine mountain massifs. Most reach about 5,940 feet, though the highest point is Monti della Meta (7,415 feet). The Sangro valley cuts through their heart, scattered about with the area's only villages: Barrea, Villetta Barrea, Civitella Alfedena, Opi, and Pescasseroli. All of these have a handful of hotels and campgrounds. The most developed spot is Pescasseroli, home to the park's main museum and information center. Old ways still predominate here: national costume is sometimes seen, sheep farming flourishes, and you are as likely to encounter old men bringing firewood from the forests on donkeys as you are tractors.

History Italy's environmental protection record is generally poor, but in the Abruzzo national park it can claim one of the best-administered parks in Europe. It started life—like many Italian parks—as a royal hunting reserve. This was dismantled in 1877 and an embryonic park created in its place in 1917. Most of the real work, however, has been done in the last 20 years. Early opposition has largely been overcome through initiatives to promote the local economy. A fine balance has been struck between the range of facilities—such as excellent marked paths—and the need to protect the wilderness in its natural state.

Walking The park has over 150 numbered and well-marked trails of all standards, most of them marked on the park's own 1:50,000 map, available from park centers. Perhaps the most popular is the five-hour round trip from Civitella Alfedena to the Valle delle Rose. Sightings of the park's 500-plus chamois are almost guaranteed here.

There are easy strolls in the Canala valley immediately north of Pescasseroli, and in the Val di Fondillo east of Opi (one of the park's loveliest and most popular areas). Near Pescasseroli try trail B2 (to Monte di Valle Carrara, 2.5 hours), or C3 to the Valico di Monte Tranquillo (2.5 hours). Another favorite is the two-hour hike from Barrea to Lago Vivo, or the walk in the Camosciara—another pretty area—to the Belvedere della Liscia (two hours).

Flora The park claims over 1,200 species of plants and trees (and 267 types of fungi). Around two-thirds of its area is covered in ancient forests of beech and maple (beautifully colored in autumn), interspersed with ash, hawthorn, and hornbeam, and blossom-bearing trees like wild apple, pear, cherry, and blackthorn. Spring ushers in swathes of asphodels, crocuses, gentians, and snow-drops, easily seen on even the shortest walks, followed by wild orchids and rarities like endemic irises and Apennine edelweiss.

Wolves Italy has an estimated 150–200 wolves. Their numbers are increasing all the time, despite constant human harassment and the ever-increasing threat from feral dogs (the country has 800,000 wild dogs, which interbreed with wolves and challenge them for their food sources). The park has perhaps 15–20 individual wolves in the wild, plus several that are kept in special reserves near Civitella Alfedena and Pescasseroli. These are used for study and to preserve the thoroughbred characteristics of the Apennine wolf.

Bears The park's most jealously protected fauna are Italy's last Apennine brown bears (*Ursus arctos marsicanus*). Although descended from Alpine forebears, the Abruzzo's bears have developed enough indigenous features to be classified as a subspecies (named after the *Marsicano*, the generic name for much of the park, deriving from the Marsi, one of the area's earliest tribes). Bears were common until the 16th century, and bounties were still paid on every bear killed until as recently as 1915. About 80–100 are thought to survive, and numbers are gradually increasing but the possibility of a sighting is minimal.

CHAMOIS
The beautiful and graceful chamois are some of the most easily seen of the park's 40 species of mammal. Like the park's bears, they are descended from Alpine ancestors, but have developed individual characteristics that allow them to be considered a subspecies (*Rupicapra rupicapra ornata*). The Valle delle Rose above Civitella Alfedena is one of their favored haunts. Many of the park's 500-strong herd are being introduced into other parts of the Abruzzo.

195

BIRDS
Over 300 species of birds have been spotted within the national park. The park centers (and park map) identify areas where you are likely to see particular birds—notably the ten or so pairs of golden eagles that nest in the region.

The Apennine brown bear clings precariously to existence in the national park, while numbers of wolves are steadily increasing

Campania

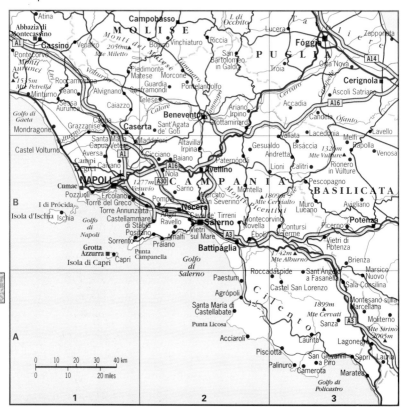

Atina
Abbazia di Montecassino
A1 Cassino
Pontecorvo
C 1575m Mte Petrella
Minturno
Teano
Sessa Aurunca
Golfo di Gaeta
Mondragone
Castel Volturno
Venafro
Monti del Matese
2050m Mte Miletto
Roccamonfina
Alvignano
Santramondi
Caiazzo
Grazzanise
Santa Maria Capua Vetere
Aversa
Campi
Cancello
Calvano
Cumae
Pozzuoli
I di Prócida
Isola d'Ischia Ischia
Golfo di Napoli
B
Sorrento
Grotta Azzurra
Isola di Capri Capri
Punta Campanella
Torre del Greco
Ercolano
Torre Annunziata
Castellammare di Stábia
Positano
Praiano
MOLISE
Campobasso
Bojano Vinchiaturo
Piedimonte Matese
Guardia
Morcone
Telese
Portelangolfo
Calore
Benevento
Caserta
Maddaloni
Cicciano
Baiano
Nola
A30 1277m Vesuvio
Pompei
Sarno
Angri
Cava de' Tirreni
Ravello
Amalfi
Vietri sul Mare
Sant'Agata de' Goti
Altavilla Irpina
Paternópoli
Mercato San Severino
Nocera
Salerno
A3
Battipáglia
Golfo di Salerno
Paestum
Roccadáspide
Castel San Lorenzo
L di Occhito
Lucera
San Bartolomeo in Galdo
Troia
Ariano Irpino
Grottaminarda
Vallata
Gesualdo
Andretta
Lioni
Calitri
Montella
Mte Cervialto
1809m
Monti Picentini
Muro Lucano
Montecorvino Rovella
Éboli
Contursi Terme
Picerno
42m Mte Alburno
PUGLIA
Fóggia
A14
Orta Nova
Cerignola
Ascoli Satriano
Accadia
A16
Candela Ofanto
Lacedonia
Bisáccia
1326m Mte Vulture
Rionero in Vúlture
Pescopagno
BASILICATA
Avigliano
Potenza
Vietri di Potenza
Brienza
Marsico Nuovo
Sala Consilina
Montesano sulla Marcellana
A3 Moliterno
Mte Sirino 2005m
Lauria
Sapri
Golfo di Policastro
Maratea
Melfi
Rapolla
Venosa
Lavello
Sant'Angelo a Fasanella
1899m Mte Cervati
Sanza
Lagonegro
San Giovanni a Piro
Camerota
Agrópoli
Santa Maria di Castellabate
Punta Licosa
Acciaroli
Pisciotta
Palinuro
CAMPANIA

0 10 20 30 40 km
0 10 20 miles

A

1   2   3

CAMPANIA To the Romans Campania was *campania felix* (the happy land), a sort of dream vacation destination—all views, fine wines, sunny skies, and bountiful countryside. It is hardly surprising, therefore, that some of the country's greatest ancient sites are here. The Greek temples at Paestum look much as they must have 2,000 years ago; so, too, do the remarkable Roman cities of Pompeii and Herculaneum, buried and preserved for posterity by the ash and mud of erupting Vesuvius—Goethe's "peak of hell rising out of paradise." Visitors still come to Campania in droves, to see the ancient sites certainly, but also to enjoy the unrivaled coastal scenery of the Sorrentino peninsula and the islands of Capri and Ischia.

NAPLES No place is quite like Naples. On first acquaintance it appears a sprawling, teeming city, the epitome of the urban nightmare. Many people leave at the earliest opportunity. Many more, intimidated by its reputation for petty crime, avoid it altogether. The Neapolitans, however—some of the wiliest and liveliest Italians going—like to say that you hate the city after a day, love it after a week, and never want to leave after a year. It is well worth testing the theory, perhaps not over a year, but certainly over several days. With your valuables safely hidden, and your courage in both hands, wander the streets, visit one of Europe's finest museums, and, most importantly, sample pizza in the city where it was born.

ISLAND IDYLLS History's hedonists have long luxuriated on Campania's famous islands. Tiberius, for one, built a dozen villas on Capri to indulge his sexual whims. Later residents have included dancer Rudolph Nureyev and droves of artists and writers. These days, day-trippers

Positano, a jewel of the Amalfi coast

SCENIC DRIVES
(*Amalfi Coast*): SS 145/
SS 163 Sorrento–
Positano–Amalfi–Salerno;
(*Monti Alburni*):
SS 19/SS 488
Battipaglia–Sant'Angelo
a Fasanella; (*Cilento
coast*): SS 267/SS 447
Agropoli–Acciaroli–
Pisciotta–Palinuro–
Camerota; (*Cilento
interior*): SS 447a
Camerota–Foria–Laurito–
Rofrano–Sanza–
Torterella–Sapri.

TOURIST INFORMATION
Amalfi: Corso delle
Repubbliche
Marinare 19–21
(tel: 089 871 107).
Benevento: Piazza Roma
31 (tel: 0824 319 938).
Capri: Piazza Umberto I 19
(tel: 081 837 0918).
Naples: Piazza dei Mastri
(tel: 081 405 311); Piazza
del Plebiscito, Palazzo
Reale (tel: 081 2525 711).
Pompeii: Via Sacra 1
(tel: 081 850 7255).
Ravello: Piazza del Duomo
10 (tel: 089 857 096).
Sorrento: Via L. de Maio
35 (tel: 081 807 4033).

make up the bulk of the visitors, diminishing the island's social cachet but unable to tarnish its incomparable beauty. Brave the crowds to share in the escapism, and leave time, perhaps, to visit the region's other islands—Ischia and tiny Procida—less beautiful, just as crowded, but equally alluring.

CAMPANIAN COASTS Where Grand Tourists once visited the Bay of Naples, package tourists now settle for the Sorrento peninsula—Italy's most renowned stretch of coastline. Whitewashed towns such as Amalfi, Positano, and Ravello rear up high above a turquoise sea, fringed by plunging cliffs and a stunning mountainous backdrop. Crowds flock to the region as they do to the islands—but fortunately its beauty is one that commercialism cannot taint. The area's main town, Sorrento, is less striking and often busy with package tours, but nonetheless makes an appealing and convenient base. You might also want to explore the Cilento, Campania's less sybaritic coastline, a long arc of cliffs, beaches, and small resorts that skirts the mountains near the Calabrian border. It is best to see it after visiting Paestum, and use Santa Maria di Castellabate as a base.

PASTA AND PIZZA Two Italian (and now international) culinary staples originated in Campania—pizza, and that most archetypal of pastas, spaghetti. Naples is the pizza's homeland (so ignore the killjoys who claim it was created earlier elsewhere). The classic Neapolitan versions are *napoletana* (tomatoes, anchovies, and mozzarella) and *Margherita* (created for Italy's first queen, using basil, tomato and mozzarella as a topping to suggest the colors of the Italian flag). Be sure to try a pizza in one of the city's old *pizzerie* such as Da Michele or Trianon da Ciro. Alternatively, buy it by the slice (*pizza taglia*) from a café. Other local specialties are: the famous *insalata caprese* (Capri salad)—slices of tomato and mozzarella; fish and seafood, mussels (*cozze*), and clams (*vongole*) in particular (though watch your wallet if you're on a budget, for seafood can be expensive).

Pizza made in the traditional wood-fired oven

▶▶▶ Amalfi   196B2

Amalfi is the largest town on Italy's most breathtaking coastline and was formerly one of the Mediterranean's sea powers. Although it can often be very congested, its hotels and restaurants are generally more affordable than many in the area.

Poised between the mountains and the sea, the town's narrow streets and dark passageways weave among monuments that testify to its former grandeur. The **Duomo▶▶**, dominating the central square from the top of a large flight of steps, shows more than a hint of Saracen influence, even stronger in the adjoining **Chiostro del Paradiso▶▶** (*Open* daily. *Admission: inexpensive*), full of palms and voluptuously intertwined twin columns.

Amalfi is known for its high-quality paper: the Museo della Carta houses Europe's oldest working paper mill, as well as a paper museum. The **Museo Civico▶** (*Closed* Sat–Sun in winter. *Admission free*) displays the *Tavole Amalfitane*, a codex of maritime law that was powerful enough to held sway over the entire Mediterranean until 1570.

Amalfi's highly decorated Duomo

▶ Benevento   196C2

Benevento was bombed heavily in World War II, and its center—despite an atmospheric appeal—still has a half-built feel. However, it remains one of the more interesting towns of the Campanian interior. The best sights are Roman, notably the 2nd-century AD **Arco di Traiano▶▶** (also known as Porta Aurea) and the ruins of the 20,000-seat **Theater▶**. There is also the church of Santa Sofia, part of a Benedictine abbey founded by the Lombards in 760. Its cloisters hold the **Museo del Sannio▶** (*Open* daily. *Admission: moderate*), a collection of Roman antiquities.

▶ Campi Flegrei   196B1

The "fiery fields" west of Naples are the Phlegrean Fields of classical myth, Homer's and Virgil's entrance to Hades. They are also the Elysian Fields, long eulogized for their transcendental beauty. Nearby Naples has largely destroyed the beauty, though one or two spots deserve a visit, and there are still signs of the volcanic activity that gave the region its name.

199

Vesuvius (Vesuvio) is neither the highest nor most dangerous volcano in the world, but the eruption that buried Pompeii and Herculaneum has made it one of the most famous. "Many a calamity has happened in the world," wrote Goethe, "but never one that has caused so much entertainment to posterity as this one."

The big bang On August 24, AD 79, Vesuvius had been belching smoke and debris for several days. Early that morning, however, its basalt plug collapsed, unleashing the full force of the volcano. A huge cloud blotted out the sun, raining dust, stone, and lava onto the surrounding countryside. Pompeii was buried within hours, some 2,000 of its inhabitants killed by falling rocks and asphyxiating gases (many of its 20,000 population had already left). That evening, the volcano's internal walls disintegrated, sending further torrents of ash over the town (Herculaneum was engulfed at this point by a flood of superheated mud). Only late on August 26 did a feeble light return to the region.

Statistically, Vesuvius' next eruption is overdue, but if you are still interested in peering down into the crater of the famous volcano, it is easily reached

Vesuvius today What you see today when you look up at the volcano from Naples is actually the truncated cone of Monte Somma (3,736 feet). Vesu-vius proper (4,214 feet) rises from its floor, a cone created by the eruption of AD 79. Vesuvius has erupted around a hundred times since that fateful morning, the last in 1944. This works out at an eruption rate of around once every 20 years, so the next cataclysm is long overdue. When it arrives Naples will be in the firing line—which makes it strange that there are no contingency plans to deal with an eruption.

Reaching the crater There are several ways to get a closer look at Vesuvius. The easiest is to take the Circumvesuviana, a local railway that runs in a broad circle around the volcano (2 hours). Alternatively, you can take the railway as far as Ercolano, where six SITA buses daily leave the station for the cafés and souvenir shops at Vesuvius' former chair-lift station (*seggovia*). You can also drive to this point (or take a taxi from Ercolano—but fix a price first). From here it is a 30-minute climb to the summit (wear sturdy shoes). Views into the crater and over Naples are breathtaking. You can walk around the crater (2 hours), but watch out for the crumbling paths and rickety fences.

Pompeii's fate was the archeologists' fortune, for the volcanic eruption of AD 79 that buried it left posterity not only the world's finest surviving Roman town, but also an unparalleled insight into the minutiae of 1st-century life. An instant in the city's existence was captured by the disaster that overwhelmed its people.

History Pompeii (Pompei in Italian) (*Open* daily 8:30–7:30. *Admission: expensive, but includes Herculaneum*) was never as famous in its own time as it is today. It started life in the 6th century BC as a Greek trading post. After falling to the Samnites, it became a thriving Roman colony. Much was damaged by an earthquake in AD 63, the remainder obliterated by Vesuvius 16 years later. The city remained forgotten until around 1600, when the study of ancient texts suggested its existence. Excavations began in 1748 and have since revealed most of the site.

Sightseeing The site is huge, and even spending a day here still leaves many stones unturned. Some houses are little more than foundations, and after a time one ruin looks much like another, so be selective. Also be sure to see Naples' Museo Archeologico, which contains most of the site's movable treasures.

The civic buildings Almost the first area you encounter (at the site's western entrance) is the **Forum**, the center of Roman civic life. Its surviving buildings include the **Basilica** (a business center and law courts), marketplace, and temples to Apollo, Venus, Jupiter, and Vespasian. In the **Antiquarium** close by are body casts taken from the volcanic ash, figures whose contorted shapes graphically illustrate the horror of that fateful morning. Beyond the forum lie the **Terme Stabiane**, the town's earliest bathhouses. Still preserved are swimming pools, men's and women's sections, even niches in the changing room for clothes. Alongside runs **Vico del Lupinare**, one of the main red-light districts. A small brothel at one end has bed stalls and frescoes describing the services on offer.

More salutary performances took place in the 5,000-seat **Teatro Grande** and the smaller indoor **Teatro Piccolo** (or *Odeon*). The 20,000-seat **Anfiteatro**, built in 80 BC, is Italy's oldest surviving amphitheater, and one of the most complete in the Roman world.

Casa dei Vetii This is Pompeii's best-preserved and most artistically rewarding house. Once the home of two

201

Waiting for the visiting hordes at Pompeii

Pompeii

PAST VISITORS

When Charles Dickens visited Vesuvius, he was carried to the summit in a litter borne by 15 attendants. In 1765, James Boswell noted sourly in his diary: "…on foot to Vesuvius. Monstrous mounting. Smoke: saw hardly anything."

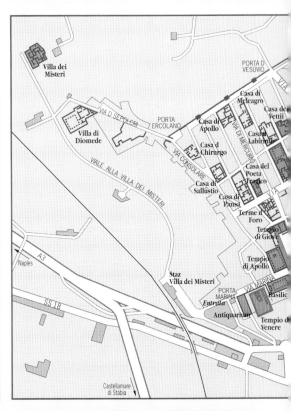

Pompeii possesses one of the most complete of all Roman amphitheaters

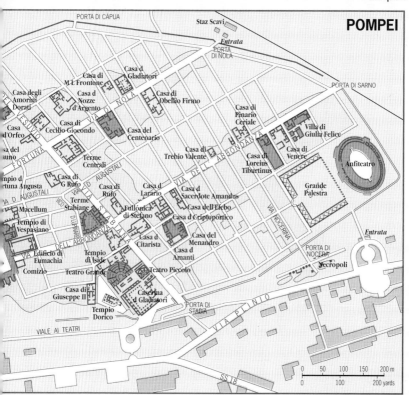

wealthy merchants, it possesses the site's finest wall paintings. The frieze of the cupids is of special note. The vestibule contains the famously well-endowed Priapus, not to mention a roomful of explicit erotica (usually closed). Phallic symbols appear all over Pompeii, probably attempts to ward off the evil eye.

Three houses The largest of the town's houses is the **Casa del Menandro**, a patrician villa with a lovely peristyle and many appealing frescoes. Other noteworthy homes include the Casa del Fauno, source of many of the finest paintings in Naples' museum; and the **Casa di Loreio Tiburtino**, an elegant mansion typical of many of the town's grand homes. In its courtyard stands the *impluvium*, a basin for collecting rainwater. To the rear spreads the peristyle, an open area of columns and fountains. Around it extend the house's private apartments.

Dogs and Dionysus Other well-kept houses include the Casa degli Amorini Doratí, Casa di M. L. Frontone, Villa di Giulia Felice, and Casa del Centenario. You might hunt out the **Casa del Poeta Tragico**, a middle-class home built in Pompeii's final days. It is known for the sign above its door—*Cave canem*—"Beware of the Dog." Some 15,000 graffiti have been found around Pompeii, many salacious, others political or cultural. Finally, be certain to visit the **Villa dei Misteri**, for beautiful frescoes describing the initiation of women into the Dionysiac mysteries.

Vesuvius, now quiet, broods over the ruins of Pompeii

Boats and hydrofoils run year round to Capri from Sorrento and Naples (Molo Beverello). During the summer there are also connections from Ischia and towns along the Amalfi coast. Buses link the island's main centers (including the Blue Grotto). Hotels are limited in July and August (reservations essential). Capri's reputation for high prices is deserved. To save money, use Sorrento as a base: a couple of day trips at most are enough to see the island.

204

THE BLUE GROTTO
Capri's most famous sight—La Grotta Azzurra—is an overrated, frustrating, and overpriced experience. First you have to pay for a boat to take you from Marina Grande; then you cough up an entrance fee; then you pay for a small boat to whisk you in and out of the turquoise-hued grotto. You are better off taking the more rewarding two-hour boat trips around the whole island.

▶▶▶ Capri   196B1

Capri's legendary beauty attracts day-trippers by the thousand. Most people come for sybaritic pursuits—Augustus called the island *Capri Apragopolis* (City of Sweet Idleness)—which means lazy walks, lovely views, and sipping drinks from flower-decked terraces.

Boats dock at Marina Grande, from where you can take a funicular to the village of **Capri▶▶▶**, whose central *piazzetta* is the place to see and be seen. Nearby, visit the Certosa San Giacomo, a crumbling monastery, and the Giardini di Augusto, gardens with tremendous views of the coast's cliffs. Below, the steep Via Krupp leads to Marina Piccola, the best place to swim (though it becomes uncomfortably crowded in summer). **Anacapri▶▶** is the island's other main village, linked by chair lift to Monte Solaro (1,967 feet), a good spot for views over the island.

▶ Caserta   196C1

Caserta's Palazzo Reale (*Closed* Mon) is Italy's largest royal palace (1,200 rooms, 1,790 windows, and 94 staircases). The so-called "Versailles of Naples" was begun in 1752 for the Bourbon King Charles III and finished 20 years later. Size for its own sake, however, is the palace's most impressive feature. Its apartments—though suitably painted, stuccoed, and decorated—are insipid and uninspiring places. The gardens, by contrast, are enchanting. Caserta Vecchia (Old Caserta), a medieval village, is about 6 miles to the north.

▶▶ Ischia   196B1

Although this island is less pretty and less chic than Capri, Ischia's spas, beaches, and hot springs still make it popular. The southern shores are nicest, around the villages of Fontana and **Sant'Angelo▶▶**, and the old volcanic peak, **Monte Epomeo▶▶**, is well worth climbing for the views. The town of **Ischia▶** divides into Ischia Porto, the tourist center and Ischia Ponte, the less commercialized fishing village. Its only real sight is the Castello, an old Aragonese fortress.

The lovely island of Capri has attracted pleasure-seekers since Roman times

When Vesuvius erupted in AD 79 it destroyed at least two towns. Although Pompeii is the better known, nearby Herculaneum is almost as interesting—and its size makes it an easier place to visit.

Origins Whereas Pompeii was a thriving commercial town, Herculaneum (*Open* daily 8:30–7:30. *Admission: expensive, but includes Pompeii*) was a chic residential suburb, built to take advantage of the area's sea breezes and magnificent views. Houses here belonged to wealthy patrician families and were built as sophisticated villas, a cut above the town houses of Pompeii's business class. The wave of superheated mud that swept over the town in AD 79, however, was no respecter of class or property, and it entombed the town until its rediscovery in 1709. Excavations began in earnest in 1927, but since then less than half the site has been revealed. Herculaneum lies at the seaward end of modern Ercolano's main street. Allow about two hours to see its highlights. On the whole it is better preserved than Pompeii, though there are fewer communal spaces or impressive civic buildings. Instead it preserves its Roman grid plan, based on two main streets—the *Cardine IV* and *Decumano Inferiore*. About 35 buildings are open to the public—special permission is needed to see the others. Among the public buildings, note the **Terme**, a bathhouse with its benches and basins intact (plus separate warm, hot, and cold rooms); the *palaestra* (gymnasium), dominated by a fountain; and the remnants of the 2,500-seat theater.

THE CASA DEI CERVI
The house that best evokes Herculaneum's luxurious past is the Casa dei Cervi (House of the Deer), by virtue of its elegant gardens and its statues: one of a drunken Hercules (Ercolo), the town's legendary founder, the other of groups of deer being hunted by dogs.

205

Herculaneum, risen from the mud of Vesuvius

▶▶ Napoli (Naples)   *196B1*

Naples is a place that arouses fierce passions. On the one hand its traffic, city center, and much of its bureaucracy can be chaotic. On the other it is the most Italian of all cities —the place where family, food, religion, and other Latin passions reign as strongly as ever; the place that gave birth to the pizza, Sophia Loren, and *O Sole Mio*; a city that was once so beautiful—thanks to Mount Vesuvius and the Bay of Naples—it formed the culmination of the Grand Tour.

Although much has been done to improve its reputation for street crime and the state of its monuments, this has not addressed all of the city's troublès. Petty crime can be a problem for the unwary, and poverty is still rife. To enjoy the city you need to be ready for its fast and furious pace. Be sure to see the **Museo Archeologico Nazionale▶▶▶**, one of Europe's greatest museums (see opposite page). Otherwise, sights are few. However, soaking up the atmosphere is as much a part of the experience as sightseeing.

What to see Start a tour near the waterfront with the **Castel Nuovo** (*Open* Mon–Sat 9–7. *Admission: expensive*), built in 1279 by Charles of Anjou (related to the French monarchy) and refurbished by Alfonso I of Aragon as a royal palace two centuries later (the Aragonese were an illegitimate branch of the Spanish monarchy, rulers of Naples until succeeded in 1734 by the Bourbons). Behind the palace lies the **Teatro San Carlo▶▶**, one of Europe's grandest opera houses built in 1737 (guided tours).

Among the churches, the **Duomo▶** is notable only for the phials of San Gennaro's blood and fragments of a basilica (Santa Restituta) founded by Constantine in AD 324. Nearby **San Lorenzo Maggiore▶** is a fine Gothic church, and **Santa Anna dei Lombardi▶** offers excellent pieces of Renaissance sculpture.

The city's most worthwhile sight (after the museum) is the picture gallery of the **Palazzo Reale di Capodimonte▶▶** (*Closed* Mon. *Admission: expensive*). Most Italian masters are represented, including Raphael, Michelangelo, Botticelli, Giovanni Bellini, Filippino Lippi, Simone Martini, and many more.

Staying It's best to avoid the mainly grim hotels near the station (around Piazza Garibaldi). Better budget options cluster between Piazza Dante and the Duomo. Farther out, the upscale hotels tend to congregate in the Mergellina district on the western side of the Bay of Naples.

Naples' grand arcade, the glass-domed Galleria Umberto I

206

Naples' Museo Archeologico Nazionale is among the best archeological museums in Europe. Its collection covers classical sculpture, finds from Campania's ancient sites, and the finest artifacts and wall paintings taken from Pompeii and Herculaneum.

The museum's exhibits are poorly labeled and whole sections are often closed—though even if you see only a fraction of what it has to offer, you should come away satisfied. Invest in an English-language guide if you want to be thorough—they are on sale at the ticket office (*Closed* Tue. *Admission: expensive*).

The ground floor The ground floor is devoted mainly to sculpture, the bulk of it from the Farnese collection, established in the 17th century by one of Rome's leading patrician families (mostly from sites in Lazio and Campania). Its most astounding pieces are the *Farnese Hercules*, a triumphant muscular figure, and the *Farnese Bull*, the largest sculptural group to have survived from antiquity (restored after its discovery by Michelangelo). Both came from the Terme di Caracalla in Rome.

Other outstanding works include the famous *Javelin-thrower;* the Augustan-era *Eurydice and Hermes;* the *Venus Callipyge* (literally "Venus of the Beautiful Bottom"); and a figure of *Doyphorous* from Pompeii, one of the most accomplished Roman copies of a Greek original.

The upper floors Many upper-floor rooms are devoted to mosaics and wall paintings, the majority removed from either Pompeii or Herculaneum. Among the mosaics look in particular for the *Battle of Issus*, a wonderfully realistic tableau showing Alexander the Great in battle with the Persians. Also hunt out the *Seascape* (a squid attacking a lobster), the *Street Musicians, Sorcerers,* and *The Meeting of the Platonic Academy.*

SMALLER EXHIBITS
Leave plenty of time to study some of the smaller exhibits, too. Other rooms contain a wealth of artistic objects and household items from Pompeii. Two famous examples are the Tazza Farnese, a cup of veined sardonyx, and a 115-piece table service from the Casa del Menandro. Elsewhere, pieces of gladiatorial equipment—helmets, swords, and trumpets—compete for attention with everyday items like shoes, pans, even dates, olives, onions, and cakes.

FOR AND AGAINST
Naples and its archeological treasures have evoked different reactions over the years. In 1869, the writer Henry James remarked: "I conceived at Naples a tenfold deeper loathing than ever of the hideous heritage of the past." In 1645, the diarist John Evelyn described Naples as the "most magnificent city in Europe," while Goethe in 1787 wrote that "Naples is a paradise: everyone lives in a state of intoxicated self-forgetfulness, myself included."

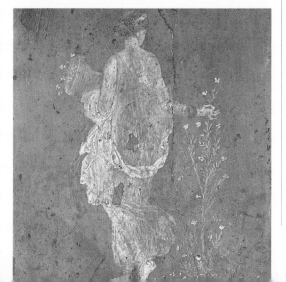

Maiden gathering flowers, *wallpainting from Stabiae*

►►► Paestum *196A2*

Open: daily 9 AM–one hour before sunset. Admission: expensive
Poseidonia was founded by the Greeks in the 6th century BC and renamed *Paestum* when it became a Roman colony in 273 BC. After falling into virtual abandonment in the 9th century, the site was rediscovered in the 18th century. Today it is dominated by three honey-colored temples, among the greatest surviving Greek temples of antiquity. It was famous for its roses and violets—Virgil mentions them—which were used in a scent industry.

The best-preserved is the **Tempio di Nettuno►►►** (actually dedicated to Hera), built in the 5th century BC and considered by many to be the greatest surviving Doric temple of antiquity. Despite its age, only the roof and a few interior walls are missing. Alongside it stands the so-called **Basilica di Hera►►**, larger but more ruined than its neighbor (its nine-column width makes it broader by three columns than the Parthenon). Somewhat apart rests the **Tempio di Cerere**, built around 500 BC. The colony's Roman monuments are less impressive, though the on-site museum fills in many of the gaps. Its most celebrated exhibits are a statue of Zeus; 6th-century BC metopes (friezes); eight bronze hydrias (water vessels); and several rare, painted Greek panels.

208

The superb Temple of Neptune at Paestum

►► Positano *196B2*

Few places are as picturesque as Positano, a pyramid of whitewashed houses spilling down from the mountains to the sea. Despite its small size it is one of the most exclusive resorts on the Amalfi coast. This generally makes hotels an expensive proposition, but there are plenty of cafés and restaurants in which to while away an idle afternoon (as well as a couple of popular little beaches). Nearby **Praiano►►** is even smaller than Positano, but rapidly beginning to match it for prices and popularity.

▶ Procida, Isola di   196B1

Tiny Procida is less varied and spectacular than Capri or Ischia. It is, therefore, less popular, which means the possibility of swimming and eating in relative peace and quiet. Ferries and hydrofoils run here from Ischia, Pozzuoli, and Naples (Mergellina). Chiaiolella has the most attractive of the beaches, while the islets of Vivara's peaceful olive groves are the nicest places to walk.

▶▶▶ Ravello   196B2

"Closer to the sky than the seashore," wrote André Gide of Ravello, an enchantingly beautiful small town whose lofty setting (1,155 feet) offers stupendous views of the Amalfi coast. But Ravello's main attractions are quiet lanes and two romantic villas. The **Villa Cimbrone**▶▶ (*Open daily. Admission: moderate*) is known for its wild gardens, lush and full of arbors, and lichen-covered terraces. They shelter Ravello's loveliest spot, a belvedere providing unrivaled views of the coast. The **Villa Rufolo**▶▶ (*Open daily. Admission: moderate*) is slightly less spectacular, a Saracen-Romanesque building begun in the 11th century. Home over the centuries to several popes, its most famous guest was Richard Wagner, who used its gardens as the inspiration for his opera *Parsifal*.

Ravello's Duomo, an 11th-century church renovated in 1786, has bronze doors (1179)—modeled on those of Amalfi's cathedral—cast with 54 scenes from the Passion. Inside are pulpits from the 12th and 13th centuries, decorated with mosaics and reliefs.

Otherwise in Ravello there is little to do—one of its charms. It is also relatively quiet: being away from the coast, it has fewer visitors than Amalfi and Positano, and most of the tourists have left by mid-afternoon, making Ravello a tempting place to stay.

Top: Ravello
Above: pulpit, Ravello cathedral

▶ Salerno   196B2

Salerno is a modern, ramshackle city, most famous as the site of the Allied landings of September 9, 1943. Its workaday atmosphere does little to entice visitors, though its position makes it a convenient base for exploring Amalfi, Positano, and Ravello. The **Duomo**▶ in the small medieval quarter is worth a few minutes for its bronze doors and inlaid pulpits (1173), similar to those of Amalfi and Ravello. The adjacent Museo Diocesano (*Open daily. Admission free*) contains an early medieval altarfront, embellished with 54 ivory panels, the largest work of its kind.

GROTTA DI SMERALDO
About 8 miles along the coast road from Positano to Amalfi is the Grotta di Smeraldo, named after the eerie emerald glow that bathes its stalagmites and stalactites. An escalator takes you to the grotto from the road, or take a boat from Amalfi (trips every two hours).

209

TERRA DI LAVORO

Northwest of Capua stretches the *Terra di Lavoro*, literally the "Land of Work," long one of Campania's prime agricultural regions. It is perhaps best known for its herds of water buffalo, which yield the milk that makes Italy's finest mozzarella cheese.

EXCURSIONS IN THE CILENTO

The Cilento's rugged interior is scarcely explored, but almost any drive along its remote roads offers numerous scenic rewards. Try in particular the mountain roads in the north around the Monti Alburni; the desolate road from Laurito to Padula (on the A3 highway); the SS 18 from Vallo di Lucania to Scario; and the short SS 447 loop from Palinuro to Centola and Camerota.

▶ Santa Maria Capua Vetere   196C1

The approaches to Capua are unprepossessing—endless impoverished and semi-derelict suburbs—making it hard to believe that during Roman times this was the second most important city in Italy after Rome. Invading Arabs destroyed the old city around AD 830. Its **Amphitheater▶▶**, once second only in size to the Colosseum, is these days in a fairly poor state of preservation: most of the seats and arches have collapsed—only the network of tunnels around the arena remains largely intact. Close by lies Italy's finest surviving **Mithraeum▶▶**, a temple to the Persian god Mithras. Its underground chamber has a vaulted ceiling painted with stars. Modern Capua, about 13 miles away, offers the **Museo Campano▶** (*Closed* Mon and PM daily. *Admission: moderate*), which houses archeological finds from the ancient city. The **Duomo**, destroyed in 1942, has been rebuilt, but a 9th-century campanile survives.

▶ Santa Maria di Castellabate   196A2

Santa Maria is one of several small resorts clinging to the coast of the **Cilento▶▶**, a wild mountainous region recently added to the list of Italy's proposed national parks. A low-key place, the village gathers around a small harbor and a clean, golden beach stretching away to the north. **San Marco▶**, 13 miles south, is another picturesque fishing village, dead in winter, but buzzing with life in summer. The region's spectacular coast road (the SS 267-447) links with other resorts, most notably Acciaroli and cosmopolitan **Palinuro▶**, famous for the Grotte di Ulisse. You might also take a look at the rather patchy Roman ruins at *Velia*, close to the village of Marina di Velia.

▶▶ Sorrento   196B1

Sorrento: boats at rest

Sorrento is popular with package tourists (80 percent of whom are British). It is easy to see why, for the town is an attractive and unpretentious place, perfectly placed for trips to Pompeii and Herculaneum (via the Circumvesuviana railway), and for trips to Amalfi, Positano, and Ravello—there is a local bus service. Boats run around the Sorrento peninsula to these towns, and in summer also ply regularly to the islands of Capri and Ischia.

The great pleasures of Sorrento itself are its lush, shady gardens and its views. The belvedere behind the Museo Correale (*Closed* Tue and PM daily. *Admission: moderate*) is a favorite viewing point, and there are few sights to equal a dramatic Sorrento sunset. You can swim locally at nearby Marina Grande, at Regina Giovanna (on Punta del Capo), or the Villa di Pollio, a small park with old Roman ruins. Otherwise there is little to do but relax in the sunshine—something for which the town is tailor-made.

THE SORRENTO PENINSULA

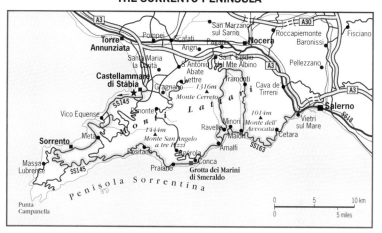

Drive

The Amalfi Coast

This drive takes in the Amalfi Coast, Italy's most spectacular stretch of coastline, and its dramatically set towns and villages.

Start from the end of the A3 highway spur at Castellammare di Stabia, just a few miles east of Naples and Pompeii, and then follow the coastal road (the SS 145) to **Sorrento** (page 210). Notice the tangle of roads beyond Massa Lubrense leading to the tip of the peninsula. Beyond Sorrento, continue on the SS 145, climbing to the ridges of the craggy mountains (the Monti Lattari) that form the peninsula's rocky backbone. The next 24 miles past **Positano** (page 208), **Praiano**, and **Amalfi** (page 199) are breathtaking. Just past Amalfi, head inland to **Ravello** (page 209), and then either loop farther inland to climb the slopes of Monte Cerreto, or return to Amalfi to pick up the SS 163 coast road to Vietri sul Mare and **Salerno** (page 209).

The popular resort of Sorrento, on the dramatic Amalfi Coast

The Deep South

TOURIST INFORMATION
Bari: Piazza Aldo
Moro 33/A
(tel: 080 524 2361).
Lecce: Castello Carlo V,
Via XXV Luglio
(tel: 0832 248 092).
Matera: Via Viti
de Marco 9
(tel: 0835 331 983).
Taranto: Corso Umberto
113 (tel: 099 453 2392).
Trani: Piazza Trieste 10
(tel: 0883 588 825).
Tropea: Piazza Ercole
(tel: 0963 61 475).
Gargano: (Vieste) Corso
Lorenzo Fuzzini 8
(tel: 0884 707 495).

212

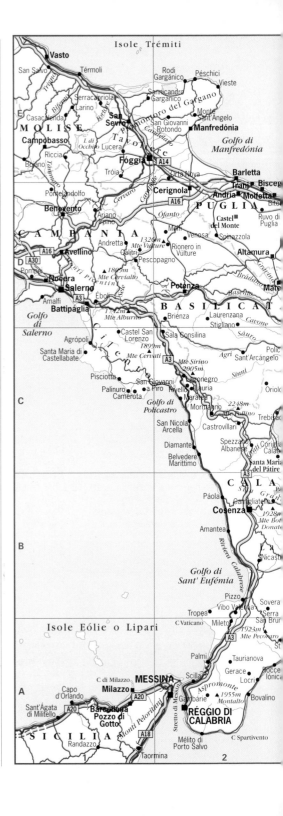

The Deep South

213

▶▶▶ REGION HIGHLIGHTS

The Deep South

MAGNA GRAECIA
The south's main Greek colonies were: (Basilicata) Metaponto; (Apulia) Otranto, Gallipoli, and Taranto; (Calabria) Crotone, Reggio di Calabria, Locri, and Sibari (home to the luxuriously living Sybarites). Today little remains of any of the cities, though artifacts excavated from their sites fill many regional museums, notably in Taranto and Reggio di Calabria.

APULIAN WINES
Apulia rivals Sicily as Italy's largest producer of wine and table grapes, yet although renowned for centuries, few of its wines are known outside the region. Many are used for blending or for making vermouth. The outstanding vintages include Torre Quarto, Favonio (red or white), Castel del Monte; Donna Marzia (red or white); Copertino (the *riserva* in particular); Locorotondo, the region's best white; and Rosa del Golfo (produced by Giuseppe Calò), widely regarded as among Italy's finest rosés.

THE DEEP SOUTH Calabria, Basilicata, and Apulia are the heart of the south—an area cut off for centuries by history and geography from the rest of Italy. Despite considerable efforts, it is still poorer and more backward than northern Italy, an imbalance worsening with the north's apparently increasing antagonism.

The south, with relatively little in the way of art or monuments, still evokes in atmosphere the Mediterranean Italy of old. Its landscapes are unspoiled, its villages ancient, and many places never see a tourist. Its downside lies in a Byzantine bureaucracy, a decaying infrastructure and a shortage of tourist facilities. But approach the south in the right spirit and it has much to recommend it, not least the fact that it costs less for eating and sleeping.

HISTORY The Greeks colonized all three regions, establishing cities in what become known as Magna Graecia (Greater Greece). The Romans were less influential, though Brindisi—connected to Rome by the Via Appia—became one of their most important links with the East. The Arabs and Byzantines held sway in the Dark Ages and influenced the region's architecture (Basilicata takes its name from *basilikos*, the term for the Byzantine administration). They were succeeded in the 11th century by the Normans, and later by the Swabians, most notably Frederick II (see panel) and the Angevins (French). For centuries after, the south stagnated under the Spanish.

CALABRIA The "toe" of the Italian boot, though bereft of any special artistic treasures, has an unspoiled coastline and grand, wild interior. The eastern (Ionian) coast is largely monotonous; except for a few towns such as Stilo and Rossano, the resort-dotted western (Tyrrhenian) littoral is more spectacular. The Calabrian interior comprises sun-baked plains and the rounded, wooded slopes of the Sila mountains, a large, and—thanks to long distances and winding roads—rather laborious area to explore, but brimming with natural beauty and half-forgotten villages.

BASILICATA Basilicata is Italy's poorest region. Its towns and villages are the country's least discovered, its intractable landscapes some of Europe's least developed. The Pollino mountains and hills of the Sauro valley offer some magnificent drives, while Matera has the unforgettable *sassi*, ancient cave dwellings that riddle the ravines around the town. Melfi, the Normans' first southern power base, is an attractive town and makes a good center for exploring some of the region's more appealing abbeys and castles.

APULIA (PUGLIA) Apulia is by far the most rewarding part of the south. Rocky and sun-bleached, or smothered in vineyards and olive groves, it offers little fine scenery, except in the Gargano, a promontory of beaches, cliffs, and forest that forms the spur of the Italian boot. But white-washed, Greek-looking villages dot the coast, and the famous *trulli* (curious, beehivelike buildings of unknown antiquity, some still in use) punctuate the countryside around Alberobello. Many towns are showcases for Apulian-Romanesque architecture, and in Lecce the Italian baroque finds its greatest expression.

▶▶ **Alberobello (see page 223)** *213D3*

▶▶ **Bari** *213D3*

Bari's warren of medieval streets is in marked contrast to the mundane promenades of the modern city. At its heart lies the **Basilica di San Nicola**▶▶▶, a prototype for many of the region's Apulian-Romanesque churches. Started in the 11th century, it was built to house the body of St. Nicholas, the patron saint of Holy Russia, pawnbrokers, sailors, and children (he is the St. Nicholas of Santa Claus fame). Inside, the ciborium (altar canopy) and episcopal throne are two of the finest such works in Italy. Note also the silver altarpiece (1684) and the exhibits of the church Treasury. St. Nicholas (San Nicola) is buried in the crypt.

The **Cattedrale di San Sabino**▶▶▶ is another exceptional Romanesque church. It contains an icon said to be the truest likeness of the Madonna. Also worth seeing are the **Pinacoteca (Art Gallery)**▶▶ (*Closed* Mon and PM daily. *Admission: inexpensive*) and **Castello**▶ (*Closed* Mon and PM daily. *Admission: inexpensive*), rebuilt by Frederick II in around 1240, and the **Museo Archeologico**▶▶ (*Closed* for restoration) housing Apulia's most complete collection of antiquities. Bitonto's streets, 10 miles to the west, shelter a 13th-century Apulian-Romanesque cathedral with an unusual *matroneum* (women's gallery).

BARLETTA
Barletta is a shabby town famous for the *Colosso*, the largest Roman bronze statue in existence (16.5 feet high). It dates from the 4th century AD and probably depicts the Byzantine emperor Valentinian (d AD 375). Stolen by the Venetians from Constantinople in the 13th century, the statue was abandoned on the beach near Barletta when the boat bringing it to Venice foundered in a storm.

215

*Left: decorated doorway of San Nicola, Bari
Below: Frederick II's enigmatic fortress, Castel del Monte*

▶▶▶ **Castel del Monte** *212D2*

This mighty fortress (*Open* daily. *Admission: moderate*) built around 1240 by Frederick II is one of the great medieval buildings of Europe. It is also one of the most mysterious, scholars having puzzled for centuries over its purpose and mathematical obsession. It is an octagonal building, built around an octagonal courtyard, flanked by eight octagonal towers. Each floor has eight rooms.

It may be that eight was a symbol of the crown, or that Frederick was imitating Jerusalem's octagonal Omar mosque. Another theory is that the castle's mathematical precision was astrological, for its proportions are supposed to relate to the movements of the planets. Others claim that it was a hunting lodge or a refuge for pilgrims in search of the Holy Grail. In any event, it has few of the defensive features normally associated with medieval castles—only a magnificent position, its gloriously isolated bastions visible for miles around.

Part of the rocky coastline of the Gargano peninsula

▶▶▶ (II) Gargano   212E2

The "spur" of the Italian boot is a hilly and largely wooded limestone peninsula edged with rocky cliffs, whitewashed villages, and broad sandy beaches. While the interior remains unvisited, the coast—in summer at least—is crowded and commercialized. Visit out of season, however, and the resorts are delightfully quiet.

Siponto▶ (Roman *Sipontum*) boasts a fine museum and the lovely 11th-century Romanesque church of **Santa Maria di Siponto**, but the Gargano starts in earnest at **Monte Sant'Angelo▶▶**. This windblown mountaintop eyrie was for almost 1,500 years one of Italy's most revered Christian shrines following several apparitions of the Archangel Michael in the 5th century. The most famous took place in a cave now contained in the **Santuario di San Michele▶▶** (note the beautiful bronze doors).

Moving around the coast, **Mattinata▶** is a small resort with a magnificent beach, linked by a scenic road to **Pugnochiuso▶**, set in a panoramic bay, and **Vieste▶▶**, the Gargano's busiest town. Nearby **Peschici▶▶** makes a more attractive base, being quieter, prettier, and well placed for access to beaches (and numerous small grottoes).

Stonework on the Santuario di San Michele, Monte Sant'Angelo

▶ Gerace   212A2

Rugged Gerace, perched on an impregnable crag, boasts Calabria's largest church, a Norman cathedral built in 1045 and enlarged by Frederick II in 1222. Its unadorned interior is supported by 20 ancient columns, many taken from the ruins of old Greek temples at nearby Locri. Be sure to see the Treasury (*Open* daily. *Admission: moderate*) with its exquisite Renaissance ivory crucifix. When you tire of exploring this unspoiled town, you might like to shop around for Gerace's distinctive local pottery.

►►► Lecce 213D4

Lecce is to the baroque what Florence is to the Renaissance. Counter-Reformationary zeal and mercantile money transformed much of the city in the 17th century. Churches, palaces—even houses and simple courtyards—were given a glorious baroque veneer of *putti*, gargoyles, garlands, stone curlicues, and wreaths of exuberant decoration. There is so much to see, but start with the 16th-century **Basilica di Santa Croce►►►**, the apotheosis of Lecce's airy baroque style. Next door stands the **Palazzo del Governo►**, designed by Zimbalo and Giuseppe Cino, architects responsible for many of the city's buildings. They also worked on **Piazza del Duomo's►►** cathedral and Palazzo del Seminario, as well as the Carmine, Gesù, Rosario, and Santa Chiara churches. Non-baroque sights include Romanesque **SS Nicola e Cataldo►**, the art and antiquities of the **Museo Provinciale►►** (currently mostly *closed* for modernization; a small section is *open* Sun–Fri) and the ruins of the amphitheater, built at the time of Hadrian and capable of accommodating 20,000 spectators.

► Lucera 212E1

Lucera's windy hilltop site and tangle of inviting streets make it a wonderful place to explore. The **Duomo►►** is one of the region's more alluring medieval buildings, though the tremendous **Frederick II fortress►►** is more likely to command your attention. The second largest in southern Italy, it has walls that stretch over a mile.

217

THE TAVOLIERE
Lucera's lofty position and its immense fortress look down over the plains of the Tavoliere, or "chessboard," named after the chequered pattern created by the region's wheatfields. The land has looked like this since Roman times, when it was divided up into squares for distribution to retired army officers.

Basilica di Santa Croce, Lecce

Apulia is perhaps best known for its remarkably vast number of Romanesque churches and cathedrals. Each in its way is a monument to the architectural styles bequeathed over the centuries by the region's many invaders. The influences of the Normans, Arabs, Lombards, and Byzantines all coalesce to produce the magnificent hybrid known as Apulian-Romanesque.

218

Why Apulia? Building a church was no easy matter. Political stability was needed for a start. Long-term projects required sustained peace and finance if they were to be completed. In Apulia, the strong government of Norman, Swabian, and Angevin rulers allowed craftsmen long periods of creative endeavour. It also meant they could travel unmolested, absorbing new trends, and moving their workshops to where demand was highest. Apulia in this respect was a religious crucible, for it lay on several vital pilgrimage routes. Its ports were also points of embarkation for pilgrims bound for the Holy Land.

Rome and Byzantium No two Apulian churches are alike, and no set rules govern their architectural styles, but the variety, richness of decoration, and sculptural skill that make them one of the glories of Italian medieval art are bound by a few unifying strands. The earliest classical models reached Apulian church builders via Byzantium. They contributed decorative motifs—crisp-cut and stylized—such as acanthus leaves, vine tendrils, animals, and birds. Later, Roman portraiture and sarcophagi also played their part.

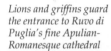
Lions and griffins guard the entrance to Ruvo di Puglia's fine Apulian-Romanesque cathedral

The Lombards Lombard sculpture also had a great influence on Apulian churches: lions, snakes, centaurs, hunters, fishes, and bizarre menageries frequently feature on church portals. Architecturally the Lombards contributed high central naves (with lower aisles), triform apsidal ends, and the arched corbel table below the roof. They also provided the beautiful lateral galleries formed of open arcades.

Arabs and Normans Norman supremacy in the 11th century brought influences from France and Normandy, notably a grandeur of design and execution. Tuscan craftsmen were employed in northern Apulia, taking the "striped" Pisan churches as their model. Oriental features filtered through from Arab Sicily, notably interlaced arches and pointed Saracenic arches. Finally, Frederick II reintroduced further classical Roman refinements.

▶▶ Maratea   212C2

Pretty Maratea, on the Basilicata coast, is as pleasant as any of the resorts on the Calabrian seaboard to the south. It divides into several districts: Maratea Porto, with fishermen's cottages, bars, and restaurants; hill town Maratea Inferiore, home to most of the hotels and fun to explore; and Maratea Superiore, the upper town, from which you can climb to the evocative ruins of Maratea Vecchia (walk a little farther and you reach the top of Monte San Biagio, with views over the Gulf of Policastro and Maratea's 72-foot statue of the Redeemer). The best beaches are 3 miles away at Maratea Marina, but the coast is studded with bays where you are able to swim in complete privacy.

▶ Martina Franca   213D3

Martina Franca's high-rise outskirts do not look promising, but the town center is a marvelous showcase of baroque and rococo architecture. Its centerpiece is the church of **San Martino▶▶**, fronted by a soaring baroque facade. Walk down Via Cavour and you are also treated to numerous exuberantly decorated houses and *palazzi*. The 300-roomed **Palazzo Ducale▶** (*Open* daily. *Admission free*) should not be missed, nor the churches of the Carmine and San Domenico. Wander the old **walls▶** for a lovely panorama over the *trulli*-dotted patchwork of fields and vineyards of the Itria valley. The area's prime tourist attraction lies 17 miles north of the town, the **Grotte di Castellana▶▶** (*Open* daily for guided tours. *Admission: expensive*), a great cave system ending in the impressive Caverna Bianca.

SCENIC DRIVES
Calabria: the SS 105 Belvedere Marittimo–Castrovillari; SS 177 Rossano–Cosenza; SS 179/SS 109 San Giovanni in Fiore–Catanzaro; SS 179 Stilo–Serra San Bruno; (*Aspromonte*) SS 183/184 Reggio di Calabria–Gambarie–Melito. (*Basilicata*): SS 7 Potenza–Matera; SS 19 Lagonegro–Rivello–Mormanno–(Rotonda)–Castrovillari. (*Apulia*): SS 89 Manfredonia–Monte Sant'Angelo–Vieste–Peschici–Rodi-Garganico; SS 528 Monte Sant'Angelo–Vico del Gargano; SS 172 Putignano–Alberobello–Martina Franca.

219

Martina Franca: the restrained elegance of the fountain (left) contrasts with the baroque flamboyance of the architectural detail (above)

▶ Massafra   213D3

Massafra bears striking similarities to Matera (see page 221). Divided in two by a deep ravine, the Gravina di San Marco, it is riddled with grottoes, troglodyte dwellings, and early Greek Christian cave churches (which date from the 9th to 14th centuries). The best churches are San Marco, La Candelora, and San Leonardo. Some of the town's buildings are not well marked by signs and are difficult to reach, but a dramatic baroque staircase leads clearly to **Madonna della Scala▶▶**, built around an early cave church—with delicate 12th-century frescoes—and a primitive 8th-century crypt.

▶▶ **Matera (see opposite page)**   *212D2*

▶▶ **Melfi**   *212D2*

The Normans' occupation of Apulia began when eleven brothers came from Normandy offering their mercenary army in the service of local barons. In 1041 they captured Melfi and two years later elected William de Hauteville their leader. William's sons, Drogo and Humphrey, were succeeded by Robert Guiscard, recognized as "Duke of Apulia and Calabria" by Pope Nicholas II after campaigns against the Saracens (in 1059).

Dark and medieval Melfi still lies in the shadow of its Norman castle (1155), standing proud despite the earthquakes that have laid the town low over the centuries. Inside is a small museum with Greek, Roman, and Byzantine finds, its prize exhibit a 1st-century Roman sarcophagus, the *Sarcofago di Rapolla*.

▶ **Metaponto**   *213C3*

Once home to Pythagoras, *Metapontion* in the 7th century BC was among the most flourishing colonies of Magna Graecia. Although its ruins today are the region's most extensive, they are spread over a large area and their effect is patchy—nor is modern Metaponto, despite its beaches, anything to write home about. The **Museo Archeologico**▶▶ (*Closed* Mon AM. *Admission: moderate*), however, is worthwhile, a museum of finds from the site. On its grounds is the **Tavole Paladine**▶▶, the 15-columned ruins of a 6th-century BC Doric temple. Most of the other remains lie scattered across the **Parco Archeologico**▶.

The Tavole Paladine at Metaponto, a temple dedicated to the goddess Hera

▶ **Otranto**   *213C4*

Greek in origin, Italy's easternmost town nestles around a small harbor. It is an attractive fishing village, increasingly popular despite its mediocre beach. Its cathedral, **Santa Maria Annunziata**▶▶ (*Open* daily. *Admission free*), is remarkable for the fresco-covered crypt (1088), supported by 42 tiny columns, and a beautiful mosaic (1165) that runs the length of the nave. It portrays Biblical stories, illustrates the *Months of the Year* and *The Tree of Life*, and includes characters as diverse as King Arthur, Alexander the Great, and the Queen of Sheba. Also see the town's mighty **Castello**▶ (*Open* daily, AM only Nov–Apr), an Aragonese fortress, and the 10th-century church of **San Pietro**▶.

Bizarrely picturesque Matera is unique for its sassi, *cave dwellings dug from the living rock in the ravines around the town. Many have been inhabited since prehistoric times. A few have been turned into cave churches; others form a honeycomb of streets and alleys.*

Disease and designer dwellings Although Matera's *sassi* appear romantic today, in the early 20th century they represented the ugly face of Italy, racked by unimaginable poverty and riddled with diseases like malaria, dysentery, and trachoma. Over the years their inhabitants have been rehoused in the modern apartments of the new town, only for the old caves to become the latest in designer homes for more affluent town residents. About 700 people now live in the *sassi*.

The best way to get an overall picture of the labyrinth is on the Strada Panoramica, a scenic road specially built for sightseers. To see some of the nooks and crannies, and the rock churches, slip into the smaller back streets or employ one of the children who, for a tip, will take you to places you might not otherwise find.

Seeing the *sassi* The *sassi* divide into two main districts, the Sasso Caveoso (nearest the eastern end of the Strada Panoramica) and Sasso Barisano. Broadly speaking there are four types of cave: the oldest are the niches cut into the sides of the ravine, inhabited up to 7,000 years ago; the second type date from 2000 BC (and form the heart of the Sasso Caveoso); the third are 1,000 years old and lie along Via B. Buozzi; the fourth are the dwellings around Via Fiorentini, most of which were excavated during the 17th century.

Rock churches Of special interest are the *chiese rupestri*, or cave churches, of which there are about 120 around the town. Most were carved by monks between the 8th and 13th centuries. Two of the best, San Pietro Caveoso and Santa Maria de Idris, lie near one another and boast 14th-century Byzantine rock paintings. Santa Lucia alle Malve, a 10th-century church, is worth visiting.

221

The gray labyrinth of sassi, *extraordinary cave houses of Matera*

▶ **Reggio di Calabria** *212A2*

Visit Calabria's capital for the **Museo Nazionale**▶▶ (*Closed* 1st and 3rd Mon of month. *Admission: moderate*), a splendid collection of material from archeological sites all over the region. Prominent works include votive tablets from the Temple of Persephone at *Locri* and two paintings by Antonello da Messina. However, Reggio's pride and joy, the *Bronzi di Riace*, retrieved from the sea in a chance discovery in 1972, are housed in the Museo della Magna Croecia (*Closed* 1st and 3rd Mon. *Admission: moderate*). The two 5th-century BC sculptures depict a pair of Greek warriors, one believed to be the work of Phidias, regarded as the greatest sculptor of antiquity.

One of the Greek Bronzi di Riace in Reggio di Calabria's Museo Nazionale

▶ **Riviera Calabrese (Calabrian Riviera)** *212B2*

The Calabrian Riviera is a term of convenience for a fairly uniform succession of resorts, beaches, and unassuming countryside on the Tyrrhenian coast. Development is often less marked than in Italy's northern resorts, but towns still have a wide choice of hotels, restaurants, and nightlife. Most spots are crowded with Italians on vacation in summer, but sleepy and undisturbed out of season. Tropea (see page 225) is the best destination, but other pleasant places include San Nicola Arcella; Diamante (an unusually chic resort); Amantea; and Pizzo (a reasonable alternative to Tropea).

▶▶ **Rossano** *213C3*

This picturesque little hill town was the most important Byzantine center in the south during the 9th century. The greatest monument to its illustrious past is the *Codex Purpureus*, a beautifully illuminated 6th-century manuscript kept in the **Museo Diocesano**▶▶ (*Closed* Mon in winter. *Admission: moderate*). The 188-page volume contains the Gospels of St. Matthew and St. Mark, and was probably brought to Italy by monks fleeing Muslim persecution. While you are in Rossano, do not miss 10th-century **San Marco**▶▶, Calabria's finest Byzantine church, lent a Middle Eastern flavor by its palm trees and tiny cupolas. Its terrace offers a fine view over Rossano's cave-riddled gorge. The town has several frescoed Byzantine churches, notably La Panaghia and Santa Maria del Pilerio.

▶▶ **Ruvo di Puglia** *212D2*

Ruvo's **Museo Jatta**▶▶ (*Closed* Sat and Sun PM. *Admission free*) offers a collection of the 5th- to 3rd-century BC ceramics for which the town was famous. Among its 1,700-plus terra-cottas is the red-figured Greek vase known as the *Krater of Talos*. The **Duomo**▶▶ is one of the region's important pieces of Apulian-Romanesque architecture, its rather severe facade relieved by a richly decorated portal and exquisite rose window. The griffins flanking the main doorway and the pagan figures are thought to have been copied from pieces of classical pottery.

ASPROMONTE
The "Bitter Mountain" is an incredibly wild region east of Reggio di Calabria. It is one of Italy's most isolated areas, and ways of life here have changed little in centuries. Aspromonte's mountain wilderness is a traditional haunt of Calabria's kidnappers (though the area is perfectly safe). Excursions on its high roads offer astounding landscapes and ancient villages where Greek dialects are still spoken.

Nobody knows the real age or origins of Apulia's trulli, *the strange, conical dwellings that are found solely in a small region around Alberobello and nowhere else in Europe.*

Practical but puzzling *Trulli* are round, single-story buildings made with uncemented stones. They are invariably whitewashed, and their tapered roofs are usually crowned with hieroglyphics—often a cross or some more arcane symbol (possibly of unknown magical significance). The oldest surviving example dates back to the 13th century, though most are no more than 300 years old. Their origins, however, are certainly more ancient.

At their most basic, the houses are eminently practical—there is plenty of local limestone available and they are simple to build; they remain cool in summer and are easily heated in winter. By these criteria, you would expect them to be found all over the Mediterranean. Why they occur only in Apulia is not known—though there is no shortage of theories.

Tax evasion? For a time it was thought they were built to outwit Ferdinand I of Aragon who, during his reign, forbade the Apulians to build permanent houses (in this way he could move laborers around as they were needed). The peasants responded by constructing houses that could be dismantled very quickly and easily when the king's inspectors were spotted. This theory has now been discredited, along with the notion that the houses were designed as a wily form of tax evasion. During Spanish rule a tax was levied on individual houses, and only unfinished buildings were exempt, a clause, it is claimed, the *trulli* owners exploited with their loose-stoned, easily removed roofs.

Greece or the Middle East A more persuasive theory links them with similar buildings at Mycenae, an idea which, if true, would connect the *trulli* with the Greek civilization of 3000 BC. Apulian ports are the closest to Greece, and for centuries the region was part of Magna Graecia. On the same lines, and perhaps closer to the truth, is the theory that they were imported from the Middle East—a conjecture based on their similarity to the "sugar loaf" houses of Syria and elsewhere. It is possible that they were introduced by Eastern monks—and used initially as tombs. Either that or they could have been copied by soldiers returning from the Crusades.

TRAIN RIDE
To visit the best of Puglia's *trulli*, take the private railway operated by the *Ferrovie Sud-Est*. The line begins at Bari and ends at Taranto. *En route* it passes close to the Grotte di Castellana (see page 219), then it travels to Putignano, beyond which you begin to see *trulli*. The largest concentration is found in and around Alberobello, 12 miles beyond, a busy place whose 1,500 *trulli* make it a popular destination. You could leave the train here, and then reboard a later connection to take you on to Martina Franca (see page 219).

One of Apulia's mysterious trulli

▶ Sila   212B2

Calabria's mountainous interior divides into three jumbled massifs—the Sila Grande, Sila Piccola, and Sila
Greca—large areas of which are protected by the Parco
Nazionale della Calabria. Almost the Apennines' last
gasp, they have long been famous for their forests (from
about the 6th century onward, timber from the Sila provided the wooden roofs for many of Rome's churches).
Today the scenery is wild and unspoiled, though the long
rolling ridges and endless woods can become
monotonous. Camigliatello and San Giovanni in Fiore (a
less attractive town) are the main bases, Lakes Arvo,
Cecita, and Ampollino the most picturesque areas. Roads
off the SS 107 (SS 177, SS 179 and SS 108bis) offer the best
drives, and there is a superbly scenic little railway from
Cosenza to San Giovanni in Fiore. The villages in the
mountains are not generally very pretty—life is hard and
poverty rife—but they come alive during the numerous
centuries-old festivals still held in many centers.

▶ Stilo   212A2

Any fan of early church architecture should head for Stilo,
home to **La Cattolica**▶▶, an important if ramshackle
Byzantine church of indeterminate age (estimates range
from 10th-century to 12th-century). Its brick and stone
weathered to a red-brown hue, the church looks out over a
valley, a retreat for Basilian monks in southern Calabria
(as Rossano was for their counterparts in the region's
north). Note the upturned ancient column in the nave,
reputedly a symbol of Christianity's triumph over pagan-
ism. The town has other churches of lesser antiquity.

*The rolling forested
landscape of the Sila*

▶ Taranto   213D3

A large port and naval base, Taranto has one important
tourist attraction, the **Museo Nazionale**▶▶▶ (currently
closed; one part of collection on display in Palazzo
Pantaleo. *Open* daily. *Admission: inexpensive*). The emphasis is on Magna Graecia, embracing a range of Greek
statues, ceramics, and the world's largest collection of
Greek terra-cottas. Its centerpiece is the *Sala degli Ori*,
devoted to goldware. Other highlights include a pair of
korai (figurines of young girls); Roman portraits; actors'
masks; and busts of Apollo and Aphrodite.

▶▶ Trani   212D2

Trani is an elegant and picturesque Apulian port, once a rival to Bari as the region's most important maritime power and still a cosmopolitan town. Today its fame rests on the **Duomo▶▶▶**, one of the area's finest examples of Apulian-Romanesque architecture. The cathedral's beauty is given added impact by the fact that it sits virtually on the sea's edge. Tremendous bronze doors, cast in 1180, usher you into a three-tiered church. Most of the interior is Norman, though part rests on the Ipogea di San Leucio, a 6th-century paleo-Christian tomb. In the rest of town, try not to miss the church of Ognissanti, built as a hospice by the Knights Templar; the Palazzo Caccetta, a 15th-century Gothic palace (Gothic buildings are rare in Apulia); and the Castello, built for Frederick II in 1233 (but since rebuilt). Also walk around the medieval quarter, centered around Via Mario Pagano, and relax in the Villa Comunale (Public Gardens) near the seafront.

▶▶ Troia   212E1

Quiet and windblown, Troia is a pretty village, distinguished by its splendid **cathedral▶▶▶**. Built in 1093, it has a sumptuous rose window, as well as a pair of 12th-century bronze doors, all tinged with the classical, Saracen, and Byzantine motifs that characterize Apulian-Romanesque architecture. Inside the cathedral, take a look at the curious carved 12th-century pulpit, the capitals, and the paintings.

▶▶ Tropea   212B2

A huddle of pastel-colored houses perched above the sea and surrounded by golden beaches, Tropea is by far the nicest resort on the Calabrian coast (the Riviera Calabrese). Although very fashionable and popular, the town manages to retain its original charm, and has hotels and *trattorie* in most price ranges.

When not enjoying Tropea's beaches, seafood, or picturesque streets, visit the church of Santa Maria dell'Isola, dramatically set on a limestone crag near the sea. Also visit the Duomo, known for two strange works of art: an inlaid 16th-century Black Crucifix and the Giotto school *Madonna of Rumania*, by a follower of Giotto, but supposedly painted by St. Luke.

Trani's cathedral, a jewel of the Apulian-Romanesque style

225

SCYLLA AND CHARYBDIS
The legendary sea monsters of Homer's *Odyssey* were probably whirlpools created in the Straits of Messina by the meeting of the Ionian and Tyrrhenian seas. Ships to this day must navigate with care in these waters. Scylla corresponds to Calabria's modern-day village of Scilla: Charybdis is Cariddi on the Sicilian mainland.

The church of Santa Maria dell'Isola, Tropea

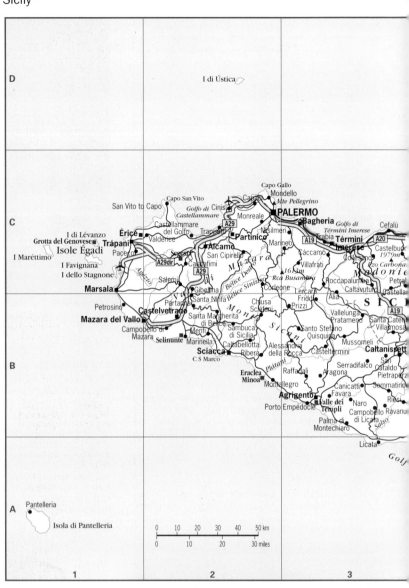

The island of Sicily

Colorful Sicilian
ceramics for the
tourist market

SICILY Cross the sea to Sicily and you do more than leave the Italian mainland. You cross to an island that stands on the edge of Europe, a place whose history and culture conspire to make it a world apart. Almost every Mediterranean power over the last 2,000 years has ruled its shores, not only leaving a mark on its art and architecture, but also molding its cuisine and shaping its attitude to foreigners (a breed that for some Sicilians also includes other Italians). Although subjugation—together with poverty and the Mafia—have often crippled the island, they have rarely cowed its population. As a result you will find Sicilians some of the most singular and most hospitable of Italians.

HISTORY Sicily is named after its early Siculo and Sicano tribes (1250 BC). Given the 500 years of Greek domination (from 800–300 BC), it could as easily have kept its Greek name, *Trinacria* (after the island's triangular shape: Greek *treis*—three—and *akra*—point). During this period cities like Syracuse and Agrigento were among the most powerful in Europe. Roman rule followed, superseded by the Vandals and then by the Byzantines. Two centuries of Arab rule from 827 produced another golden age, followed by a further upbeat period under the Normans (1061–1194). Henry IV, son of Frederick Barbarossa, imposed a period of imperial Swabian rule, soon followed by Angevin domination under Charles of Anjou (brother of the French king). The famous Sicilian Vespers (1282), after a brief period of independence, brought in the Spanish, who ruled Sicily in one guise or another until the 19th century.

The Greek temple of Segesta in its magnificent flower-strewn setting

ART AND ARCHITECTURE Sicily is laden with monuments from each of its historical epochs; archeological sites make up some of the island's most enticing attractions. The Greeks bequeathed the theaters of Syracuse and Taormina, and the temples of Agrigento, Selinunte, and Segesta. The Romans created the mosaics of Piazza Armerina; Arabs, Byzantines, and Normans left numerous fine buildings and influenced the architecture of countless others. Swabians and Angevins built palaces and churches, many overlaid with the baroque stamp of the Spanish (most notably those in Noto and Ragusa). All the strands come together in Palermo, moribund and slightly battered in places, but still one of Italy's great artistic capitals. Few towns, however, are without treasures from one or more periods.

LANDSCAPES The last 30 years have not been kind to the Sicilian coast. Time and again you come across ranks of derelict factories or half-built houses destroying what must once have been an idyllic coast. Cefalù and lovely Taormina are notable exceptions, and things are better on the islands—the unspoiled Egadi, for example, or the volcanic Lipari. In the interior they are better still, with landscapes as strange and spectacular as any in Italy. Modern housing has left its mark, but few could fail to be moved by Mount Etna, Europe's greatest volcano, or by the stark grandeur and lunar emptiness of the rolling interior plateaux. The mountains, too, are a revelation, especially the Madonie and Nebrodi, whose high, wooded ridges run along much of the northern coast.

FOOD Eating is one of Sicily's great pleasures—Greek, Arab, Norman, and Spanish influences combining to form a unique cuisine. The quality and variety of fruit and vegetables in the markets is superb, and in restaurants the array of specialties is overwhelming. Seafood figures heavily, notably mussels (*cozze*), tuna (*tonno*), sardines (*sardi*), and swordfish (*pesce spada*). Fish sauces for pasta are good, especially *pasta con le sarde*. Chillis, capers, olives, peppers, and eggplant are widely used (notably in *caponata*, a local "sweet-and-sour" specialty). Sicilian desserts are legendary. Ice cream was reputedly first made by the Arabs using snow from Etna. *Cassata* is an ice cream cake, *granita* crushed ice flavored with coffee or lemon. *Zabaglione*, a frothy whip of eggs and Marsala wine, and *cannoli*, a cream-filled pastry, must both be sampled at least once.

WHEN AND HOW TO GO Spring is the best time to visit Sicily, when the weather is warm and the hills covered in wildflowers. July and August are uncomfortably hot and crowded, while September and October are more pleasant (and you can often swim as late as November). Be warned, however, that in the interior, and particularly in the mountains, the weather can be cold, and occasionally severe—snow is not unknown in April and May.

There are several ways of reaching Sicily from the mainland, including regular car ferries to Messina from Villa San Giovanni and Reggio di Calabria. Overnight car ferries operate daily from Naples to Palermo, and once a week to Catania and Syracuse.

TOURIST INFORMATION
Agrigento: Via Cesare Battisti 15
(tel: 0922 20 454).
Cefalù: Corso Ruggero 77
(tel: 0921 421 050).
Enna: Via Roma 413 (tel: 0935 528 228) and
Piazza Colajanni 6 (tel: 0935 26 119).
Lipari: Corso Vittorio Emanuele 202 (tel: 090 988 0095).
Monreale: Piazza Duomo (tel: 091 640 2448).
Palermo: Piazza Castelnuovo 34–35
(tel: 091 605 8351 or 583 847).
Piazza Armerina: Via Cavour 15
(tel: 0935 680 201).
Siracusa: Via Maestranza 33 (tel: 0931 464 255) and Via San Sebastiano 45 (tel: 0931 67 710).
Taormina: Piazza Santa Catarina, Palazzo Corvaja (tel: 0942 23 243).

229

SCENIC DRIVES
(*Mount Etna*): Catania–Nicolosi–Rifugio Sapienza; Linguaglossa–Rifugio Citelli–Milo; SS 120 Adrano–Bronte–Randazzo.
(*Madonie mountains*): Cefalù–Collesano–Piano Battaglia–Petralia Soprana; SS 286/SS 120 Cefalù–Gibilmanna–Castelbuono–Gangi–Nicosia; SS 117 Mistretta–Nicosia–Enna.

Mount Etna seen from Taormina

The Temple of Concord at Agrigento (ancient Acragas), one of the most complete Greek temples remaining

OPERATIC TASTE
There is a famous pasta specialty named after one of the operas of Catania-born composer Vincenzo Bellini. You should be able to sample *pasta alla Norma* (a tomato and eggplant sauce garnished with basil and cheese) in any of the trattorias on Via Etnea.

▶▶▶ **Agrigento**   *226B3*

Although modern Agrigento detracts from the setting, the **Valle dei Templi**▶▶▶ (Valley of the Temples) is one of Europe's greatest archeological sites. Only ruins now remain of perhaps Magna Graecia's foremost city.

The eastern zone (*Open* daily 8:30 AM–9 PM. *Admission free*) of the site contains the **Tempio di Ercole (Hercules)**▶▶, a temple built around the time of the colony's foundation in 582 BC. Nearby are the ruins of a paleo-Christian necropolis and the tawny-stoned **Tempio della Concordia (Concord)**▶▶▶, the best-preserved Greek temple in the world after the Theseion in Athens. From here a path follows the old walls to the **Tempio di Giunone (Juno)**▶▶, a lonely and majestic ruin at the edge of the site.

In the western zone is the **Tempio di Giove (Jupiter)**▶ (*Open* daily 8:30–7. *Admission: inexpensive*), planned as the largest Greek temple, but unfinished after an attack by the Carthaginians in 405 BC. Here is a *telamone*, a column carved as a human figure, and the Tempio dei Dioscuri, a fake temple built in 1832 from miscellaneous fragments.

The **Museo Nazionale Archeologico**▶▶▶ (*Open* daily 9–1 and Wed–Sat 1:30–5:30. *Admission: moderate*) a mile from the site, houses an overwhelming collection of artifacts removed from Agrigento and its environs. Outstanding are its *telamone*; a *krater*, or vase, depicting the *Battle of the Amazons*; the *Efebo*, a statue of a young man; a statuette known as the *Sitting Venus*; and several lion's head carvings removed from the temples. Also pop into the adjacent church of **San Nicola**▶, for its views of the temples, and the Greek and Roman fragments incorporated in its walls.

▶ **Catania**   *227B5*

Sicily's second city is a modern, industrial place, whose chaotic streets may deter you from exploring its handful of ancient and medieval monuments (most of which have suffered over the years from earthquakes). The **Duomo**▶ and Sicily's largest church, San Nicolò, are worth a glance; so, too, the artistic and archeological displays of the **Museo Civico**▶ (*Open* daily 9–1).

Magna Graecia *(Greater Greece) was the net-work of scattered Greek colonies that sprang up over much of Sicily and southern Italy from about the 8th century* BC. *Greece had an established trade with parts of Italy, most notably with the Etruscan cities of Tuscany, and it was inevitable that in time settlers should start to colonize areas near the Greek mainland. Over the centuries, the splendor of their cities came to rival and sometimes exceed those of Greece itself.*

The colonies According to the historian Thucydides, the first settlers in Sicily established a foothold at Naxos (now Giardini-Naxos near Taormina) in 735 BC. They then quickly founded other colonies on Sicily's eastern coast at *Catana* (Catania), *Leontinoi* (Lentini), and *Zancle* (Messina). Within a year Greeks from Corinth had raised *Ortigia* (Syracuse), Magna Graecia's most powerful city, and five years later Megaran colonists, neighbors of the Corinthians in Greece, founded Megara Hyblaea, 15 miles to the north. Settlers from Crete and Rhodes created Gela in 689 BC, expanding westward a century later to settle *Acragas* (Agrigento). Pioneers from Rhodes founded Lipari, Sicily's last Greek colony, in 580 BC.

Sicilian riches Although the colonies retained links with Greece, they quickly became independent cities. Sicily's immense resources—especially its wheat-growing potential—brought them considerable wealth, a prosperity that can still be gauged from the splendor of the ruins in Syracuse and Agrigento. At the same time, however, the colonies were torn by internal jealousies and internecine warfare.

Greek jealousy As well as suffering civil war, the cities remained prey to two external adversaries. The first threat came from the mainland Greek states, who became jealous of Magna Graecia's increasing power. In 415 BC Athens sent an armada to attack Syracuse, suffering a defeat—after one of the greatest sea battles in ancient history—that left Syracuse and Magna Graecia at the peak of their powers.

Carthage The second threat came from Carthage, a North African power founded by the Phoenicians, who had cities of their own in western Sicily (Marsala and Palermo in particular). Battles raged between the two powers for centuries (and Carthage often sided with cities against their neighbors). In the 3rd century BC, the two sides laid aside their differences and united to confront the growing power of Rome. The alliance was to no avail. The sack of Syracuse by Rome in 211 BC marked Magna Graecia's effective demise. For 700 years thereafter Sicily remained under Roman rule.

MAGNA GRAECIA TODAY
Archeological and historical remnants of the great Greek-influenced cities that once lay scattered across Sicily today make up some of the most enticing and rewarding sights on the island. The most obvious things to see are Magna Graecia's great surviving temples, particularly those at Segesta (see page 240), which is noted for its beautiful surroundings, and Agrigento (see page 230), celebrated as some of the best-preserved monuments from the ancient world. There are also the remains of no fewer than seven temples at Selinunte (see page 240), two of which are in an excellent state of preservation. You might also want to visit the Greek theaters at Taormina and Siracusa (Syracuse), and the museums of antiquities in these and other towns.

231

LA MATTANZA
Tuna are caught all over Sicily, but the most famous catch is Favignana's ritualized slaughter, *La Mattanza*. The age-old rite takes place around three times weekly in May and June. Under the head fisherman, or *rais* (an Arabic title), the fish are surrounded, netted, and then impaled and beaten to death. To many, in these days of ecological awareness, the ritual seems to be a bloodthirsty tourist attraction.

Charming Cefalù is dominated by its superb Norman-Romanesque cathedral

▶▶ Cefalù   226C3

Of all Sicily's coastal towns, except for Taormina, Cefalù is perhaps the most attractive. Nestled under a huge crag, it boasts good beaches and a tangle of tempting medieval streets. Its prime attraction is the beautiful **Duomo▶▶▶**, whose glorious mosaics (1148) are the earliest of any church in Sicily. Equally captivating is its Norman-Romanesque facade, best seen from one of the outdoor cafés in the palm-fringed **Piazza del Duomo▶▶**. Close by lies the **Museo Mandralisca▶▶** (*Open* daily. *Admission: moderate*) with a collection of Greek and Arab artifacts, and a painting by Sicily's most famous artist, Antonello da Messina, the *Portrait of an Unknown Man* (1472).

▶ Egadi, Isole   226C1

Ferries and hydrofoils run from Trapani to this archipelago off Sicily's western coast. Favignana is the largest and most popular island, with many rocky coves but just one sandy beach, Cala Burrone. **Marettimo▶▶** is wilder and grander, an important sanctuary for wildlife, with gentle walks and hidden beaches. **Levanzo▶** is more primitive, rocky and sun-bleached, and known for the neolithic cave paintings of the Grotta del Genovese.

▶ Enna   227B4

If you explore Sicily's remote and beautiful interior, then consider making your base in Enna (the so-called "navel of Sicily"). There is little to see, but the town has a welcoming air and—from its incredible crag-top position—some of the finest views on the island. Two small museums, the Museo Alessi (*Open* daily. *Admission: inexpensive*) and Museo Archeologico (*Open* daily. *Admission: inexpensive*), have displays of Greco-Roman finds and medieval church art. The **Castello▶** (*Open* daily. *Admission free*) was built by Frederick II, on a site probably used as a citadel for over 5,000 years.

▶▶ Erice   226C1

Erice is a mountain town, a sacred place and mighty fortress (*Eryx*) since time immemorial. Tourists crowd in during the summer, drawn by the views from its limestone ramparts and the piazzas and cobbled streets, but there are quiet corners in which to escape the throng.

▶▶ Etna
227B5

Etna (10,965 feet) is one of the world's largest and most active volcanoes. One of the Mediterranean's greatest landforms, its smoking summit is a landmark over much of Sicily. The Arabs called it *Jebel*, the Mountain of Mountains. Ancient navigators thought it the highest point on earth. Pindar described it as the "column which supports the sky." The Greeks called it *Aipho* (I burn), from

Etna smoulders under its blanket of snow

233

which the present name derives. Reputedly, Arabs used ice from its summit to create *gelato* in the 8th century.

Eruptions For all its majesty, Etna is little more than 60,000 years old—a mere stripling in geological terms. There have been about 90 major eruptions since 475 BC (when the first was recorded)—minor eruptions occur almost annually. The most catastrophic came in 1669, when a 15-mile fissure opened up in the mountain (Etna has a tendency to split at the seams, unlike most volcanoes, which erupt through the central cone; around 350 minor craters have been created by these lateral eruptions). The rent unleashed a tongue of magma over a mile wide, engulfing Catania (24 miles away) and surrounding its castle with molten lava. The eruption continued for 122 days, throwing out ash that carried over 60 miles. In places the lava took eight years to cool. Chronicles describe peasants boiling water on the rocks long after the eruption.

Around the volcano Etna is an awe-inspiring sight, and a quarter of a million people a year now visit the crater (see panel). Its environs, however, offer as much to see as the melancholy desolation of its highest slopes. For a good view of these varied surroundings you can either drive one of several scenic roads or take the Circumetnea railway that circles Etna's base, starting at Catania's Circumetnea station and finishing at Giarre-Riposto. Five trains daily ply the route. Most motorists approach from Catania, but roads from **Linguaglossa▶▶** and Adrano are equally spectacular—and less busy. All routes offer beautiful countryside, ranging from thick forests of oak and chestnut to the citrus and olive groves on Etna's fertile lower slopes.

REACHING THE SUMMIT
All-inclusive tours to Etna's summit run from Catania or Taormina. It is as easy (and cheaper), however, to make the trip by car or take a bus from Catania's FS railway station to the *Rifugio Sapienza* (6,207 feet). From here you can walk to the summit on a rough road provided for tourist minibuses. Allow 3 to 4 hours for the walk, wear boots or strong shoes, and take plenty of warm and waterproof clothing.

STROMBOLI

Stromboli is packed in summer with visitors drawn to its still-active volcano (which performs around four times hourly). Hotels are busy, so make the island a day trip from Salina or Lipari. A path leads to the cone (3,059 feet) from Piscita, a hamlet close to the harbor at San Vicenzo (a five-hour walk there and back). Many people camp near the summit to enjoy the volcano at night.

AEOLUS

Aeolus, god of the winds and navigation, kept all the world's winds in one of the islands' many caves. Ulysses was given a sack of them, and they blew his boat back to port when his curious crew opened the bag.

The Duomo at Messina: what is claimed as the world's largest astronomical clock is housed in the campanile

ANTONELLO DA MESSINA (1414–1479)

This great Sicilian painter was one of the few southern artists to leave a mark on the Italian Renaissance. He was one of the first painters to experiment with oils, his virtuoso technique—particularly in portraiture—greatly influencing the Venetian artists of his day (Antonello himself was much influenced by Flemish art). Only a handful of his works survive in Sicily, notably in Messina, Cefalù, Syracuse, and Palermo.

▶ Gela   227A4

Gela is a town ravaged by textile factories and petrochemical plants. It is redeemed only by its **Museo Archeologico▶** (*Open* daily. *Admission: moderate*), known for the collection of 5th-century BC pottery for which Greek Gela was famous. About 2 miles out of town is the attractive **Capo Soprano▶▶**, where part of the fortifications that once surrounded the city have been excavated.

▶▶ Lipari, Isola di   227D4

Lipari is the main island of the Isole Eolie (Aeolian Islands), a seven-island volcanic archipelago off Sicily's northern coast. The group has become popular recently, visited mainly for its beaches and Stromboli's regular volcanic eruptions. The Aeolian islands were named after Aeolus, the Greek god of the winds and navigation (see panel).

Lipari is the busiest of the islands, easily reached by regular ferries from Milazzo, Messina, Naples, and Reggio di Calabria. From its capital, Lipari, a picturesque port (with a good little museum), you can take boat trips around the coast or pick up bus connections to the rest of the island. You can also rent bikes and motor scooters (many roads offer lovely panoramas of Sicily and the archipelago). Good targets include Aquacalda, interesting for its pumice and obsidian quarries; San Calogero, which has mud baths and hot springs; and Canneto, a mile from Lipari's best beach, the Spiaggia Bianca. Much of the rugged interior also offers excellent walking.

To escape the crowds, visit the tiny yet dazzling island of Panarea, or the still unspoiled islets of Filicudi and Alicudi (each has a hotel and a few private rooms).

▶ Messina   227C5

Most people see no more of the gateway to Sicily than is absolutely necessary. Despite an enchanting view from the ferry, Messina is a battered and modern city (the result of earthquakes and 1943 bombing raids). If you have to linger there, try to be in Piazza del Duomo at noon for the performance of one of the world's largest astronomical clocks (housed in the campanile, located to the side of the main cathedral building). It is also worth paying a visit to the outlying **Museo Regionale▶** (*Closed* Mon and PM Sun, Wed, and Fri. *Admission: moderate*), which is graced with paintings by Caravaggio and Antonello da Messina.

▶▶▶ Monreale 226C2

Little outside the famous Norman cathedral of Monreale, 5 miles east of Palermo, suggests the splendor of what is within—the most extensive and accomplished Christian mosaics in the world. Probably the work of Greek and Byzantine craftsmen, they were started around 1174 and completed in only 10 years. The apse portrays Christ, arms outstretched, flanked by St. Peter and St. Paul (the panels show the saints' martyrdoms—crucifixion and beheading respectively). The nave's gold-backed mosaics illustrate episodes from the Old and New Testaments.

Climb the tower for its views, then visit the cloister, an elegant arcade supported by 216 twin columns (no two of which are the same). To the cathedral's rear lies a garden, filled with banyan trees and other exotic vegetation. Little else in the town is worth exploring, though the views over Palermo and the Conca d'Oro, or "Golden Shell," (the coastal area) are magnificent.

▶▶ Noto 227A5

The earthquake that devastated much of eastern Sicily in 1693 had at least one silver lining—many of the cities it razed were beautifully rebuilt in the baroque style of the day. Noto's tawny-stoned churches and palaces are the most complete expression of this transformation. It is also one of the more heavily promoted of the region's tourist attractions, so if you wish to stay—and the town makes a nice stopover—then be prepared for high-season crowds.

During rebuilding, the town's residential and religio-political districts were deliberately separated. Most of the latter's buildings lie along Corso Vittorio Emanuele, the best on **Piazza del Municipio▶▶**, one of the most harmonious little squares in Sicily. Most of the *palazzi* have beautifully decorated facades, but perhaps the most famous is the **Palazzo Villadorata▶▶**, known for its billowing balconies (located in Via Corrado Nicolaci, first right west of Piazza del Municipio).

235

Baroque splendor in Noto, one of the gems of Sicily

RAPPORTI MAFIA - POLITICA:
INFLUENZA NELLE AMMINISTRAZIONI LOCALI
VENERDÌ 7 MAGGIO 1993 - Ore 18,30
CARMINE MANCUSO

Many ambiguities surround the origins and identity of the Mafia. These days the old image of a criminal fraternity bound by family ties and codes of honor is a thing of the past. Mafia bosses are now slick-suited supremos (with politicians in their pockets), involved in every dubious trade from arms to heroin.

PLUS ÇA CHANGE...

One of the earliest allusions to the Mafia came in a report from the the British consul in 1866, who wrote: "*Maffie*-elected *juntas* share the earnings of the workmen, keep up intercourse with outcasts, and take male-factors under their wing and protection."

THE MAFIA FAMILY

Mafia "families" are groups united in crime—which do not always include blood relations. Each takes its name from its village of origin (Corleone, for example), or the city quarter it con-trols (in Palermo, the *Ciaculli*, *Porta Nova*, etc). Each has foot soldiers, lieutenants, and a *capo*, or *padrino* (godfather). Families ally themselves in *cosche*, named after artichoke crowns (to sym-bolize the unity of many), but the network is often fractured by disputes both within and between families.

THE AMERICAN MAFIA

The hundreds of thousands of Sicilians who emigrated to the United States at the beginning of the century were a breeding ground for Mafia-style organiza-tions (the so-called "Black Hand"). During the period of Fascist rule, many Italian *mafiosi* also fled to the U.S. Today, few doubt that there are links between Italian and American organized crime.

Mafia and mafia Everything about the Mafia is mysterious—even where its name comes from. The word may derive from the Arabic *mu'afàh* meaning "protection" (though it also means "skill," "ability," "beauty," and "safety"). It appeared in Italian for the first time around 1860. Many commentators underline the idea of mafia as a mentality, "a state of mind, a philosophy of life, a moral code, prevailing among all Sicilians" (Luigi Barzini, *The Italians*). This small "m" mafia does not mean all Sicilians are criminals (nor that they condone criminality). It does, however, have a bearing on its upper-case cousin—the criminal underworld known as the Mafia.

Origins How and why the Mafia (and mafia) developed are vexed questions. The answers lie in the gap that has always existed between southerners and authority— a breach historically filled by the Mafia. Two cultural phenomena go some way to explaining it: first, the value Sicilians attach to the ability to impose one's will on others; second, the historic distrust felt by southerners for the state. This feeling stems from Sicily's catalogue of foreign rulers, as well as from the island's isolation— its rugged interior has always proved a barrier to the imposition of authority—and from the alienation of peasants from their feudal overlords, forced to work on Sicily's estates (*latifondi*) as serfs for absentee landlords in Naples or Palermo.

History Mafia activities go back hundreds of years, some say to the 12th century, when a secret sect was formed to oppose imperial rule. Under the Bourbons, ex-brigands were used to "police" the interior, often taking kickbacks instead of arresting their erstwhile colleagues. Elsewhere, middlemen known as *gabellotti* acted as mediators between peasants and landowners. By intimidating one group and becoming agents for the other, they quickly grew rich, becoming a distinct class, bound by mutual self-interest, and established codes of honor and a semi-formal organization.

Mussolini and the Mafia Little is known of the Mafia before World War II. It was under fascism that Mussolini became the only political figure in Italy's history to dam-age the organization. Through his legendary prefect, Cesare Mori, he set about the Mafia with a lethal—and illegal—efficiency. The Mafia was dealt a dose of its own medicine. It might well have proved fatal—but for the intervention of the Americans.

Allied deliverance When the Allies prepared to land in Sicily in 1943, they had only one organized source of intelligence and logistical support—the Mafia. In New York they talked to men like Lucky Luciano, who provided "introductions" to the island's Mafia bosses (Luciano's 50-year prison sentence was repealed as a reward). This cleared the way for the Allies, and, in the aftermath of the invasion, also helped create the Allied Military Government. In organizing political and military control of the island, the Allies entrusted responsibility for 62 of Sicily's 66 towns and cities to men with Mafia connections. Don Vito Genovese, on whom Mario Puzio based *The Godfather*, was one of these men.

The new Mafia Allied intervention left the Mafia well placed to exploit Italy's postwar economic boom. With its criminal muscle and political connections it amassed huge fortunes (mainly from the construction business). Much of the money was "laundered" through "respectable" businesses, or used to finance the Mafia's expansion into arms and drug-dealing (trades that brought immeasurable riches and changed the Mafia's character forever). Mafia tactics became increasingly ruthless as the stakes grew higher. Threats to its power were met by violent clan battles and the assassination of all who stood in its way. Despite recent "maxi-trials" of hundreds of *mafiosi*, and the "confessions" of men like Tommaso Buscetta, the Mafia's inextricable links with most aspects of Sicilian life make it highly unlikely that it will ever be eradicated.

WORDS
Italians call the Mafia *la piovra*, or the "octopus," because its tentacles infiltrate so many aspects of national life. The *mafiosi* themselves, however, are more circumspect. They would never address each other as such: Mafia men are *amici* (friends) or *uomini d'onore* (men of honor). They are members of *Cosa Nostra* (Our Thing) and protected by a code of silence—*omertà*.

237

ILLUSTRIOUS CORPSES
Since the 1970s the Mafia has murdered politicians, journalists, and anyone else who threatened its position. These *cadaveri eccellenti* (illustrious corpses) reached a peak in 1982 with the assassination of General dalla Chiesa, gunned down as he prepared to investigate links between politicians and organized crime. In 1992, Italy was shocked by the killings of Giovane Falcone, one of the most effective and highly respected of Sicily's investigating magistrates, and of Judge Paolo Borsellino.

Sicily, 1950s: The coffin of another police officer killed in the daily fight against the Mafia

Glowing mosaics decorate the arches in Palermo's 12th-century Palatine Chapel

▶▶ **Palermo**   *226C2*

Past meets present head-on in Palermo, Sicily's capital. Norman, Arab, and baroque monuments rise amid slums and back streets riddled with poverty and petty crime. Traffic and squalor assault the senses at every turn, ingredients in the city's strange mixture of criminal threat and decaying grandeur. Like Naples, this is not a place to suit all tastes, but in its grungy streets, its vibrant markets, and magnificent art, it captures all the color and contradictions that are so peculiarly Sicilian.

History Palermo started life as an 8th-century BC Phoenician trading post (though it takes its name from the Greek *Panormus*—"all port"). Later it became a Carthaginian and then Roman stronghold. Its golden age came under the Arabs, when for 240 years (from 831) it became Europe's second most important city after Constantinople. It remained preeminent under the Normans (1072) and the Swabians (1194). Decline set in with the Angevins (1266) and—most markedly—with the Spanish, who ruled for almost 600 years from 1282 on.

Cathedral and palace The Norman stamp is evident in the **Cattedrale**▶▶, at least in the exterior (1185); the interior was ruined by 18th-century alterations. Its interesting features are the royal tombs of Henry VI, Roger II, and Frederick II (contained in two chapels of the south aisle). A reliquary (1631) contains the remains of St. Rosalia, Palermo's patron saint. The treasury is full of precious objects, notably a jewel-encrusted crown removed from the tomb of Constance of Aragon, wife of Frederick II.

By the cathedral stands the **Palazzo dei Normanni**▶▶▶ (*Open* Mon, Fri–Sat 9–noon. *Admission free*), a monumental complex started by the Arabs and enlarged by the Normans (under whom it became one of Europe's leading courts). At its heart are the Sala di Re Ruggero (Hall of Roger II), decorated with mosaics of hunting scenes, and Palermo's undoubted artistic highlight, the **Cappella Palatina**▶▶▶ (*Open* Mon–Fri 9–11:45, 3–4:45; Sat 9–11:45;

Sun 9–9:45, noon–12:45. *Admission free*). The latter, built by Roger II in 1132, is largely Romanesque, though the interior rests on Roman columns and glitters with Byzantine-influenced mosaics. The wooden ceiling is Moorish, a honeycomb of exquisite carving.

Churches Nearby **San Giovanni degli Eremiti**▶▶ stands on the edge of the *Albergheria* district, a quarter teeming with baroque churches, busy markets, and back streets. The church (1132), on the site of an old mosque (Palermo once had 200 mosques), retains its original Arab-influenced domes, as well as a picturesque double cloister, filled with palms, shrubs, and lemon trees. Three other important churches lie grouped around **Piazza Pretoria**▶▶. The finest, **La Martorana**▶▶, contains 12th-century mosaics, while both **San Giuseppe**▶ and **Santa Caterina**▶ have wonderfully extravagant baroque interiors.

Museum and gallery The **Museo Archeologico**▶▶ (*Open daily 9–1:30; also 3–7 on Tue, Wed, Fri. Admission: moderate*), is a small but excellent collection, prized for the carved friezes (or metopes) taken from the temples at Selinunte (see page 240). Other highlights include prehistoric cave paintings; lion's head fountains from temples at Himera; the *Ram of Syracuse*, a 3rd-century BC Greek bronze; and two Roman sculptures—*Hercules and the Stag* and *The Satyr Preparing to Drink*. The cream of Sicily's medieval treasures are contained in Palazzo Abatellis's **Galleria Nazionale Siciliana**▶▶▶ (*Open Mon–Sat 9–2; also 3–8 Tue and Thu. Admission: moderate*). Paintings are downstairs, sculptures upstairs, including Antonello da Messina's *Three Saints* and *Annunciation*, the Arab-styled *Malaga Vase*, and a 15th-century *Bust of Eleanor of Aragon.*

Convento dei Cappuccini Italy has no eerier sight than the thousands of mummies lining the catacombs of Palermo's Capuchin convent (*Open daily. Admission: donation*; west of the city at the corner of Via G. Mosca and Via Pindemonte). The figures have parchment-yellow skin stretched across bones. Still wearing clothes—crumbling silks and dusty top hats—each is bizarre, comical, or macabre by turns.

Fishy decisions in Palermo's market

Residents of the Catacombs

▶ **Ragusa** *227A4*

Ragusa suffered in the same earthquake as Noto (see page 235) and was rebuilt along similar baroque lines. It is less visited than its neighbor, however, and you can wander around the atmospheric old town (*Ragusa Ibla*) in virtual solitude. The streets here are decrepit without being depressing, the locked doors and shuttered windows creating the impression of an abandoned ghost town. While exploring, be sure to visit **San Giorgio**▶▶, among the more stately of Sicily's baroque churches.

▶▶▶ **Segesta** *226C2*

Segesta's windswept **Greek temple**▶▶▶ (*Open* daily 9 AM –one hour before sunset. *Admission: moderate*) rises in glorious isolation amid beautiful countryside, the grandest and most inspiring of all Sicily's great Hellenistic monuments. Started around 425 BC, it is all that remains of ancient *Segesta*, a colony with pre-Greek roots in the 12th century BC. The temple was never finished, though from its 36 columns and well-rounded appearance you would never know. Close up, you see that the columns remain unfluted and parts of the walls are missing, but this doesn't detract from the temple's harmonious proportions or the splendor of its setting.

Take the short road (1 mile) that wends through flower-strewn slopes to a small Greek theater on a hilltop nearby. The views are remarkable, especially at sunset, stretching to the sea across Monte Erice and the pastoral plains below.

The unfinished Greek temple of Segesta

▶▶▶ **Selinunte** *226B2*

Open: daily 9 AM–one hour before sunset. Admission: moderate
Founded in 628 BC and probably named after a wild parsley (*selinon* in Greek), Selinunte quickly became one of Magna Graecia's most prosperous colonies. It attracted many rivals, notably Segesta, and suffered devastating attacks from the Carthaginians in 409 BC and 250 BC (blows from which it never recovered). The site today is among Sicily's finest, two of its original seven **temples**▶▶▶ as impressive as any on the island. Nobody knows to which gods Selinunte's temples were dedicated, so each is indicated only by a letter. They divide into two groups: the nearest to the entrance stand in a group (E, F, G)—Temple E was reerected in the 1950s; the others lie together on the old acropolis. Many of the treasures have been taken to Palermo's Museo Archeologico, but the ruins are still a lovely place to explore. The fishing village of Marinella just below the site makes a good base for the ruins.

> *Even in the ruins of Pompeii and Herculaneum, even in Rome itself, there are no classical mosaics to compare in quality or extent with those of the Villa Casale near Piazza Armerina. Spread over 50 rooms, they are Sicily's finest Roman remains and one of the island's foremost attractions.*

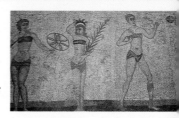

A steep, cobbled lane leads from Piazza Armerina in central Sicily toward the Villa Casale, wending through open countryside before arriving at the little forested valley that shelters the ruins (3 miles). The villa probably served as a retreat and occasional hunting lodge, possibly for Emperor Maximianus Herculius, co-emperor with Diocletian between AD 286 and 305. It was used until as late as the 12th century, when a landslide covered it, preserving the mosaics until full-scale excavations began in the 1950s. The site has been skilfully laid out, new roofs serving to protect the mosaics and to suggest how the villa might have looked in its heyday.

The mosaics All the elements of Roman houses are here, from the atrium, peristyle, and baths to vast public halls and private apartments. Everything pales alongside the mosaics, however, 38,000 square feet of exquisite works that unfold dramatically from room to room. Their style is reminiscent of Roman villas in North Africa, suggesting they are the work of Carthaginian craftsmen, a notion that helps to explain some of the more exotic scenes and animals they portray. Certainly the villa's centerpiece seems set in Africa, the great *Hunting Scene* that stretches about 200 feet along the edge of the court-yard's covered corridor. Its detailed and intertwined narrative depicts tigers, ostriches, elephants—even rhinos—being captured and caged for return to Rome to take part in circuses and gladiatorial games.

241

Detail from a hunting scene: one of the mosaics in the Villa Casale

Equally captivating are a circus scene and chariot race, or an enchanting children's hunt, where youngsters are chased by the hares and peacocks they are supposed to be catching. Another fine room vividly (and bloodily) depicts the labors of Hercules. Most people's favorite room, however, is the one that proves there is nothing new under the sun—with a mosaic showing ten women athletes in Roman "bikinis."

The baroque facade of Syracuse's cathedral

Syracuse: a fishing port for thousands of years

FONTANA ARETUSA
The Delphic oracles that first guided settlers to Syracuse spoke of the spring feeding Ortigia's Arethusa fountain. In Greek myth the nymph Arethusa rose here after swimming from Greece, transformed into a spring by Artemis to escape the clutches of the river god Alpheus. The spot is planted with papyrus and surrounded by a number of pleasant cafés.

▶▶▶ **Siracusa (Syracuse)** 227A5

Syracuse was founded by Greeks from Corinth in 733 BC. Within a hundred years it had become one of Europe's greatest cities. Today it divides into three areas: a dull modern town; Ortigia, the city's heart for 2,700 years; and the Parco Archeologico, a large area of Greek, Roman, and early Christian remains.

The old town Ortigia▶▶, part medieval and part baroque, is an island, linked to the rest of the town by a bridge. It is graced with two pretty squares—**Piazza Duomo▶▶** and Piazza Archimede (both popular meeting places with plenty of nice cafés). See the **Tempio di Apollo▶**, Sicily's oldest Doric temple (565 BC), and spend plenty of time wandering around the port area and its old streets. Pay special attention to the **Duomo▶▶**, a fascinating patchwork of styles, its Norman walls embedded with columns from a 5th-century BC temple (much of the interior was also hacked from the temple). Further fragments hail from the 7th century, the date of the site's consecration as a Christian cathedral. The facade is 17th century.

The **Museo Regionale▶▶** (*Open* Tue–Sun AM, Wed PM. *Admission: moderate*), part of the Palazzo Bellomo, offers paintings, including an *Annunciation* by Antonello da Messina and Caravaggio's *Burial of St. Lucia*. There is also sculpture, silverware, furniture, and religious vestments.

From the ancient world At the **Parco Archeologico▶▶▶** (*Open* Tue–Sun 9 AM–one hour before sunset. *Admission: expensive*—for both Parco and Museo) the first thing you see after the souvenir stalls is the Ara di Ierone, the base of a 3rd-century BC altar. In the past it was the scene of sacrifice; orgies of blood-letting that saw up to 450 bulls slaughtered in one day. Much of its stone was taken by the Spanish in the 16th century. Close by is the 15,000-seat **Teatro Greco▶▶**, the most complete theater in the Greek world (5th-century BC). Near it extends the Latomia del Paradiso, famous for the cave known as the *Orecchio di Dionisio* (Ear of Dionysius).

Near the park, the **Museo Archeologico Nazionale▶▶▶** (*Open* Tue–Sun AM and Mon, Wed, Fri, Sat PM. *Admission: moderate*) has as its star attractions the *Venus Anadiomene* (Venus Rising from the Sea) and Greek statuettes.

▶▶ Taormina
227C5

Taormina is Sicily's most beautiful town, backed by mountains and perched above a turquoise sea. Etna rises majestically in the background. The climate is mild, the views matchless, and its vegetation a semitropical garden of palms, bougainvillea, and orange trees.

What to see The town center forms an intimate collection of tiny streets and flower-filled balconies. Wandering its twisting alleys or exploring its dark staircases is pleasure enough, with the chance of stumbling onto quiet piazzas or of catching sudden views of the sea below.

Beyond the town's back-street charm, there is really only one sight, the magnificently sited **Teatro Greco▶▶▶** (*Open* daily 9 AM–one hour before sunset. *Admission: moderate*). Built by the Greeks in the 3rd century BC, it was almost completely remodeled by the Romans. A small museum holds archeological fragments from the site.

What to do After seeing the theater, many people confine themselves to a drink in one of the expensive but irresistible cafés on Piazza IX Aprile, Taormina's main square (or those on Corso Umberto I, its main street). You should also take time to stroll in the public gardens (on Via Croce) and to climb to the **Castello▶▶** (currently *closed* for restoration) for more all-embracing views. Paths and roads (and buses) beyond the castle lead to Castelmola (3 miles), a tiny crag-top village with more nice bars and fine views.

Sadly, Taormina is too enticing to have to yourself. In peak season (Apr–Sep) it becomes crowded and almost a caricature of itself. The streets are thronged, their attractive shops outnumbered by souvenir stalls. Glitzy pizzerias compete at night with pounding discos. Ranks of glitterati attending film and theater festivals parade. Don't be deterred, but try to come off peak if possible.

TAORMINA ALTERNATIVES
If hotel prices and peak-season crowds prevent you staying in Taormina, consider putting up in Spisone or Letojanni, less elegant but more affordable resorts nearby. Better still, try Giardini-Naxos, the best place to stay near Taormina. It is a modern town, with a broad sandy beach and plenty of hotels at all prices. Regular buses run up to Taormina.

243

The Greek theater above Taormina, with Etna beyond

Sardinia

SARDINIA (SARDEGNA) Italy's second-largest island differs from the Italian mainland in almost every respect, but for visitors its most vital difference is the lack of conventional sightseeing. You come here not for museums and monuments, but for some of Europe's finest beaches, or for the spectacle of the island's mountainous interior. The main cities, Cagliari and Sassari, are provincial spots and—like most of the smaller towns—amount to little more than bases from which to venture farther afield. If you do want to sightsee, you could happily wander around one of the island's classical or prehistoric sites (see page 249), or make a beeline for the string of Pisan-Romanesque churches near Sassari (see page 251).

SEA AND SAND Glorious beaches and aquamarine seas are what bring most people to Sardinia. The most famous beach resorts are on the Costa Smeralda, but there are plenty of smaller resorts, and a plethora of sandy coves and rocky inlets await those who make the effort to get off the beaten track. For the most part the sea is clean and beautifully clear, safe for swimming and ideal for any number of activities from sailing to snorkeling. Facilities at larger resorts allow you to indulge most seaside whims, though there are still plenty of unspoiled and scarcely developed spots.

THE INTERIOR Sardinia's interior is varied and in many parts strikingly beautiful, ranging from gently rolling plains and endless scrub-covered hills to the upland hamlets and desolation of the Barbagia and Gennargentu mountains. Here, sheep and shepherds are often the only living creatures you encounter as you drive the lonely roads. Villages often preserve ancient customs and ceremonies, and you may still come across people in traditional costume. For the most part, inland Sardinia is also unused to seeing many tourists, so expect facilities to be few and far between.

Sardinia

Mosaic in Cagliari's cathedral

TOURIST INFORMATION
Alghero: Piazza Porta Terra 9 (tel: 079 979 054).
Cagliari: Piazza Matteotti 9 (tel: 070 669 255).
Nuoro: Piazza Italia 19 (tel: 078 432 307 or 30 083).
Oristano: Piazza Eleonora 19 (tel: 078 336 831).
Sassari: Viale Caprera 36 (tel: 079 299 579) and Viale Umberto 72 (tel: 079 233 534).

HISTORY Although prehistory bequeathed Sardinia's finest monuments—its great stone *nuraghi*—the Phoenicians, some of antiquity's greatest seafarers, are the first culture of which much is known. They arrived in the 8th century BC, followed by the Carthaginians and the Romans (238 BC). During the Middle Ages, Vandals, Byzantines, and Arabs all left their mark. For a brief period, however, the island was ruled by the Giudicati, four independent duchies with close ties to Pisa and Genoa (hence the island's many Pisan-Romanesque churches). The Spanish gained control in 1479, remaining in charge until 1720, when the island passed by treaty to Piedmont's dukes of Savoy (the future kings of Italy). The island joined a united Italy in 1861.

FOOD Sardinian cuisine is the simple food of peasant and fisherman. On the coast you can sample just about every type of Mediterranean seafood, and in the interior cheeses such as *pecorini, casu marzu,* and the yogurtlike *gioddu* are common. First-course specialties include *malloreddus* (small dumplings); *culingiones* (ravioli); *favata* (pork and bean stew); *leppudrida* (meat and vegetable soup); and *sa fregula* (Sardinian couscous). For main courses you might be offered *aragosta* (crayfish); *burrida* (marinated fish); *porceddu* (suckling pig); or *buttarga* (tuna or mullet roe). *Sebadas* are cheese and honey pastries fried in oil; *suspirus* and *gueffus* are desserts bursting with almonds.

FACTS AND FIGURES
Sardinia lies 108 miles from mainland Italy, and is 162 miles long by about 72 miles wide. It is Italy's third largest region, but has the country's lowest population density (the population is 1.6 million, a third that of Sicily). The capital is Cagliari and there are three provincial capitals—Nuoro, Oristano, and Sassari.

WINE Several of Sardinia's unique grape varieties were introduced by the Phoenicians and Carthaginians. Despite their venerable provenance, they have not always been used to best effect, and the island's wines can be idiosyncratic—to say the least. The most famous vintage is the dry, sherry-like Vernaccia di Oristano (Contini is a good producer). The basic reds are Cannonau and Monica di Sardegna, slightly overshadowed by whites like Vermentino and Torbato di Alghero (the latter is produced by Sella & Mosca, one of Europe's largest estates). Malvasia di Bosa is a prized dessert wine. *Filu ferru* (literally "steel thread") is the local grappa, named because shepherds traditionally distilled it illegally and hid bottles underground—with a protruding piece of wire to locate them later. Almost every cork in a bottle of Italian wine, incidentally, comes from the cork oak forests of northern Sardinia.

► **Alghero**   *244D1*

Alghero is one of Sardinia's busiest resorts, saved by its proud Catalan roots and down-to-earth fishing harbor from the tackiness that often blights tourist towns. There were so many Catalans here in the 14th century that the region became known as *Barcelonetta* (Little Barcelona). Many streets and monuments have Catalan names—*carrer* not *via*, for example; *plaça* not *piazza*; and *iglesia* not *chiesa*.

Among the cobbled streets within the medieval walls, look for the town's seven large 15th-century towers, particularly the **Porta Torre**► and **Torre Sulis**►, and fine Aragonese-Gothic buildings like the **Casa Doria**►, **Palau Reial**►, and **Palazzo d'Albis**►. The octagonal *campanile* is all that survives from the original 16th-century **Duomo**►. San Francesco is the most interesting church.

►► **Cagliari**   *244A2*

A large port, lots of industry, and around 250,000 people should make Cagliari an unappetizing prospect. In fact, it is a pleasant place, blessed with a medieval center, several monuments, and exquisite beaches and flamingo-filled lagoons. The citadel above the harbor was founded by the Phoenicians, the forerunner of a port that has remained one of the most important in the Mediterranean.

The **Citadella dei Musei-Museo Archeologico**►► (*Closed* Mon. *Admission: moderate*) is the island's premier museum, home to the cream of its prehistoric, pre-Roman, and medieval treasures. Of these, the most important are the bronze figurines and other displays devoted to Sardinia's ancient Nuraghic culture (see page 249). The **Duomo**► nearby is known for its crypt and two Pisan pulpits (1165). Elsewhere, see the **Torre San Pancrazio**►, which with the Torre dell'Elefante formed the cornerstone of the city's medieval defenses, and **San Saturnino**►►, Sardinia's oldest church (5th century). Also well worth seeing are the **Botanic Gardens**►► (*Closed* PM daily in winter. *Admission: moderate*) and the ruins of the old amphitheater, which are among Italy's finest.

Bottom: Sunday market in Cagliari
Below: marshland wildlife near Alghero

247

BOAT TRIPS
Two of the best coves south of Cala Gonone are Cala di Luna and Cala Sisine. Boats run to both, offering views of the deep gorges that cut through the coast's 2,970-foot-high mountains. Boats also visit the *Grotta del Bue Marino*, reputedly one of the last refuges of the Mediterranean monk seal (*bue marino*), and a magical spot filled with stalactites and stalagmites.

L'ELEFANTE
This little curiosity stands 2.5 miles out of Castelsardo on the SS 134. It is an odd ele-phant-shaped rock that hangs over the road. Inside are several *domus de janas* tombs (see page 249), many etched with mysterious symbols and bull's head motifs. At Sedini (9 miles) another five-chambered *domus* has been turned into the Gothic church of San Andrea (1517).

The lovely bay at Cala Gonone

►► Cala Gonone   244C3

Sardinia is so well known for its beaches that it is easy to forget the tremendous variety of its other coastal scenery. None is more spectacular than the mountainous cliffs on the east coast surrounding the bay at Cala Gonone. Approach the area on the SS 125 if possible (from Arbatax), a majestic road that climbs to over 3,300 feet high as it wends through some of the island's wildest scenery. Its most breathtaking stretch offers views over the gorge of the **Gola su Gorruppu ►► ►**.

Cala Gonone itself is approached from Dorgali, a town growing increasingly busy as more people discover the beauty of the coastline. Until a few years ago the bay and its tiny hamlet were accessible only from the sea. New hotels and villas that have sprouted since the building of a road have not yet spoiled the area's incomparable scenery. The best way to the area is to take a boat trip, either to mar-vel at the views, or to be dropped at one of the secluded coves up and down the coast (see panel).

►► Castelsardo   244D2

Castelsardo, on the north coast, is a citadel town, founded in 1102 by the Genovese, whose formidable castle offers sweeping views over the sea and the town's maze of medieval streets. Similar views are to be had from the cliff-edge Duomo, worth popping into for its 15th-century icon, the *Madonna degli Angeli*, by an unknown local painter. For good beaches follow the scenic road to Porto Torres, fringed by a broad crescent of white sands and turquoise seas.

Castelsardo is also known for its handicrafts, many of which are of dubious quality and authenticity. Bargains are to be had, though, if you rummage through the junk and stick to the weaving and palm-leaf baskets for which the town is most famous. Cork and coral goods, rugs, wrought iron, and souvenir Sardinian masks (*mamathones*) are also available.

Sardinia's prehistoric monuments provide some of the island's most memorable sights, from the great stone nuraghi *that dot the countryside to the delicate bronze figurines of Cagliari's archeological museum. That almost nothing is known of the culture that produced them only adds to the appeal of the remains, as intriguing as any in Europe.*

The earliest ruins The Sardinians could have come from almost anywhere: were they descended from Sardus, legendary son of Hercules, or from the Shardana tribes of ancient Libya? Or did they come from one of the countries around the Mediterranean? Nobody knows. Their earliest memorials are the *domus de janas* (elves' dwellings), tiny tombs cut into the rock dating from 2000–1800 BC. According to popular tradition they were the homes of elves, witches, and fairies. Their other major monuments were the *tombe dei giganti* (giants' tombs), believed by locals to be the graves of their gigantic ancestors—in fact, they were the temples and mausoleums of the Nuraghic tribes that dominated prehistoric Sardinia from 1500–500 BC.

249

TOMBE DEI GIGANTI
Sardinia's most significant concentration of *tombe* are at Anghelu Ruiu (6 miles north of Alghero on the road to Porto Torres). About 35 tombs riddle the hillside, eerie chambers connected by corridors and sloping passages. Some have lintels carved with symbolic shapes. Others are protected by a large standing stone.

Nuraghi These same tribes also left the 7,000 or more *nuraghi* that scatter the island. These enigmatic structures are visible everywhere—on hills, at roadsides, or half-buried in scrub—either singly or in clusters. Most are conical in shape, with a round vaulted interior, linked by corridors and stairways to an upper terrace. Many are more than two or three stories high. No two are the same. Some may have been dwellings, others fortified citadels.

The Sant'Antine nuraghe

Statuettes Sardinia has yielded around 500 nuraghic statuettes, quirky bronze figurines between 6 inches and 18 inches tall, probably made around the 8th century BC from copper and tin ore imported from as far afield as Etruria and Cornwall. Many were votive offerings, made to decorate Nuraghic temples. They show immense vigor and invention, depicting not only people—anything from warriors to nursing mothers—but also objects such as houses, boats, gods, *nuraghi,* and domestic animals.

These figures marked the apogee of Nuraghic culture. Around 1000 BC, Sardinia began to fall prey to invading Phoenicians and Etruscans, far more skilled than the local tribes in the art of warfare (whose only weapons, according to the chroniclers, were stones and boulders rolled from hilltops).

FINDING *NURAGHI*
Sardinia's best *nuraghi* are Su Nuraxi, outside Barumini; Losa, near Abbasanta; and Sant' Antine, between Macomer and Sassari. The most interesting of the smaller sites are Palmavera, west of Fertilia; Serra Orrios, near Dorgali; Bruncu de Madili, near Gesturi. You should have no trouble in discovering many more for yourself.

▶▶ (La) Costa Smeralda   244E3

The Emerald Coast started life as one resort—**Porto Cervo▶▶**—an upscale resort village built by the Aga Khan in the 1960s. Since then it has come to describe the string of chic resorts that have sprung up along Sardinia's northeastern coast. Many of its villages are in the Porto Cervo mold—undeniably chic and tasteful, but also rather soulless and lacking in local color. As oases of hedonistic retreat, however, they can hardly be bettered.

Other spots are still quite undeveloped, and therefore give you Porto Cervo's beaches and facilities at a fraction of the cost. Close to **Santa Teresa Gallura▶**, for example, a relaxed and carefree resort on Sardinia's northern tip, lie three of the island's best beaches—Punta Falcone, La Marmorata, and **Capo Testa▶▶**. Beyond them, more beach-fringed bays stretch as far as **Palau▶**, the main port for the Maddalena archipelago (see page 253). Further east, villages like **Cannigione▶** on the Golfo di Arzachena are also still relatively quiet. Nearby Baia Sardinia, Portisco, and Porto Rotondo, however, are similar in style to Porto Cervo.

▶▶ Gennargentu, Monti del   244C2

The Gennargentu is Sardinia's mountainous heart, a region of ancient landscapes and ways of life that have scarcely changed in centuries. Its isolated and self-contained farming villages offer your best hope of seeing local costumes or stumbling on age-old festivals. It is also among Europe's last wilderness areas, recently having been designated a national park. Driving is the only practical way to explore, using either Mandas or Nuoro as your base (though infrequent trains from Cagliari run through the region to Sorgono and Arbatax). Most roads here offer lonely excursions, but try the Arbatax–Dorgali (SS 125) drive in particular for its exhilarating views of the gorge of the **Gola su Gorruppu▶▶▶**. To reach other breezy vantage points for views, follow the Fonni to Aritzo road (and the spur to Bruncu Spina at 5,181 feet) or the scenic drives from Aritzo to Arcu Guddetorgiu (6 miles northeast of Aritzo) and Seui (27 miles southeast).

A quiet stretch of the Costa Smeralda

THE LOGUDORO

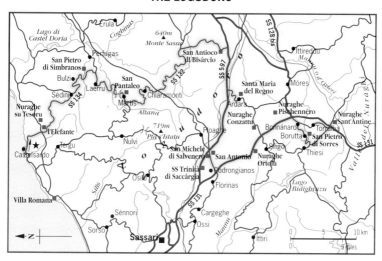

Drive

The Logudoro

This route explores Sardinia's north-west corner—the Logudoro (Land of Gold)—famous for its remote 12th-century Pisan-Romanesque churches and several of the island's grandest prehistoric *nuraghi*.

You could start the tour in Sassari, but by starting at **Castelsardo** (page 248), a magnificently sited old town, you have the chance of seeing not only San Pietro di Simbranos, one of the remotest of the Pisan churches, but also the famous Elefante rock and its prehistoric tombs. Tumbledown **San Antioco di Bisarcio** is the next church, followed by **Santa Maria del Regno**, a large, granite-fronted affair near Ardara (this now nondescript village was once important as the capital of the Logudoro).

Moving southwest, you reach **San Antonio**, Pisan in style, but—as the red-and-white facade suggests—renovated by the Aragonese. Next comes **San Michele di Salvenero**, then **Santissima Trinità di**

Saccargia▶▶, part of a once famous abbey (1116), now perhaps Sardinia's most notable church.

Pick up the main road (SS 131) and turn off to Borutta, beyond which stands the beautifully sited church of **San Pietro di Sorres**▶. Returning to the SS 131 you come to the **Valle dei Nuraghi**▶▶, peppered with dozens of these enigmatic buildings, including the outstanding **Nuraghe Sant'Antine**▶▶▶. It dates from the 14th century BC, and centers on an impressive 53-foot bastion.

Be sure to visit the **Museo di Torralba**, the best of several *nuraghi* museums in the vicinity (1 mile north in Torralba. *Closed* Mon in winter).

The eye-catching church of Trinità di Saccargia

BUGGERRU
This beach resort lies 24 miles north of Iglesias, surrounded by impressive beaches and dramatic countryside. To stay ahead of the crowd, explore the beautifully unspoiled Costa Verde north of Buggerru, reached on wild and picturesque roads from Guspini. Marina di Arbus is developed, but the cliffs and mountains to the south are still pristine.

Giara di Gesturi: basalt and wildflowers

GARIBALDI AND CAPRERA
Garibaldi first came to Caprera in 1855, seven years after his abortive attempt to form a Roman republic. In 1860 he set off from Maddalena with the thousand redshirts (the famous *Mille*), his spectacular conquest of Sicily and Naples a prelude to the creation of a united Italy a year later. He then retired to lead the life of a simple farmer on Caprera. His house, garden, and tomb are kept as a museum.

▶▶ Giara di Gesturi 244B2

Giare are strange basalt plateaux found all over Sardinia. None are odder or more alluring than the Giara di Gesturi. About 1,980 feet high and 7 miles across, its herb- and *maquis*-covered plains stretch to the horizon, broken by outcrops of pinkish-black basalt and vast woods of cork oak (the forests contain an estimated 250,000 trees). After rain, trickling streams appear and areas of marsh form on the plateau, rich in spring flowers and host to many migrating birds (the biggest such areas are Pauli Maiori and Pauli Minori). Roaming the heathland you may spot one of the plateau's famous wild horses—shy, tiny creatures similar to Shetland ponies and once common all over Sardinia. The area makes excellent walking country and is easily reached from surrounding villages. To get there, take the SS 131 from Cagliari and after 24 miles branch east on the SS 197 for Barumini: Gesturi village is 3 miles beyond.

You can combine a visit to the Giara di Gesturi with a trip to **Las Plassas▶▶**, a remarkable conical hill whose dramatic silhouette and ruined 12th-century castle are a landmark all around, and to **Su Nuraxi▶▶▶**, one of the island's finest *nuraghi*. *Su Nuraxi* means simply "the *nuraghe*," a blunt title for the oldest, most splendid and most extensive *nuraghe* in Sardinia. It was probably deliberately buried by Sards or Cathaginians: only a severe storm in 1949 brought it to the notice of the modern world. If you see no other *nuraghi*, be sure to see this one, only half a mile west of Barumini.

▶ Iglesias 244B1

Gold, silver, iron, lead, and zinc have been mined from the countryside around Iglesias for centuries. The town itself bears remarkably few signs of its industrial past. On the contrary, it is a pleasant and elegant spot, whose name derives from its numerous churches (Spanish *iglesia*—church). Its hub is Piazza Sella, a lively little square, backed by an old quarter of balconied houses and quiet cobbled streets. The secluded **Duomo▶** is worth a quick glance, and there is also a museum devoted to the town's extensive mining heritage.

▶▶ La Maddalena   *244E3*

This seven-isle archipelago has always had a naval presence. Britain's Admiral Nelson spent 15 months in its waters pursuing the French prior to the Battle of Trafalgar. Today, the island of Maddalena still has a huge NATO base, though assaults on the islands now come only from visitors flooding in from the Costa Smeralda. Most are here for the beaches, but the archipelago also has its scenic side—worn granite rocks, sparse *maquis*, and wind-bent pines. Many people also come to pay homage to Garibaldi, Italy's nationalist hero, who lived for many years on the island of Caprera (see panel on page 252).

▶▶ Nora   *244A2*

Sardinia's most compelling archeological site (*Open* daily 9–sunset. *Admission: moderate*) occupies a narrow neck of land at Capo di Pula (19 miles west of Cagliari). Founded by the Phoenicians, the colony was later settled by the Carthaginians and then by the Romans. It was abandoned in the 3rd century AD, possibly in the wake of some natural disaster. Among the ruins you can see part of a burial ground, a Carthaginian temple to their chief goddess Astarte, a fine Roman theater, fragments of four Roman baths, and a miscellany of houses, streets, and mosaic pavements. Part of the city is submerged, but still remains visible under the water close to the shore-line. Alongside the site stand the ruins of the 11th-century church of Sant' Efisio. Immediately below is a tempting sandy bay.

▶ Nuoro   *244C2*

Nuoro has a grand mountain setting, but as D. H. Lawrence observed when he visited the town in the 1920s: "There is nothing to see...which to tell the truth is always a relief. Sights are an irritating bore." Little has changed, though these days the town boasts a folk museum, the **Museo della Vita e Tradizioni Popolari**▶▶ (*Open* daily. *Admission: moderate*). Sardinia's most complete collection of costumes, handicrafts, and other mementos of its rural past. Otherwise, it is a rather shabby place, useful mainly as a springboard for excursions into the former bandit country to the south.

▶ Olbia   *244D3*

Mainland ferries dock at Olbia, a modern but not unduly industrialized port. This makes it a lively but unprepossessing place, and after seeing the 12th-century church of **San Simplicio**▶▶ it makes sense to head for the string of resorts and beaches strung along the SS 125. Lanes off the main road lead to small bays and sandy beaches. More developed facilities cluster around San Teodoro (15 miles) and Siniscola (33 miles), and around the coast's most picturesque little resorts, La Caletta and Santa Lucia (both about 4 miles east of Siniscola).

COSTUMES

Elderly people still wear traditional dress in Sardinia's interior villages. Styles vary from village to village, but colors are usually black and white for men, scarlet and green for women. Many garments are richly embroidered, or embellished with jewelry handed down over generations. Many are extremely valuable. The Museo della Vita in Nuoro has an excellent display of such costumes.

253

Costume display in Nuoro's Museo della Vita

THARROS
Little remains of Tharros, founded by the Phoenicians in 800 BC and later occupied by the Romans and Carthaginians. One of the most important classical sites in Sardinia nonetheless, it has the added attraction of a wild and beautiful setting, edged by clear seas and alluring beaches.

▶ Oristano 244C1

You often come to Sardinian towns only to leave them again for more interesting sights in the surrounding countryside. Oristano is no exception: it serves as a base for the **Sinis peninsula▶▶**, a patchwork of lagoons and desertlike dunes east of the town. As well as providing the background to ancient **Tharros▶▶** (see panel), this is an area of solitary churches, ghost towns, and virtually deserted white-sand beaches. As a sanctuary for flora and birds, notably flamingos, it is also a haven for botanists and naturalists. In Oristano itself, the bustling Piazza Roma and the tight historic core should detain you only briefly. South of the town, however, leave time for the majestic 12th-century church of **Santa Giusta▶▶**.

▶▶ Porto Conte 244D1

Porto Conte is the main destination for many of Alghero's visitors, a sweeping bay of fine beaches and beautifully limpid seas that forms part of the *Riviera del Corallo* (named after the coral collected off the coast, much of which is then made into jewelry and sold in Alghero's shops). Two rocky promontories hold the bay in a protective embrace. The crook of the southern arm contains the **Nuraghi di Palmavera▶▶**, some 50 or so *nuraghi* gathered around a central domed "palace." Two attractive beaches occupy the promontory's southern shore, Lazzaretto and Le Bombarde.

The northern arm, Capo Caccia, rears up from the sea in a series of spectacular cliffs, easily seen by boat (from Alghero) or from the promontory's fine coastal road. It also harbors the **Grotta di Nettuno▶▶▶**, one of the Mediterranean's most fabulous sea caves. Single-file tours (on the hour) are conducted along a natural corridor past incredible displays of stalagmites and stalactites. The whole cavern is beautifully and dramatically lit. You can approach by boat from Alghero (15 minutes) or from Capo Caccia, where 654 dizzying steps—the *escala del cabriol* (literally, "goat's stairway")—drop to the cave's entrance at the foot of the cliffs. The stairway was only completed in 1954; before that the only access was via a precipitous and dangerous path.

Top: the marshland blooms near Oristano
Above: painting in the church of Santa Giusta, Oristano

▶ Sant'Antioco, Isola di   *244A1*

Access to Sant'Antioco, off southwest Sardinia, is via a causeway built by the Carthaginians. Halfway across, look for the two rocks known as *Su Pàra* and *Sa Mongia* (the monk and the nun), two illicit lovers turned to stone by God as they fled the island. The town of Sant'Antioco on the other side has been inhabited since Phoenician times. Its main attractions date from later, principally the early Christian catacombs (*Open* daily, depending on presence of priest. *Admission: inexpensive*) under the Romanesque church of Sant'Antioco. Dark, dank, and chilling, these tombs still contain skeletons, some perhaps from an earlier Carthaginian tomb on the site. A more extensive Carthaginian burial site, or *tophet*, covers a hillside nearby (follow signs from the village). The site has a small museum (*Open* daily) and the remains of several ancient temples.

Many popular beaches dot the island, notably on the western coast, all linked by road to Calasetta and Sant'Antioco. Most are still pleasantly undeveloped.

▶ San Pietro, Isola di   *244A1*

Carloforte▶ on San Pietro can be reached by ferry from Portoscuro (13 miles southwest of Iglesias, page 252), or from Calasetta on its near neighbor, Sant'Antioco. Although partly spoiled by a large power station, individual parts of the island are attractive, notably **Capo Sandalo**▶ ▶ and **La Caletta**▶ ▶, both accessible by road from Carloforte (8 miles). The island has endless stretches of rocky shoreline, perfect for swimming and snorkeling.

▶ Sassari   *244D1*

Sardinia's second city has little to recommend it other than as a supplies stop to be visited from more agreeable spots on the coast. If you happen to pass through, spend a little time in the old quarter, whose claustrophobic maze of streets contrasts strikingly with the bland modern boulevards on the town's outskirts. See the **Duomo**▶ with its intricate baroque facade, and the **Museo Sanna**▶ (*Closed* Sun PM), almost a carbon copy of Cagliari's archeological museum. It offers similar displays of Nuraghic, Roman, and Carthaginian artifacts, and examples of local costumes and handicrafts.

BEACHES
A fine succession of beaches curve in a wide arc along the coast north of Sassari from Porto Torres to Castelsardo. All are linked by the SS 200, a scenic coast road.

SCENIC DRIVES
SS 125 Arbatax–Dorgali–Nuoro; SS 128/197 Nuoro–Fonni–Sorgono–Barumini; SS 292 Oristano–Cuglieri–Bosa–Alghero; SS 200/ SS 127 Sassari–Castelsardo–Costa Smeralda.

255

Traces of former elegance in Sassari

Sardinia's coastline is synonymous with beaches and the pleasures of sand and sea, but the interior's vast tracts of lonely, sunbaked mountains have been associated from time immemorial with banditry, kidnapping, and lethal, blood-soaked "tribal" vendettas.

BLOOD ON THE WALLS
Visitors to Orgosolo now search in vain for traces of its violent past, though locals have painted many houses with murals depicting some of the village's more blood-curdling historical episodes.

Sardinian banditry has flourished for centuries

The beginnings Banditry (the word comes from the Catalan *bandejat*, or *bandeado* in Spanish) has plagued Sardinia from Roman times. It has its roots in the traditional animosity and conflict of interests between the shepherds of the mountains—who required land for grazing—and the more peaceable peasants of the lowlands who sought to tame the land for cultivation. At its simplest, lawlessness probably started with the looting of a few sheep, or the rustling of a few cattle, even today not seen as terribly heinous crimes among shepherds, who are more likely to be outraged at the theft of money, or the more practical items needed for everyday existence.

The blood feud If banditry's simple give-and-take were breached, or its basic rules broken—notably when blood was spilled—then blood feuds and vendettas (*bardana*) could develop that might escalate over decades to embrace not simply individuals but entire villages and districts. One notable *disamistade*, or enmity, for example, festered for years in Orgosolo, deep in the Barbagia mountains, banditry's traditional fortress, prompted by the disputed inheritance of the village's chief clansman. From 1903, over the course of 14 years, virtually every member of the two families involved was wiped out. Between then and 1954, the village (population 4,000) had on average a killing every two months.

Le Petit Journal
SUPPLÉMENT ILLUSTRÉ

Capture de deux voyageurs français par des brigands en Sardaigne

Robbery and kidnapping Highway robbery also became endemic, particularly after the war. One of the more infamous heists was the holdup of 250 people in broad daylight in 1952 while the police force celebrated its annual *festa*. Another came in 1973 when thieves made off with 230 sheep from the state agricultural penal colony.

More recently, kidnapping has become the crime of choice, Sardinia's harsh interior providing cover for captors who know the terrain better than their pursuers. Kidnappings have increased, but foreigners should not fear. Most victims come from wealthy Italian families because ransoms are invariably met, despite Italian laws, designed to neutralize the problem, which freeze family's bank accounts to prevent payment.

Travel Facts

Arriving

Passports only (no visas) are required for visitors from the U.K. and other E.U. (European Union) countries, the U.S., Canada, the Republic of Ireland, Australia, and New Zealand.

By air Direct scheduled flights from the U.S. fly to Rome and Milan. From the U.K. and Europe, you can fly to Rome, Venice, Milan, Verona, Bologna, Turin, Genoa, Florence, Pisa, and Naples. Most long-haul flights fly to either Milan (Malpensa) or Rome (Leonardo da Vinci). Charter flights operate to the main cities plus Ancona, Alghero, Brindisi, Cagliari, Catania, Lamezia (Calabria), Olbia, Palermo, Pescara, Rimini, and Verona.

By rail Trains run directly to Rome, Milan, Venice, and Naples via Calais and Paris from London Victoria to the Channel ferry ports and via the Eurostar from London Waterloo.

By road Entry to Italy by road is best made via the Mont Blanc tunnel (France); the Brenner Pass (Austria); and the St. Bernard tunnel, Chiasso, or Simplon Pass (from Switzerland).

Camping

Most Italian campgrounds are on the coast or around lakes. Many Italian campgrounds open seasonally (typically June–September) and are extremely busy during July and August (so reserve ahead or arrive by 10 AM). Tourist offices have full details of current prices for sites, but if you are camping extensively invest in the widely available *Campeggi e Villaggi Turistici*, published by the Touring Club of Italy (T.C.I.).

Car breakdowns see page 261.

Car rentals see page 262.

Children

All but inexpensive hotels accept children and it is normal to take young children to restaurants in the evening. Diapers, accessories, and baby foods are widely available. Children under four ride free on buses, trams, and trains, and enjoy free admission to museums and galleries. Children between four and 12 qualify for half-price reductions.

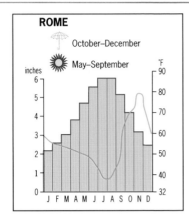

ROME

☂ October–December
☀ May–September

Climate

Despite its basically mild winters and warm summers, Italy has a surprisingly varied and extreme climate. In winter, Venice and Milan are nearly as cold as New York City, and you can ski in several parts of the country during September. The best months for sightseeing are April, May, June, September, and October, though rain and cold are more persistent in northern and mountain areas throughout spring and fall. July and August are the hottest months everywhere. Winters can be severe, particularly in the Alps and fog-bound plains of Lombardy and Emilia-Romagna.

Crime

The sheer number of visitors to Italy makes them an obvious target for the unscrupulous, especially in the cities and areas of the south. Of the horror stories told of unwitting tourists fleeced by Italy's criminal élite, however, few have much basis in fact. Common sense and a few precautions should keep you safe.

● Always carry cash in a belt or pouch—never in a pocket.

● Do not carry large amounts of cash: use credit cards or traveler's checks.

● Wear your camera and never put it down on café tables—and beware of strap-cutting thieves.

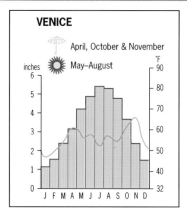

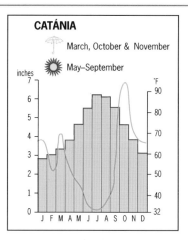

- Do not flaunt valuables—better still, leave them at home.

- Leave all jewelry in the hotel safe (not rooms). Chains and earrings worn in the street are easily snatched by bold thieves.

- Women should hold bags across their front, never hung over one shoulder, where they can be easily rifled through or grabbed.

- Be careful of pickpockets on crowded buses or trains, street markets, and where large groups of tourists congregate.

- After dark, women especially should not linger in noncommercial parts of town, in parks, or around train stations.

- When driving, lock your car and never leave luggage, cameras, or valuables inside.

Report any theft immediately to your hotel and then to the police at the local *questura* (police station), many of which have a special department to deal with tourists' problems. They will issue you with documents (*denuncia*) to forward along with any insurance claims that you may need to make.

If you lose a passport, report the loss first to the police and then contact your country's local consulate or embassy. To contact the police in an emergency, call 113.

Customs regulations

You may bring home up to $400 of foreign goods duty-free, provided you've been out of the country for at least 48 hours and haven't used all or part of the allowance on an international trip in the past 30 days. Each member of the family is entitled to the same exemption; exemptions may be pooled.

For the next $1,000 of goods, a flat 10 percent rate is assessed; above $1,400, duties vary according to the merchandise. Travelers 21 years or older are allowed to export one liter of alcohol, 100 cigars, and 200 cigarettes, and one bottle of perfume trademarked in the United States. Antiques and works of art that are over 100 years old are duty-free. Exceed these limits, and you'll be taxed at the port of entry and additionally in your home state.

Gifts under $200 for personal use may be mailed duty-free to stateside friends or relatives, with a limit of one package per day per addressee. However, perfumes worth over $5, tobacco, and liquor are banned from being posted abroad.

The import of wildlife souvenirs sourced from rare or endangered species may be either illegal or require a special permit. Before purchase, check your home country's customs regulations.

Travelers with disabilities

Italy is not an easy country for people with disabilities, though facilities are slowly improving and staff at airports, stations, and museums are helpful (St. Peter's and the Vatican Museums are wheelchair accessible). Italian Tourist Offices in foreign countries (see page 270) provide a list of hotels equipped for people with disabilities, and addresses of helpful Italian associations. Some trains have wheelchair lifts (wheelchairs are carried free by law): buses do not, though seats are reserved for disabled passengers.

Useful addresses

● **Australia**: A.C.R.O.D. (Australian Council for the Rehabilitation of the Disabled), P.O. Box 60, Curtin, ACT 2605 (tel: 02/6282 4333).

● **Canada**: Canadian Paraplegic Association, Suite 320, 1101 Prince of Wales Drive, Ottawa, Ontario K2C 3W7 (tel: 613/723-1033).

● **Republic of Ireland**: National Rehabilitation Board, 24–25 Clyde Road, Ballsbridge, Dublin 4 (tel: 01/668 4181).

● **New Zealand**: Disabled Persons Assembly, P.O. Box 27-524, Wellington (tel: 04/801 9100).

260

An alternative form of travel in Rome

● **U.K.**: R.A.D.A.R., 12 City Forum, 250 City Road, London, EC1V 8AF (tel: 020-7250 3222); Holiday Care Service, 2nd Floor, Imperial Buildings, Victoria Road, Horley, Surrey, RH6 7PZ (tel: 01293 774 535).

● **U.S.**: S.A.T.H. (Society for the Advancement of Travel for the Handicapped), 347 Fifth Avenue, Suite 610, New York NY 10016 (tel: 212/447-7284 or 212/447-0027).

Domestic travel

Air Alitalia, its domestic affiliate A.T.I., and several smaller national carriers offer frequent services between cities and islands. Prices are high and it is often cheaper and more convenient to travel by train. Students and passengers between 12 and 25 qualify for 25 percent discounts on certain Alitalia flights, and there are 30 percent reductions on some night flights, plus 50 percent savings for family groups.

Boat The F.S. (see under **Rail**) and numerous private companies provide car ferries and hydrofoils to Sicily, Sardinia, Elba, and the Tuscan archipelago, the Tremiti islands (Apulia), the Sicilian islands, and the Bay of Naples islands. There are connections to Corsica, Malta, Tunisia, Egypt, and Israel. Car ferry reservations for summer travel to Sardinia and Elba should be made several months in advance.

Bus Long-haul buses (*pullman*) operate between most Italian cities, but timetables, departure points, and frequency can be hard to pin down. It's best to ask about services at tourist offices or to visit the local bus terminal (*autostazione*), often located outside the town's train station. Tickets must usually be bought before you travel from *tabacchi* (tobacconists) or the bus terminal. For city buses see page 268.

Rail Train is the best way of traveling around Italy without a car. The system is cheap and efficient. Except for a few private lines, the network is run by the Ferrovie dello Stato (F.S.). There are several train categories: *Rapido* and *Inter City*, which stop only at major stations and charge a 30 percent supplement (*un supplemento*) that must be be bought in addition to the normal ticket; Eurostar, which requires a supplement and compulsory reservations; *Espressi* and *diretti* stop at more stations, while *locali* stop at every station along the line. Two other categories known as *Regionali* and *Inter-Regionali* are similar to *espressi* and *diretti*.

● **Tickets** (*biglietti*) are available as a one-way (*andata*) or round-trip (*andata e ritorno*) in first (*prima*) or second class (*seconda classe*). Be sure to validate return tickets in yellow platform machines before traveling.

● **Fares** are calculated on a milage basis and are some of the cheapest in Europe. Round-trip (3-day) tickets are discounted 15 percent on distances up to 150 miles; 1-day round-trip tickets are discounted 15 percent on distances up to 30 miles.

● **Validity** Tickets are valid for one day from the day of issue up to 150 miles, plus an extra day of validity for each additional 120 miles up to a maximum of 6 days. This validity takes effect from the moment you punch your ticket on platform machines. Tickets must be used within two months of purchase.

● **Reservations** Stations usually have separate ticket windows for reservations and sleepers (*cucetta*), the former worth considering for long journeys in summer when trains can be crowded.

● **Discounts** of 30 percent are available for families with a *Carta Famiglia* (Family Card); for travelers between 12 and 26 with a *Carta Verde* (reductions are 20 percent June 26–August 14); and for men over 65, women over 60 (with a *Carta d'Argento*). Cards are available from main stations and are valid for a year (except June 26–August 14 and December 18–28 for *Carta d'Argento*). Children between four and 12 travel half fare.

● **Passes** The F.S. issues two main passes: the *Chilometrico*, valid for 1,800 miles of travel over a maximum of 20 journeys; and the *Italy Railcard*, a travel-as-you-please card available for 8-, 15-, 21-, and 30-day periods (1st and 2nd class).

● **Timetables** If you use trains regularly be sure to buy the *Pozzorario*, a cheap biannual timetable widely available in bookstores and station kiosks.

Driving
While many city centers are congested, the rest of Italy has a superb network of *autostrade* (limited access highways), *superstrade* (main roads), and *strade statali* (minor roads). Tolls are charged on the *autostrade*.

Accidents If you have an accident, place a warning triangle 165 feet behind the car and call the police (tel: 112 or 113). Do not admit liability or make statements that might later incriminate you. Ask any witness(es) to remain, make a statement to the police, and exchange names, addresses, car details, and insurance companies' names and addresses with other driver(s) involved.

Breakdowns Put on your blinkers and place a warning triangle behind the car. Call the Automobile Club d'Italia (A.C.I.) on its 24-hour emergency number (tel: 116) and give the operator your location, license plate number, and make of vehicle. Roadside assistance will be given, or the car will be towed to the nearest A.C.I.-affiliated garage. The service is free to any visiting motorist who is driving a foreign-registered vehicle.

❏ For information on routes, road conditions, gas stations, and garages that repair foreign makes of cars, contact the Automobile Club d'Italia (A.C.I.), Via Marsala 8, Rome (tel: 06/49 981). For road conditions call 1518. ❏

CONVERSION CHARTS

FROM	TO	MULTIPLY BY
Inches	Centimeters	2.54
Centimetres	Inches	0.3937
Feet	Meters	0.3048
Metres	Feet	3.2810
Yards	Metres	0.9144
Metres	Yards	1.0940
Miles	Kilometers	1.6090
Kilometres	Miles	0.6214
Acres	Hectares	0.4047
Hectares	Acres	2.4710
Gallons	Liters	4.5460
Litres	Gallons	0.2200
Ounces	Grams	28.35
Grams	Ounces	0.0353
Pounds	Grams	453.6
Grams	Pounds	0.0022
Pounds	Kilograms	0.4536
Kilograms	Pounds	2.205
Tons	Tonnes	1.0160
Tonnes	Tons	0.9842

MEN'S SUITS

UK	36	38	40	42	44	46	48
Rest of Europe	46	48	50	52	54	56	58
US	36	38	40	42	44	46	48

DRESS SIZES

UK	8	10	12	14	16	18
France	36	38	40	42	44	46
Italy	38	40	42	44	46	48
Rest of Europe	34	36	38	40	42	44
US	6	8	10	12	14	16

MEN'S SHIRTS

UK	14	14.5	15	15.5	16	16.5	17
Rest of Europe	36	37	38	39/40	41	42	43
US	14	14.5	15	15.5	16	16.5	17

MEN'S SHOES

UK	7	7.5	8.5	9.5	10.5	11
Rest of Europe	41	42	43	44	45	46
US	8	8.5	9.5	10.5	11.5	12

WOMEN'S SHOES

UK	4.5	5	5.5	6	6.5	7
Rest of Europe	38	38	39	39	40	41
US	6	6.5	7	7.5	8	8.5

Documents Visitors bringing their own (foreign-registered) car to Italy must be at least 18 years of age and carry the vehicle's registration documents (logbook) and a full, valid driver's license (*patente* in Italian). Third-party insurance is compulsory; an international green card, though not compulsory, is recommended. A foreign driver's license is acceptable if accompanied by a translation, available free from the A.C.I. or the Italian State Tourist Office in the country of origin. The translation is not required for the new, pink E.U., U.K., or Republic of Ireland license.

Gas Gasoline (*benzina*) in Italy is among the most expensive in Europe. Diesel (*gasolio*) is cheaper.
Gas stations except those on highways (*Open* all day) tend to follow normal store hours (*Closed* 1–4 PM) and most close all day on Sunday (except on the *autostrade*). Self-service and 24-hour pumps that take large-denomination notes are increasingly common.

Parking Parking is often a nightmare in towns: parking spots (*parcheggi*) are invariably full and most historic centers are partially or fully closed to traffic. Try to leave your car in guarded parking areas, and always take valuables or luggage with you. Cars may be towed away if illegally parked: contact the local offices of the *Vigili Urbani* to effect recovery.

Renting a car Leading rental firms have offices in most cities and airports and, with local agencies, are listed in the Yellow Pages under "Autonoleggio." Fly-drive deals can be organized through travel agents. Drivers must be over 21 and hold a valid license (an international driver's license is sometimes required).

Rules of the road Italy employs international road signs and driving is on the right, and you should yield at intersections to vehicles coming from your right. The speed limit in built-up areas is 50kph (30mph); outside urban areas it is 110kph

(70mph), unless otherwise marked (when it is usually 90kph/56mph). The limit on highways is 130kph (81mph) for vehicles over 1,100cc. Carrying warning triangles and wearing front seat belts are compulsory.

Electricity
The current is 220 volts AC, 50 cycles, with plugs of the two round pin type: a voltage converter and adaptor plug are therefore useful items. In older hotels and houses you will find two-pin plugs of different specifications, but adaptors are available.

Embassies and consulates
All major countries are represented by an embassy in Rome. They include:
Australia: Via Alessandri 215 (tel: 06/852 721)
Canada: Via Zara 30 (tel: 06/440 3028 or 06/445 981)
Republic of Ireland: Piazza Campitelli 3 (tel: 06/697 9121)
New Zealand: Via Zara 28 (tel: 06/440 2928)
U.K.: Via XX Settembre 80a (tel: 06/482 5441)
U.S.: Via Vittorio Veneto 119a–121 (tel: 06/46 741)

Emergency telephone numbers

Police (*Carabinieri*) **112**
Emergency services (police, fire, ambulance) **113**
Fire (*Vigili di Fuoco*) **115**
Car breakdown **116**

Etiquette
● Wearing shorts, short skirts, or skimpy tops when visiting churches is considered disrespectful.

● Do not intrude (or cause any sort of disturbance) while church services are in progress.

● Many churches forbid flash photography or ban photos altogether.

● There are few nonsmoking areas in restaurants and public places but it is banned on buses and subways.

● Topless sunbathing is tolerated on out-of-the-way beaches.

● Bargaining is not appropriate in shops, though in markets (except food markets) and budget hotels you may be able to negotiate lower rates.

Health and Insurance
It is vital to ensure that your travel insurance has adequate provisions for medical emergencies. Though Italian hospitals may be a little disorganized, and the lines long, the standards of care and treatment are very high.
Key health points to remember are:

● Vaccinations are unnecessary for entry into Italy unless you are traveling from a known infected area.

● Take out health insurance; keep all receipts for medicines and treatment from doctors, dentists, and hospitals.

● For minor ailments visit a pharmacist (see **Pharmacies**, page 267).

● If you need a doctor (*un medico*), ask at your hotel or drugstore, or consult the Yellow Pages under "Unita Sanitaria Locale" (U.S.L.).

● If you need first aid, visit the nearest hospital (*ospedale*) emergency department (*pronto soccorso*).

● If you need an ambulance (*ambulanza*), call the emergency services (tel: 113) or the Red Cross.

● Water is safe to drink unless marked *acqua non potabile*.

● To avoid heat exhaustion and sunstroke, drink plenty of water, wear a hat, and avoid long exposed periods in the sun.

● Levels of air pollution are high in most Italian cities.

● Snakebites are rarely fatal. If bitten, make a note of the snake's appearance and visit a doctor or pharmacy for the appropriate serum.

● Condoms (*profilatici*) are available at drugstores and supermarkets.

Language

Italians respond well to foreigners who make an effort to speak their language. In the more high-class hotels and restaurants and in tourist cities, you should have few problems.

All Italian words are pronounced as written, with each vowel and consonant sounded. Points to remember are:

● Use the polite, third person (*Lei*) to speak to strangers: use the second person (*tu*) to friends or children.

● The letter **c** is hard, as in the English "cat" except when followed by **i** or **e**, when it becomes the soft *ch* of "children."

● The same applies to **g** followed by **i** or **e**—soft in *giardino*, as in the English "giant"; hard in *gatto*, as in "gate."

Courtesies:
Good morning: buon giorno
Good afternoon/good evening:
  buona sera
Good night: buona notte
Hello/goodbye (informal): ciao
Goodbye: arrivederci
Please: per favore
Thank you (very much):
  grazie (mille)
You're welcome: prego
How are you? (polite/informal):
  come sta/stai?
I'm fine: bene
I'm sorry: mi dispiace
Excuse me: mi scusi
Excuse me (in a crowd):
  permesso

● Words ending in **o** are almost always masculine (plural: **i**); those ending in **a** are feminine (plural: **e**).

Lost property

● Report losses to your hotel, then to the local police station (*questura*). Most large bus terminals and rail-road stations have lost property offices.

● Report loss of passports to the police and your embassy or consulate.

Essentials

Yes: sì
No: no
OK: ok/d'accordo
OK/that's fine/sure: va bene
I don't understand: no capisco
Do you speak English: parla
  inghlese?
I don't know: non lo so
I would like: vorrei
Do you have...?: avete...?
How much is it: quant'è?
What is it?: che cos'è?
Who?: chi
What?: quale
Why?: perché?
When?: quando?
Where?: dove?
Where is/where are?:
dov'è/dove sono?
Left/right: sinistra/destra
Straight on: sempre dritto

● If you lose your traveler's checks or credit cards, notify the police, then follow the instructions that were given to you with the cards and checks and inform the issuing company's nearest office.

Maps

Excellent 1:200 000 Touring Club Italiano (T.C.I.) maps, ideal for driving and route planning, are widely available in Italy. For walking maps, the main publishers are **Kompass**, **Tabacco**, **Multigraphic**, and **Istituto Geografico Centrale** (I.G.C.).

Newsstands and bookstores sell maps, but adequate street maps of towns and cities are usually available from local tourist offices.

Media

Italy's main national newspapers (*giornali*) include the authoritative Milan-based *Corriere della Sera* (center-right); the Turin-based *La Stampa*; and the Rome-based *La Repubblica* (center-left). The biggest-selling papers are sports papers like the pink *Gazzetta dello Sport* and *Corriere dello Sport*. The leading news magazines (*riviste*) are *L'Espresso*, *Panorama*, *Europeo*, and *Epoca*.

Foreign-language newspapers and magazines are available in major tourist areas at 2 PM on the day of issue. The European editions of several newspapers are widely available at newsstands (known as *edicole*).

Italian radio and television offer a range of national and local stations. Standards are low, with local networks geared mainly to advertising, pop music, and old movies. National stations are better, dividing equally between the three channels of the state RAI network and the channels founded by Silvio Berlusconi (*Canale 5*, *Rete 4*, and *Italia Uno*).

Money matters
On January 1, 1999, the euro (€ or abbreviated as EUR) became the official currency of Italy and the lira became a denomination of the euro. Italian lire continue to be legal tender during a transitional period. After February 2002 euro bank notes and coins only will be used in the following denominations:
• **Bills**—€5; 10; 20; 50; 100; 200; 500
• **Coins**—€1 and €2, plus the 1, 2, and 5 euro cent coins, which are a bronze color and the 10, 20, and 50 euro cent coins, which are golden.

Import and export Visitors are advised to contact their banks for current information, but at present there are no restrictions on foreign currency brought into Italy. To export particularly large amounts of currency you should contact Customs for advice.

You may need to sign a form V2 at Customs on entry and show it on leaving. Keep all your receipts and the stubs of your transactions.

Traveler's checks are free of upper limit restrictions, and all major checks as well as Eurocheques are widely recognized. Most banks and exchange outlets allow you to cash up to three checks daily.

Credit cards (*carta di credito*) are widely accepted in larger hotels, stores, and restaurants, but an establishment may refuse a card, even though it displays its sticker. Check before you have to pay the bill. Also be sure it is impossible for stubs to be tampered with once you have signed. Better-known cards (Visa, Amex) can be used for cash at certain banks and ATMs. Many gas stations do not accept cards.

Exchange Most banks will change foreign currency and traveler's checks—look for the sign *cambio*— but lines are often long and service slow. Exchange outlets may offer worse rates, but, along with bureaus at airports and main rail stations, they are open beyond normal banking hours. Big hotels will change money, but at poor rates.

Dining al fresco *in Rome's Campo dei Fiori*

265

National holidays
Stores, banks, offices, and schools are closed on the following days:

January 1 (New Year's Day)
January 6 (Epiphany)
Easter Sunday
Easter Monday
April 25 (Liberation Day)
May 1 (Labor Day)
August 15 (Assumption)
November 1 (All Saints' Day)
December 8 (Immaculate Conception)
Christmas Day
December 26 (Santo Stefano)

When a public holiday falls on a Tuesday or Thursday, it is customary to make a *ponte* (bridge) to the weekend and take the Monday or Friday off as well.

Opening times
Archeological sites Many sites are open all day from 9 AM to one hour before dusk, but it is always wise to check times with local tourist offices. Tickets are usually sold up to one hour before closing.

Banks are open weekdays 8:30 AM to 1:20 PM. Larger banks open until 4 PM and Sat morning.

Sidewalk café in Verona

Churches generally open around 7 AM and close toward noon, opening again between 4 and 7 PM. Many churches remain closed except on Sundays and religious holidays; major cathedrals and basilicas like St. Peter's remain open all day.

Museums and galleries run by the state usually open Tuesday to Sunday from 9 AM to 1 or 2 PM or 9 AM–7 PM; almost all shut on Mondays and Sunday afternoons. Others may open from 4 to 7 PM on selected days. Afternoon hours during winter are more restricted, especially in smaller galleries.

Parks and gardens usually open from 9 AM to an hour before dusk.

Post offices usually open Monday to Friday 8 or 8:30 AM to 2 PM (to 12:30 PM on Saturday). Main offices often stay open until 8 PM. Offices everywhere close at noon on the last working day of the month.

Restaurants and bars traditionally close once a week for a *riposo settimanale*. Check opening times.

Stores and offices are normally open from 8:30 or 9 AM until 1 PM, reopening at 3:30 or 4 to 7:30 or 8 PM. Most close on Sundays and on Monday mornings, and food stores may also close on Wednesday or Thursday afternoons. Garages are shut on Sundays except on autostrade; barbers and hairdressers on Sundays and Mondays. Supermarkets and department stores usually open 9:30 AM to 8 PM.

Pharmacies

A drugstore (*farmacia*) is identified by a green cross. Pharmacies keep the same hours as shops, but also open late on a rotation basis. When closed (during lunch, holidays, or at night), they display a list of pharmacists open nearby.

Staff are well qualified to give advice on minor ailments, and can dispense medicines over the counter, including some only available by prescription in other countries. Brand names differ from country to country, so take your used-up medication to a pharmacist to help with identification. Remember to bring any prescription or doctor's notes that might be required to obtain medicine.

Police

Dial 113 in an emergency; in other situations go to the local police station (see **Crime** on pages 258–259). Police on the street divide into:

● The semimilitary *carabinieri*, with sharp-looking black uniforms.

● The *polizia statale*, in blue uniforms, who perform most day-to-day policing.

● The *polizia urbana* and *vigili urbani*, who deal mainly with traffic control and parking offenses.

Police registration In theory, you should register at a *questura* within three days of entering Italy. In practice, no one does (hotels pass on their register instead).

Postal services

See **Opening Times** on page 266.

Stamps (*francobolli*) can be bought from tobacconists' (*tabacchi*) that display a blue "T" sign, or from the post office (*posta* or *ufficio postale*).

Mail to and from Italy can take up to three weeks, but it is often faster than this: *raccomandata* (registered) or *espresso* (express) are quicker. Letters can be sent *poste restante* (general delivery) to a town's main post office by addressing them *Fermo Posta*, followed by the name of the town. Take a passport when collecting mail: there is a small fee to pay. Filing can be haphazard, so check under your first and last names.

Fax and telegrams can be sent from larger post offices.

The Vatican runs its own postal service, known for its efficiency. There are post offices in the square in front of St. Peter's in Rome.

267

Public transportation

Buses The urban bus (*autobus*) services of most towns and cities run along similar lines. Usually you must buy a ticket in advance from a machine, a newsstand, a *tabacchi*—or even from station bars—then validate it in a machine on the bus (roving inspectors and spot fines await anyone without a ticket). Tickets in some cities are valid for one journey, others for any number of journeys within a given time limit. Usually you will enter a bus by its rear doors (marked *salita*) and then leave by the center doors (*uscita*). A bus stop is known as *una fermata*.

Subway Several cities have an underground system (*la metropolitana*), which provides the quickest way across the city. Tickets must be bought beforehand from stores, kiosks, or subway stations.

Taxis Always check that your taxi is a registered cab and that the meter is running, as it is the best way to protect yourself from fraud. Supplements to the meter fare are levied for additional passengers, for luggage, and for journeys after 8 PM and on Sundays and public holidays. Many cities have set rates from the airport to the city center. It can be difficult to hail taxis on the street, and most congregate at taxi stands. You can phone for cabs either through your hotel or by consulting the Yellow Pages.

Senior citizens

Many discounts are available when visiting Europe, but some may require membership in a specific club. A 30 percent discount on rail fares

is offered to senior citizens with a *Carta d'Argento* (Silver Card), available from mainline stations— see **Discounts** on page 261 for further details.

Student and youth travel

Students and young travelers can enjoy discounts for train and some air travel (see pages 260 and 261) as well as at museums, galleries, and archeological sites by showing an I.S.I.C. card. There is free entrance to state museums for under-18s. Specialist youth travel agents Centro Turistico Studentesco e Giovanile (C.T.S.) have over 90 offices throughout Italy.

Bicycles and scooters
Bicycle and scooter rental outlets are increasingly springing up in popular tourist areas. Most rent by the hour or day and require a credit card or passport as deposit.

Telephones

- Italy's main telephone company (*Telecom Italia*) provides public phones in many bars, on the street, and in special Telecom Italia offices, all of which are marked by a red or yellow sign showing a telephone dial and receiver.

- Most telephones will accept coins, and phone cards are increasingly in use (*schede telefoniche*). These are available, in a number of denominations, from *tabacchi*, Telecom offices, automatic dispensers, or shops displaying a Telecom sticker. Remember to tear the corner off the card before using it.

Telephone services

Operator 12
International operator
(Europe & intercontinental) 170
International information
   176
Police 112/113
Emergency services 113
A.C.I. car breakdowns 116
Post office information 160
Time 161
Road reports 1518
Medical assistance 118
Wake-up calls 114

International calls

To call abroad from Italy dial 00, then the country code, followed by the town or city code, then the number (including the first zero in any town or city code). To call Italy from the U.S. dial 011 39 plus the town code (including any zero) and number. Country prefixes from Italy include:
Australia 00 61
Canada 001
Republic of Ireland 00 353
New Zealand 00 64
U.K. 00 44
U.S. 001

- Peak period during weekdays is from 8 AM to 1 PM, off-peak from 1 PM to 8 PM, and the cheapest rates are at all other times. The cheap international rate is on weekends and 8 PM to 8 AM during the week.

- Note that when dialing Italian numbers, whether from outside or within Italy, you must use the full number, including a town or city code, even if you are calling from within the town or city concerned.

- For international calls use phone cards or a *telefono a scatti*, where you speak first and pay later: these special telephone cabins are found in some bars and hotels, post offices, some tourist offices, and in most Telecom Italia offices.

- To make a collect or reverse-charge call, dial 170 and ask to make *una chiamata con pagamento a destinazione*.

Time

Italy is 6 hours ahead of Eastern Standard Time, 7 hours ahead of Central Standard Time, 8 hours ahead of Mountain Standard Time, and 9 hours ahead of Pacific Standard Time.
   Montréal is 6 hours behind Italian time, London is 1 hour behind, and Sydney is 8 hours ahead during the summer.

269

Tipping

● A 10 to 15 percent service charge (*servizio*) is usually added to restaurant bills, but waiters expect a small tip in addition.

● Taxi drivers should be tipped 10 percent.

● For quick service in bars you might wish to do as the locals do and put down some small change with your receipt when ordering.

● Tip hotel staff (porters, doormen, room service) depending on the standard of hotel and service.

● Movie and theater ushers expect you to give them a small tip for showing you to your seats.

● Give something to custodians or sacristans if they have opened up churches or museums especially for your benefit, or outside normal opening hours.

Toilets

Public restrooms are rare in Italy, found mainly in train stations and large museums, and most of the time you have to use the facilities in bars and cafés. Ask for *il gabinetto* or *bagno* and do not confuse *signori* (men) with *signore* (women). Some larger places may have an attendant and small dish for tips—leave small change.

Tourist offices

The tourist system is currently being reorganized, but most towns, main railroad stations, and airports have a tourist office known as an *Azienda*

Promozione del Turismo (A.P.T.). Most follow normal store hours and offer maps, information, and help with finding accommodations. The *Ente Provinciale per il Turismo* (E.P.T.) is usually more devoted to bureaucracy than providing information. Villages may only have a small office known as a *Pro Loco*, with limited opening hours.

Italian State Tourist Offices abroad
Australia/N.Z. Level 45, 1 Macquarie Street, Sydney 2000, NSW (tel: 02/9392 7900) or 36 Grant Road, Thorndon, Wellington (tel: 04/736 065 or 04/473 5339).
Canada 1 Place Ville Marie, Montréal, Québec H3B 3M9 (tel: 514/866 7667).
U.K. 1 Princes Street, London W1 8AY (tel: 020 7408 1254).
U.S. 630 5th Avenue, Suite 1565, Rockefeller Center, New York, NY 10111 (tel: 212/245-5618).

Laundry service

While Italy boasts very few coin-operated laundromats, virtually every town and village has an old-style cleaners (*una tintoria*). Service is friendly and efficient, and clothes come back pressed and packaged and looking as good as new. Most places also offer dry-cleaning (*lava a secco*).

Youth hostels

Italy has about 50 youth hostels (*Alberghi per la Gioventù*) which are affiliated to Hosteling International (H.I.). Dormitory beds can be difficult to come by without reservations in summer (many hostels are closed out of season). In theory, you should be a member of your national youth hostel association, but many hostels will allow you to join on the spot, or they simply charge a higher fee to nonmembers.

Accommodations

Inexpensive ($): under €90
Moderate ($$): €90–155
Expensive ($$$): €155–190
Luxury ($$$$): expect to pay more than €190

All prices are based on a double room. Note that all Italian hotels are classified by law from five star (luxury) down to one star. Prices are also set by law and must be displayed at receptions and in each room.

ROME

Ambasciatori ($$$$)
Via V. Veneto 62 tel: 06/47 493
Recently refurbished luxury hotel; impeccable service and facilities.
Columbus ($$)
Via della Conciliazione 33 tel: 06/686 5435
Renaissance *palazzo* and gracious atmosphere; near St. Peter's.
Excelsior ($$$$)
Via V. Veneto 125 tel: 06/4708
One of Rome's top hotels; polished and prestigious, but relaxed atmosphere.
Hassler ($$$$)
Piazza Trinità dei Monti 6 tel: 06/699 340
Grand position above Spanish Steps and one of Rome's top hotels.
Hotel d'Inghilterra ($$$$)
Via Bocca di Leone 14
tel: 06/69 981
A favorite of 19th-century writers and artists; good location in Rome's shopping district.
Locarno ($$)
Via della Penna 22 tel: 06/361 0841
Atmospheric old favorite in side street near Piazza del Popolo.
Lord Byron ($$$$)
Via G. de Notaris 5 tel: 06/322 4541
Parkland setting in Parioli; perhaps the most splendid of Rome's luxury hotels.
Margutta ($$)
Via Laurina 34 tel: 06/322 3674
Pretty, with average rooms in quiet location near Piazza del Popolo.
Perugia ($)
Via del Colosseo 7 tel: 06/679 7200
On quiet side street near Colosseum.
Pomezia ($)
Via dei Chiavari 12 tel: 06/686 1371
Bargain rooms near Piazza Navona.
Portoghesi ($$)
Via dei Portoghesi 1 tel: 06/686 4231
Although once a bargain this restaurant near Piazza Navona is no longer cheap, but is still popular; fine roof terrace.
Sistina ($$)
Via Sistina 136
tel: 06/4890 0316 or 06/474 5000
Quiet and reliable hotel near Piazza di Spagna.
Smeraldo ($)
Via dei Chiodaroli 9 tel: 06/687 5929
Refitted, comfortable and popular hotel two minutes from Campo dei Fiori.

Sole ($)
Via del Biscione 76
tel: 06/6880 6873 or 06/687 9446
Well-known backpackers' favorite; busy rooms just off Campo dei Fiori.

THE NORTHWEST

Aosta

Europe ($$$)
Piazza Narbonne 8 tel: 0165/236 363
Central 5-story hotel.

Asti

Alermo ($$$)
Via E. Filiberto 13 tel: 0141/595 661
Best hotel in town.
Cavour ($)
Piazza Marconi 18 tel: 0141/530 222
A good, modern, and inexpensive hotel in the town center.

Cinque Terre

Porto Roca ($$$)
Via Corone 1, Monterosso tel: 0187/817 502
Quiet location on a hill near the town, with sea views.

Genova (Genoa)

Bristol Palace ($$$)
Via XX Settembre 35 tel: 010/592 541
Top-class hotel in fashionable part of the city.
Major ($)
Vico Spada 4 tel: 010/247 4174
A bargain; central, modern, and clean.

Riviera di Levante

Cenobio dei Dogi ($$$)
Via Cuneo 34, Camogli
tel: 0185/7241
Modernized former summer villa of Genoa's doges.
Eden ($–$$)
Vico Dritto 20, Portofino tel: 0185/269 091
Nice 2-star in 1920s Ligurian house, close to village square.
Piccolo Hotel ($$)
Via Duca degli Abruzzi 31, Portofino
tel: 0185/269 015
Small and modern, overlooking the harbor; attracts a younger set.
Royal Sporting ($$)
Via dell'Olivo 345, Portovenere
tel: 0187/790 326
Modern beach hotel with excellent sports facilities.
Splendido ($$$$)
Salita Baratta 13, Portofino
tel: 0185/269 551
This is about as luxurious and expensive as any Italian hotel gets. There is a sister hotel, Spendido Mare, in Via Roma (tel: 0185 267802).

Riviera di Ponente

Grand Hotel del Mare ($$$)
Via Portico della Punta 34, Bordighera
tel: 0184/262 201
Top-quality hotel on a hill above the beach.
Paradiso ($$)
Via Roccasterone 12, San Remo
tel: 0184/571 211
Quiet, modern hotel set in its own garden.
Royal ($$$$)
Corso Imperatrice 80, San Remo
tel: 0184/53 91
Luxury hotel near the casino.

Torino (Turin)

Astoria ($)
Via XX Settembre 4 tel: 011/562 0653
A good inexpensive hotel.
Principe di Piemonte ($$$$)
Via P. Gobetti 15 tel: 011/562 9693
Elegant hotel patronized by the rich and famous.
Victoria ($$)
Via Nino Costa 4 tel: 011/561 1909
Central, pleasant and modern, decorated in
idiosyncratic style.

LOMBARDY AND EMILIA-ROMAGNA

Bergamo

Agnello d'Oro ($)
Via Gombito 22 tel: 035/249 883
An inexpensive place in the old town.
Excelsior San Marco ($$$)
Piazza della Repubblica 6 tel: 035/366 111
Top hotel with a renowned restaurant.

Bologna

Apollo ($)
Via Drapperie 5 tel: 051/223 955
Clean, spacious, and central. Recently
renovated.
Corona d'Oro ($$$)
Via Oberdan 12 tel: 051/236 456
Old hotel, in a former printing house.
Orologio ($$)
Via IV Novembre 10 tel: 051/ 231 253
Reserve well in advance for this quiet, central,
and popular hotel.

Como, Lago di

Barchetta Excelsior ($$$)
Piazza Cavour 1, Como tel: 031/3221
Hotel with lakefront setting.
Du Lac ($$)
Piazza Mazzini 32, Bellagio tel: 031/950 320
Lakeside hotel in village center; great views
from roof terrace.
Villa d'Este ($$$$)
Via Regina 40, Cernobbio
tel: 031/3481
The most famous and expensive hotel in the
Lakes region.

Ferrara

Ripagrande ($$$)
Via Ripagrande 21 tel: 0532/765 250
Restored medieval *palazzo* in the old town.
San Paolo ($–$$)
Via Baluardi 9 tel: 0532/762 040
Quiet budget rooms in the old Jewish quarter.

Garda, Lago di

Grifone($)
Via Bocchio 4 tel: 030/916 014
On the waterfront with views of the castle.
Sirmione ($$)
Piazza Castello 19, Sirmione
tel: 030/916 331
Lakeside hotel in a charming garden setting.
Villa del Sogno ($$$)
Corso Zanardelli 107, Gardone Riviera
tel: 0365/290 181
Located above the lake; very relaxing.

Lago Maggiore

Des Iles Borromes ($$$$)
Lungolago Umberto I 67, Stresa
tel: 0323/938 938
Famous, palatial, and very expensive hotel.
Milan au Lac ($$)
Piazza Marconi, Stresa tel: 0323/31 178
Large, traditional hotel with views of dock.
Primavera ($$)
Via Cavour 39, Stresa
tel: 0323/31 286
Clean, simple, 3-star rooms in quiet, pedestri-
anized center of town.

Mantova (Mantua)

San Lorenzo ($$$)
Piazza Concordia 14 tel: 0376/220 500
Modernized hotel in old *palazzo* in the historic
center. Pleasantly characterful.

Milano (Milan)

Diana Majestic ($$$)
Viale Piave 42 tel: 02/20581
Lovely, stylish, art deco hotel.
Manzoni ($$)
Via Santo Spirito 20 tel: 02/7600 5700
Excellent, central and popular—reserve.
Rovello ($)
Via Rovello 18a tel: 02/8646 4654
Basic décor in this small budget *pensione*, a
favorite with the young.
Spadari al Duomo ($$$)
Via Spadari II tel: 021/7200 2371
An intimate hotel in set in a characteristic side
street very close to the cathedral.

Parma

Button ($$)
Via Saline 7 tel: 0521/208 039
Excellent central 3-star hotel, in a quiet
side street.

273

Accommodations and Restaurants

Torino ($$)
Via Mazza 7 tel: 0521/281 047
An agreeable, friendly place; central yet quiet.

Ravenna

Bisanzio ($$$)
Via Salara 30 tel: 0544/217 111
Smooth, comfortable central hotel.
Ravenna ($)
Via Maroncelli 12 tel: 0544/212 204
Modern hotel, handy for the station.

VENICE

Accademia ($$)
*Fondamenta Bollani, Dorsoduro 1058
tel: 041/521 0188*
Ample rooms, but not always quiet; homey;
reasonable rates. Reserve up to a year ahead.
Agli Alboretti ($$)
*Rio Terrà Sant'Agnese, Dorsoduro 882/4
tel: 041/523 0058*
Simple, attractive family-run hotel; modern
rooms but cozy atmosphere; central location.
American ($$)
*Fondamenta Bragadin, Rio di San Vio,
Dorsoduro 628 tel: 041/520 4733*
Good 3-star just a few minutes from the
Accademia in pretty location.
Ca' Foscari ($)
*Calle della Frescada, Dorsoduro 3888
tel: 041/522 5817*
Quiet, attractive, and easygoing.
Canova ($)
*Ramo della Fava, Castello 5515
tel: 041/522 8118*
Close to the Rialto but still quiet; most rooms
overlook a canal.
Casa Petrarca ($)
*Calle delle Colonne, San Marco 4386
tel: 041/520 0430*
Friendly, only seven rooms. Near San Marco.
Casa Verardo ($)
Ruga Giuffa, Castello 4765 tel: 528 6127
The best budget choice in this part of the city.
Cipriani ($$$$)
Giudecca 10 tel: 041/520 7744
Famous and luxurious, away from the center.
Danieli ($$$$)
*Riva degli Schiavoni, Castello 4196
tel: 522 6480*
Famous since 1822; still celebrity-packed
despite a fading reputation; avoid the annex.
Flora ($$)
*Calle Bergamaschi, off Calle Larga XXII Marzo,
San Marco 2283a tel: 041/520 5844*
Delightful, relaxing hotel (though some rooms
are dark or cramped); garden.
Gritti Palace ($$$$)
*Campo Santa Maria del Giglio, San Marco
2467 tel: 041/794 611*
Superb location and setting; elegant service
and supreme luxury.
La Fenice et des Artistes ($$)
*Campiello della Fenice 1936, San Marco
tel: 041/523 2333*
Slightly arty; rooms in the old wing are best.

Monaco and Grand Canal ($$$$)
*Calle Vallaresso, San Marco 1325
tel: 041/520 0211*
Intimate hotel on the Grand Canal; some
rooms rather small; excellent service.
Pausania ($$)
*Fondamenta Gherardini, Dorsoduro 2824
tel: 041/522 2083*
Quiet, 3-star hotel close to Campo Santa
Margherita.
La Residenza ($)
*Campo Bandiera e Moro 3608
tel: 041/528 5315*
Small, low-key hotel with a feeling of old
Venice.
San Samuele ($)
*Piscina San Samuele, San Marco 3358
tel: 041/522 8045*
A good budget choice with a friendly welcome
close to Campo Santo Stefano.
Santo Stefano ($$)
*Campo Santo Stefano, San Marco 2957
tel: 041/520 0166*
Tiny, immaculate 3-star hotel near the
Accademia; modest-sized rooms with nice décor.

THE NORTHEAST

Asolo

Villa Cipriani ($$$$)
Via Canova 298 tel: 0423/952 166
One of the most beautiful and alluring of all the
CIGA chain's hotels.

Bolzano (Bozen)

Luna-Mondschein ($$)
Via Piave 15 tel: 0471/975 642
Established and run by the same family for
two centuries, this hotel is central, tranquil,
and friendly.
Park Hotel Laurin ($$$)
Via Laurin 4 tel: 0471/311 000
A beautiful hotel in a park just east of town
center; outdoor pool; excellent restaurant.

Padova (Padua)

Europa ($$)
Largo Europa 9 tel: 049/661 200
Central hotel, but unexciting.
Igeau ($)
Via Ospedale Civile 87 tel: 049/875 05 77
A welcoming, simple hotel just a few steps
from the Basilica di Sant'Antonio.

Trento

America ($$)
Via Torre Verde 50 tel: 0461/983 010
Central and amiable hotel in medieval building.

Treviso

Campeol ($)
Piazza Ancillotto 4–8 tel: 0422/56 601
A reliable mid-range hotel in the center.

Trieste

Alabarda ($)
Via Valdirivo 22 tel: 040/630 269
The best inexpensive hotel in Trieste.
Duchi d'Aosta ($$$)
*Piazza dell'Unità d'Italia 2
tel: 040/760 0011*
Central, beautifully appointed hotel with
elegant restaurant.

Verona

Giulietta e Romeo ($$)
Vicolo Tre Marchetti 3 tel: 045/800 3554
Unpretentious hotel; good value and well
placed for sightseeing around the city.
Il Torcolo ($$)
Vicolo Listone 3 tel: 045/800 7512
Close to the Arena; like all Verona's hotels,
reserve in advance during the opera season.
Victoria ($$$)
Via Adua 8 tel: 045/590 566
Small, plush, and quiet.

Vicenza

Palladio ($)
Via Oratorio dei Servi 25 tel: 0444/321 072
A friendly 2-star close to Piazza dei Signori.

FLORENCE

Annalena ($$)
Via Romana 34 tel: 055/222 402
Famous 14th-century hotel near Pitti and
Boboli gardens.
Casci ($$)
Via Cavour 13 tel: 055/211 686
Well-positioned close to Duomo; pleasant
rooms and welcoming owners.
Excelsior ($$$$)
Piazza Ognissanti 3 tel: 055/264 201
A top-rate hotel, its renowned *Il Cestello*
restaurant has great views of the city from the
summer roof terrace.
Hermitage ($$)
Vicolo Marzio 1 tel: 055/287 216
Popular with U.K. and U.S. visitors. Good 3-star
overlooking the Arno.
Kraft ($$)
Via Solferino 2 tel: 055/284 273
Quiet, comfortable, and spacious; small pool
and panoramic roof terrace.
Loggiato dei Serviti ($$)
*Piazza della Santissima Annunziata 3
tel: 055/289 592*
19th-century elegance and 21st-century
comfort in a quiet, pleasant square.
Maxim ($)
11 Via dei Calzaiuoli tel: 055/217 474
Welcoming, very central budget choice; some
quiet courtyard rooms.
Monna Lisa ($$$)
Borgo Pinti 27 tel: 055/247 9751
Cozy, rather small rooms, but aristocratic
fittings and communal spaces; located in a
Renaissance *palazzo* close to the Duomo.

Regency ($$$$)
Piazza d'Azeglio 3 tel: 055/245 247
Quiet and charming, with a noted restaurant.
Sorelle Bandini ($)
Piazza Santo Spirito 9 tel: 055/215 308
Fine choice in Oltrarno; lofty rooms with views.
Villa San Michele ($$$$)
Via Doccia 4, Fiesole tel: 055/59 451
Small, romantic, and exclusive hotel in hills
outside the city.

TUSCANY

Arezzo

Continentale ($$)
Piazza Guido Monaco 7 tel: 0575/20251
Well-equipped; near station and sights.

Lucca

Piccolo Puccini ($$)
Via di Poggio 9 tel: 0583/ 55 421
Small, very pleasant 3-star hotel, close to the
center and to the composer Puccini's house.
Universo ($$)
*Piazza del Giglio, off Piazza Napoleone
tel: 0583/493 678*
Highest-ranking spot in the town center.

Pisa

Cavalieri ($$$)
Piazza della Stazione 2 tel: 050/43 290
Modern and handy for the station and airport.
Royal Victoria ($$)
Lungarno Pacinotti 12 tel: 050/940 111
Comfortable *palazzo* 10 minutes from the
cathedral square.

San Gimignano

La Cisterna ($$)
Piazza della Cisterna tel: 0577/940 328
Venerable old inn in the center of town.

Siena

Certosa di Maggiano ($$$$)
Via Certosa 82 tel: 0577/288 180
Exclusive hotel in former monastery.
Palazzo Ravizza ($$)
Via Pian dei Mantellini 34 tel: 0577/280 462
Traditional hotel in 17th-century *palazzo*.
Santa Caterina ($$)
Via Piccolomini 7 tel: 0577/221 105
A small modern town-house hotel with an
attractive garden.

Volterra

San Lino ($$)
*Via San Lino 26, near Porta San Francesco
tel: 0588/85 250*
Central choice with pool; formerly a convent.
Villa Nencini ($$)
Borgo Santo Stefano 55 tel: 0588/ 86 386
Just out of town center; pool and garden.

Accommodations and Restaurants

UMBRIA & THE MARCHES

Assisi

Hotel Umbra ($$)
Via degli Archi 6 tel: 075/812 240
A 400-year-old building in traffic-free location; rooms have terraces.
Subasio ($$$)
Via Frate Elia 2 tel: 075/812 206
Traditional elegance to be found in a good location close to the Basilica.

Gubbio

Ai Cappuccini ($$$)
Via Tifernate tel: 075/922 9234
This luxurious hotel is built in a converted 14th-century monastery.
Bosone ($$)
Via XX Settembre 22 tel: 075/922 0688
In a frescoed palace in the heart of Gubbio.
Hotel Gattapone ($)
Via Ansidei 6 tel: 075/927 2489
Comfortable and informal hotel in the center.

Orvieto

La Badia ($$$$)
*La Badia, 3 miles south of Orvieto
tel: 0763/301 959*
An old monastery has been converted into this famous hotel.
Maitani ($$)
Via Maitani 5 tel: 0763/342 011
Baroque palace in town center with comfortable, if not overly modern rooms.

Perugia

Locanda della Posta ($$$)
Corso Vannucci 97 tel: 075/572 8925
Lovely small hotel in the old quarter with views over the town.
Palace Hotel Bellavista ($$)
Piazza d'Italia 12 tel: 075/572 0741
Grand hotel in a 19th-century *palazzo*.
Umbria ($)
Via Boncambi 37 tel: 075/572 1203
A reasonable 2-star hotel with 18 rooms.

Spoleto

Aurora ($)
Via dell'Apollinare 4 tel: 0743/220 315
Small, central, yet quiet place in the upper town, making it a good base.
Gattapone ($$$)
Via del Ponte 6 tel: 0743/223 447
This may be a tiny hotel, but the views are wonderfully tempting. The rooms are lovely too.

Todi

Fonte Cesia ($$$)
Via Lorenzo Leoni 3 tel: 075/894 3737
Superbly converted *palazzo* 4-star hotel, right in the heart of town.

Urbino

Bonconte ($$$)
Via delle Mura 28 tel: 0722/2463
Avoid the small top-floor rooms in this otherwise pleasant hotel.
Hotel San Giovanni ($$)
Via Barocci 13 tel: 0722/2827
Unpretentious but comfortable hotel in a converted medieval building.

LAZIO & ABRUZZO

L'Aquila

Castello ($$)
Piazza B. Alpini tel: 0862/419 147
Stands close to the park by the town castle just north of the center.
Duomo ($)
Via Dragonetti 10 tel: 0862/410 893
A 2-star hotel in a quiet, very central position.

Parco Nazionale d'Abruzzo

Cristiania ($$)
Pescasseroli tel: 0863/910 795
Popular and welcoming wooden chalet-type mountain hotel.

Sulmona

Italia ($)
*Piazza Tommaso 3, off Piazza XX Settembre
tel: 0864/52 308*
Popular, central, and inexpensive; Puccini was one of the first guests.

CAMPANIA

Amalfi

Amalfi ($$)
Via dei Pastai 3 tel: 089/872 440
A good mid-range choice with spotless rooms; reservations essential.
Hotel Luna Convento ($$$)
*Via P. Comite 33
tel: 089/871 002 or 871 050*
A lovely, converted 13th-century abbey; avoid street-side rooms.
Lidomare ($$)
Via Piccolomini 9 tel: 089/871 332
Classy, small and clean.
Santa Caterina ($$$)
Strada Amalfitana 9 tel: 089/871 012
One of the area's best hotels; swimming pool and lovely grounds.
Sole ($)
Largo della Zecca 3 tel: 089/871 147
Inexpensive place near the cathedral.

Capri

Quattro Stagioni ($)
*Via Marina Piccola 1, Capri Town
tel: 081/837 0041*
Cozy rooms with views.

Quisisana ($$$$)
Via Camerelle 2, Capri Town
tel: 081/837 0788
Island's top hotel and a favorite of visiting Americans; very expensive.

Villa Brunella ($$)
Via Tragara 24, Capri Town
tel: 081/837 0122
Tasteful hotel with terraces, views, pool, and noted restaurant.

Villa Eva ($)
Via La Fabbrica 8, Anacapri
tel: 081/837 2040
Secluded and simple.

Villa Krupp ($$)
Via Matteotti 12, near Giardini di Augusto
tel: 081/837 0362
Quiet and small; Lenin and Gorky stayed here.

Ischia

La Villarosa ($$)
Via Giacinto Gigante 5 tel: 081/991 316
Tasteful hotel in lovely garden. Private pool.

Regina Isabella ($$$$)
Piazza Restituita, Lacco Ameno
tel: 081/994 322
The island's top luxury hotel.

Napoli (Naples)

Excelsior ($$$$)
Via Partenope 48 tel: 081/764 0111
The city's top hotel.

Mercure Angioino ($$)
De Pretis 123 tel: 081/552 9500
Excellent central position; good facilities; housed in 19th-century *palazzo*.

Rex ($$)
Via Palepoli 12 tel: 081/764 9389
In a convenient and relatively quiet location near the Santa Lucia waterfront.

Positano

Casa Albertina ($$$)
Via Tavolozza 3 tel: 089/875 143
Friendly, family-owned; small hotel; view from terrace and roof garden.

Palazzo Murat ($$)
Via dei Mulini 23 tel: 089/875 177
Elegant charm, in the center; garden setting.

San Pietro ($$$$)
Amalfi Coast Road tel: 089/875 455
The best in the area; extravagance and exclusivity; very expensive.

Ravello

Belvedere Caruso ($$)
Via San Giovanni del Toro 52
tel: 089/857 111
Charming old-fashioned villa hotel; lovely garden and restaurant; first choice in the range.

Palumbo ($$$$)
Palazzo Confalone tel: 089/857 244
Just eight attractive rooms here; very elegant and very expensive.

Villa Maria ($)
Via Santa Chiara 2 tel: 089/857 255
Small and quiet *pensione* with pretty garden.

Sorrento

Eden ($$)
Via Correale 25 tel: 081/878 1909
Central but reasonably quiet; pleasant rooms.

Excelsior Vittoria ($$$$)
Piazza Tasso 34
tel: 081/807 1044 or 878 1900
Sorrento's best-known hotel; faded grandeur but cozy.

THE DEEP SOUTH

Alberobello

Dei Trulli ($$$$)
Via Cadore 28 tel: 080/432 3555
This 5-star hotel is built around a group of traditional *trulli* dwellings (see page 223).

Bari

Boston ($$)
Via Piccinni 155 tel: 080/521 6633
Medium-sized modern hotel near the Old Town.

Gargano

Al Castello ($)
Via Castello 29, Peschici tel: 0884/964 038
Hotel with noted restaurant.

Pizzomunno ($$$)
Lungomare Enrico Mattei, Vieste
tel: 0884/708 741
Upscale complex; numerous facilities.

Lecce

Risorgimento ($$)
Via Augusto Imperatore 19
tel: 0832/242 125
Large *palazzo* in old town; old-fashioned charm.

Matera

Italia ($$)
Via Ridola 5 tel: 0835/333 561
Just south of the town center, with views of the famous *sassi* cave dwellings.

Trani

Royal ($$)
Via De Robertis 29 (tel: 0883/588 777
A 4-star hotel in the center; elegant facilities.

SICILY

Agrigento

Villa Athena ($$$)
Via dei Templi 33 tel: 0922/596 288
Only hotel near the temples, so busy as a result; reserve ahead.

Cefalù

Cangelosi ($)
Via Umberto I 26 tel: 0921/421 591
Good value; central.
Kalura ($$$)
Contrada Caldura
tel: 0921/421 354 or 422 501
Beautifully set hotel with private beach and terraces with panoramic views.

Enna

Grande Albergo Sicilia ($)
Piazza N. Colajanni 7, off via Roma
tel: 0935/500 850
Friendly, reliable, and central.

Erice

Elimo ($$)
Via V. Emanuele 75 tel: 0923/869 377
Comfortable hotel in medieval house.

278

Palermo

Grande Albergo e delle Palme ($$$)
Via Roma 398 tel: 091/583 933
Famous and faded, but still the best hotel in central Palermo; rooms vary greatly in quality.
Mediterraneo ($$)
Via Rosolino Pilo 43 tel: 091/581 133
A modern, comfortable hotel close to the Museo Archeologico.
Villa Archirafi ($–$$)
Via Lincoln 30 tel: 091/616 8827
In a relatively quiet and pleasant position by the botanical gardens just south of the center.
Villa Igiea ($$$$)
Via Belmonte 43, Acquasanta
tel: 091/543 744
Art nouveau; the city's most luxurious hotel.

Siracusa (Syracuse)

Gran Bretagna ($$$)
Via Savoia 21 tel: 0931/68 765
Easily the best Ortigia choice and often full as a result (refurbished for July 2001).
Jolly Hotel ($$$)
Corso Gelone 45 tel: 0931/461 111
Reliable big-chain hotel near the station and archeological zone.

Taormina

San Domenico Palace ($$$$)
Piazza San Domenico 5 tel: 0942/23 701
First choice for atmosphere and luxury.
Svizzera ($)
Via Pirandello 26 tel: 0942/23 790
Excellent and popular choice; lovely building; clean rooms and sea views.
Villa Fiorita ($$)
Via Pirandello 39 tel: 0942/24 122
Swimming pool and small garden; rooms with fine views of the coast.

SARDINIA

Alghero

San Francesco ($)
Via Machin 2 tel: 079/980 330
At the center of the old town; quiet and clean rooms; book in advance.
Villa Las Tronas ($$$)
Lungomare Valencia 1 tel: 079/981 818
Top hotel; characterful villa just east of center.

Cagliari

La Perla ($)
Via Sardegna 18 tel: 070/669 446
One of many budget options on this street.
Regina Margherita ($$$)
Viale Regina Margherita 44 tel: 070/670 342
The city's top hotel.

Costa Smeralda

Balocco ($$$)
Liscia di Vacca, Porto Cervo tel: 0789/91 555
A bit cheaper than most hotels in Porto Cervo.
Pitrizza ($$$$)
Porto Cervo tel: 0789/991 500; closed Oct–May
A very exclusive hotel.

Oristano

Cama ($)
Via V. Veneto 119 tel: 0783/74 374
Convenient for the station and the old town.
Mistral ($$)
Via Martiri di Belfiore tel: 0783/212 505
Edge of town hotel; new annex in town center.

RESTAURANTS

The restaurants listed below are divided into three categories (prices are based on a three-course meal without alcohol):
Inexpensive ($): under €25
Moderate ($$): €25–50
Expensive ($$$): over €50

ROME

Al Leoncino ($)
Via del Leoncino 38
Superb pizzeria one block off Via del Corso; woodfired oven.
Al Pompiere ($$)
Via Santa Maria dei Calderari 38
tel: 066/868 377
Famous Jewish/Roman cuisine.
Il Campo ($$)
Piazza della Cancellaria 64
Italian dishes in a feng shui atmosphere. Lunchtime buffet.
Checchino dal 1887 ($$$)
Testaccio 30 tel: 06/574 6318
Long renowned for classic Roman dishes— tripe, brains, and other rarely eaten parts; varied wine list.

Il Convivio ($$$–$$$$)
Viccolo dei Soldati 31 tel: 06/686 9432
Some of the best and most innovative cooking in the city; booking is essential.
Ivo ($)
Via di San Francesco a Ripa 157
Quintessential Roman pizzeria; fast turnover; arrive early to avoid the lines.
La Moreta ($)
Piazza della Moreta tel: 06/686 1900
Typical Italian food and fresh fish. Very friendly service.
Papà Giovanni ($$$)
Via dei Sediari 4 tel: 061/686 5308
Light, innovative cooking; a pleasant dining room close to Piazza Navona.
La Rosetta ($$$)
Via della Rosetta 9 tel: 06/686 1002
Elegant dining room in small alley immediately north of the Pantheon. For years one of the city's best-known fish restaurants.
El Toulà ($$$$)
Via della Lupa 29b tel: 06/687 3498
High prices, swanky and often rated Rome's best; plenty of famous faces.

THE NORTHWEST

Aosta

Taverna da Nando ($)
Via De Tillier 41 tel: 0165/44 455
Founded in 1957; a good local *trattoria* just 50 yards from the main square.
Vecchio Ristoso ($$)
Via Tourneuve 4 tel: 0165/33 238
The best place in town; located in a converted mill; excellent regional cooking.

Asti

Gener Neuv ($$$$)
Lungo Tanaro 4 tel: 0141/557 270
Among Italy's top restaurants; very good.

Genova (Genoa)

Enoteca Sola ($$)
Corso Barabino 120r tel: 010/594 513
Small, old-fashioned place; Ligurian cooking.
Gran Gotto ($$$)
Via Brigata Bisoprio 69, near Piazza della Vittoria tel: 010/564 344
Small and classy. A classic spot.

Riviera di Levante

Eden ($$)
Via Diaz 5, Rapallo tel: 0185/50 553
Top-rate fish and seafood.
Corsaro ($$)
Calata Doria 102, Portovenere tel: 0187/790 622
Portovenere's best restaurant: fine fish and seafood, and a good choice of wines.
Manuelina ($$)
Via Roma 300, Recco tel: 0185/576 128
One of the Riviera's more celebrated spots.

Riviera di Ponente

Bagatto ($$)
Via Matteotti 145, San Remo tel: 0184/531 925
Serves national and regional dishes.
La Reserve Tastevin ($$$)
Via Arziglia 20, Capo Sant'Ampelio, Bordighera tel: 0184/261 3222
Excellent views and seafood.

Torino (Turin)

Balbo ($$$$)
Via A. Doria 11 tel: 011/839 57 75
Sublime food, but stratospheric prices.
C'Era Una Volta ($–$$)
Corso V. Emanuele 41 tel: 011/650 4589
A simple restaurant; good Piemontese food. Dinner only.

LOMBARDY AND EMILIA-ROMAGNA

Bergamo

Da Vittorio ($$$$)
Via Giovanni XXIII 21 tel: 035/218 060
One of Italy's top restaurants.
Taverna del Colleoni ($$$)
Piazza Vecchia tel: 035/232 596
Handsome place in the heart of the old town.

Bologna

Battibecco ($$–$$$)
Via Battibecco 4 tel: 051/223 298
Some of the best fish cooking in the city.
Bertino ($)
Via delle Lame 55 tel: 051/522 230
Inexpensive, popular *trattoria*.
Da Cesari ($$)
Via de Carbonesi 8 tel: 051/226 769
Interesting dishes at a reasonable price.

Como, Lago di

Barchetta ($$)
Salita Mella 13, Bellagio tel: 031/951 389
Some of the lake's best fish cooking.
La Scuderia ($)
Piazza Matteotti 4, Como tel: 041/272 6518
Lively pizzeria.

Ferrara

Il Gatto Bianco ($)
Via Carlo Mayr 59 tel: 0532/762 007
Popular pizzeria.
La Provvidenza ($$$)
Corso Ercole d'Este 92 tel: 0532/205 187
Worthy and well known; reservations advisable.

Garda, Lago di

Vecchia Lugana ($$)
Piazzale Vecchia Lugana 1, Sirmione tel: 030/919 012
One of the region's leading restaurants.

279

Accommodations and Restaurants

Lago Maggiore

L'Emiliano ($$$)
Corso Italia 50, Stresa tel: 0323/31 396
An elegant, high-quality restaurant.

Mantova (Mantua)

L'Aquila Nigra ($$)
*Vicolo Bonacolsi 4, near Palazzo Ducale
tel: 0376/327 180*
Mantuan specialties in frescoed dining room.

Milano (Milan)

Aimo e Nadia ($$$)
Via Monte-Cuccoli 6 tel: 02/416 886
The best restaurant in Milan, a cab ride west of
the city center. Lunch menus are good value.
Bice ($$$)
Borgo Spesso 12 tel: 02/7600 2572
Expertly cooked local and Tuscan dishes.
Boeucc ($$$$)
Piazza Belgioioso 2 tel: 02/7602 0224
Venerable Milanese dining spot near La Scala,
with luxurious décor.

280

Parma

Enoteca Fontana di Parma ($)
Via Farini 24a tel: 0521/286 037
Excellent selection of wines and light meals.
La Greppia ($$$)
Via Garibaldi 39a tel: 0521/233 686
Parma's best restaurant.

Ravenna

La Gardela ($)
Via Ponte Marino 3 tel: 0544/217 147
Fine, homely *trattoria* by Piazza del Popolo.
Tre Spade ($$)
Via Faentina 136 tel: 0544/500 522
Converted mill near Duomo; inventive food.

VENICE

Agli Alboretti ($$)
*Rio Terrà Sant'Agnese, Dorsoduro 882
tel: 041/523 0058*
Pleasant place near the Accademia.
Ai Promessi Sposi ($)
Calle dell'Oca, Castello 4367
Seafood dishes and lively bar.
Al Mascaron ($)
*Calle Lunga S. M. Formosa 5225
tel: 041/522 5995*
Informal and often busy with Venetians.
Antica Mola ($–$$)
Fondamenta degli Ormesini 2800, Cannaregio.
Excellent, family-run *trattoria* near Ghetto.
Antico Martini ($$$)
Campo San Fantin 1983 tel: 041/522 4121
A Venetian institution.
Da Fiore ($$$)
*Calle dello Scaleter, San Polo 2202
tel: 041/721 308*
Has an international reputation for quality.

Fiaschetteria Toscana ($$$)
*Campo San Giovanni Crisostomo, Cannaregio
5719 tel: 041/528 5281*
Friendly atmosphere, setting, and food make
this popular with locals.
Montin ($$)
*Fondamenta di Borgo, Dorsoduro 1147
tel: 041/522 7151*
Favored by Pound, Hemingway, *et al*;
atmospheric dining rooms and superb garden.
San Bartolomeo ($)
Calle della Bissa, San Marco 5424a
Good self-service selection.
Vini da Gigio ($$)
*Fondamente San Felice 36289, Cannaregio
tel: 041/528 5140*
Romantic place with wood-beamed interior,
good food, and a very welcoming atmosphere.

THE NORTHEAST

Bolzano (Bozen)

Luna Mondschein ($$)
Via Piave 15 tel: 0471/975 642
Top-quality Italian and Tyrolean dishes. Garden
dining in summer.

Padova (Padua)

Antico Brolo ($$)
Corso Milano 22 tel: 049/664 555
Housed in a 15th-century *palazzo*, good food.

Trento

Rue Spade ($$–$$$)
Via Don a Rizzi 11 tel: 0461/234 343
Elegant restaurant with the best food in town.

Trieste

Antica Suban ($$)
Via Emilio Comici 2 tel: 040/54 368
Good local dishes in a historic restaurant.

Verona

Dodici Apostoli ($$$$)
Corticella San Marco 3 tel: 045/596 999
One of Verona's top places; medieval setting.
Il Desco ($$$$)
Via dietro San Sebastiano 7 tel: 045/595 358
Vies with Dodici Apostoli for the role of the
city's best restaurant.
La Greppia ($$)
Vicolo Samaritana 3 tel: 045/800 4577
Good local dishes in old-fashioned décor.

Vicenza

Antica Casa Della Maluasia ($–$$)
Contrà delle Morette 5 tel: 0444/543 704
A superb, central restaurant with a large dining
room and informal atmosphere.
Zi Teresa ($–$$)
Contrada S. Antonio 1 tel: 0444/321 411
Restaurant specializing in pizza and pasta dishes.

FLORENCE

Alle Murate ($$–$$$)
Via Ghibellina 52r tel: 055/240 618
Light, innovative cuisine in a smart restaurant.
Angiolino ($$)
Via Santo Spirito 36r tel: 055/239 8976
Busy place, with wood-burning stove and
charcoal grill. The cooking is erratic at times.
Baldovino ($–$$)
Via San Giuseppe 22r tel: 055/241 773
A delightful place just behind Santa Croce.
Caffè Italiano ($–$$)
Via San Giuseppe 22r tel: 055/289 368
Terra-cotta floors and big wooden beams;
restaurant, wine bar, and lunch *trattoria*.
Da Mario ($)
Via Rosina 2r, Piazza del Mercato
tel: 055/218 550
Low prices, friendly atmosphere, shared
tables, traditional no-frills food.
Enoteca Pinchiorri ($$$$)
Via Ghibellina 87 tel: 055/242 777
Often called Italy's best restaurant, though
perhaps over-formal; 80,000 bottles of
the best French and Italian wine.
Reservations required.
Il Cibrèo ($$)
Via de' Macci 118r tel: 055/234 1100
Sometimes over-adventurous Tuscan
specialties and Italian standards; great
desserts and wine list.

TUSCANY

Arezzo

Buca di San Francesco ($$)
Piazza San Francesco I tel: 0575/23 271
Tourist filled, but offers reliable food.

Cortona

Locarda nel Loggiato ($$)
Piazza Pescheria 3 tel: 0575/30575
Lovely medieval room, fine food and wines.

Lucca

Buca di Sant'Antonio ($$)
Via della Cervia 3 tel: 0583/55 881
This former inn is now considered Lucca's
finest restaurant. Some unusual dishes.
Da Giulio ($)
Via delle Conce 47 tel: 0583/55 948
Packed and popular, so book or arrive early.

Montalcino

Grappola Blu ($$)
Via Scale di Moglio 1 tel: 0577/847 150
Medieval dining room with innovative cooking.

Pisa

Mescita ($)
Via Domenico Cavalca 2 tel: 050/544 294
Lively, bustling place close to university.

Osteria dei Cavalieri ($$)
Via San Frediano 16 tel: 050/580 858
Relaxed restaurant at the heart of the old city.

San Gimignano

Bel Soggiorno ($$)
Via San Giovanni 91 tel: 0577/940 375
A 19th-century inn serving local dishes.
Le Terrazze ($$)
Hotel La Cisterna, Piazza della Cisterna 23
tel: 0577/940 328
Tuscan specialties and good views.

Siena

Al Marsili ($$)
Via del Castoro 3 tel: 0577/47 154
Siena's best; reservations essential.
Le Logge ($$)
Via del Porrione 33 tel: 0577/48 013
Pretty and popular spot offering Tuscan
specialties; reserving a table is recommended.

Volterra

Etruria ($$)
Piazza dei Priori 6 tel: 0588/86 064
Local dishes are good.

UMBRIA AND THE MARCHES

Assisi

Fortezza ($$)
Vicolo della Fortezza tel: 075/812 418
Unpretentious food and setting.
Il Medio Evo ($$$)
Via dell'Arco dei Priori 43 tel: 075/813 068
Medieval rooms; some of Umbria's best food.
Palotta ($)
Via San Rufino 4 tel: 075/812 649 or 812 307
Arrive early to be sure of a table (12:30 lunch).

Montefalco

Il Coccorone ($)
Via Fabbri-Largo Tempestivi
tel: 0742/379 535
One of Umbria's most pleasing restaurants.

Norcia

Grotta Azzurra ($$)
Via Alfieri 12 tel: 0743/816 513
Truffle dishes and medieval dining rooms.

Orvieto

Etrusca ($$)
Via Maritani 10 tel: 0763/344 016
Medieval dining room; traditional food.

Perugia

Falchetto ($$)
Via Bartolo 20 tel: 075/573 1775
Two small dining rooms and good food.

Accommodations and Restaurants

Spello

La Cantina ($)
Via Cavour 2 tel: 0742/651 775
Local specialties in medieval setting.

Spoleto

Apollinare ($$)
Via Sant'Agata tel: 0743/223 256
Medieval interior and rustic Umbrian dishes.

Todi

Umbria ($$)
Via S. Bonaventura 13, off Piazza del Popolo tel: 075/894 2737
Superb outside terrace.

Urbino

Vecchia Urbino ($$)
Via dei Vasari 3 tel: 0722/4447
The best place in Urbino.

LAZIO & ABRUZZO

L'Aquila

Ernesto ($–$$)
Piazza Palazzo 22 tel: 0862/21 094
Varied local cooking.
Tre Marie ($$)
Via Tre Marie 3 tel: 0862/413 191
Classic Abruzzese food and wines. Reserve.

Tivoli

Adriano ($$$)
Via Villa Adriano 194 tel: 0774/382 235
Located close to Hadrian's Villa; prices are high, but outside dining in summer is a plus.
Cinque Statue ($$)
Via Quintilio Varo 2-Largo S. Angelo tel: 0774/335 366
At the entrance to the Villa Gregoriana; veranda for al fresco eating.

CAMPANIA

Amalfi

Eolo ($$–$$$)
Via P. Comite 3 tel: 089/871 241
The terrace is a wonderfully romantic spot.
La Caravella ($$)
Via M. Camera 12 tel: 089/871 029
Intimate interior; mainly fish dishes.

Capri

Campanile ($$)
Via Roma 4 tel: 081/837 0266
A good place close to Piazza Umberto I.
La Capannina ($$$$)
Via delle Botteghe 14, Capri Town tel: 081/837 0732
Widely considered the island's top restaurant.

La Pigna ($$$)
Via lo Palazzo 30, Capri Town tel: 081/837 0280
Veranda and al fresco dining; one of Capri's favorite restaurants. Very large.

Ischia

Giardini Eden ($$)
Ischia Ponte, Via Nuova Cartaromana tel: 081/985 0151
The island's top restaurant.

Napoli (Naples)

Bellini ($)
Via Santa Maria di Constantinopli 80, corner of Via San Pietro tel: 081/459 774
One of the most popular restaurants with Neapolitans; somewhat slow service but great pizzas and other dishes.
Bersagliera ($$)
Borgo Marinaro 10 tel: 081/764 6016
On the waterfront and touristy as a result, but still fun for a first night—and the food is good.
Ciro a Santa Brigida ($$)
Via Santa Brigida 71, off Via Toledo tel: 081/552 4072
Pizza and fish specialties; favored by artists, journalists, and the like.
La Sacrestia ($$)
Via Orazio 116 tel: 081/664 186
One of southern Italy's finest restaurants.
Masaniello ($$)
Via Donnalbina 28 (on Riviera di Chiaia) tel: 081/552 8863
Small restaurant near Piazza dei Martini. Serves excellently prepared simple dishes and particularly good antipasti.

Positano

Buca di Bacco ($$)
Via Rampa Teglia 4 tel: 089/875 699
Above the town's most fashionable café; terrace overlooks the beach. Reservations required in the evening.
O'Capurale ($$)
Via Regina Giovanna 12 tel: 089/875 374
Reserve outdoor tables in the cheapest and best restaurant on Positano's waterfront.

Ravello

Cumpa Cosimo ($)
Via Roma 44 tel: 089/857 156
Friendly and pleasant good-sized restaurant, popular with tourists.
Villa Maria ($)
Via di Santa Chiara tel: 089/857 255
Romantic place with garden overlooking the sea.

Sorrento

Parrucchiano ($$)
Corso Italia 71 tel: 081/878 1321
One of the town's most popular restaurants; beautiful setting and tempting local dishes; reservations advised.

Sant'Antonino ($)
Via Santa Maria delle Grazie 6
Popular with locals and visitors; low prices and flower-filled patio.

THE DEEP SOUTH

Alberobello

Il Poeta Contadino ($$)
Via Indipendenza 21 tel: 080/4321 917
Best restaurant in the area; almost worth a special trip.
Trullo d'Oro ($$)
Via F. Cavallotti 29 tel: 080/4321 820
Rustic and atmospheric restaurant arranged in five *trulli*.

Bari

La Pignata ($$)
Corso Vittorio Emanuele 173
tel: 080/523 2481
Although there are many to choose from, this is the best of Bari's many fine restaurants.

Lecce

Guido e Figli ($)
Via XXV Luglio 14
tel: 0832/305 868
A long-established city institution; restaurant, pizzeria, and self-service combined, close to central Piazza Sant'Oronzo.

Matera

Il Terrazzino ($)
Piazza Vittorio Veneto-Vico S. Giuseppe 7
tel: 0835/332 503
In an old *sasso* dug into the rock; outdoor terrace.
Lucana ($)
Via Lucana 48, off Via Roma
tel: 0835/336 117
Best restaurant in town.

Trani

Torrente Antico ($$$)
Via E. Fusco 3 tel: 0883/487 911
Small, elegant restaurant with innovative food (particularly fish and seafood).

SICILY

Agrigento

Caprice ($$)
Via Panoramica dei Templi 51
tel: 0922/26 469
Popular place near the town's temples.
Leon d'Oro ($)
Via Emporium, near Lungomare di San Leone
tel: 0922/414 400
Fine old *trattoria*; standards have been kept high as it has been in the same hands for 30 years.

Cefalù

Arkade Grill ($)
Via Vanni 9 tel: 0921/422 530
Typical Sicilian dishes plus a few Italian dishes.

Palermo

Capricci di Sicilia ($$)
Via I. Pignatelli 6, Piazza Sturzo
tel: 091/327 777
Rustic ambience, a warm welcome, good food, and a central location.
Charleston ($$$)
Piazza Ungheria 30 tel: 091/321 366
Palermo's most elegant restaurant.
La Scuderia ($$)
Via del Fante 9 tel: 091/520 323
Relaxed atmosphere and outstanding Palermitan specialties.

Siracusa (Syracuse)

Do Scugghiu ($)
Via Scina 11, off Piazza Archimede
Local institution with huge choice of pasta dishes.
Minosse ($$)
Via Mirabella 6 tel: 0931/66 366
The town's top restaurant.

Taormina

Maffei's ($$$)
Via San Domenico di Guzman I
tel: 0942/240 55
The town's best food, with delightful garden.

SARDINIA

Alghero

La Lepanto ($$)
Via Carlo Alberto 135 tel: 079/979 116
A leading seafood spot.

Cagliari

Antica Osteria ($$)
Via Cavour 60 tel: 070/ 665 870
Rivals Dal Corsaro as Cagliari's best restaurant, but prices are bit lower.
Da Serafino ($)
Via Sardegna 109
Good value and popular with locals.
Dal Corsaro ($$$$)
Viale Regina Margherita 28 tel: 070/664 318
One of Sardinia's best.

Oristano

Il Faro ($$$)
Via Bellini 25 tel: 0783/70 002
One of the area's top seafood restaurants.
Da Gino ($)
Via Tirso 13 tel: 0783/71 428
Good-value *trattoria* close to Piazza Roma.

Index

Index

285

Index

288

Picture credits

The Automobile Association would like to thank the following for their assistance in the preparation of this book. **J ALLAN CASH PHOTO LIBRARY** 72 San Remo harbour, 77a St Bernard Tunnel, 119a Traditional houses, Bolzano, 119b Bassano del Grappa market, 124 Equestrian statue Padua, 126 Trieste. **ASSOCIATED PRESS/TOPHAM** 237a Funeral at Palermo. **MARTIN BLACK/IMPACT PHOTOS** 70 Walkers. **BRIDGEMAN ART LIBRARY** front cover c, 26b *Napoleon crossing the Alps* by David, Jacques Louis (1748–1825) Schloss Charlottenburg, Berlin, 27b *General Garibaldi* by Barucco, F (fl 1864–6) Guildhall Art Gallery, Corporation of London, 30b Golden Etruscan bowl, 7th century BC by courtesy of the Board of Trustees of the V & A, 38b *The Melancholy of Departure* by Chirico, Giorgio de (1888–1978) Tate Gallery, London, 98b *The Tempest* by Giorgione, Giorgio (1476/8–1510) Galleria dell'Accademia, Venice, 99a *The Miracle of the Cross on San Lorenzo Bridge* by Bellini, Gentile (ca1429–1507) Galleria dell'Accademia, Venice, 136b *Venice: San Giorgio from the Dogana, Sunrise* by Turner, Joseph Mallord William (1775–1851) British Museum, London, 187 Etruscan vase showing boxers fighting ca 500 BC British Museum, London, 207 Spring—maiden gathering flowers—wall painting from Stabiae (1st century AD) Archeological Museum, Naples. **JAMES DAVIS** 234 Messina. **STEVE DAY** 120, 121, 122b Dolomites. **CHRIS DONAGHUE** 131 San Giorgio Maggiore. **E T ARCHIVE** 75b Turin Shroud. **MARY EVANS PICTURE LIBRARY** 21a Punic Wars, 22b Assassination of Caesar, 24b Pope Gregory VII, 256b Bandits. **RONALD GRANT ARCHIVE** 18a *Città Aperta*, 18b *Ossessione*. **HULTON DEUTSCH COLLECTION LTD** 28a, 28b Mussolini, 29b Student riot. **INTERNATIONAL PHOTOBANK** Cover Amalfi Coast. **T JEPSON** 68 Parco Nazionale del Gran Paradiso. **NATURE PHOTOGRAPHERS LTD** 195a Grey wolf (E A Janes), 195b European brown bear (P R Sterry). **PICTURES COLOUR LIBRARY** front cover a. **REX FEATURES LTD** 14b Coins, 15 Italian election. **ROYAL GEOGRAPHICAL SOCIETY** 25b Map. **SPECTRUM COLOUR LIBRARY** 67 Genoa Campanile, 74 Turin, 75a Replica of Turin Shroud, 75c Turin San Giovanni Cathedral, 122–3a Skiers Vigo di Fassa, 123 Skiers Dolomites, 127a Verona Aida, 162a,b Siena Palio, 200a,b Vesuvius, 204 Capri, 256a Sheep. **THE GARDEN PICTURE LIBRARY** 73a,b,c, Hanbury Gardens. **THE MANSELL COLLECTION LTD** 20b Phoenician merchant ships, 21b Julius Caesar, 23a Barbarians, 23b Charlemagne, 24a Henry IV, 99b Titian. **TONY STONE IMAGES** front cover b. **TOPHAM PICTURE SOURCE** 237b Coffin of policeman. **ZEFA PICTURE LIBRARY (UK) LTD** Spine.

All remaining pictures are held in the Association's own library (AA PHOTO LIBRARY) with contributions from: **ADRIAN BAKER** 77b. **PETE BENNETT** 26a. **JERRY EDMANSON** 34a,b, 137, 141, 142, 144a, 145, 152. **JIM HOLMES** 257. **ALEX KOUPRIANOFF** 265, 267, 268. **DARIO MITIDIERI** 12b, 19, 22c, 27a, 31b, 35, 36b, 37a,b, 39, 45a,b, 47, 48a, 52, 53, 58, 60, 61, 109. **ERIC MEACHER** 13b. **RICHARD NEWTON** 98a, 101, 103, 104a, 106, 108. **KEN PATERSON** 11a, b, 16a, 30a,c, 33a, 135, 139, 140, 143a,b, 144b, 146, 147, 149, 150, 151, 153, 154, 156, 157, 158, 159, 160, 161a,b, 163, 164–5, 168, 169a,b, 170, 171, 173, 174a,b, 175a, 176a,b, 177, 179b, 186a. **CLIVE SAWYER** 2, 3, 4, 5a,b, 6–7a, 7b, 9, 10b, 14a, 16b,c, 17a,b, 19, 20a, 31a, 32c, 36a, 39, 42, 46, 48b, 49b, 50a, 54, 56, 63, 65, 70, 71, 76a,b, 79, 80a, 82, 83, 85, 87a,b, 88, 89, 90a,b, 95, 96, 97, 100a,b, 104b, 105a,b, 107, 110a,b, 111a,b, 112, 113, 115, 117, 125, 127b, 128, 129, 130, 132, 134, 165, 166, 167, 175b, 180, 181, 184, 185, 188, 189a,b, 190, 192, 193, 194a,b, 196–7, 19, 201a,b, 202, 203, 209b, 210, 211, 215a,b, 216a,b, 217, 219a,b, 222, 223a,b, 224, 225b, 226, 227, 228, 229, 230, 231, 232, 233, 235a,b, 236, 238, 239a,b, 240, 242a,b, 243, 245, 246, 247a,b, 248, 249a,b, 250, 251, 252, 253, 254a,b, 255, 260, 266, 270, 271. **BARRIE SMITH** front cover d, 25a, 29a, 33c, 132, 138. **ANTONY SOUTER** 2,8, 13a, 21c, 32a,b, 55b, 66, 69, 84, 91, 92, 93a,b, 131a, 172, 178, 179a, 182a,b, 183, 186b, 187b, 191, 197, 198, 205a,b, 207a,b, 208, 209a, 213, 218a,b, 220, 221a,b, 225a, 271. **PETER WILSON** 10a, 12a, 22a, 37c, 43, 49a, 50b, 51, 55a, 57, 59.

Contributors

Original copy editor: Audrey Horne
Revision verifiers: Tim Jepson and Praxilla Trabattoni